HEART OF DARKNESS

AN AUTHORITATIVE TEXT

BACKGROUNDS AND SOURCES

CRITICISM

❧ ❧

SECOND EDITION

JOSEPH CONRAD
HEART OF DARKNESS

SECOND EDITION

AN AUTHORITATIVE TEXT
BACKGROUNDS AND SOURCES
CRITICISM

➤➤ ➤➤

Edited by

ROBERT KIMBROUGH
UNIVERSITY OF WISCONSIN

➤➤ ➤➤

W · W · NORTON & COMPANY

New York · London

W. W. Norton & Company, Inc., 500 Fifth Avenue, New York, N.Y. 10110

Copyright © 1971, 1963 by W. W. Norton & Company, Inc.

Library of Congress Catalog Card No. 78-152308

ISBN 0-393-04347-9 {Cloth Edition}

ISBN 0-393-09773-0 {Paper Edition}

PRINTED IN THE UNITED STATES OF AMERICA

6 7 8 9 0

Contents

Preface to the Second Edition

Because of the continuing fascination over Joseph Conrad's *Heart of Darkness*, the need became clear for a second edition of this Norton Critical Edition. Within the Text three typographical errors have been corrected and some annotation has been altered. In this last regard I am particularly indebted to Derek Hughes, a former examiner of marine engineers, for pointing out two misconceptions of mine regarding Marlow's steamer.

In the Backgrounds and Sources section, the prime addition is the reproduction of four pages from Conrad's manuscript. Here, my thanks are to Yale University for giving permission for their inclusion.

The major changes in the edition occur in the Essays in Criticism, which have been rearranged, with six former ones dropped and nine new ones added. Susan Quinn, Carol Kawalczyk, and Robert DuPont were most helpful in the search and selection of these pieces.

Finally, the bibliographies at the end have been expanded and brought up to date, mainly through the efforts of Sandra Snell and Susan Quinn.

My own major task has been the pleasant one of immersing myself once again in the story, its background, and its reception.

ROBERT KIMBROUGH

MADISON, WISCONSIN
SEPTEMBER 1971

Preface

In the fall of 1889, Joseph Conrad simultaneously began his first piece of fiction, *Almayer's Folly*, and his search for a way to get command of a river-boat on the Congo. The first act was impulsive and casual; the second, long-planned and calculatingly carried out. The first seemed mere whim; the second, the natural extension of a boyhood dream and present vocation as a seaman. But the actual significance of these two acts proved to be just the reverse of their appearance, for his Congo adventure so broke Conrad's health that he was delayed in resuming a life on ship, while his period of convalescence was occupied with increasingly satisfying creative writing. Although Conrad returned to sea twice before *Almayer* was finished in 1894, his new career as a writer began to take definite shape when he sat down to start *An Outcast of the Islands* even before *Almayer* had been accepted. These two novels were published in 1895 and 1896, and, in spite of losing time on two abortive projects, Conrad completed *The Nigger of the "Narcissus"* and a volume of five short stories, *Tales of Unrest*, in 1897. During 1898 he wrote and published *Youth*, the first of his Marlow tales, and in the fall began *Heart of Darkness*, the second.

Thus, *Heart of Darkness*, which had its inception nine years earlier, rounds out a period of Conrad's life. For half of those nine years Conrad worked in obscurity, sharing only with his aunt news of his progress in writing. With the publication of *Almayer*, however, fame and publicity came quickly, and by the time of *Heart of Darkness* Conrad was an established literary figure on intimate terms with John Galsworthy, Stephen Crane, H. G. Wells, Ford Madox Ford, and Henry James—just to mention fellow novelists. This rapid transition from a life of isolation to one of fellowship, from seaman to landsman, from captain to writer—indeed, from bachelor to family man—is part of the romance of Conrad's biography. But what is immediately important is that by the fall of 1898 Conrad was so securely established as a master of his new craft and so settled in a new way of life that he was ready to experiment artistically with very private material. *Heart of Darkness*, while in one sense ending a phase of Conrad's life, also indicates the beginning of a new one.

Conrad's earlier narratives are primarily objective, descriptive, and thematically clear; *Heart of Darkness* tends to be interior, suggestively analytic, and highly psychological. In short, it introduces a new mode into Conrad's fiction: the symbolic. To work successfully within such a mode a writer must know well his craft—how to manipulate words and events in the most suggestive ways—and himself—the ultimate source of all symbols—and by 1898 Conrad was ready to try. At a later point he seemed doubtful about his success: "What I distinctly admit is the fault of having made Kurtz too symbolic or rather symbolic at all. But the story being mainly a vehicle for conveying a batch of personal impressions I gave rein to my mental laziness and took the line of least resistance" (letter, December 2, 1902). The present book has been designed to allow the reader to evaluate how just this casual remark may or may not be.

The text itself, based upon a full study of all extant states of the story, from original draft through collected edition, offers the most reliable one printed since Conrad's death (see "A Note on the Text") and is the first to publish extensive portions of Conrad's manuscript. The "Backgrounds and Sources" section which follows the text has been subdivided into four. The first gives, after a modern historical sketch, views and opinions of Belgian activity in the Congo contemporary with Conrad's "personal impressions." All the printed sources of these impressions have been collected for the first time in the second subsection, "Conrad in the Congo." The actual matter-of-fact way in which Conrad went about translating this highly personal experience into art is revealed in the third subsection, "Writing the Story," while the last is a collection of Conrad's views on life and art, each of which was selected in order to shed light on either the meaning or art of *Heart of Darkness*. "Essays in Criticism" reveals a variety of "readings" of the story, ranging from specific to general, from parody of style to analysis of meaning. These selections have been included mainly as aids, as means, not as ends in themselves, the editor hoping that the reader will start with Conrad's text and work as far back from that as he pleases.

My aim in every respect has been reliability and completeness, but I could not have hoped to accomplish this end had I not received help from many quarters: from the secretaries of the Department of English of the University of Wisconsin who did much of the typing; from the staff of the Wisconsin Memorial Library who tracked down and obtained through Inter-Library Loan all editions and important reprints of the story; from the Newberry Library who allowed me to use their 1921 Heinemann edition for a copy-text; from the Yale University Library, which granted permission to publish readings from Conrad's manuscript; from Herman W. Liebert, Curator of the Rare Book Room at Yale, for patient and full answers to many questions regarding the manuscript and various editions; from Standish Henning, who heard me out on numerous bibliographical frustrations; from the authors who gave permission to reprint their material; and from Paul L. Wiley, who not only shared with me his detailed knowledge of Conrad but who also graciously wrote a study of *Heart of Darkness* specifically for this edition. To all I am most grateful.

ROBERT KIMBROUGH

MADISON, WISCONSIN

MAY 1962

The Text of
Heart of Darkness

Heart of Darkness appeared in print many times during Conrad's lifetime, but the version of the story found in the 1921 collected edition of his works may be considered his final text; it has been used as the basis for the present edition (see the "Note" which follows the text). Because there are, however, three significant forms of the text behind the "final" one—the manuscript of 1898–99, the *Blackwood's Magazine* version of February, March, and April of 1899, and the Blackwood book form of 1902—the present edition carries in its footnotes a selection of variant readings which permits the reader to follow Conrad as he worked toward establishing the final meaning and art of his text. The manuscript is a "clean" one; it moves steadily forward, having no long insertions, taking no false tacks, showing few second thoughts, and containing almost no revisions longer than a sentence in length. Because it is the most explicit of the three, many passages which were later supressed help one understand the meaning of the final text of *Heart of Darkness*. The magazine version is less explicit, omitting words, phrases, and one whole scene, but has only one totally rewritten passage and only one other fully revised. As a result the 1902 version differs from the magazine mainly in matters of style, in smoothness of phrase and syntax, but Conrad did tone down noticeably two descriptions of the native woman who appears toward the end of the story. Although no major changes appear in the 1921 edition, it is the most polished and consistent in style of all previous editions and reprints.

In the following annotation, readings from the manuscript are identified as *Ms*; from the magazine, as *Maga*; and from the first book form, as 1902. Note †, on page 3, is an example of a reading in the *Maga* version that differs from 1902 and 1921 (the extant *Ms* does not begin until page 5 of the present text). Note *, page 5, is an example of a phrase in the *Ms* which was eliminated either in the typescript or galleys of the *Maga* version. And note †, page 19, is an example of a reading in the *Ms* which Conrad crossed out before the manuscript was typed. Not all variants have been included, only those which the editor feels lead toward fuller, richer understanding of Conrad's art, either technically or thematically.

The remaining annotation has been restricted to the definition of obscure words and phrases and the identification of proper nouns. No notes try to identify people and places that had a real existence outside the story, for Conrad's letter to Richard Curle, below, p. 155, makes it quite clear that such annotation does him a disservice. Nor has the editor given hints toward a "reading" of the story, either by quoting analogues and sources or through direct suggestion. All the help a reader may need can be found in the "Backgrounds and Sources" and "Essays in Criticism" sections which follow the text.

Heart of Darkness

I

The *Nellie*, a cruising yawl, swung to her anchor without a flutter
of the sails, and was at rest. The flood had made, the wind was nearly
calm, and being bound down the river, the only thing for it† was to
come to and wait for the turn of the tide.

The sea-reach of the Thames stretched before us like the beginning of an interminable waterway. In the offing the sea and the
sky were welded together without a joint, and in the luminous space
the tanned sails of the barges drifting up with the tide seemed to
stand still in red clusters of canvas sharply peaked, with gleams of
varnished sprits. A haze rested on the low shores that ran out to sea
in vanishing flatness. The air was dark above Gravesend,[1] and farther
back still seemed condensed into a mournful gloom, brooding motionless over the biggest, and the greatest, town on earth.

The Director of Companies was our captain and our host. We
four affectionately watched his back as he stood in the bows looking
to seaward. On the whole river there was nothing that looked half
so nautical. He resembled a pilot, which to a seaman is trustworthi-
ness personified. It was difficult to realise his work was not out there
in the luminous estuary, but behind him, within the brooding gloom.

Between us there was, as I have already said somewhere, the bond
of the sea. Besides holding our hearts together through long periods
of separation, it had the effect of making us tolerant of each other's
yarns—and even convictions. The Lawyer—the best of old fellows—
had, because of his many years and many virtues, the only cushion
on deck, and was lying on the only rug. The Accountant had brought
out already a box of dominoes, and was toying architecturally with
the bones. Marlow sat cross-legged right aft, leaning against the miz-
zen-mast. He had sunken cheeks, a yellow complexion, a straight
back, an ascetic aspect, and, with his arms dropped, the palms of
hands outwards, resembled an idol. The Director, satisfied the anchor
had good hold, made his way aft and sat down amongst us. We exchanged a few words lazily. Afterwards there was silence on board
the yacht. For some reason or other we did not begin that game of
dominoes. We felt meditative, and fit for nothing but placid staring.

† *Maga:* us
1. Gravesend is the last major town in
the Thames estuary, 26 miles east of
London, on the south shore (in Kent)
where Essex forms the north shore.

The day was ending in a serenity of still and exquisite brilliance. The water shone pacifically; the sky, without a speck, was a benign immensity of unstained light; the very mist on the Essex marshes was like a gauzy and radiant fabric, hung from the wooded rises inland, and draping the low shores in diaphanous folds. Only the gloom to the west, brooding over the upper reaches, became more sombre every minute, as if angered by the approach of the sun.

And at last, in its curved and imperceptible fall, the sun sank low, and from glowing white changed to a dull red without rays and without heat, as if about to go out suddenly, stricken to death by the touch of that gloom brooding over a crowd of men.

Forthwith a change came over the waters, and the serenity became less brilliant but more profound. The old river in its broad reach rested unruffled at the decline of day, after ages of good service done to the race that peopled its banks, spread out in the tranquil dignity of a waterway leading to the uttermost ends of the earth. We looked at the venerable stream not in the vivid flush of a short day that comes and departs for ever, but in the august light of abiding memories. And indeed nothing is easier for a man who has, as the phrase goes, "followed the sea" with reverence and affection, than to evoke the great spirit of the past upon the lower reaches of the Thames. The tidal current runs to and fro in its unceasing service, crowded with memories of men and ships it has borne to the rest of home or to the battles of the sea. It had known and served all the men of whom the nation is proud, from Sir Francis Drake to Sir John Franklin,[2] knights all, titled and untitled—the great knights-errant of the sea. It had borne all the ships whose names are like jewels flashing in the night of time, from the *Golden Hind* returning with her round flanks full of treasure, to be visited by the Queen's Highness and thus pass out of the gigantic tale, to the *Erebus* and *Terror*, bound on other conquests—and that never returned. It had known the ships and the men. They had sailed from Deptford, from Greenwich, from Erith—the adventurers and the settlers; kings' ships and the ships of men on 'Change; captains, admirals, the dark "interlopers" of the Eastern trade, and the commissioned "generals" of East India fleets.[3] Hunters for gold or pursuers of fame, they all had gone out on that stream, bearing the sword, and often the torch, messengers of the might within the land, bearers of a spark from the sacred fire. What greatness had not floated on the

---

2. Sir Francis Drake sailed the "Golden Hind" in the service of Elizabeth I; Sir John Franklin (1786–1847) in 1845 led an exploring party in the "Erebus" and "Terror" in search of the Northwest Passage, but by the winter of 1848–49 all hands were dead. See below, p. 100.

3. Deptford, Greenwich, and Erith are three ports between London and Gravesend; the 'Change is the "Wall Street" of London; and "interlopers" were ships which trespassed on the rights of the trade monopolies such as the East India Company with its large transports engaged in regular general trade.

...nknown earth! . . . The
...hs, the germs of empires.
..., and lights began to ap-
...ouse, a three-legged thing
... of ships moved in the fair-
...going down. And farther
...monstrous town was still
...loom in sunshine, a lurid

...'has been one of the dark

...owed the sea." The worst
...ot represent his class. He
...while most seamen lead,
...Their minds are of the
...ys with them—the ship;
and so is their country—the sea. One ship is very much like another,
and the sea is always the same. In the immutability of their surroundings the foreign shores, the foreign faces, the changing immensity of life, glide past, veiled not by a sense of mystery but by a
slightly disdainful ignorance; for there is nothing mysterious to a
seaman unless it be the sea itself, which is the mistress of his existence and as inscrutable as Destiny. For the rest, after his hours of
work, a casual stroll or a casual spree on shore suffices to unfold for
him the secret of a whole continent, and generally he finds the secret
not worth knowing. The yarns of seamen have a† direct simplicity,
the whole meaning of which lies within the shell of a cracked nut.
But Marlow was not typical (if his propensity to spin yarns be ex-
cepted), and to him the meaning of an episode was not inside like
a kernel but outside,* enveloping the tale which brought it out only
as a glow brings out a haze, in the likeness of one of these misty
halos that sometimes are made visible by the spectral illumination
of moonshine.

His remark did not seem at all surprising. It was just like Marlow.
It was accepted in silence. No one took the trouble to grunt even;
and presently he said, very slow:

"I was thinking of very old times, when the Romans first came
here, nineteen hundred years ago—the other day. . . . Light came
out of this river since—you say Knights? Yes; but it is like a running
blaze on a plain, like a flash of lightning in the clouds. We live in
the flicker—may it last as long as the old earth keeps rolling! But
darkness was here yesterday. Imagine the feelings of a commander
of a fine—what d'ye call 'em?—trireme[4] in the Mediterranean,

† *Ms begins here, but reads* an effective
for a direct
* *Ms:* outside in the unseen

4. A "trireme" was a galley with three
ranks of oars, one above another;
"Falernian wine," below, was a fa-

ordered suddenly to the north; run overland across the Gauls in a
hurry; put in charge of one of these craft the legionaries—a wonderful lot of handy men they must have been too—used to build, apparently by the hundred, in a month or two, if we may believe what
we read. Imagine him here—the very end of the world, a sea the
colour of lead, a sky the colour of smoke, a kind of ship about as
rigid as a concertina—and going up this river with stores, or orders,
or what you like. Sandbanks, marshes, forests, savages—precious
little to eat fit for a civilised man, nothing but Thames water to
drink. No Falernian wine here, no going ashore. Here and there a
military camp lost in a wilderness, like a needle in a bundle of hay—
cold, fog, tempests, disease, exile, and death—death skulking in the
air, in the water, in the bush. They must have been dying like flies
here. Oh yes—he did it. Did it very well, too, no doubt, and without
thinking much about it either, except afterwards to brag of what he
had gone through in his time, perhaps. They were men enough to
face the darkness. And perhaps he was cheered by keeping his eye
on a chance of promotion to the fleet at Ravenna by and by, if he
had good friends in Rome and survived the awful climate. Or think
of a decent young citizen in a toga—perhaps too much dice, you
know—coming out here in the train of some prefect, or tax-gatherer,
or trader, even, to mend his fortunes. Land in a swamp, march
through the woods, and in some inland post feel the savagery, the
utter savagery, had closed round him—all that mysterious life of the
wilderness that stirs† in the forest, in the jungles, in the hearts of wild
men. There's no initiation either into such mysteries. He has to live
in the midst of the incomprehensible, which is also detestable. And
it has a fascination, too, that goes to work upon him. The fascination of the abomination—you know. Imagine the growing regrets,
the longing to escape, the powerless disgust, the surrender, the
hate."

He paused.

"Mind," he began again, lifting one arm from the elbow, the palm
of the hand outwards, so that, with his legs folded before him, he
had the pose of a Buddha preaching in European clothes and without a lotus-flower—"Mind, none of us would feel exactly like this.
What saves us is efficiency—the devotion to efficiency. But these
chaps were not much account, really. They were no colonists; their
administration was merely a squeeze, and nothing more, I suspect.
They were conquerors, and for that you want only brute force—
nothing to boast of, when you have it, since your strength is just an
accident arising from the weakness of others. They grabbed what

mous ancient wine from Campania and
should not be confused with Neopolitan
Falerno; and "Ravenna," below, now
inland, was the chief Roman naval base
in northern Italy on the upper Adriatic.
† *Ms* p. 14, *running from this word
through* But these chaps were, *is missing.*

they could get for the sake of what was to be got.† It was just robbery with violence, aggravated murder on a great scale, and men going at it blind—as is very proper for those who tackle a darkness. The conquest of the earth, which mostly means the taking it away from those who have a different complexion or slightly flatter noses than ourselves, is not a pretty thing when you look into it too much. What redeems it is the idea only. An idea at the back of it; not a sentimental* pretence but an idea; and an unselfish belief in the idea—something you can set up, and bow down before, and offer a sacrifice to. . . ."

He broke off. Flames glided in the river, small green flames, red flames, white flames, pursuing, overtaking, joining, crossing each other—then separating slowly or hastily. The traffic of the great city went on in the deepening night upon the sleepless river.‡ We looked on, waiting patiently—there was nothing else to do till the end of the flood; but it was only after a long silence, when he said, in a hesitating voice, "I suppose you fellows remember I did once turn fresh-water sailor for a bit," that we knew** we were fated, before the ebb began to run, to hear about one of Marlow's inconclusive experiences.

"I don't want to bother you much with what happened to me personally," he began, showing in this remark the weakness of many tellers of tales who seem so often unaware of what their audience would best like to hear; "yet to understand the effect of it on me you ought to know how I got out there, what I saw, how I went up that river to the place where I first met the poor chap. It was the farthest point of navigation and the culminating point of my experience. It seemed somehow to throw a kind of light on everything about me—and into my thoughts. It was sombre enough too—and pitiful —not extraordinary in any way—not very clear either. No, not very clear. And yet it seemed to throw a kind of light.

"I had then, as you remember, just returned to London after a lot of Indian Ocean, Pacific, China Seas—a regular dose of the East— six years or so, and I was loafing about, hindering you fellows in your work and invading your homes, just as though I had got a heavenly

† *Ms:* got. That's all. The best of them is they didn't get up pretty fictions about it. Was there, I wonder, an association on a philanthropic basis to develop Britain, with some third rate king for a president and solemn old senators discoursing about it approvingly and philosophers with uncombed beards praising it, and men in market places crying it up. Not much! And that's what I like! No! No! It was just, *etc.*
* *Ms:* mouthing
‡ *Ms:* river. A big steamer came down all a long blaze of lights like a town viewed from the sea bound to the uttermost ends of the earth and timed to the day, to the very hour with nothing unknown in her path[,] no mystery on her way, nothing but a few coaling stations. She went fullspeed, noisily, an angry commotion of the waters followed her spreading from bank to bank—passed, vanished all at once—timed from port to port, to the very hour. And the earth suddenly seemed shrunk to the size of a pea spinning in the heart of an immense darkness full of sparks born, scattered, glowing, going out beyond the ken of men. We looked on, *etc.*
** *Ms* p. 17 *ends;* pp. 18–29 *missing.*

mission to civilise you. It was very fine for a time, but after a bit I did get tired of resting. Then I began to look for a ship—I should think the hardest work on earth. But the ships wouldn't even look at me. And I got tired of that game too.

"Now when I was a little chap I had a passion for maps. I would look for hours at South America, or Africa, or Australia, and lose myself in all the glories of exploration. At that time there were many blank spaces on the earth, and when I saw one that looked particularly inviting on a map (but they all look that) I would put my finger on it and say, When I grow up I will go there. The North Pole was one of these places, I remember. Well, I haven't been there yet, and shall not try now. The glamour's off. Other places were scattered about the Equator, and in every sort of latitude all over the two hemispheres. I have been in some of them, and . . . well, we won't talk about that. But there was one yet—the biggest, the most blank, so to speak—that I had a hankering after.

"True, by this time it was not a blank space any more. It had got filled since my boyhood with rivers and lakes and names. It had ceased to be a blank space of delightful mystery—a white patch for a boy to dream gloriously over. It had become a place of darkness. But there was in it one river especially, a mighty big river, that you could see on the map, resembling an immense snake uncoiled, with its head in the sea, its body at rest curving afar over a vast country, and its tail lost in the depths of the land. And as I looked at the map of it in a shop-window, it fascinated me as a snake would a bird—a silly little bird. Then I remembered there was a big concern, a Company for trade on that river. Dash it all! I thought to myself, they can't trade without using some kind of craft on that lot of fresh water—steamboats! Why shouldn't I try to get charge of one? I went on along Fleet Street,[5] but could not shake off the idea. The snake had charmed me.

"You understand it was a Continental concern, that Trading Society; but I have a lot of relations living on the Continent, because it's cheap and not so nasty as it looks, they say.

"I am sorry to own I began to worry them. This was already a fresh departure for me. I was not used to get things that way, you know. I always went my own road and on my own legs where I had a mind to go. I wouldn't have believed it of myself; but, then—you see—I felt somehow I must get there by hook or by crook. So I worried them. The men said, 'My dear fellow,' and did nothing. Then—would you believe it?—I tried the women. I, Charlie Marlow, set the women to work—to get a job. Heavens! Well, you see, the notion drove me. I had an aunt, a dear enthusiastic soul. She wrote: 'It will be delightful. I am ready to do anything, anything for

5. A central business street in London.

you. It is a glorious idea. I know the wife of a very high personage in the Administration, and also a man who has lots of influence with,' etc. etc. She was determined to make no end of fuss to get me appointed skipper of a river steamboat, if such was my fancy.

"I got my appointment—of course; and I got it very quick. It appears the Company had received news that one of their captains had been killed in a scuffle with the natives. This was my chance, and it made me the more anxious to go. It was only months and months afterwards, when I made the attempt to recover what was left of the body, that I heard the original quarrel arose from a mis-understanding about some hens. Yes, two black hens. Fresleven—that was the fellow's name, a Dane—thought himself wronged some-how in the bargain, so he went ashore and started to hammer the chief of the village with a stick. Oh, it didn't surprise me in the least to hear this, and at the same time to be told that Fresleven was the gentlest, quietest creature that ever walked on two legs. No doubt he was; but he had been a couple of years already out there engaged in the noble cause, you know, and he probably felt the need at last of asserting his self-respect in some way. Therefore he whacked the old nigger mercilessly, while a big crowd of his people watched him, thunderstruck, till some man—I was told the chief's son—in desper-ation at hearing the old chap yell, made a tentative jab with a spear at the white man—and of course it went quite easy between the shoulder-blades. Then the whole population cleared into the forest, expecting all kinds of calamities to happen, while, on the other hand, the steamer Fresleven commanded left also in a bad panic, in charge of the engineer, I believe. Afterwards nobody seemed to trouble much about Fresleven's remains, till I got out and stepped into his shoes. I couldn't let it rest, though; but when an opportunity offered at last to meet my predecessor, the grass growing through his ribs was tall enough to hide his bones. They were all there. The supernatural being had not been touched after he fell. And the village was deserted, the huts gaped black, rotting, all askew within the fallen enclosures. A calamity had come to it, sure enough. The people had vanished. Mad terror had scattered them, men, women, and children, through the bush, and they had never returned. What became of the hens I don't know either. I should think the cause of progress got them, anyhow. However, through this glorious affair I got my appointment, before I had fairly begun to hope for it.

"I flew around like mad to get ready, and before forty-eight hours I was crossing the Channel to show myself to my employers, and sign the contract. In a very few hours I arrived in a city that always makes me think of a whited sepulchre. Prejudice no doubt. I had no difficulty in finding the Company's offices. It was the biggest thing in the town, and everybody I met was full of it. They were going to run an oversea empire, and make no end of coin by trade.

"A narrow and deserted street in deep shadow, high houses, innumerable windows with venetian blinds, a dead silence, grass sprouting between the stones, imposing carriage archways right and left, immense double doors standing ponderously ajar. I slipped through one of these cracks, went up a swept and ungarnished staircase, as arid as a desert, and opened the first door I came to. Two women, one fat and the other slim, sat on straw-bottomed chairs, knitting black wool. The slim one got up and walked straight at me —still knitting with downcast eyes—and only just as I began to think of getting out of her way, as you would for a somnambulist, stood still, and looked up. Her dress was as plain as an umbrella-cover, and she turned round without a word and preceded me into a waiting-room. I gave my name, and looked about. Deal table in the middle, plain chairs all round the walls, on one end a large shining map, marked with all the colours of a rainbow. There was a vast amount of red—good to see at any time, because one knows that some real work is done in there, a deuce of a lot of blue, a little green, smears of orange, and, on the East Coast, a purple patch, to show where the jolly pioneers of progress drink the jolly lager-beer. However, I wasn't going into any of these. I was going into the yellow. Dead in the centre. And the river was there—fascinating—deadly—like a snake. Ough! A door opened, a white-haired secretarial head, but wearing a compassionate expression, appeared, and a skinny forefinger beckoned me into the sanctuary. Its light was dim, and a heavy writing-desk squatted in the middle. From behind that structure came out an impression of pale plumpness in a frock-coat. The great man himself. He was five feet six, I should judge, and had his grip on the handle-end of ever so many millions. He shook hands, I fancy, murmured vaguely, was satisfied with my French. *Bon voyage.*

"In about forty-five seconds I found myself again in the waiting-room with the compassionate secretary, who, full of desolation and sympathy, made me sign some document. I believe I undertook amongst other things not to disclose any trade secrets. Well, I am not going to.

"I began to feel slightly uneasy. You know I am not used to such ceremonies, and there was something ominous in the atmosphere. It was just as though I had been let into some conspiracy—I don't know—something not quite right; and I was glad to get out. In the outer room the two women knitted black wool feverishly. People were arriving, and the younger one was walking back and forth introducing them. The old one sat on her chair. Her flat cloth slippers were propped up on a foot-warmer, and a cat reposed on her lap. She wore a starched white affair on her head, had a wart on one cheek, and silver-rimmed spectacles hung on the tip of her nose. She glanced at me above the glasses. The swift and indifferent placidity of that look troubled me. Two youths with foolish and cheery countenances were being piloted over, and she threw at them the same quick glance of unconcerned wisdom. She seemed to know all about them and about me too. An eerie feeling came over me. She seemed uncanny and fateful. Often far away there I thought of these two, guarding the door of Darkness, knitting black wool as for a warm pall, one introducing, introducing continuously to the unknown, the other scrutinising the cheery and foolish faces with unconcerned old eyes. *Ave!* Old knitter of black wool. *Morituri te salutant.*[6] Not many of those she looked at ever saw her again—not half, by a long way.

"There was yet a visit to the doctor. 'A simple formality,' assured me the secretary, with an air of taking an immense part in all my sorrows. Accordingly a young chap wearing his hat over the left eyebrow, some clerk I suppose—there must have been clerks in the business, though the house was as still as a house in a city of the dead —came from somewhere upstairs, and led me forth. He† was shabby and careless, with ink-stains on the sleeves of his jacket, and his cravat was large and billowy, under a chin shaped like the toe of an old boot. It was a little too early for the doctor, so I proposed a drink, and thereupon he developed a vein of joviality. As we sat over our vermuths he glorified the Company's business, and by and by I expressed casually my surprise at him not going out there. He became very cool and collected all at once. 'I am not such a fool as I look, quoth Plato to his disciples,' he said sententiously, emptied his glass with great resolution, and we rose.

"The old doctor felt my pulse, evidently thinking of something else the while. 'Good, good for there,' he mumbled, and then with a certain eagerness asked me whether I would let him measure my head. Rather surprised, I said Yes, when he produced a thing like callipers and got the dimensions back and front and every way, taking notes carefully. He was an unshaven little man in a thread-bare coat like a gaberdine, with his feet in slippers, and I thought him a harmless fool. 'I always ask leave, in the interests of science, to measure the crania of those going out there,' he said. 'And when they come back too?' I asked. 'Oh, I never see them,' he remarked; 'and, moreover, the changes take place inside, you know.' He smiled, as if at some quiet joke. 'So you are going out there. Famous. Interesting too.' He gave me a searching glance, and made another note. 'Ever any madness in your family?' he asked, in a matter-of-fact tone. I felt very annoyed. 'Is that question in the interests of science

6. "Hail! . . . Those who are about to   † *Ms p. 30 begins here.*
die salute you."

too?' 'It would be,' he said, without taking notice of my irritation, 'interesting for science to watch the mental changes of individuals, on the spot, but . . .' 'Are you an alienist?' I interrupted. 'Every doctor should be—a little,' answered that original imperturbably. 'I have a little theory which you Messieurs who go out there must help me to prove. This is my share in the advantages my country shall reap from the possession of such a magnificent dependency. The mere wealth I leave to others. Pardon my questions, but you are the first Englishman coming under my observation . . .' I hastened to assure him I was not in the least typical. 'If I were,' said I, 'I wouldn't be talking like this with you.' 'What you say is rather profound, and probably erroneous,' he said, with a laugh. 'Avoid irritation more than exposure to the sun. Adieu. How do you English say, eh? Good-bye. Ah! Good-bye. Adieu. In the tropics one must before everything keep calm.' . . . He lifted a warning forefinger. . . . '*Du calme, du calme. Adieu.*'

"One thing more remained to do—say good-bye to my excellent aunt. I found her triumphant. I had a cup of tea—the last decent cup of tea for many days—and in a room that most soothingly looked just as you would expect a lady's drawing-room to look, we had a long quiet chat by the fireside. In the course of these confidences it became quite plain to me I had been represented to the wife of the high dignitary, and goodness knows to how many more people besides, as an exceptional and gifted creature—a piece of good fortune for the Company—a man you don't get hold of every day. Good Heavens! and I was going to take charge of a two-penny-half-penny river-steamboat with a penny whistle attached! It appeared, however, I was also one of the Workers, with a capital—you know. Something like an emissary of light, something like a lower sort of apostle. There had been a lot of such rot let loose in print and talk just about that time, and the excellent woman, living right in the rush of all that humbug, got carried off her feet. She talked about 'weaning those ignorant millions from their horrid ways,' till, upon my word, she made me quite uncomfortable. I ventured to hint that the Company was run for profit.

" 'You forget, dear Charlie, that the labourer is worthy of his hire,' she said brightly. It's queer how out of touch with truth women are. They live in a world of their own, and there had never been anything like it, and never can be. It is too beautiful altogether, and if they were to set it up it would go to pieces before the first sunset. Some confounded fact we men have been living contentedly with ever since the day of creation would start up and knock the whole thing over.

"After this I got embraced, told to wear flannel, be sure to write

7. In Conrad's day, a kind of psychiatrist.

often, and so on—and I left. In the street—I don't know why—a queer feeling came to me that I was an impostor. Odd thing that I, who used to clear out for any part of the world at twenty-four hours' notice, with less thought than most men give to the crossing of a street, had a moment—I won't say of hesitation, but of startled pause, before this commonplace affair.† The best way I can explain it to you is by saying that, for a second or two, I felt as though, instead of going to the centre of a continent, I were about to set off for the centre of the earth.

"I left in a French steamer, and* she called in every blamed port they have out there, for, as far as I could see, the sole purpose of landing soldiers and custom-house officers. I watched the coast. Watching a coast as it slips by the ship is like thinking about an enigma. There it is before you—smiling, frowning, inviting, grand, mean, insipid, or savage, and always mute with an air of whispering, Come and find out. This one was almost featureless, as if still in the making, with an aspect of monotonous grimness. The edge of a colossal jungle, so dark green as to be almost black, fringed with white surf, ran straight, like a ruled line, far, far away along a blue sea whose glitter was blurred by a creeping mist. The sun was fierce, the land seemed to glisten and drip with steam. Here and there greyish-whitish specks showed up clustered inside the white surf, with a flag flying above them perhaps—settlements some centuries old, and still no bigger than pin-heads on the untouched expanse of their background. We pounded along, stopped, landed soldiers; went on, landed custom-house clerks to levy toll in what looked like a God-forsaken wilderness, with a tin shed and a flag-pole lost in it; landed more soldiers—to take care of the custom-house clerks presumably. Some, I heard, got drowned in the surf; but whether they did or not, nobody seemed particularly to care. They were just flung out there, and on we went. Every day the coast looked the same, as though we had not moved; but we passed various places—trading places—with names like Gran' Bassam, Little Popo; names that seemed to belong to some sordid farce acted in front of a sinister back-cloth.‡ The idleness of a passenger, my isolation amongst all these men with whom I had no point of contact, the oily and languid sea, the uniform sombreness of the coast, seemed to keep me away from the truth of things, within the toil of a mournful and senseless delusion. The voice of the surf heard now and then was a positive pleasure, like the speech of a brother. It was something natural, that had its reason, that had a meaning. Now and then a boat from the shore gave one a momentary contact with reality. It was paddled by black fellows. You could see from afar the white of

† *Ms:* affair as though it had been an unheard of undertaking.
* *Ms:* and beginning with Dakar

‡ *Ms:* back-cloth. Of all my life this passage is the part the most unreal.

their eyeballs glistening. They shouted, sang; their bodies streamed with perspiration; they had faces like grotesque masks—these chaps; but they had bone, muscle, a wild vitality, an intense energy of movement, that was as natural and true as the surf along their coast. They wanted no excuse for being there. They were a great comfort to look at. For a time I would feel I belonged still to a world of straightforward facts; but the feeling would not last long. Something would turn up to scare it away. Once, I remember, we came upon a man-of-war anchored off the coast. There wasn't even a shed there, and she was shelling the bush. It appears the French had one of their† wars going on thereabouts. Her ensign dropped limp like a rag; the muzzles of the long six-inch* guns stuck out all over the low hull; the greasy, slimy swell swung her up lazily and let her down, swaying her thin masts. In the empty immensity of earth, sky, and water, there she was, incomprehensible, firing into a continent. Pop, would go one of the six-inch guns; a small flame would dart and vanish, a little white smoke would disappear, a tiny projectile would give a feeble screech—and nothing happened. Nothing could happen. There was a touch of insanity in the proceeding, a sense of lugubrious drollery in the sight; and it was not dissipated by somebody on board assuring me earnestly there was a camp of natives—he called them enemies!—hidden out of sight somewhere.

"We gave her her letters (I heard the men in that lonely ship were dying of fever at the rate of three a day) and went on. We called at some more places with farcical names, where the merry dance of death and trade goes on in a still and earthy atmosphere as of an overheated catacomb; all along the formless coast bordered by dangerous surf, as if Nature herself had tried to ward off intruders; in and out of rivers, streams of death in life, whose banks were rotting into mud, whose waters, thickened into slime, invaded the contorted mangroves, that seemed to writhe at us in the extremity of an impotent despair. Nowhere did we stop long enough to get a particularised impression, but the general sense of vague and oppressive wonder grew upon me. It was like a weary pilgrimage amongst hints for nightmares.

"It was upward of thirty days before I saw the mouth of the big river.‡ We anchored off the seat of the government. But my work

---

† Ms: their heroic wars
* Ms: ten-inch *and below; Maga:* eight-inch *and below; 1902:* six-inch *and below*
‡ Ms: river where my work was waiting for me. We went up some twenty miles and anchored off the seat of the government. I had heard enough in Europe about its advanced state of civilization: the papers, nay the very paper vendors in the sepulchral city were boasting about the steam tramway and

the hotel—especially the hotel. I beheld that wonder. It was like a symbol at the gate. It stood alone, a grey high cube of iron with two tiers of galleries outside towering above one of those ruinous-looking foreshores you come upon at home in out-of-the-way places where refuse is thrown out. To make the resemblance complete it wanted only a drooping post bearing a board with the legend: rubbish shot here, and the symbol would have had the clearness of

would not begin till some two hundred miles farther on. So as soon as I could I made a start for a place thirty miles higher up.

"I had my passage on a little sea-going steamer. Her captain was a Swede, and knowing me for a seaman, invited me on the bridge. He was a young man, lean, fair, and morose, with lanky hair and a shuffling gait. As we left the miserable little wharf, he tossed his head contemptuously at the shore. 'Been living there?' he asked. I said, 'Yes.' 'Fine lot these government chaps—are they not?' he went on, speaking English with great precision and considerable bitterness. 'It is funny what some people will do for a few francs a month. I wonder what becomes of that kind when it goes up country?' I said to him I expected to see that soon. 'So-o-o!' he exclaimed. He shuffled athwart, keeping one eye ahead vigilantly. 'Don't be too sure,' he continued. 'The other day I took up a man who hanged himself on the road. He was a Swede, too.' 'Hanged himself! Why, in God's name?' I cried. He kept on looking out watchfully. 'Who knows? The sun too much for him, or the country perhaps.'†

"At last we opened a reach. A rocky cliff appeared, mounds of turned-up earth by the shore, houses on a hill, others with iron roofs, amongst a waste of excavations, or hanging to the declivity. A continuous noise of the rapids above hovered over this scene of inhabited devastation. A lot of people, mostly black and naked, moved about like ants. A jetty projected into the river. A blinding sunlight drowned all this at times in a sudden recrudescence of glare. 'There's your Company's station,' said the Swede, pointing to three wooden

the naked truth. Not that a man could not be found even there, just as a precious stone is sometimes found in a dust-bin.

I had one dinner in the hotel and found out the tramway ran only twice a day, at mealtimes. It brought I believe the whole government with the exception of the governor general down from the hill to be fed by contract. They filled the dining room, uniforms and civil clothes[,] sallow faces, purposeless expressions. I was astonished at their number. An air of weary bewilderment at finding themselves where they were sat upon all the faces, and in their demeanour they pretended to take themselves seriously just as the greasy and dingy place that was like one of those infamous eating shops you find near the slums of cities, where everything is suspicious, the linen, the crockery, the food[,] the owner[,] the patrons, pretended to be a sign of progress; as the enormous baobab on the barren top of the hill amongst the government buildings[,] soldier's huts, wooden shanties, corrugated iron hovels, soared, spread out a maze of denuded boughs as though it had been a shade giving tree, as ghastly as a skeleton that posturing in showy attitudes would pretend to be, a man.

I was glad to think my work only began two hundred miles away from there. I could not be too far away from that comedy of light at the door of darkness. As soon as I could I left for a place thirty miles higher up. From there I would have to walk on the caravan road some hundred and seventy miles more to the starting point of inland navigation.

I had my passage, *etc.*
† *Ms:* perhaps.

The little steamer had no speed to speak of and I was rather impatient to see the first establishment, the shore station of my company. We had left the coast belt of forest and barren, stony hills came to view right and left of the stream, bordering flat strips of reedy coarse grass. [*Canceled:* As we rounded a point I heard far ahead a powerful and muffled detonation as of a big gun. After a time there was another. It reminded me of the ship shelling the continent. "What's that?" I asked. "Railway station," answered the Swede curtly, preparing to make a crossing to the south bank.]

At last we opened a reach, *etc.*

barrack-like structures on the rocky slope. 'I will send your things up. Four boxes did you say? So. Farewell.'

"I came upon a boiler wallowing in the grass, then found a path leading up the hill. It turned aside for the boulders, and also for an undersized railway truck lying there on its back with its wheels in the air. One was off. The thing looked as dead as the carcass of some animal. I came upon more pieces of decaying machinery, a stack of rusty rails. To the left a clump of trees made a shady spot, where dark things seemed to stir feebly. I blinked, the path was steep. A horn tooted to the right, and I saw the black people run. A heavy and dull detonation shook the ground, a puff of smoke came out of the cliff, and that was all. No change appeared on the face of the rock. They were building a railway. The cliff was not in the way or anything; but this objectless blasting was all the work going on.

"A slight clinking behind me made me turn my head. Six black men advanced in a file, toiling up the path. They walked erect and slow, balancing small baskets full of earth on their heads, and the clink kept time with their footsteps. Black rags were wound round their loins, and the short ends behind waggled to and fro like tails. I could see every rib, the joints of their limbs were like knots in a rope; each had an iron collar on his neck, and all were connected together with a chain whose bights swung between them, rhythmically clinking. Another report from the cliff made me think suddenly of that ship of war I had seen firing into a continent. It was the same kind of ominous voice; but these men could by no stretch of imagination be called enemies. They were called criminals, and the outraged law, like the bursting shells, had come to them, an insoluble mystery from the sea. All their meagre breasts panted together, the violently dilated nostrils quivered, the eyes stared stonily uphill. They passed me within six inches, without a glance, with that complete, deathlike indifference of unhappy savages. Behind this raw matter one of the reclaimed, the product of the new forces at work, strolled despondently, carrying a rifle by its middle. He had a uniform jacket with one button off, and seeing a white man on the path, hoisted his weapon to his shoulder with alacrity. This was simple prudence, white men being so much alike at a distance that he could not tell who I might be. He was speedily reassured, and with a large, white, rascally grin, and a glance at his charge, seemed to take me into partnership in his exalted trust. After all, I also was a part of the great cause of these high and just proceedings.

"Instead of going up, I turned and descended to the left. My idea was to let that chain-gang get out of sight before I climbed the hill. You know I am not particularly tender; I've had to strike and to fend off. I've had to resist and to attack sometimes—that's only one way of resisting—without counting the exact cost, according to the demands of such sort of life as I had blundered into. I've seen the devil of violence, and the devil of greed, and the devil of hot desire; but, by all the stars! these were strong, lusty, red-eyed devils, that swayed and drove men—men, I tell you. But as I stood on this hillside, I foresaw that in the blinding sunshine of that land I would become acquainted with a flabby, pretending, weak-eyed devil of a rapacious and pitiless folly. How insidious he could be, too, I was only to find out several months later and a thousand miles farther. For a moment I stood appalled, as though by a warning. Finally I descended the hill, obliquely, towards the trees I had seen.

"I avoided a vast artificial hole somebody had been digging on the slope, the purpose of which I found it impossible to divine. It wasn't a quarry or a sandpit, anyhow. It was just a hole. It might have been connected with the philanthropic desire of giving the criminals something to do. I don't know. Then I nearly fell into a very narrow ravine, almost no more than a scar in the hillside. I discovered that a lot of imported drainage-pipes for the settlement had been tumbled in there. There wasn't one that was not broken. It was a wanton smash-up. At last I got under the trees. My purpose was to stroll into the shade for a moment; but no sooner within than it seemed to me I had stepped into the gloomy circle of some Inferno. The rapids were near, and an uninterrupted, uniform, headlong, rushing noise filled the mournful stillness of the grove, where not a breath stirred, not a leaf moved, with a mysterious sound—as though the tearing pace of the launched earth had suddenly become audible.

"Black shapes crouched, lay, sat between the trees, leaning against the trunks, clinging to the earth, half coming out, half effaced within the dim light, in all the attitudes of pain, abandonment, and despair. Another mine[8] on the cliff went off, followed by a slight shudder of the soil under my feet. The work was going on. The work! And this was the place where some of the helpers had withdrawn to die.

"They were dying slowly—it was very clear. They were not enemies, they were not criminals, they were nothing earthly now—nothing but black shadows of disease and starvation, lying confusedly in the greenish gloom. Brought from all the recesses of the coast in all the legality† of time contracts, lost in uncongenial surroundings, fed on unfamiliar food, they sickened, became inefficient, and were then allowed to crawl away and rest. These moribund shapes were free as air—and nearly as thin. I began to distinguish the gleam of the eyes under the trees. Then, glancing down, I saw a face near my hand. The black bones reclined at full length with one shoulder against the tree, and slowly the eyelids rose and the sunken eyes looked up at me, enormous and vacant, a kind of blind, white flicker in the depths of the orbs, which died out slowly. The man seemed

8. British for a high-explosive charge.　　† *Ms:* pomp

young—almost a boy—but you know with them it's hard to tell. I found nothing else to do but to offer him one of my good Swede's ship's biscuits I had in my pocket. The fingers closed slowly on it and held—there was no other movement and no other glance. He had tied a bit of white worsted round his neck—Why? Where did he get it? Was it a badge—an ornament—a charm—a propitiatory act? Was there any idea at all connected with it? It looked startling round his black neck, this bit of white thread from beyond the seas.

"Near the same tree two more bundles of acute angles sat with their legs drawn up. One, with his chin propped on his knees, stared at nothing, in an intolerable and appalling manner: his brother phantom rested its forehead, as if overcome with a great weariness; and all about others were scattered in every pose of contorted collapse, as in some picture of a massacre or a pestilence. While I stood horror-struck, one of these creatures rose to his hands and knees, and went off on all-fours towards the river to drink. He lapped out of his hand, then sat up in the sunlight, crossing his shins in front of him, and after a time let his woolly head fall on his breastbone.

"I didn't want any more loitering in the shade, and I made haste towards the station. When near the buildings I met a white man, in such an unexpected elegance of get-up that in the first moment I took him for a sort of vision. I saw a high starched collar, white cuffs, a light alpaca jacket, snowy trousers, a clean† necktie, and varnished boots. No hat. Hair parted, brushed, oiled, under a green-lined parasol held in a big white hand. He was amazing, and had a pen-holder behind his ear.

"I shook hands with this miracle, and I learned he was the Company's chief accountant, and that all the book-keeping was done at this station. He had come out for a moment, he said, 'to get a breath of fresh air.' The expression sounded wonderfully odd, with its suggestion of sedentary desk-life. I wouldn't have mentioned the fellow to you at all, only it was from his lips that I first heard the name of the man who is so indissolubly connected with the memories of that time. Moreover, I respected the fellow. Yes; I respected his collars, his vast cuffs, his brushed hair. His appearance was certainly that of a hairdresser's dummy; but in the great demoralisation of the land he kept up his appearance. That's backbone. His starched collars and got-up shirt-fronts were achievements of character. He had been out nearly three years; and, later, I could not help asking him how he managed to sport such linen. He had just the faintest blush, and said modestly, 'I've been teaching one of the native women about the station. It was difficult. She had a distaste for the work.' Thus this man had verily accomplished something. And he was devoted to his books, which were in apple-pie order.

† *Ms:* clear silk; *Maga and 1902:* clear

"Everything else in the station was in a muddle,—heads, things, buildings. Strings of dusty niggers with splay feet arrived and departed; a stream of manufactured goods, rubbishy cottons, beads, and brass-wire set into the depths of darkness, and in return came a precious trickle of ivory.

"I had to wait in the station for ten days—an eternity. I lived in a hut in the yard, but to be out of the chaos I would sometimes get into the accountant's office. It was built of horizontal planks, and so badly put together that, as he bent over his high desk, he was barred from neck to heels with narrow strips of sunlight. There was no need to open the big shutter to see. It was hot there too; big flies buzzed fiendishly, and did not sting, but stabbed. I sat generally on the floor, while, of faultless appearance (and even slightly scented), perching on a high stool, he wrote, he wrote. Sometimes he stood up for exercise. When a truckle-bed with a sick man (some invalided agent from up-country) was put in there, he exhibited a gentle annoyance. 'The groans of this sick person,' he said, 'distract my attention. And without that it is extremely difficult to guard against clerical errors in this climate.'

"One day he remarked, without lifting his head, 'In the interior you will no doubt meet Mr. Kurtz.'† On my asking who Mr. Kurtz was, he said he was a first-class agent; and seeing my disappointment at this information, he added slowly, laying down his pen, 'He is a very remarkable person.' Further questions elicited from him that Mr. Kurtz was at present in charge of a trading-post, a very important one, in the true ivory-country, at 'the very bottom of there. Sends in as much ivory as all the others put together . . .' He began to write again. The sick man was too ill to groan. The flies buzzed in a great peace.

"Suddenly there was a growing murmur of voices and a great tramping of feet. A caravan had come in. A violent babble of uncouth sounds burst out on the other side of the planks. All the carriers were speaking together, and in the midst of the uproar the lamentable voice of the chief agent was heard 'giving it up' tearfully for the twentieth time that day. . . . He rose slowly. 'What a frightful row,' he said. He crossed the room gently to look at the sick man, and returning, said to me, 'He does not hear.' 'What! Dead?' I asked, startled. 'No, not yet,' he answered, with great composure. Then, alluding with a toss of the head to the tumult in the station-yard, 'When one has got to make correct entries, one comes to hate those savages—hate them to the death.' He remained thoughtful for a moment. 'When you see Mr. Kurtz,' he went on, 'tell him from me that everything here'—he glanced at the desk—'is very satisfactory. I don't like to write to him—with those messengers of ours you

† *Ms canceled:* Klein (*and the next three times; thereafter,* Kurtz).

never know who may get hold of your letter—at that Central Station.' He stared at me for a moment with his mild, bulging eyes. 'Oh, he will go far, very far,' he began again. 'He will be a somebody in the Administration before long. They, above—the Council in Europe, you know—mean him to be.'

"He turned to his work. The noise outside had ceased, and presently in going out I stopped at the door. In the steady buzz of flies the homeward-bound agent was lying flushed and insensible; the other, bent over his books, was making correct entries of perfectly correct transactions; and fifty feet below the doorstep I could see the still tree-tops of the grove of death.

"Next day I left that station at last, with a caravan of sixty men, for a two-hundred-mile tramp.

"No use telling you much about that. Paths, paths, everywhere; a stamped-in network of paths spreading over the empty land, through long grass, through burnt grass, through thickets, down and up chilly ravines, up and down stony hills ablaze with heat; and a solitude, a solitude, nobody, not a hut. The population had cleared out a long time ago. Well, if a lot of mysterious niggers armed with all kinds of fearful weapons suddenly took to travelling on the road between Deal and Gravesend, catching the yokels right and left to carry heavy loads for them, I fancy every farm and cottage thereabouts would get empty very soon. Only here the dwellings were gone too. Still, I passed through several abandoned villages. There's something pathetically childish in the ruins of grass walls. Day after day, with the stamp and shuffle of sixty pair of bare feet behind me, each pair under a 60-lb. load. Camp, cook, sleep; strike camp, march. Now and then a carrier dead in harness, at rest in the long grass near the path, with an empty water-gourd and his long staff lying by his side. A great silence around and above. Perhaps on some quiet night the tremor of far-off drums, sinking, swelling, a tremor vast, faint; a sound weird, appealing, suggestive, and wild—and perhaps with as profound a meaning as the sound of bells in a Christian country. Once a white man in an unbuttoned uniform, camping on the path with an armed escort of lank Zanzibaris,[9] very hospitable and festive —not to say drunk. Was looking after the upkeep of the road, he declared. Can't say I saw any road or any upkeep, unless the body of a middle-aged negro, with a bullet-hole in the forehead, upon which I absolutely stumbled three miles farther on, may be considered as a permanent improvement. I had a white companion too, not a bad chap, but rather too fleshy and with the exasperating habit of fainting on the hot hillsides, miles away from the least bit of shade and water. Annoying, you know, to hold your own coat like a parasol over a man's head while he is coming to. I couldn't help

9. The natives of Zanzibar were used as mercenaries throughout Africa.

asking him once what he meant by coming there at all. 'To make money, of course. What do you think?' he said scornfully. Then he got fever, and had to be carried in a hammock slung under a pole. As he weighed sixteen stone[1] I had no end of rows with the carriers. They jibbed, ran away, sneaked off with their loads in the night—quite a mutiny. So, one evening, I made a speech in English with gestures, not one of which was lost to the sixty pairs of eyes before me, and the next morning I started the hammock off in front all right. An hour afterwards I came upon the whole concern wrecked in a bush—man, hammock, groans, blankets, horrors. The heavy pole had skinned his poor nose. He was very anxious for me to kill somebody, but there wasn't the shadow of a carrier near. I remembered the old doctor—'It would be interesting for science to watch the mental changes of individuals, on the spot.' I felt I was becoming scientifically interesting. However, all that is to no purpose. On the fifteenth day I came in sight of the big river again, and hobbled into the Central Station. It was on a back water surrounded by scrub and forest, with a pretty border of smelly mud on one side, and on the three others enclosed by a crazy fence of rushes. A neglected gap was all the gate it had, and the first glance at the place was enough to let you see the flabby devil was running that show. White men with long staves in their hands appeared languidly from amongst the buildings, strolling up to take a look at me, and then retired out of sight somewhere. One of them, a stout, excitable chap with black moustaches, informed me with great volubility and many digressions, as soon as I told him who I was, that my steamer was at the bottom of the river. I was thunderstruck. What, how, why? Oh, it was 'all right.' The 'manager himself' was there. All quite correct. 'Everybody had behaved splendidly! splendidly!'—'You must,' he said in agitation, 'go and see the general manager at once. He is waiting.'

"I did not see the real significance of that wreck at once. I fancy I see it now, but I am not sure—not at all. Certainly the affair was too stupid—when I think of it—to be altogether natural. Still . . . But at the moment it presented itself simply as a confounded nuisance. The steamer was sunk. They had started two days before in a sudden hurry up the river with the manager on board, in charge of some volunteer skipper, and before they had been out three hours they tore the bottom out of her on stones, and she sank near the south bank. I asked myself what I was to do there, now my boat was lost. As a matter of fact, I had plenty to do in fishing my command out of the river. I had to set about it the very next day. That, and the repairs when I brought the pieces to the station, took some months.

1. 224 pounds.

"My first interview with the manager was curious. He did not ask me to sit down after my twenty-mile walk that morning. He was commonplace in complexion, in feature, in manners, and in voice. He was of middle size and of ordinary build. His eyes, of the usual blue, were perhaps remarkably cold, and he certainly could make his glance fall on one as trenchant and heavy as an axe. But even at these times the rest of his person seemed to disclaim the intention. Otherwise there was only an indefinable, faint expression of his lips, something stealthy—a smile—not a smile—I remember it, but I can't explain.† It was unconscious, this smile was, though just after he had said something it got intensified for an instant. It came at the end of his speeches like a seal applied on the words to make the meaning of the commonest phrase appear absolutely inscrutable. He was a common trader, from his youth up employed in these parts—nothing more. He was obeyed, yet he inspired neither love nor fear, nor even respect. He inspired uneasiness. That was it! Uneasiness. Not a definite mistrust—just uneasiness—nothing more. You have no idea how effective such a . . . a . . . faculty can be. He had no genius for organising, for initiative, or for order even. That was evident in such things as the deplorable state of the station. He had no learning, and no intelligence. His position had come to him—why? Perhaps because he was never ill . . . He had served three terms of three years out there . . . Because triumphant health in the general rout of constitutions is a kind of power in itself. When he went home on leave he rioted on a large scale—pompously. Jack ashore—with a difference—in externals only. This one could gather from his casual talk. He originated nothing, he could keep the routine going—that's all. But he was great. He was great by this little thing that it was impossible to tell what could control such a man. He never gave that secret away. Perhaps there was nothing within him. Such a suspicion made one pause—for out there there were no external checks. Once when various tropical diseases had laid low almost every 'agent' in the station, he was heard to say, 'Men who come out here should have no entrails.' He sealed the utterance with that smile of his, as though it had been a door opening into a darkness he had in his keeping. You fancied you had seen things—but the seal was on. When annoyed at meal-times by the constant quarrels of the white men about precedence, he ordered an immense round table to be made, for which a special house had to be built. This was the station's mess-room. Where he sat was the first place—the rest were nowhere. One felt this to be his unalterable conviction. He was neither civil or uncivil. He was quiet. He allowed his 'boy'—an overfed young negro from the coast—to treat

† *Ms:* explain. It could be seen from a distance as he walked about the station grounds, a silent perambulating, glancing figure—with the air of being very much alone. It was unconscious, *etc.*

the white men, under his very eyes, with provoking insolence.

"He began to speak as soon as he saw me. I had been very long on the road. He could not wait. Had to start without me. The up-river stations had to be relieved. There had been so many delays already that he did not know who was dead and who was alive, and how they got on—and so on, and so on. He paid no attention to my explanations, and, playing with a stick of sealing-wax, repeated several times that the situation was 'very grave, very grave.' There were rumours that a very important station was in jeopardy, and its chief, Mr. Kurtz, was ill. Hoped it was not true. Mr. Kurtz was . . . I felt weary and irritable. Hang Kurtz, I thought. I interrupted him by saying I had heard of Mr. Kurtz on the coast. 'Ah! So they talk of him down there,' he murmured to himself. Then he began again, assuring me Mr. Kurtz was the best agent he had, an exceptional man, of the greatest importance to the Company; therefore I could understand his anxiety. He was, he said, 'very, very uneasy.' Certainly he fidgeted on his chair a good deal, exclaimed, 'Ah, Mr. Kurtz!' broke the stick of sealing-wax and seemed dumbfounded by the accident. Next thing he wanted to know 'how long it would take to' . . . I interrupted him again. Being hungry, you know, and kept on my feet too, I was getting savage. 'How can I tell?' I said. 'I haven't even seen the wreck yet—some months, no doubt.' All this talk seemed to me so futile. 'Some months,' he said. 'Well, let us say three months before we can make a start. Yes. That ought to do the affair.' I flung out of his hut (he lived all alone in a clay hut with a sort of verandah) muttering to myself my opinion of him. He was a chattering idiot. Afterwards I took it back when it was borne in upon me startlingly with what extreme nicety he had estimated the time requisite for the 'affair.'

"I went to work the next day, turning, so to speak, my back on that station. In that way only it seemed to me I could keep my hold on the redeeming facts of life. Still, one must look about sometimes; and then I saw this station, these men strolling aimlessly about in the sunshine of the yard. I asked myself sometimes what it all meant. They wandered here and there with their absurd long staves in their hands, like a lot of faithless pilgrims bewitched inside a rotten fence. The word 'ivory' rang in the air, was whispered, was sighed. You would think they were praying to it. A taint of imbecile rapacity blew through it all, like a whiff from some corpse. By Jove! I've never seen anything so unreal in my life. And outside, the silent wilderness surrounding this cleared speck on the earth struck me as something great and invincible, like evil or truth, waiting patiently for the passing away of this fantastic invasion.

"Oh, those months! Well, never mind. Various things happened. One evening a grass shed full of calico, cotton prints, beads, and I don't know what else, burst into a blaze so suddenly that you would have thought the earth had opened to let an avenging fire consume all that trash. I was smoking my pipe quietly by my dismantled steamer, and saw them all cutting capers in the light, with their arms lifted high, when the stout man with moustaches came tearing down to the river, a tin pail in his hand, assured me that everybody was 'behaving splendidly, splendidly,' dipped about a quart of water and tore back again. I noticed there was a hole in the bottom of his pail.

"I strolled up. There was no hurry. You see the thing had gone off like a box of matches. It had been hopeless from the very first. The flame had leaped high, driven everybody back, lighted up everything—and collapsed. The shed was already a heap of embers glowing fiercely. A nigger was being beaten near by. They said he had caused the fire in some way; be that as it may, he was screeching most horribly. I saw him, later, for several days, sitting in a bit of shade looking very sick and trying to recover himself: afterwards he arose and went out—and the wilderness without a sound took him into its bosom again. As I approached the glow from the dark I found myself at the back of two men, talking. I heard the name of Kurtz pronounced, then the words, 'take advantage of this unfortunate accident.' One of the men was the manager. I wished him a good evening. 'Did you ever see anything like it—eh? it is incredible,' he said, and walked off. The other man remained. He was a first-class agent, young, gentlemanly, a bit reserved, with a forked little beard and a hooked nose. He was stand-offish with the other agents, and they on their side said he was the manager's spy upon them. As to me, I had hardly ever spoken to him before. We got into talk, and by and by we strolled away from the hissing ruins. Then he asked me to his room, which was in the main building of the station. He struck a match, and I perceived that this young aristocrat had not only a silver-mounted dressing-case but also a whole candle all to himself. Just at that time the manager was the only man supposed to have any right to candles. Native mats covered the clay walls; a collection of spears, assegais,[2] shields, knives, was hung up in trophies. The business entrusted to this fellow was the making of bricks—so I had been informed; but there wasn't a fragment of a brick anywhere in the station, and he had been there more than a year—waiting. It seems he could not make bricks without something, I don't know what—straw maybe. Anyway, it could not be found there, and as it was not likely to be sent from Europe, it did not appear clear to me what he was waiting for. An act of special creation perhaps. However, they were all waiting—all the sixteen or twenty pilgrims of them—for something; and upon my word it did not seem an uncongenial occupation, from the way they took it,

2. Slender South African throwing spears.

though the only thing that ever came to them was disease—as far as I could see. They beguiled the time by backbiting and intriguing against each other in a foolish kind of way. There was an air of plotting about that station, but nothing came of it, of course. It was as unreal as everything else—as the philanthropic pretence of the whole concern, as their talk, as their government, as their show of work. The only real feeling was a desire to get appointed to a trading-post where ivory was to be had, so that they could earn percentages. They intrigued and slandered and hated each other only on that account—but as to effectually lifting a little finger—oh no. By Heavens! there is something after all in the world allowing one man to steal a horse while another must not look at a halter. Steal a horse straight out. Very well. He has done it. Perhaps he can ride. But there is a way of looking at a halter that would provoke the most charitable of saints into a kick.

"I had no idea why he wanted to be sociable, but as we chatted in there it suddenly occurred to me the fellow was trying to get at something—in fact, pumping me. He alluded constantly to Europe, to the people I was supposed to know there—putting leading questions as to my acquaintances in the sepulchral city, and so on. His little eyes glittered like mica discs—with curiosity—though he tried to keep up a bit of superciliousness. At first I was astonished, but very soon I became awfully curious to see what he would find out from me. I couldn't possibly imagine what I had in me to make it worth his while.† It was very pretty to see how he baffled himself, for in truth my body was full only of chills, and my head had nothing in it but that wretched steamboat business. It was evident he took me for a perfectly shameless prevaricator. At last he got angry, and, to conceal a movement of furious annoyance, he yawned. I rose. Then I noticed a small sketch in oils, on a panel, representing a woman, draped and blindfolded, carrying a lighted torch. The background was sombre—almost black. The movement of the woman was stately, and the effect of the torchlight on the face was sinister.

"It arrested me, and he stood by civilly, holding an empty half-pint champagne bottle (medical comforts) with the candle stuck in it. To my question he said Mr. Kurtz had painted this—in this very station more than a year ago—while waiting for means to go to his trading-post. 'Tell me, pray,' said I, 'who is this Mr. Kurtz?'

" 'The chief of the Inner Station,' he answered in a short tone, looking away. 'Much obliged,' I said, laughing. 'And you are the brickmaker of the Central Station. Every one knows that.' He was silent for a while. 'He is a prodigy,' he said at last. 'He is an emissary of pity, and science, and progress, and devil knows what else. We want,' he began to declaim suddenly, 'for the guidance of the cause

† *Ms and Maga:* while. His allusions were Chinese to me. It was, *etc.*

entrusted to us by Europe, so to speak, higher intelligence, wide sympathies, a singleness of purpose.' 'Who says that?' I asked. 'Lots of them,' he replied. 'Some even write that; and so *he* comes here, a special being, as you ought to know.' 'Why ought I to know?' I interrupted, really surprised. He paid no attention. 'Yes. To-day he is chief of the best station, next year he will be assistant-manager, two years more and . . . but I daresay you know what he will be in two years' time. You are of the new gang—the gang of virtue. The same people who sent him specially also recommended you. Oh, don't say no. I've my own eyes to trust.' Light dawned upon me. My dear aunt's influential acquaintances were producing an unexpected effect upon that young man. I nearly burst into a laugh. 'Do you read the Company's confidential correspondence?' I asked. He hadn't a word to say. It was great fun. 'When Mr. Kurtz,' I continued severely, 'is General Manager, you won't have the opportunity.'

"He blew the candle out suddenly, and we went outside. The moon had risen. Black figures strolled about listlessly, pouring water on the glow, whence proceeded a sound of hissing; steam ascended in the moonlight; the beaten nigger groaned somewhere. 'What a row the brute makes!' said the indefatigable man with the moustaches, appearing near us. 'Serve him right. Transgression—punishment—bang! Pitiless, pitiless. That's the only way. This will prevent all conflagrations for the future. I was just telling the manager . . .' He noticed my companion, and became crestfallen all at once. 'Not in bed yet,' he said, with a kind of servile† heartiness; 'it's so natural. Ha! Danger—agitation.' He vanished. I went on to the river-side, and the other followed me. I heard a scathing murmur at my ear, 'Heaps of muffs—go to.' The pilgrims could be seen in knots gesticulating, discussing. Several had still their staves in their hands. I verily believe they took these sticks to bed with them. Beyond the fence the forest stood up spectrally in the moonlight, and through the dim stir, through the faint sounds of that lamentable courtyard, the silence of the land went home to one's very heart—its mystery, its greatness, the amazing reality of its concealed life. The hurt nigger moaned feebly somewhere near by, and then fetched a deep sigh that made me mend my pace away from there. I felt a hand introducing itself under my arm. 'My dear sir,' said the fellow, 'I don't want to be misunderstood, and especially by you, who will see Mr. Kurtz long before I can have that pleasure. I wouldn't like him to get a false idea of my disposition. . . .'

"I let him run on, this papier-mâché Mephistopheles, and it seemed to me that if I tried I could poke my forefinger through him, and would find nothing inside but a little loose dirt, maybe. He, don't you see, had been planning to be assistant-manager by and

† *Ms and Maga:* obsequious.

by under the present man, and I could see that the coming of that Kurtz had upset them both not a little. He talked precipitately, and I did not try to stop him. I had my shoulders against the wreck of my steamer, hauled up on the slope like a carcass of some big river animal. The smell of mud, of primeval mud, by Jove! was in my nostrils, the high stillness of primeval forest was before my eyes; there were shiny patches on the black creek. The moon had spread over everything a thin layer of silver—over the rank grass, over the mud, upon the wall of matted vegetation standing higher than the wall of a temple, over the great river I could see through a sombre gap glittering, glittering, as it flowed broadly by without a murmur. All this was great, expectant, mute, while the man jabbered about himself. I wondered whether the stillness on the face of the immensity looking at us two were meant as an appeal or as a menace. What were we who had strayed in here? Could we handle that dumb thing, or would it handle us? I felt how big, how confoundedly big, was that thing that couldn't talk and perhaps was deaf as well. What was in there? I could see a little ivory coming out from there, and I had heard Mr. Kurtz was in there. I had heard enough about it too—God knows! Yet somehow it didn't bring any image with it—no more than if I had been told an angel or a fiend was in there. I believed it in the same way one of you might believe there are inhabitants in the planet Mars. I knew once a Scotch sailmaker who was certain, dead sure, there were people in Mars. If you asked him for some idea how they looked and behaved, he would get shy and mutter something about 'walking on all-fours.' If you as much as smiled, he would—though a man of sixty—offer to fight you. I would not have gone so far as to fight for Kurtz, but I went for him near enough to a lie. You know I hate, detest, and can't bear a lie, not because I am straighter than the rest of us, but simply because it appals me. There is a taint of death, a flavour of mortality in lies—which is exactly what I hate and detest in the world—what I want to forget. It makes me miserable and sick, like biting something rotten would do. Temperament, I suppose. Well, I went near enough to it by letting the young fool there believe anything he liked to imagine as to my influence in Europe. I became in an instant as much of a pretence as the rest of the bewitched pilgrims. This simply because I had a notion it somehow would be of help to that Kurtz whom at the time I did not see—you understand. He was just a word for me. I did not see the man in the name any more than you do. Do you see him? Do you see the story? Do you see anything? It seems to me I am trying to tell you a dream—making a vain attempt, because no relation of a dream can convey the dream-sensation, that commingling of absurdity, surprise, and bewilderment in a tremor of struggling revolt, that notion of being captured by the incredible which is of the very essence of dreams. . . ."

He was silent for a while.

". . . No, it is impossible; it is impossible to convey the life-sensation of any given epoch of one's existence—that which makes its truth, its meaning—its subtle and penetrating essence. It is impossible. We live, as we dream—alone. . . ."

He paused again as if reflecting, then added:

"Of course in this you fellows see more than I could then. You see me, whom you know. . . ."

It had become so pitch dark that we listeners could hardly see one another. For a long time already he, sitting apart, had been no more to us than a voice. There was not a word from anybody. The others might have been asleep, but I was awake. I listened, I listened on the watch for the sentence, for the word, that would give me the clue to the faint uneasiness inspired by this narrative that seemed to shape itself without human lips in the heavy night-air of the river.

". . . Yes—I let him run on," Marlow began again, "and think what he pleased about the powers that were behind me. I did! And there was nothing behind me! There was nothing but that wretched, old, mangled steamboat I was leaning against, while he talked fluently about 'the necessity for every man to get on.' 'And when one comes out here, you conceive, it is not to gaze at the moon.' Mr. Kurtz was a 'universal genius,' but even a genius would find it easier to work with 'adequate tools—intelligent men.' He did not make bricks—why, there was a physical impossibility in the way—as I was well aware; and if he did secretarial work for the manager, it was because 'no sensible man rejects wantonly the confidence of his superiors.' Did I see it? I saw it. What more did I want? What I really wanted was rivets, by Heaven! Rivets. To get on with the work—to stop the hole. Rivets I wanted. There were cases of them down at the coast—cases—piled up—burst—split! You kicked a loose rivet at every second step in that station yard on the hillside. Rivets had rolled into the grove of death. You could fill your pockets with rivets for the trouble of stooping down—and there wasn't one rivet to be found where it was wanted. We had plates that would do, but nothing to fasten them with. And every week the messenger, a lone negro, letter-bag on shoulder and staff in hand, left our station for the coast. And several times a week a coast caravan came in with trade goods—ghastly glazed calico that made you shudder only to look at it, glass beads value about a penny a quart, confounded spotted cotton handkerchiefs. And no rivets. Three carriers could have brought all that was wanted to set that steamboat afloat.

"He was becoming confidential now, but I fancy my unresponsive attitude must have exasperated him at last, for he judged it necessary to inform me he feared neither God nor devil, let alone any mere man. I said I could see that very well, but what I wanted was a certain quantity of rivets—and rivets were what really Mr. Kurtz wanted, if he had only known it. Now letters went to the coast every week. . . . 'My dear sir,' he cried, 'I write from dictation.' I demanded rivets. There was a way—for an intelligent man. He changed his manner; became very cold, and suddenly began to talk about a hippopotamus; wondered whether sleeping on board the steamer (I stuck to my salvage night and day) I wasn't disturbed. There was an old hippo that had the bad habit of getting out on the bank and roaming at night over the station grounds. The pilgrims used to turn out in a body and empty every rifle they could lay hands on at him. Some even had sat up o' nights for him. All this energy was wasted, though. 'That animal has a charmed life,' he said; 'but you can say this only of brutes in this country. No man—you apprehend me?—no man here bears a charmed life.' He stood there for a moment in the moonlight with his delicate hooked nose set a little askew, and his mica eyes glittering without a wink, then, with a curt Good-night, he strode off. I could see he was disturbed and considerably puzzled, which made me feel more hopeful than I had been for days. It was a great comfort to turn from that chap to my influential friend, the battered, twisted, ruined, tin-pot steamboat. I clambered on board. She rang under my feet like an empty Huntley & Palmer biscuit-tin kicked along a gutter; she was nothing so solid in make, and rather less pretty in shape, but I had expended enough hard work on her to make me love her. No influential friend would have served me better. She had given me a chance to come out a bit—to find out what I could do. No, I don't like work. I had rather laze about and think of all the fine things that can be done. I don't like work—no man does—but I like what is in the work—the chance to find yourself. Your own reality—for yourself, not for others— what no other man can ever know. They can only see the mere show, and never can tell what it really means.

"I was not surprised to see somebody sitting aft, on the deck, with his legs dangling over the mud. You see I rather chummed with the few mechanics there were in that station, whom the other pilgrims naturally despised—on account of their imperfect manners, I suppose. This was the foreman—a boiler-maker by trade—a good worker. He was a lank, bony, yellow-faced man, with big intense eyes. His aspect was worried, and his head was as bald as the palm of my hand; but his hair in falling seemed to have stuck to his chin, and had prospered in the new locality, for his beard hung down to his waist. He was a widower with six young children (he had left them in charge of a sister of his to come out there), and the passion of his life was pigeon-flying. He was an enthusiast and a connoisseur. He would rave about pigeons. After work hours he used sometimes to come over from his hut for a talk about his children and his pigeons; at work, when he had to crawl in the mud under the bottom of the steamboat, he would tie up that beard of his in a kind of white serviette³ he brought for the purpose. It had loops to go over his ears. In the evening he could be seen squatted on the bank rinsing that wrapper in the creek with great care, then spreading it solemnly on a bush to dry.

"I slapped him on the back and shouted 'We shall have rivets!' He scrambled to his feet exclaiming 'No! Rivets!' as though he couldn't believe his ears. Then in a low voice, 'You . . . eh?' I don't know why we behaved like lunatics. I put my finger to the side of my nose and nodded mysteriously. 'Good for you!' he cried, snapped his fingers above his head, lifting one foot. I tried a jig. We capered on the iron deck. A frightful clatter came out of that hulk, and the virgin forest on the other bank of the creek sent it back in a thundering roll upon the sleeping station. It must have made some of the pilgrims sit up in their hovels. A dark figure obscured the lighted doorway of the manager's hut, vanished, then, a second or so after, the doorway itself vanished too. We stopped, and the silence driven away by the stamping of our feet flowed back again from the recesses of the land. The great wall of vegetation, an exuberant and entangled mass of trunks, branches, leaves, boughs, festoons, motionless in the moonlight, was like a rioting invasion of soundless life, a rolling wave of plants, piled up, crested, ready to topple over the creek, to sweep every little man of us out of his little existence. And it moved not. A deadened burst of mighty splashes and snorts reached us from afar, as though an ichthyosaurus⁴ had been taking a bath of glitter in the great river. 'After all,' said the boiler-maker in a reasonable tone, 'why shouldn't we get the rivets?' Why not, indeed! I did not know of any reason why we shouldn't. 'They'll come in three weeks,' I said confidently.

"But they didn't. Instead of rivets there came an invasion, an infliction, a visitation. It came in sections during the next three weeks, each section headed by a donkey carrying a white man in new clothes and tan shoes, bowing from that elevation right and left to the impressed pilgrims. A quarrelsome band of footsore sulky niggers trod on the heels of the donkey; a lot of tents, camp-stools, tin boxes, white cases, brown bales would be shot down in the courtyard, and the air of mystery would deepen a little over the muddle of the station. Five such instalments came, with their absurd air of disorderly flight with the loot of innumerable outfit shops and provision stores, that, one would think, they were lugging, after a raid, into the wilderness for equitable division. It was an inextricable mess of things decent in themselves but that human folly made look like the spoils

3. French form for table napkin.   4. A huge prehistoric kind of crocodile.

of thieving.

"This devoted band called itself the Eldorado Exploring Expedition, and I believe they were sworn to secrecy. Their talk, however, was the talk of sordid buccaneers: it was reckless without hardihood, greedy without audacity, and cruel without courage; there was not an atom of foresight or of serious intention in the whole batch of them, and they did not seem aware these things are wanted for the work of the world. To tear treasure out of the bowels of the land was their desire, with no more moral purpose at the back of it than there is in burglars breaking into a safe. Who paid the expenses of the noble enterprise I don't know; but the uncle of our manager was leader of that lot.

"In exterior he resembled a butcher in a poor neighbourhood, and his eyes had a look of sleepy cunning. He carried his fat paunch with ostentation on his short legs, and during the time his gang infested the station spoke to no one but his nephew. You could see these two roaming about all day long with their heads close together in an everlasting confab.

"I had given up worrying myself about the rivets. One's capacity for that kind of folly is more limited than you would suppose. I said Hang!—and let things slide. I had plenty of time for meditation, and now and then I would give some thought to Kurtz. I wasn't very interested in him. No. Still, I was curious to see whether this man, who had come out equipped with moral ideas of some sort, would climb to the top after all, and how he would set about his work when there."

II

"One evening as I was lying flat on the deck of my steamboat, I heard voices approaching—and there were the nephew and the uncle strolling along the bank. I laid my head on my arm again, and had nearly lost myself in a doze, when somebody said in my ear, as it were: 'I am as harmless as a little child, but I don't like to be dictated to. Am I the manager—or am I not? I was ordered to send him there. It's incredible.' . . . I became aware that the two were standing on the shore alongside the forepart of the steamboat, just below my head. I did not move; it did not occur to me to move: I was sleepy. 'It *is* unpleasant,' grunted the uncle. 'He has asked the Administration to be sent there,' said the other, 'with the idea of showing what he could do; and I was instructed accordingly. Look at the influence that man must have. Is it not frightful?' They both agreed it was frightful, then made several bizarre remarks: 'Make rain and fine weather—one man—the Council—by the nose'—bits of absurd sentences that got the better of my drowsiness, so that I had pretty near the whole of my wits about me when the uncle said, 'The climate may do away with this difficulty for you. Is he alone there?' 'Yes,' answered the manager; 'he sent his assistant down the river with a note to me in these terms: "Clear this poor devil out of the country, and don't bother sending more of that sort. I had rather be alone than have the kind of men you can dispose of with me." It was more than a year ago. Can you imagine such impudence?' 'Anything since then?' asked the other hoarsely. 'Ivory,' jerked the nephew; 'lots of it—prime sort—lots—most annoying, from him.' 'And with that?' questioned the heavy rumble. 'Invoice,' was the reply fired out, so to speak. Then silence. They had been talking about Kurtz.

"I was broad awake by this time, but, lying perfectly at ease, remained still, having no inducement to change my position. 'How did that ivory come all this way?' growled the elder man, who seemed very vexed. The other explained that it had come with a fleet of canoes in charge of an English half-caste clerk Kurtz had with him; that Kurtz had apparently intended to return himself, the station being by that time bare of goods and stores, but after coming three hundred miles, had suddenly decided to go back, which he started to do alone in a small dugout with four paddlers, leaving the half-caste to continue down the river with the ivory. The two fellows there seemed astounded at anybody attempting such a thing. They were at a loss for an adequate motive. As for me, I seemed to see Kurtz for the first time. It was a distinct glimpse: the dugout, four paddling savages, and the lone white man turning his back suddenly on the headquarters, on relief, on thoughts of home—perhaps; setting his face towards the depths of the wilderness, towards his empty and desolate station. I did not know the motive. Perhaps he was just simply a fine fellow who stuck to his work for its own sake. His name, you understand, had not been pronounced once. He was 'that man.' The half-caste, who, as far as I could see, had conducted a difficult trip with great prudence and pluck, was invariably alluded to as 'that scoundrel.' The 'scoundrel' had reported that the 'man' had been very ill—had recovered imperfectly. . . . The two below me moved away then a few paces, and strolled back and forth at some little distance. I heard: 'Military post—doctor—two hundred miles—quite alone now—unavoidable delays—nine months—no news—strange rumours.' They approached again, just as the manager was saying, 'No one, as far as I know, unless a species of wandering trader—a pestilential fellow, snapping ivory from the natives.' Who was it they were talking about now? I gathered in snatches that this was some man supposed to be in Kurtz's district, and of whom the manager did not approve. 'We will not be free from unfair competition till one of these fellows is hanged for an example,' he said. 'Certainly,' grunted the other; 'get him hanged! Why not? Anything—anything can be done in this country. That's what I say; nobody here, you understand, *here*, can endanger your position. And why? You stand the climate—you outlast them all. The danger is in Europe; but there before I left I took care to——' They moved off and whispered, then their voices rose again. 'The extraordinary series of delays is not my fault. I did my possible.'† The fat man sighed, 'Very sad.' 'And the pestiferous absurdity of his talk,' continued the other; 'he bothered me enough when he was here. "Each station should be like a beacon on the road towards better things, a centre for trade of course, but also for humanising, improving, instructing." Conceive you—that ass! And he wants to be manager! No, it's——' Here he got choked by excessive indignation, and I lifted my head the least bit. I was surprised to see how near they were—right under me. I could have spat upon their hats. They were looking on the ground, absorbed in thought.* The manager was switching his leg with a slender twig: his sagacious relative lifted his head. 'You have been well since you came out this time?' he asked. The other gave a start. 'Who? I? Oh! Like a charm—like a charm. But the rest—oh, my goodness! All sick. They die so quick, too, that I haven't the time to send them out of the country—it's incredible!' 'H'm. Just so,' grunted the uncle. 'Ah! my boy, trust to this—I say, trust to this.' I saw him extend his short flipper of an arm for a gesture that took in the forest, the creek, the mud, the river—seemed to beckon with a dishonouring flourish before the sunlit face of the land a treacherous appeal to the lurking death, to the hidden evil, to the profound darkness of its heart. It was so startling that I leaped to my feet and looked back at the edge of the forest, as though I had expected an answer of some sort to that black display of confidence.‡ You know the foolish notions that come to one sometimes. The high stillness confronted these two figures with its ominous patience, waiting for the passing away of a fantastic invasion.

"They swore aloud together—out of sheer fright, I believe—then, pretending not to know anything of my existence, turned back to the station. The sun was low; and leaning forward side by side, they seemed to be tugging painfully uphill their two ridiculous shadows of unequal length, that trailed behind them slowly over the tall grass without bending a single blade.

"In a few days the Eldorado Expedition went into the patient wilderness, that closed upon it as the sea closes over a diver. Long

† *Ms canceled after* possible: Can I help him being alone?
* *Ms canceled twice:* in their atrocious thoughts
‡ *Ms:* confidence. But there was nothing, there could be nothing. The thick voice was swallowed up, the confident gesture was lost in the high stillness that fronted these two mean and atrocious figures with its ominous air [of] patient waiting, *etc.* [*Canceled: a comparison of the voice and gesture to* bursting shells *and* blasted rocks.]

afterwards the news came that all the donkeys were dead. I know nothing as to the fate of the less valuable animals. They, no doubt, like the rest of us, found what they deserved. I did not inquire. I was then rather excited at the prospect of meeting Kurtz very soon. When I say very soon I mean it comparatively. It was just two months from the day we left the creek when we came to the bank below Kurtz's station.

"Going up that river was like travelling back to the earliest beginnings of the world, when vegetation rioted on the earth and the big trees were kings. An empty stream, a great silence, an impenetrable forest. The air was warm, thick, heavy, sluggish. There was no joy in the brilliance of sunshine. The long stretches of the waterway ran on, deserted, into the gloom of overshadowed distances. On silvery sandbanks hippos and alligators sunned themselves side by side. The broadening waters flowed through a mob of wooded islands; you lost your way on that river as you would in a desert, and butted all day long against shoals, trying to find the channel, till you thought yourself bewitched and cut off for ever from everything you had known once—somewhere—far away—in another existence perhaps. There were moments when one's past came back to one, as it will sometimes when you have not a moment to spare to yourself; but it came in the shape of an unrestful and noisy dream, remembered with wonder amongst the overwhelming realities of this strange world of plants, and water, and silence. And this stillness of life did not in the least resemble a peace. It was the stillness of an implacable force brooding over an inscrutable intention. It looked at you with a vengeful aspect. I got used to it afterwards; I did not see it any more; I had no time. I had to keep guessing at the channel; I had to discern, mostly by inspiration, the signs of hidden banks; I watched for sunken stones; I was learning to clap my teeth smartly before my heart flew out, when I shaved by a fluke some infernal sly old snag that would have ripped the life† out of the tin-pot steamboat and drowned all the pilgrims; I had to keep a look-out for the signs of dead wood we could cut up in the night for next day's steaming. When you have to attend to things of that sort, to the mere incidents of the surface, the reality—the reality, I tell you—fades. The inner truth is hidden—luckily, luckily. But I felt it all the same; I felt often its mysterious stillness watching me at my monkey tricks, just as it watches you fellows performing on your respective tight-ropes for—what is it? half a crown a tumble——"

"Try to be civil, Marlow," growled a voice, and I knew there was at least one listener awake besides myself.

"I beg your pardon. I forgot the heartache which makes up the

† *Ms:* bowels

rest of the price. And indeed what does the price matter, if the trick be well done? You do your tricks very well. And I didn't do badly either, since I managed not to sink that steamboat on my first trip. It's a wonder to me yet. Imagine a blindfolded man set to drive a van over a bad road. I sweated and shivered over that business considerably, I can tell you. After all, for a seaman, to scrape the bottom of the thing that's supposed to float all the time under his care is the unpardonable sin. No one may know of it, but you never forget the thump—eh? A blow on the very heart. You remember it, you dream of it, you wake up at night and think of it—years after—and go hot and cold all over. I don't pretend to say that steamboat floated all the time. More than once she had to wade for a bit, with twenty cannibals splashing around and pushing. We had enlisted some of these chaps on the way for a crew. Fine fellows—cannibals—in their place. They were men one could work with, and I am grateful to them. And, after all, they did not eat each other before my face: they had brought along a provision of hippo-meat which went rotten, and made the mystery of the wilderness stink in my nostrils. Phoo! I can sniff it now. I had the manager on board and three or four pilgrims with their staves—all complete. Sometimes we came upon a station close by the bank, clinging to the skirts of the unknown, and the white men rushing out of a tumble-down hovel, with great gestures of joy and surprise and welcome, seemed very strange—had the appearance of being held there captive by a spell. The word 'ivory' would ring in the air for a while—and on we went again into the silence, along empty reaches, round the still bends, between the high walls of our winding way,† reverberating in hollow claps the ponderous beat of the stern-wheel. Trees, trees, millions of trees, massive, immense, running up high; and at their foot, hugging the bank against the stream, crept the little begrimed steamboat, like a sluggish beetle crawling on the floor of a lofty portico. It made you feel very small, very lost, and yet it was not altogether depressing, that feeling. After all, if you were small, the grimy beetle crawled on—which was just what you wanted it to do. Where the pilgrims imagined it crawled to I don't know. To some place where they expected to get something, I bet! For me it crawled towards Kurtz—exclusively; but when the steam-pipes started leaking we crawled very slow. The reaches opened before us and closed behind, as if the forest had stepped leisurely across the water to bar the way for our return. We penetrated deeper and deeper into the heart of darkness. It was very quiet there. At night sometimes the roll of drums behind the curtain of trees would run up the river and

† *Ms:* way higher than the corridor of a temple, as still, as sonorous, reverberating, etc.

remain sustained faintly, as if hovering in the air high over our heads, till the first break of day. Whether it meant war, peace, or prayer we could not tell. The dawns were heralded by the descent of a chill stillness; the woodcutters slept, their fires burned low; the snapping of a twig would make you start. We were wanderers on a prehistoric earth, on an earth that wore the aspect of an unknown planet. We could have fancied ourselves the first of men taking possession of an accursed inheritance, to be subdued at the cost of profound anguish and of excessive toil. But suddenly, as we struggled round a bend, there would be a glimpse of rush walls, of peaked grass-roofs, a burst of yells, a whirl of black limbs, a mass of hands clapping, of feet stamping, of bodies swaying, of eyes rolling, under the droop of heavy and motionless foliage. The steamer toiled along slowly on the edge of a black and incomprehensible frenzy. The prehistoric man was cursing us, praying to us, welcoming us—who could tell? We were cut off from the comprehension of our surroundings;† we glided past like phantoms, wondering and secretly appalled, as sane men would be before an enthusiastic outbreak in a madhouse. We could not understand because we were too far and could not remember, because we were travelling in the night of first ages, of those ages that are gone, leaving hardly a sign—and no memories.

"The earth seemed unearthly. We are accustomed to look upon the shackled form of a conquered monster, but there—there you could look at a thing monstrous and free. It was unearthly, and the men were—— No, they were not inhuman. Well, you know, that was the worst of it—this suspicion of their not being inhuman. It would come slowly to one. They howled and leaped, and spun, and made horrid faces;* but what thrilled you was just the thought

† *Ms:* surroundings. It could only be obtained by conquest—or by surrender, but we passed on indifferent, surprising, less than phantoms, wondering and secretly *etc.*

* *Ms:* faces. You know how it is when we hear the band of a regiment. A martial noise—and you pacific father, mild guardian of a domestic heartstone [*sic*] suddenly find yourself thinking of carnage. The joy of killing—hey? Or did you never, when listening to another kind of music, did you never dream yourself capable of becoming a saint—if—if. Aha! Another noise, another appeal, another response. All true. All there—in you. Not for you tho' the joy of killing—or the felicity of being a saint. Too many things in the way, business, houses, omnibuses, police[,] the man next door. You don't know my respectable friends how much you owe to the man next door. He is a great fact. There[']s very few places on earth where you haven't a man next door to you or something of him, the merest trace, his footprint—that's enough. You heard the yells and saw the dance and there was the man next door to call you names if you felt an impulse to yell and dance yourself. Another kindly appeal too, and, by Jove, if you did not watch yourself, if you had no weak spot in you where you could take refuge, you would perceive a responsive stir. Why not! Especially if you had a brain. There's all the past as well as all the future in a man's mind. And no kind neighbor to hang you promptly. The discretion of the wilderness, the night, the darkness of the land that would hide everything. Principles? Principles—acquisitions, clothes, rags, rags that fall off if you gave yourself a good shake. There was the naked truth—dancing, howling, praying, cursing. Rage. Fear. Joy. Who can tell. It was an appeal. Who's that grunting?

of their humanity—like yours—the thought of your remote kinship
with this wild and passionate uproar. Ugly. Yes, it was ugly enough;
but if you were man enough you would admit to yourself that there
was in you just the faintest trace of a response to the terrible frank-
ness of that noise, a dim suspicion of there being a meaning in it
which you—you so remote from the night of first ages—could comprehend. And why not? The mind of man is capable of anything—
because everything is in it, all the past as well as all the future.
What was there after all? Joy, fear, sorrow, devotion, valour, rage—
who can tell?—but truth—truth stripped of its cloak of time. Let
the fool gape and shudder—the man knows, and can look on without a wink. But he must at least be as much of a man as these on
the shore. He must meet that truth with his own true stuff—with
his own inborn strength. Principles? Principles won't do. Acquisitions, clothes, pretty rags—rags that would fly off at the first good
shake. No; you want a deliberate belief. An appeal to me in this
fiendish row—is there? Very well; I hear; I admit, but I have a
voice too, and for good or evil mine is the speech that cannot be
silenced. Of course, a fool, what with sheer fright and fine sentiments, is always safe. Who's that grunting? You wonder I didn't
go ashore for a howl and a dance? Well, no—I didn't. Fine sentiments, you say? Fine sentiments be hanged! I had no time. I had
to mess about with white-lead and strips of woollen blanket helping
to put bandages on those leaky steam-pipes—I tell you. I had to
watch the steering, and circumvent those snags, and get the tin-pot
along by hook or by crook. There was surface-truth enough in these
things to save a wiser man. And between whiles I had to look after
the savage who was fireman. He was an improved specimen; he
could fire up a vertical boiler.[5] He was there below me, and, upon
my word, to look at him was as edifying as seeing a dog in a parody
of breeches and a feather hat, walking on his hind legs. A few
months of training had done for that really fine chap. He squinted
at the steam-gauge and at the water-gauge with an evident effort of
intrepidity—and he had filed teeth too, the poor devil, and the
wool of his pate shaved into queer patterns, and three ornamental
scars on each of his cheeks. He ought to have been clapping his
hands and stamping his feet on the bank, instead of which he was
hard at work, a thrall to strange witchcraft, full of improving knowledge. He was useful because he had been instructed; and what he
knew was this—that should the water in that transparent thing
disappear, the evil spirit inside the boiler would get angry through

You don't think I went ashore to dance
too. Not I. I had to mess about with
white lead and strips of blanket band-
aging those leaky steam pipes—I tell
you. And I had to watch the steering,
and I had to look after the savage who
was fireman. He was being improved
—he was improved. He could fire up
a vertical boiler, *etc.*
5. Boiler of relatively simple construction, easily fired, and requiring little
space.

the greatness of his thirst, and take a terrible vengeance. So he sweated and fired up and watched the glass fearfully (with an impromptu charm, made of rags, tied to his arm, and a piece of polished bone, as big as a watch, stuck flatways through his lower lip), while the wooded banks slipped past us slowly, the short noise was left behind, the interminable miles of silence—and we crept on, towards Kurtz. But the snags were thick, the water was treacherous and shallow, the boiler seemed indeed to have a sulky devil in it, and thus neither that fireman nor I had any time to peer into our creepy thoughts.

"Some fifty miles below the Inner Station we came upon a hut of reeds, an inclined and melancholy pole, with the unrecognisable tatters of what had been a flag of some sort flying from it, and a neatly stacked wood-pile. This was unexpected. We came to the bank, and on the stack of firewood found a flat piece of board with some faded pencil-writing on it. When deciphered it said: 'Wood for you. Hurry up. Approach cautiously.' There was a signature, but it was illegible—not Kurtz—a much longer word. 'Hurry up.' Where? Up the river? 'Approach cautiously.' We had not done so. But the warning could not have been meant for the place where it could be only found after approach. Something was wrong above. But what —and how much? That was the question. We commented adversely upon the imbecility of that telegraphic style. The bush around said nothing, and would not let us look very far, either. A torn curtain of red twill hung in the doorway of the hut, and flapped sadly in our faces. The dwelling was dismantled; but we could see a white man had lived there not very long ago. There remained a rude table—a plank on two posts; a heap of rubbish reposed in a dark corner, and by the door I picked up a book. It had lost its covers, and the pages had been thumbed into a state of extremely dirty softness; but the back had been lovingly stitched afresh with white cotton thread, which looked clean yet. It was an extraordinary find. Its title was, *An Inquiry into some Points of Seamanship*, by a man Towser, Towson—some such name—Master in His Majesty's Navy. The matter looked dreary reading enough, with illustrative diagrams and repulsive tables of figures, and the copy was sixty years old. I handled this amazing antiquity with the greatest possible tenderness, lest it should dissolve in my hands. Within, Towson or Towser was inquiring earnestly into the breaking strain of ships' chains and tackle, and other such matters. Not a very enthralling book; but at the first glance you could see there a singleness of intention, an honest concern for the right way of going to work, which made these humble pages, thought out so many years ago, luminous with another than a professional light. The simple old sailor, with his talk of chains and purchases, made me forget the jungle and the pilgrims in a delicious sensation of having come upon something unmistakably real. Such a book being there was wonderful enough; but still more astounding were the notes pencilled in the margin, and plainly referring to the text. I couldn't believe my eyes! They were in cipher! Yes, it looked like cipher. Fancy a man lugging with him a book of that description into this nowhere and studying it—and making notes—in cipher at that! It was an extravagant mystery.

"I had been dimly aware for some time of a worrying noise, and when I lifted my eyes I saw the wood-pile was gone, and the manager, aided by all the pilgrims, was shouting at me from the river-side. I slipped the book into my pocket. I assure you to leave off reading was like tearing myself away from the shelter of an old and solid friendship.

"I started the lame engine ahead. 'It must be this miserable trader—this intruder,' exclaimed the manager, looking back malevolently at the place we had left. 'He must be English,' I said. 'It will not save him from getting into trouble if he is not careful,' muttered the manager darkly. I observed with assumed innocence that no man was safe from trouble in this world.

"The current was more rapid now, the steamer seemed at her last gasp, the stern-wheel flopped languidly, and I caught myself listening on tiptoe for the next beat of the float,[6] for in sober truth I expected the wretched thing to give up every moment. It was like watching the last flickers of a life. But still we crawled. Sometimes I would pick out a tree a little way ahead to measure our progress towards Kurtz by, but I lost it invariably before we got abreast. To keep the eyes so long on one thing was too much for human patience. The manager displayed a beautiful resignation. I fretted and fumed and took to arguing with myself whether or no I would talk openly with Kurtz; but before I could come to any conclusion it occurred to me that my speech or my silence, indeed any action of mine, would be a mere futility. What did it matter what any one knew or ignored? What did it matter who was manager? One gets sometimes such a flash of insight. The essentials of this affair[†] lay deep under the surface, beyond my reach, and beyond my power of meddling.

"Towards the evening of the second day we judged ourselves about eight miles from Kurtz's station. I wanted to push on; but the manager looked grave, and told me the navigation up there was so dangerous that it would be advisable, the sun being very low already, to wait where we were till next morning. Moreover, he pointed out that if the warning to approach cautiously were to be

6. Each blade on the paddle-wheel.　　† *Ms:* affair, its meaning and its lesson, lay deep, *etc.*

followed, we must approach in daylight—not at dusk, or in the dark. This was sensible enough. Eight miles meant nearly three hours' steaming for us, and I could also see suspicious ripples at the upper end of the reach. Nevertheless, I was annoyed beyond expression at the delay, and most unreasonably too, since one night more could not matter much after so many months. As we had plenty of wood, and caution was the word, I brought up in the middle of the stream. The reach was narrow, straight, with high sides like a railway cutting. The dusk came gliding into it long before the sun had set. The current ran smooth and swift, but a dumb immobility sat on the banks. The living trees, lashed together by the creepers and every living bush of the undergrowth, might have been changed into stone, even to the slenderest twig, to the lightest leaf. It was not sleep—it seemed unnatural, like a state of trance. Not the faintest sound of any kind could be heard. You looked on amazed, and began to suspect yourself of being deaf—then the night came suddenly, and struck you blind as well. About three in the morning some large fish leaped, and the loud splash made me jump as though a gun had been fired. When the sun rose there was a white fog, very warm and clammy, and more blinding than the night. It did not shift or drive; it was just there, standing all round you like something solid. At eight or nine, perhaps, it lifted as a shutter lifts. We had a glimpse of the towering multitude of trees, of the immense matted jungle, with the blazing little ball of the sun hanging over it—all perfectly still—and then the white shutter came down again, smoothly, as if sliding in greased grooves. I ordered the chain, which we had begun to heave in, to be paid out again. Before it stopped running with a muffled rattle, a cry, a very loud cry, as of infinite desolation, soared slowly in the opaque air. It ceased. A complaining clamour, modulated in savage discords, filled our ears. The sheer unexpectedness of it made my hair stir under my cap. I don't know how it struck the others: to me it seemed as though the mist itself had screamed, so suddenly, and apparently from all sides at once, did this tumultuous and mournful uproar arise. It culminated in a hurried outbreak of almost intolerably excessive shrieking, which stopped short, leaving us stiffened in a variety of silly attitudes, and obstinately listening to the nearly as appalling and excessive silence. 'Good God! What is the meaning——?' stammered at my elbow one of the pilgrims—a little fat man, with sandy hair and red whiskers, who wore side-spring boots, and pink pyjamas tucked into his socks. Two others remained open-mouthed a whole minute, then dashed into the little cabin, to rush out incontinently and stand darting scared glances, with Winchesters at 'ready' in their hands. What we could see was just the steamer we were on, her outlines blurred as though she had been on the point of dissolving, and a misty strip of water, perhaps two feet broad, around her—and that was all. The rest of the world was nowhere, as far as our eyes and ears were concerned. Just nowhere. Gone, disappeared; swept off without leaving a whisper or a shadow behind.

"I went forward, and ordered the chain to be hauled in short, so as to be ready to trip the anchor and move the steamboat at once if necessary. 'Will they attack?' whispered an awed voice. 'We will all be butchered in this fog,' murmured another. The faces twitched with the strain, the hands trembled slightly, the eyes forgot to wink. It was very curious to see the contrast of expressions of the white men and of the black fellows of our crew, who were as much strangers to that part of the river as we, though their homes were only eight hundred miles away. The whites, of course greatly discomposed, had besides a curious look of being painfully shocked by such an outrageous row. The others had an alert, naturally interested expression; but their faces were essentially quiet, even those of the one or two who grinned as they hauled at the chain. Several exchanged short, grunting phrases, which seemed to settle the matter to their satisfaction. Their head-man, a young, broad-chested black, severely draped in dark-blue fringed cloths, with fierce nostrils and his hair all done up artfully in oily ringlets, stood near me. 'Aha!' I said, just for good fellowship's sake. 'Catch 'im,' he snapped, with a bloodshot widening of his eyes and a flash of sharp teeth—'catch 'im. Give 'im to us.' 'To you, eh?' I asked; 'what would you do with them?' 'Eat 'im!' he said curtly, and, leaning his elbow on the rail, looked out into the fog in a dignified and profoundly pensive attitude. I would no doubt have been properly horrified, had it not occurred to me that he and his chaps must be very hungry: that they must have been growing increasingly hungry for at least this month past. They had been engaged for six months (I don't think a single one of them had any clear idea of time, as we at the end of countless ages have. They still belonged to the beginnings of time—had no inherited experience to teach them, as it were), and of course, as long as there was a piece of paper written over in accordance with some farcical law or other made down the river, it didn't enter anybody's head to trouble how they would live. Certainly they had brought with them some rotten hippo-meat, which couldn't have lasted very long, anyway, even if the pilgrims hadn't, in the midst of a shocking hullabaloo, thrown a considerable quantity of it overboard. It looked like a high-handed proceeding; but it was really a case of legitimate self-defence. You can't breathe dead hippo waking, sleeping, and eating, and at the same time keep your precarious grip on existence. Besides that, they had given them every week three pieces of brass wire, each about

nine inches long; and the theory was they were to buy their provisions with that currency in river-side villages. You can see how *that*
worked. There were either no villages, or the people were hostile, or
the director, who like the rest of us fed out of tins, with an occasional old he-goat thrown in, didn't want to stop the steamer for
some more or less recondite reason. So, unless they swallowed the
wire itself, or made loops of it to snare the fishes with, I don't see
what good their extravagant salary could be to them. I must say it
was paid with a regularity worthy of a large and honourable trading
company. For the rest, the only thing to eat—though it didn't look
eatable in the least—I saw in their possession was a few lumps of
some stuff like half-cooked dough, of a dirty lavender colour, they
kept wrapped in leaves, and now and then swallowed a piece of, but
so small that it seemed done more for the look of the thing than
for any serious purpose of sustenance. Why in the name of all the
gnawing devils of hunger they didn't go for us—they were thirty to
five—and have a good tuck-in for once, amazes me now when I
think of it. They were big powerful men, with not much capacity
to weigh the consequences, with courage, with strength, even yet,
though their skins were no longer glossy and their muscles no
longer hard. And I saw that something restraining, one of those
human secrets that baffle probability, had come into play there.
I looked at them with a swift quickening of interest—not because
it occurred to me I might be eaten by them before very long, though
I own to you that just then I perceived—in a new light, as it were—
how unwholesome the pilgrims looked, and I hoped, yes, I positively
hoped, that my aspect was not so—what shall I say?—so—unap-
petising: a touch of fantastic vanity which fitted well with the
dream-sensation that pervaded all my days at that time. Perhaps
I had a little fever too. One can't live with one's finger everlastingly
on one's pulse. I had often 'a little fever,' or a little touch of other
things—the playful paw-strokes of the wilderness, the preliminary
trifling before the more serious onslaught which came in due course.
Yes; I looked at them as you would on any human being, with a
curiosity of their impulses, motives, capacities, weaknesses, when
brought to the test of an inexorable physical necessity. Restraint!
What possible restraint? Was it superstition, disgust, patience,
fear—or some kind of primitive honour? No fear can stand up to
hunger, no patience can wear it out, disgust simply does not exist
where hunger is; and as to superstition, beliefs, and what you may
call principles, they are less than chaff in a breeze. Don't you know
the devilry of lingering starvation, its exasperating torment, its black
thoughts, its sombre and brooding ferocity? Well, I do. It takes a
man all his inborn strength to fight hunger properly. It's really
easier to face bereavement, dishonour, and the perdition of one's

soul—than this kind of prolonged hunger. Sad, but true. And these chaps too had no earthly reason for any kind of scruple. Restraint! I would just as soon have expected restraint from a hyena prowling amongst the corpses of a battlefield. But there was the fact facing me—the fact dazzling, to be seen, like the foam on the depths of the sea, like a ripple on an unfathomable enigma, a mystery greater —when I thought of it—than the curious, inexplicable note of desperate grief in this savage clamour that had swept by us on the river-bank, behind the blind whiteness of the fog.

"Two pilgrims were quarrelling in hurried whispers as to which bank. 'Left.' 'No, no; how can you? Right, right, of course.' 'It is very serious,' said the manager's voice behind me; 'I would be desolated if anything should happen to Mr. Kurtz before we came up.' I looked at him, and had not the slightest doubt he was sincere. He was just the kind of man who would wish to preserve appearances. That was his restraint. But when he muttered something about going on at once, I did not even take the trouble to answer him. I knew, and he knew, that it was impossible. Were we to let go our hold of the bottom, we would be absolutely in the air— in space. We wouldn't be able to tell where we were going to— whether up or down stream, or across—till we fetched against one bank or the other—and then we wouldn't know at first which it was. Of course I made no move. I had no mind for a smash-up. You couldn't imagine a more deadly place for a shipwreck. Whether drowned at once or not, we were sure to perish speedily in one way or another. 'I authorise you to take all the risks,' he said, after a short silence. 'I refuse to take any,' I said shortly; which was just the answer he expected, though its tone might have surprised him. 'Well, I must defer to your judgment. You are captain,' he said, with marked civility. I turned my shoulder to him in sign of my appreciation, and looked into the fog. How long would it last? It was the most hopeless look-out. The approach to this Kurtz grubbing for ivory in the wretched bush was beset by as many dangers as though he had been an enchanted princess sleeping in a fabulous castle. 'Will they attack, do you think?' asked the manager, in a confidential tone.

"I did not think they would attack, for several obvious reasons. The thick fog was one. If they left the bank in their canoes they would get lost in it, as we would be if we attempted to move. Still, I had also judged the jungle of both banks quite impenetrable— and yet eyes were in it, eyes that had seen us. The river-side bushes were certainly very thick; but the undergrowth behind was evidently penetrable. However, during the short lift I had seen no canoes anywhere in the reach—certainly not abreast of the steamer. But what made the idea of attack inconceivable to me was the nature of the noise—of the cries we had heard. They had not the fierce character boding of immediate hostile intention. Unexpected, wild, and violent as they had been, they had given me an irresistible impression of sorrow. The glimpse of the steamboat had for some reason filled those savages with unrestrained grief. The danger, if any, I expounded, was from our proximity to a great human passion let loose. Even extreme grief may ultimately vent itself in violence —but more generally takes the form of apathy. . . .

"You should have seen the pilgrims stare! They had no heart to grin, or even to revile me; but I believe they thought me gone mad —with fright, maybe. I delivered a regular lecture. My dear boys, it was no good bothering. Keep a look-out? Well, you may guess I watched the fog for the signs of lifting as a cat watches a mouse; but for anything else our eyes were of no more use to us than if we had been buried miles deep in a heap of cotton-wool. It felt like it too—choking, warm, stifling. Besides, all I said, though it sounded extravagant, was absolutely true to fact. What we afterwards alluded to as an attack was really an attempt at repulse. The action was very far from being aggressive—it was not even defensive, in the usual sense: it was undertaken under the stress of desperation, and in its essence was purely protective.

"It developed itself, I should say, two hours after the fog lifted, and its commencement was at a spot, roughly speaking, about a mile and a half below Kurtz's station. We had just floundered and flopped round a bend, when I saw an islet, a mere grassy hummock of bright green, in the middle of the stream. It was the only thing of the kind; but as we opened the reach more, I perceived it was the head of a long sandbank, or rather of a chain of shallow patches stretching down the middle of the river. They were discoloured, just awash, and the whole lot was seen just under the water, exactly as a man's backbone is seen running down the middle of his back under the skin. Now, as far as I did see, I could go to the right or to the left of this. I didn't know either channel, of course. The banks looked pretty well alike, the depth appeared the same; but as I had been informed the station was on the west side, I naturally headed for the western passage.†

"No sooner had we fairly entered it than I became aware it was much narrower than I had supposed. To the left of us there was the long uninterrupted shoal, and to the right a high steep bank heavily overgrown with bushes. Above the bush the trees stood in serried ranks. The twigs overhung the current thickly, and from distance to distance a large limb of some tree projected rigidly over the stream. It was then well on in the afternoon, the face of the forest was gloomy, and a broad strip of shadow had already fallen on the

† *Ms canceled:* east *and* eastern.

water. In this shadow we steamed up—very slowly, as you may imagine. I sheered her well inshore—the water being deepest near the bank, as the sounding-pole informed me.

"One of my hungry and forbearing friends was sounding in the bows just below me. This steamboat was exactly like a decked scow. On the deck there were two little teak-wood houses, with doors and windows. The boiler was in the fore-end, and the machinery right astern. Over the whole there was a light roof, supported on stanchions. The funnel projected through that roof, and in front of the funnel a small cabin built of light planks served for a pilot-house. It contained a couch, two camp-stools, a loaded Martini-Henry[7] leaning in one corner, a tiny table, and the steering-wheel. It had a wide door in front and a broad shutter at each side. All these were always thrown open, of course. I spent my days perched up there on the extreme fore-end of that roof, before the door. At night I slept, or tried to, on the couch. An athletic black belonging to some coast tribe, and educated by my poor predecessor, was the helmsman. He sported a pair of brass earrings, wore a blue cloth wrapper from the waist to the ankles, and thought all the world of himself. He was the most unstable kind of fool I had ever seen. He steered with no end of a swagger while you were by; but if he lost sight of you, he became instantly the prey of an abject funk, and would let that cripple of a steamboat get the upper hand of him in a minute.

"I was looking down at the sounding-pole, and feeling much annoyed to see at each try a little more of it stick out of that river, when I saw my poleman give up the business suddenly, and stretch himself flat on the deck, without even taking the trouble to haul his pole in. He kept hold on it though, and it trailed in the water. At the same time the fireman, whom I could also see below me, sat down abruptly before his furnace and ducked his head. I was amazed. Then I had to look at the river mighty quick, because there was a snag in the fairway. Sticks, little sticks, were flying about—thick: they were whizzing before my nose, dropping below me, striking behind me against my pilot-house. All this time the river, the shore, the woods, were very quiet—perfectly quiet. I could only hear the heavy splashing thump of the stern-wheel and the patter of these things. We cleared the snag clumsily. Arrows, by Jove! We were being shot at! I stepped in quickly to close the shutter on the land-side. That fool-helmsman, his hands on the spokes, was lifting his knees high, stamping his feet, champing his mouth, like a reined-in horse. Confound him! And we were staggering within ten feet of the bank. I had to lean right out to swing the heavy† shutter, and I saw a face amongst the leaves on the level with my

---

7. A breech-action military rifle which takes a cartridge with an especially large powder charge.
† *Ms:* beastly heavy

own, looking at me very fierce and steady; and then suddenly, as though a veil had been removed from my eyes, I made out, deep in the tangled gloom, naked breasts, arms, legs, glaring eyes—the bush was swarming with human limbs in movement, glistening, of bronze colour. The twigs shook, swayed, and rustled, the arrows flew out of them, and then the shutter came to. 'Steer her straight,' I said to the helmsman. He held his head rigid, face forward; but his eyes rolled, he kept on lifting and setting down his feet gently, his mouth foamed a little. 'Keep quiet!' I said in a fury. I might just as well have ordered a tree not to sway in the wind. I darted out. Below me there was a great scuffle of feet on the iron deck; confused exclamations; a voice screamed, 'Can you turn back?' I caught sight of a V-shaped ripple on the water ahead. What? Another snag! A fusillade burst out under my feet. The pilgrims had opened with their Winchesters, and were simply squirting lead into that bush. A deuce of a lot of smoke came up and drove slowly forward. I swore at it. Now I couldn't see the ripple or the snag either. I stood in the doorway, peering, and the arrows came in swarms. They might have been poisoned, but they looked as though they wouldn't kill a cat. The bush began to howl. Our wood-cutters raised a war-like whoop; the report of a rifle just at my back deafened me. I glanced over my shoulder, and the pilot-house was yet full of noise and smoke when I made a dash at the wheel. The fool-nigger had dropped everything, to throw the shutter open and let off that Martini-Henry. He stood before the wide opening, glaring, and I yelled at him to come back, while I straightened the sudden twist out of that steamboat. There was no room to turn even if I had wanted to, the snag was somewhere very near ahead in that confounded smoke, there was no time to lose, so I just crowded her into the bank—right into the bank, where I knew the water was deep.

"We tore slowly along the overhanging bushes in a whirl of broken twigs and flying leaves. The fusillade below stopped short, as I had foreseen it would when the squirts got empty. I threw my head back to a glinting whiz that traversed the pilot-house, in at one shutter-hole and out at the other. Looking past that mad helmsman, who was shaking the empty rifle and yelling at the shore, I saw vague forms of men running bent double, leaping, gliding, distinct, incomplete, evanescent. Something big appeared in the air before the shutter, the rifle went overboard, and the man stepped back swiftly, looked at me over his shoulder in an extraordinary, profound, familiar manner, and fell upon my feet. The side of his head hit the wheel twice, and the end of what appeared a long cane clattered round and knocked over a little camp-stool. It looked as though after wrenching that thing from somebody ashore he had lost his balance in the effort. The thin smoke had blown away, we were clear of the snag, and looking ahead I could see that in another hundred yards or so I would be free to sheer off, away from the bank; but my feet felt so very warm and wet that I had to look down. The man had rolled on his back and stared straight up at me; both his hands clutched that cane. It was the shaft of a spear that, either thrown or lunged through the opening, had caught him in the side just below the ribs; the blade had gone in out of sight, after making a frightful gash; my shoes were full; a pool of blood lay very still, gleaming dark-red under the wheel; his eyes shone with an amazing lustre. The fusillade burst out again. He looked at me anxiously, gripping the spear like something precious, with an air of being afraid I would try to take it away from him. I had to make an effort to free my eyes from his gaze and attend to the steering. With one hand I felt above my head for the line of the steam whistle, and jerked out screech after screech hurriedly. The tumult of angry and warlike yells was checked instantly, and then from the depths of the woods went out such a tremulous and prolonged wail of mournful fear and utter despair as may be imagined to follow the flight of the last hope from the earth. There was a great commotion in the bush; the shower of arrows stopped, a few dropping shots rang out sharply—then silence, in which the languid beat of the stern-wheel came plainly to my ears. I put the helm hard a-starboard at the moment when the pilgrim in pink pyjamas, very hot and agitated, appeared in the doorway. 'The manager sends me——' he began in an official tone, and stopped short. 'Good God!' he said, glaring at the wounded man.

"We two whites stood over him, and his lustrous and inquiring glance enveloped us both. I declare it looked as though he would presently put to us some question in an understandable language; but he died without uttering a sound, without moving a limb, without twitching a muscle. Only in the very last moment, as though in response to some sign we could not see, to some whisper we could not hear, he frowned heavily, and that frown gave to his black death-mask an inconceivably sombre, brooding, and menacing expression. The lustre of inquiring glance faded swiftly into vacant glassiness. 'Can you steer?' I asked the agent eagerly. He looked very dubious; but I made a grab at his arm, and he understood at once I meant him to steer whether or no. To tell you the truth, I was morbidly anxious to change my shoes and socks. 'He is dead,' murmured the fellow, immensely impressed. 'No doubt about it,' said I, tugging like mad at the shoe-laces. 'And by the way, I suppose Mr. Kurtz is dead as well by this time.'

"For the moment that was the dominant thought. There was a sense of extreme disappointment, as though I had found out I had been striving after something altogether without a substance. I couldn't have been more disgusted if I had travelled all this way for the sole purpose of talking with Mr. Kurtz. Talking with . . . I flung one shoe overboard, and became aware that that was exactly what I had been looking forward to—a talk with Kurtz. I made the strange discovery that I had never imagined him as doing, you know, but as discoursing. I didn't say to myself, 'Now I will never see him,' or 'Now I will never shake him by the hand,' but, 'Now I will never hear him.' The man presented himself as a voice. Not of course that I did not connect him with some sort of action. Hadn't I been told in all the tones of jealousy and admiration that he had collected, bartered, swindled, or stolen more ivory than all the other agents together? That was not the point. The point was in his being a gifted creature, and that of all his gifts the one that stood out pre-eminently, that carried with it a sense of real presence, was his ability to talk, his words—the gift of expression, the bewildering, the illuminating, the most exalted and the most contemptible, the pulsating stream of light, or the deceitful flow from the heart of an impenetrable darkness.

"The other shoe went flying unto the devil-god of that river. I thought, By Jove! it's all over. We are too late; he has vanished—the gift has vanished, by means of some spear, arrow, or club. I will never hear that chap speak after all—and my sorrow had a startling extravagance of emotion, even such as I had noticed in the howling sorrow of these savages in the bush. I couldn't have felt more of lonely desolation somehow, had I been robbed of a belief or had missed my destiny in life. . . . Why do you sigh in this beastly way, somebody? Absurd? Well, absurd. Good Lord! mustn't a man ever—— Here, give me some tobacco." . . .

There was a pause of profound stillness, then a match flared, and Marlow's lean face appeared, worn, hollow, with downward folds and dropped eyelids, with an aspect of concentrated attention; and as he took vigorous draws at his pipe, it seemed to retreat and advance out of the night in the regular flicker of the tiny flame. The match went out.

"Absurd!" he cried. "This is the worst of trying to tell . . . Here you all are, each moored with two good addresses, like a hulk with two anchors, a butcher round one corner, a policeman round another, excellent appetites, and temperature normal—you hear—normal from year's end to year's end. And you say, Absurd! Absurd be—exploded! Absurd! My dear boys, what can you expect from a man who out of sheer nervousness had just flung overboard a pair of new shoes? Now I think of it, it is amazing I did not shed tears. I am, upon the whole, proud of my fortitude. I was cut to the quick at the idea of having lost the inestimable privilege of listening

to the gifted Kurtz. Of course I was wrong. The privilege was waiting for me. Oh yes, I heard more than enough. And I was right, too.
A voice. He was very little more than a voice. And I heard—him—
it—this voice—other voices—all of them were so little more than
voices—and the memory of that time itself lingers around me,
impalpable, like a dying vibration of one immense jabber, silly,
atrocious, sordid, savage, or simply mean, without any kind of sense.
Voices, voices—even the girl herself—now—"

He was silent for a long time.

"I laid the ghost of his gifts at last with a lie," he began suddenly.
"Girl! What? Did I mention a girl? Oh, she is out of it—completely. They—the women I mean—are out of it—should be out
of it. We must help them to stay in that beautiful world of their
own, lest ours gets worse.† Oh, she had to be out of it. You should
have heard the disinterred body of Mr. Kurtz saying, 'My Intended.'
You would have perceived directly then how completely she was out
of it. And the lofty frontal bone of Mr. Kurtz! They say the hair
goes on growing sometimes, but this—ah—specimen was impres-
sively bald. The wilderness had patted him on the head, and,
behold, it was like a ball—an ivory ball; it had caressed him, and
—lo!—he had withered; it had taken him, loved him, embraced
him, got into his veins, consumed his flesh, and sealed his soul to
its own by the inconceivable ceremonies of some devilish initiation.
He was its spoiled and pampered favourite. Ivory? I should think so.
Heaps of it, stacks of it. The old mud shanty was bursting with it.
You would think there was not a single tusk left either above or
below the ground in the whole country. 'Mostly fossil,' the manager
had remarked disparagingly. It was no more fossil than I am; but
they call it fossil when it is dug up. It appears these niggers do
bury the tusks sometimes—but evidently they couldn't bury this
parcel deep enough to save the gifted Mr. Kurtz from his fate. We
filled the steamboat with it, and had to pile a lot on the deck. Thus
he could see and enjoy as long as he could see, because the appreciation of this favour had remained with him to the last. You should
have heard him say, 'My ivory.' Oh yes, I heard him. 'My Intended,
my ivory, my station, my river, my——' everything belonged to him.
It made me hold my breath in expectation of hearing the wilderness burst into a prodigious peal of laughter that would shake the
fixed stars in their places. Everything belonged to him—but that
was a trifle. The thing was to know what he belonged to, how many
powers of darkness claimed him for their own. That was the reflection that made you creepy all over. It was impossible—it was

† *Ms:* worse. That's a monster-truth
with many maws to whom we've got to
throw every year—or every day—no
matter—no sacrifice is too great—a
ransom of pretty, shining lies—not very
new perhaps—but spotless, aureoled,
tender. Oh, she, *etc.*

not good for one either—trying to imagine. He had taken a high seat amongst the devils of the land—I mean literally. You can't understand. How could you?—with solid pavement under your feet, surrounded by kind neighbours ready to cheer you or to fall on you, stepping delicately between the butcher and the policeman, in the holy terror of scandal and gallows and lunatic asylums—how can you imagine what particular region of the first ages a man's untrammelled feet may take him into by the way of solitude—utter solitude without a policeman—by the way of silence—utter silence, where no warning voice of a kind neighbour can be heard whispering of public opinion? These little things make all the great difference. When they are gone you must fall back upon your own innate strength, upon your own capacity for faithfulness. Of course you may be too much of a fool to go wrong—too dull even to know you are being assaulted by the powers of darkness. I take it, no fool ever made a bargain for his soul with the devil: the fool is too much of a fool, or the devil too much of a devil—I don't know which. Or you may be such a thunderingly exalted creature as to be altogether deaf and blind to anything but heavenly sights and sounds. Then the earth for you is only a standing place—and whether to be like this is your loss or your gain I won't pretend to say. But most of us are neither one nor the other. The earth for us is a place to live in, where we must put up with sights, with sounds, with smells, too, by Jove!—breathe dead hippo, so to speak, and not be contaminated.† And there, don't you see? your strength comes in, the faith in your ability for the digging of unostentatious holes to bury the stuff in—your power of devotion, not to yourself, but to an obscure, back-breaking business. And that's difficult enough. Mind, I am not trying to excuse or even explain—I am trying to account to myself for—for—Mr. Kurtz—for the shade of Mr. Kurtz. This initiated wraith* from the back of Nowhere honoured me with its amazing confidence before it vanished altogether. This was because it could speak English to me. The original Kurtz had been educated partly in England, and—as he was good enough to say himself—his sympathies were in the right place. His mother was half-English, his father was half-French. All Europe contributed to the making of Kurtz; and by and by I learned that, most appropriately, the International Society for the Suppression of Savage Customs had entrusted him with the making of a report, for its future guidance. And he had written it too. I've seen it. I've read it. It was eloquent, vibrating with eloquence, but too high-strung, I think. Seventeen pages of close writing he had found time for! But this must have been before his—let us say—

---

† *Ms canceled after* contaminated: To say there's no dead hippo won't do. And there, *etc.*

* *Ms canceled:* ghost

nerves went wrong, and caused him to preside at certain midnight dances ending with unspeakable rites, which—as far as I reluctantly gathered from what I heard at various times—were offered up to him—do you understand?—to Mr. Kurtz himself. But it was a beautiful piece of writing. The opening paragraph, however, in the light of later information, strikes me now as ominous. He began with the argument that we whites, from the point of development we had arrived at, 'must necessarily appear to them [savages] in the nature of supernatural beings—we approach them with the might as of a deity,' and so on, and so on. 'By the simple exercise of our will we can exert a power for good practically unbounded,' etc. etc. From that point he soared and took me with him. The peroration was magnificent, though difficult to remember, you know. It gave me the notion of an exotic Immensity ruled by an august Benevolence. It made me tingle with enthusiasm. This was the unbounded power of eloquence—of words—of burning noble words. There were no practical hints to interrupt the magic current of phrases, unless a kind of note at the foot of the last page, scrawled evidently much later, in an unsteady hand, may be regarded as the exposition of a method. It was very simple, and at the end of that moving appeal to every altruistic sentiment it blazed at you, luminous and terrifying, like a flash of lightning in a serene sky: 'Exterminate all the brutes!'† The curious part was that he had apparently forgotten all about that valuable postscriptum, because, later on, when he in a sense came to himself, he repeatedly entreated me to take good care of 'my pamphlet' (he called it), as it was sure to have in the future a good influence upon his career.* I had full information about all these things, and, besides, as it turned out, I was to have the care of his memory. I've done enough for it to give me the indisputable right to lay it, if I choose, for an everlasting rest in the dust-bin of progress, amongst all the sweepings and, figuratively speaking, all the dead cats of civilisation. But then, you see, I can't choose. He won't be forgotten. Whatever he was, he was not common. He had the power to charm or frighten rudimentary souls into an aggravated witch-dance in his honour; he could also fill the small souls of the pilgrims with bitter misgivings: he had one devoted friend at least,‡ and he had conquered one soul in the world that was neither rudimentary nor tainted with self-seeking. No; I can't forget him, though I am not prepared to affirm the fellow was exactly worth the life we lost in getting to him. I missed my late helmsman awfully—I missed him even while his body was still lying in the pilot-house. Perhaps you will think it passing strange this regret for a savage who was no more account than a grain of sand in a

† *Ms canceled:* **Kill every single brute of them.**

* *Ms:* upon 'my career.' His Intended, his ivory, his future, his career.

‡ one devoted friend at least, *not in Ms.*

black Sahara. Well, don't you see, he had done something, he had steered; for months I had him at my back—a help—an instrument. It was a kind of partnership. He steered for me—I had to look after him, I worried about his deficiencies, and thus a subtle bond had been created, of which I only became aware when it was suddenly broken. And the intimate profundity of that look he gave me when he received his hurt remains to this day in my memory—like a claim of distant kinship affirmed in a supreme moment.

"Poor fool! If he had only left that shutter alone. He had no restraint, no restraint—just like Kurtz—a tree swayed by the wind. As soon as I had put on a dry pair of slippers, I dragged him out, after first jerking the spear out of his side, which operation I confess I performed with my eyes shut tight. His heels leaped together over the little door-step; his shoulders were pressed to my breast; I hugged him from behind desperately. Oh! he was heavy, heavy; heavier than any man on earth, I should imagine. Then without more ado I tipped him overboard. The current snatched him as though he had been a wisp of grass, and I saw the body roll over twice before I lost sight of it for ever. All the pilgrims and the manager were then congregated on the awning-deck about the pilot-house, chattering at each other like a flock of excited magpies, and there was a scandalised murmur at my heartless promptitude. What they wanted to keep that body hanging about for I can't guess. Embalm it, maybe. But I had also heard another, and a very ominous, murmur on the deck below. My friends the wood-cutters were likewise scandalised, and with a better show of reason—though I admit that the reason itself was quite inadmissible. Oh, quite! I had made up my mind that if my late helmsman was to be eaten, the fishes alone should have him. He had been a very second-rate helmsman while alive, but now he was dead he might have become a first-class temptation, and possibly cause some startling trouble. Besides, I was anxious to take the wheel, the man in pink pyjamas showing himself a hopeless duffer at the business.

"This I did directly the simple funeral was over. We were going half-speed, keeping right in the middle of the stream, and I listened to the talk about me. They had given up Kurtz, they had given up the station; Kurtz was dead, and the station had been burnt—and so on, and so on. The red-haired pilgrim was beside himself with the thought that at least this poor Kurtz had been properly revenged. 'Say! We must have made a glorious slaughter of them in the bush. Eh? What do you think? Say?' He positively danced, the bloodthirsty little gingery beggar.[8] And he had nearly fainted when he saw the wounded man! I could not help saying, 'You made a glorious lot of smoke, anyhow.' I had seen, from the way the tops

8. British slang for "red-headed rascal."

of the bushes rustled and flew, that almost all the shots had gone too high. You can't hit anything unless you take aim and fire from the shoulder; but these chaps fired from the hip with their eyes shut. The retreat, I maintained—and I was right—was caused by the screeching of the steam-whistle. Upon this they forgot Kurtz, and began to howl at me with indignant protests.

"The manager stood by the wheel murmuring confidentially about the necessity of getting well away down the river before dark at all events, when I saw in the distance a clearing on the river-side and the outlines of some sort of building. 'What's this?' I asked. He clapped his hands in wonder. 'The station!' he cried. I edged in at once, still going half-speed.

"Through my glasses I saw the slope of a hill interspersed with rare trees and perfectly free from undergrowth. A long decaying building on the summit was half buried in the high grass; the large holes in the peaked roof gaped black from afar; the jungle and the woods made a background. There was no enclosure or fence of any kind; but there had been one apparently, for near the house half a dozen slim posts remained in a row, roughly trimmed, and with their upper ends ornamented with round carved balls. The rails, or whatever there had been between, had disappeared. Of course the forest surrounded all that. The river-bank was clear, and on the water side I saw a white man under a hat like a cart-wheel beckoning persistently with his whole arm. Examining the edge of the forest above and below, I was almost certain I could see movements—human forms gliding here and there. I steamed past prudently, then stopped the engines and let her drift down. The man on the shore began to shout, urging us to land. 'We have been attacked,' screamed the manager. 'I know—I know. It's all right,' yelled back the other, as cheerful as you please. 'Come along. It's all right. I am glad.'

"His aspect reminded me of something I had seen—something funny I had seen somewhere. As I manœuvred to get alongside, I was asking myself, 'What does this fellow look like?' Suddenly I got it. He looked like a harlequin. His clothes had been made of some stuff that was brown holland probably, but it was covered with patches all over, with bright patches, blue, red, and yellow—patches on the back, patches on the front, patches on elbows, on knees; coloured binding round his jacket, scarlet edging at the bottom of his trousers; and the sunshine made him look extremely gay and wonderfully neat withal, because you could see how beautifully all this patching had been done. A beardless, boyish face, very fair, no features to speak of, nose peeling, little blue eyes, smiles and frowns chasing each other over that open countenance like sunshine and shadow on a wind-swept plain. 'Look out, captain!' he cried; 'there's a snag lodged in here last night.' What! Another snag? I confess I swore shamefully. I had nearly holed my cripple, to finish off that charming trip. The harlequin on the bank turned his little pug-nose up to me. 'You English?' he asked, all smiles. 'Are you?' I shouted from the wheel. The smiles vanished, and he shook his head as if sorry for my disappointment. Then he brightened up. 'Never mind!' he cried encouragingly. 'Are we in time?' I asked. 'He is up there,' he replied, with a toss of the head up the hill, and becoming gloomy all of a sudden. His face was like the autumn sky, overcast one moment and bright the next.

"When the manager, escorted by the pilgrims, all of them armed to the teeth, had gone to the house, this chap came on board. 'I say, I don't like this. These natives are in the bush,' I said. He assured me earnestly it was all right. 'They are simple people,' he added; 'well, I am glad you came. It took me all my time to keep them off.' 'But you said it was all right,' I cried. 'Oh, they meant no harm,' he said; and as I stared he corrected himself, 'Not exactly.' Then vivaciously, 'My faith, your pilot-house wants a clean-up!' In the next breath he advised me to keep enough steam on the boiler to blow the whistle in case of any trouble. 'One good screech will do more for you than all your rifles. They are simple people,' he repeated. He rattled away at such a rate he quite overwhelmed me. He seemed to be trying to make up for lots of silence, and actually hinted, laughing, that such was the case. 'Don't you talk with Mr. Kurtz?' I said. 'You don't talk with that man—you listen to him,' he exclaimed with severe exaltation. 'But now——' He waved his arm, and in the twinkling of an eye was in the uttermost depths of despondency. In a moment he came up again with a jump, possessed himself of both my hands, shook them continuously, while he gabbled: 'Brother sailor . . . honour . . . pleasure . . . delight . . . introduce myself . . . Russian . . . son of an arch-priest . . . Government of Tambov . . . What? Tobacco! English tobacco; the excellent English tobacco! Now, that's brotherly. Smoke? Where's a sailor that does not smoke?'

"The pipe soothed him, and gradually I made out he had run away from school, had gone to sea in a Russian ship; ran away again; served some time in English ships; was now reconciled with the arch-priest. He made a point of that. 'But when one is young one must see things, gather experience, ideas; enlarge the mind.' 'Here!' I interrupted. 'You can never tell! Here I met Mr. Kurtz,' he said, youthfully solemn and reproachful. I held my tongue after that. It appears he had persuaded a Dutch trading-house on the coast to fit him out with stores and goods, and had started for the interior with a light heart, and no more idea of what would happen to him than a baby. He had been wandering about that river for nearly two years alone, cut off from everybody and everything. 'I am not so young as I look. I am twenty-five,' he said. 'At first old Van Shuyten would tell me to go to the devil,' he narrated with keen enjoyment; 'but I stuck to him, and talked and talked, till at last he got afraid I would talk the hind-leg off his favourite dog, so he gave me some cheap things and a few guns, and told me he hoped he would never see my face again. Good old Dutchman, Van Shuyten. I sent him one small lot of ivory a year ago, so that he can't call me a little thief when I get back. I hope he got it. And for the rest, I don't care. I had some wood stacked for you. That was my old house. Did you see?'

"I gave him Towson's book. He made as though he would kiss me, but restrained himself. 'The only book I had left, and I thought I had lost it,' he said, looking at it ecstatically. 'So many accidents happen to a man going about alone, you know. Canoes get upset sometimes—and sometimes you've got to clear out so quick when the people get angry.' He thumbed the pages. 'You made notes in Russian?' I asked. He nodded. 'I thought they were written in cipher,' I said. He laughed, then became serious. 'I had lots of trouble to keep these people off,' he said. 'Did they want to kill you?' I asked. 'Oh no!' he cried, and checked himself. 'Why did they attack us?' I pursued. He hesitated, then said shamefacedly, 'They don't want him to go.' 'Don't they?' I said curiously. He nodded a nod full of mystery and wisdom. 'I tell you,' he cried, 'this man has enlarged my mind.' He opened his arms wide, staring at me with his little blue eyes that were perfectly round."

III

"I looked at him, lost in astonishment. There he was before me, in motley, as though he had absconded from a troupe of mimes, enthusiastic, fabulous. His very existence was improbable, inexplicable, and altogether bewildering. He was an insoluble problem. It was inconceivable how he had existed, how he had succeeded in getting so far, how he had managed to remain—why he did not instantly disappear. 'I went a little farther,' he said, 'then still a little farther—till I had gone so far that I don't know how I'll ever get back. Never mind. Plenty time. I can manage. You take Kurtz away quick—quick—I tell you.' The glamour of youth enveloped his parti-coloured rags, his destitution, his loneliness, the essential desolation of his futile wanderings. For months—for years—his life hadn't been worth a day's purchase; and there he was gallantly, thoughtlessly alive, to all appearance indestructible solely by the virtue of his few years and of his unreflecting audacity. I was seduced into something like admiration—like envy. Glamour urged him on, glamour kept him unscathed. He surely wanted nothing from the wilderness but space to breathe in and to push on through.

His need was to exist, and to move onwards at the greatest possible risk, and with a maximum of privation. If the absolutely pure, un-calculating, unpractical spirit of adventure had ever ruled a human being, it ruled this be-patched youth. I almost envied him the pos-session of this modest and clear flame. It seemed to have consumed all thought of self so completely, that, even while he was talking to you, you forgot that it was he—the man before your eyes—who had gone through these things. I did not envy him his devotion to Kurtz, though. He had not meditated over it. It came to him, and he accepted it with a sort of eager fatalism. I must say that to me it appeared about the most dangerous thing in every way he had come upon so far.

"They had come together unavoidably, like two ships becalmed near each other, and lay rubbing sides at last. I suppose Kurtz wanted an audience, because on a certain occasion, when encamped in the forest, they had talked all night, or more probably Kurtz had talked. 'We talked of everything,' he said, quite transported at the recollection. 'I forgot there was such a thing as sleep. The night did not seem to last an hour. Everything! Everything! . . . Of love too.' 'Ah, he talked to you of love!' I said, much amused. 'It isn't what you think,' he cried, almost passionately. 'It was in general. He made me see things—things.'

"He threw his arms up. We were on deck at the time, and the head-man of my wood-cutters, lounging near by, turned upon him his heavy and glittering eyes. I looked around, and I don't know why, but I assure you that never, never before, did this land, this river, this jungle, the very arch of this blazing sky, appear to me so hopeless and so dark, so impenetrable to human thought, so pitiless to human weakness. 'And, ever since, you have been with him, of course?' I said.

"On the contrary. It appears their intercourse had been very much broken by various causes. He had, as he informed me proudly, managed to nurse Kurtz through two illnesses (he alluded to it as you would to some risky feat), but as a rule Kurtz wandered alone, far in the depths of the forest. 'Very often coming to this station, I had to wait days and days before he would turn up,' he said. 'Ah, it was worth waiting for!—sometimes.' 'What was he doing? exploring or what?' I asked. 'Oh yes, of course'; he had discovered lots of villages, a lake too—he did not know exactly in what direc-tion; it was dangerous to inquire too much—but mostly his expe-ditions had been for ivory. 'But he had no goods to trade with by that time,' I objected. 'There's a good lot of cartridges left even yet,' he answered, looking away. 'To speak plainly, he raided the country,' I said. He nodded. 'Not alone, surely!' He muttered something about the villages round that lake. 'Kurtz got the tribe to follow him, did he?' I suggested. He fidgeted a little. 'They adored him,' he said. The tone of these words was so extraordinary that I looked at him searchingly. It was curious to see his mingled eagerness and reluctance to speak of Kurtz. The man filled his life, occupied his thoughts, swayed his emotions. 'What can you expect?' he burst out; 'he came to them with thunder and lightning, you know—and they had never seen anything like it—and very terrible. He could be very terrible. You can't judge Mr. Kurtz as you would an ordinary man. No, no, no! Now—just to give you an idea—I don't mind telling you, he wanted to shoot me too one day—but I don't judge him.' 'Shoot you!' I cried. 'What for?' 'Well, I had a small lot of ivory the chief of that village near my house gave me. You see I used to shoot game for them. Well, he wanted it, and wouldn't hear reason. He declared he would shoot me unless I gave him the ivory and then cleared out of the country, because he could do so, and had a fancy for it, and there was nothing on earth to prevent him killing whom he jolly well pleased. And it was true too. I gave him the ivory. What did I care! But I didn't clear out. No, no. I couldn't leave him. I had to be careful, of course, till we got friendly again for a time. He had his second illness then. Afterwards I had to keep out of the way; but I didn't mind. He was living for the most part in those villages on the lake. When he came down to the river, sometimes he would take to me, and sometimes it was better for me to be careful. This man suffered too much. He hated all this, and somehow he couldn't get away. When I had a chance I begged him to try and leave while there was time; I offered to go back with him. And he would say yes, and then he would remain; go off on another ivory hunt; disappear for weeks; forget himself amongst these people—forget himself—you know.' 'Why! he's mad,' I said. He protested indignantly. Mr. Kurtz couldn't be mad. If I had heard him talk, only two days ago, I wouldn't dare hint at such a thing. . . . I had taken up my binoculars while we talked, and was looking at the shore, sweeping the limit of the forest at each side and at the back of the house. The consciousness of there being people in that bush, so silent, so quiet—as silent and quiet as the ruined house on the hill—made me uneasy. There was no sign on the face of nature of this amazing tale† that was not so much told as suggested to me in desolate exclamations, completed by shrugs, in interrupted phrases, in hints ending in deep sighs. The woods were unmoved, like a mask—heavy, like the closed door of a prison—they looked with their air of hidden knowledge, of patient expectation, of unapproachable silence. The Russian was explaining to me that it was only lately that Mr. Kurtz had come down to the river, bringing along with

† *Ms and Maga:* tale of cruelty and greed that was, *etc.*

him all the fighting men of that lake tribe. He had been absent for several months—getting himself adored, I suppose—and had come down unexpectedly, with the intention to all appearance of making a raid either across the river or down stream. Evidently the appetite for more ivory had got the better of the—what shall I say? —less material aspirations. However, he had got much worse suddenly. 'I heard he was lying helpless, and so I came up—took my chance,' said the Russian. 'Oh, he is bad, very bad.' I directed my glass to the house. There were no signs of life, but there were the ruined roof, the long mud wall peeping above the grass, with three little square window-holes, no two of the same size; all this brought within reach of my hand, as it were. And then I made a brusque movement, and one of the remaining posts of that vanished fence leaped up in the field of my glass. You remember I told you I had been struck at the distance by certain attempts at ornamentation, rather remarkable in the ruinous aspect of the place. Now I had suddenly a nearer view, and its first result was to make me throw my head back as if before a blow. Then I went carefully from post to post with my glass, and I saw my mistake. These round knobs were not ornamental but symbolic;† they were expressive and puzzling, striking and disturbing—food for thought and also for vultures if there had been any looking down from the sky; but at all events for such ants as were industrious enough to ascend the pole. They would have been even more impressive, those heads on the stakes, if their faces had not been turned to the house. Only one, the first I had made out, was facing my way. I was not so shocked as you may think. The start back I had given was really nothing but a movement of surprise. I had expected to see a knob of wood there, you know. I returned deliberately to the first I had seen— and there it was, black, dried, sunken, with closed eyelids—a head that seemed to sleep at the top of that pole, and, with the shrunken dry lips showing a narrow white line of the teeth, was smiling too, smiling continuously at some endless and jocose dream of that eternal slumber.

"I am not disclosing any trade secrets. In fact the manager said afterwards that Mr. Kurtz's methods had ruined the district. I have no opinion on that point, but I want you clearly to understand that there was nothing exactly profitable in these heads being there. They only showed that Mr. Kurtz lacked restraint in the gratification of his various lusts, that there was something wanting in him—some small matter which, when the pressing need arose, could not be found under his magnificent eloquence. Whether he knew of this deficiency himself I can't say. I think

† *Ms and Maga:* symbolic of some cruel and forbidden knowledge. They were, *etc.*

the knowledge came to him at last—only at the very last.† But the wilderness had found him out early, and had taken on him a terrible vengeance for the fantastic invasion.* I think it had whispered to him things about himself which he did not know, things of which he had no conception till he took counsel with this great solitude—and the whisper had proved irresistibly fascinating. It echoed loudly within him because he was hollow at the core. . . . I put down the glass, and the head that had appeared near enough to be spoken to seemed at once to have leaped away from me into inaccessible distance.

"The admirer of Mr. Kurtz was a bit crestfallen. In a hurried, indistinct voice he began to assure me he had not dared to take these—say, symbols—down. He was not afraid of the natives; they would not stir till Mr. Kurtz gave the word. His ascendancy was extraordinary. The camps of these people surrounded the place, and the chiefs came every day to see him. They would crawl . . . 'I don't want to know anything of the ceremonies used when approaching Mr. Kurtz,' I shouted. Curious, this feeling that came over me that such details would be more intolerable than those heads drying on the stakes under Mr. Kurtz's windows. After all, that was only a savage sight, while I seemed at one bound to have been transported into some lightless region of subtle horrors, where pure, uncomplicated savagery was a positive relief, being something that had a right to exist—obviously—in the sunshine. The young man looked at me with surprise. I suppose it did not occur to him that Mr. Kurtz was no idol of mine. He forgot I hadn't heard any of these splendid monologues on, what was it? on love, justice, conduct of life—or what not. If it had come to crawling before Mr. Kurtz, he crawled as much as the veriest savage of them all.‡ I had no idea of the conditions, he said: these heads were the heads of rebels. I shocked him excessively by laughing. Rebels! What would be the next definition I was to hear? There had been enemies, criminals, workers—and these were rebels. Those rebellious heads looked very subdued to me on their sticks. 'You don't know how such a life tries a man like Kurtz,' cried Kurtz's last disciple. 'Well, and you?' I said. 'I! I! I am a simple man. I have no great thoughts. I want nothing from anybody. How can you compare me to . . . ?' His feelings were too much for speech, and suddenly he broke down. 'I don't understand,' he groaned. 'I've been doing my best to keep him alive, and that's enough. I had no hand in all this. I have no abilities. There hasn't been a

---

† *Ms:* last. If so, then justice was done. But, *etc.*

* *Ms and Maga:* invasion. It had tempted him with all the sinister suggestions of its loneliness. I think. *etc.*

‡ *Ms:* all. And his was a sturdy allegiance, soaring bravely above the facts which it could see with a bewilderment and a sorrow akin to despair. I had, *etc.*

drop of medicine or a mouthful of invalid food for months here. He was shamefully abandoned. A man like this, with such ideas. Shamefully! Shamefully! I—I—haven't slept for the last ten nights. . . .'

"His voice lost itself in the calm of the evening. The long shadows of the forest had slipped downhill while we talked, had gone far beyond the ruined hovel, beyond the symbolic row of stakes. All this was in the gloom, while we down there were yet in the sunshine, and the stretch of the river abreast of the clearing glittered in a still and dazzling splendour, with a murky and over-shadowed bend above and below. Not a living soul was seen on the shore. The bushes did not rustle.

"Suddenly round the corner of the house a group of men appeared, as though they had come up from the ground. They waded waist-deep in the grass, in a compact body, bearing an improvised stretcher in their midst. Instantly, in the emptiness of the landscape, a cry arose whose shrillness pierced the still air like a sharp arrow flying straight to the very heart of the land; and, as if by enchantment, streams of human beings—of naked human beings—with spears in their hands, with bows, with shields, with wild glances and savage movements, were poured into the clearing by the dark-faced and pensive forest. The bushes shook, the grass swayed for a time, and then everything stood still in attentive immobility.

" 'Now, if he does not say the right thing to them we are all done for,' said the Russian at my elbow. The knot of men with the stretcher had stopped too, half-way to the steamer, as if petrified. I saw the man on the stretcher sit up, lank and with an uplifted arm, above the shoulders of the bearers. 'Let us hope that the man who can talk so well of love in general will find some particular reason to spare us this time,' I said. I resented bitterly the absurd danger of our situation, as if to be at the mercy of that atrocious phantom† had been a dishonouring necessity. I could not hear a sound, but through my glasses I saw the thin arm extended commandingly, the lower jaw moving, the eyes of that apparition shining darkly far in its bony head that nodded with grotesque jerks. Kurtz—Kurtz—that means 'short' in German—don't it? Well, the name was as true as everything else in his life—and death. He looked at least seven feet long. His covering had fallen off, and his body emerged from it pitiful and appalling as from a winding-sheet. I could see the cage of his ribs all astir, the bones of his arm waving. It was as though an animated image of death carved out of old ivory had been shaking its hand with menaces at a motionless crowd of men made of dark and glittering bronze. I saw him open

† *Ms:* phantom who ruled this land had been, *etc.*

his† mouth wide—it gave him a weirdly voracious aspect, as though he had wanted to swallow all the air, all the earth, all the men before him. A deep voice reached me faintly. He must have been shouting. He fell back suddenly. The stretcher shook as the bearers staggered forward again, and almost at the same time I noticed that the crowd of savages was vanishing without any perceptible movement of retreat, as if the forest that had ejected these beings so suddenly had drawn them in again as the breath is drawn in a long aspiration.

"Some of the pilgrims behind the stretcher carried his arms—two shot-guns, a heavy rifle, and a light revolver-carbine—the thunderbolts of that pitiful Jupiter. The manager bent over him murmuring as he walked beside his head. They laid him down in one of the little cabins—just a room for a bed-place and a camp-stool or two, you know. We had brought his belated correspondence, and a lot of torn envelopes and open letters littered his bed. His hand roamed feebly amongst these papers. I was struck by the fire of his eyes and the composed languor of his expression. It was not so much the exhaustion of disease. He did not seem in pain. This shadow looked satiated and calm, as though for the moment it had had its fill of all the emotions.

"He rustled one of the letters, and looking straight in my face said, 'I am glad.' Somebody had been writing to him about me. These special recommendations were turning up again. The volume of tone he emitted without effort, almost without the trouble of moving his lips, amazed me. A voice! a voice! It was grave, profound, vibrating, while the man did not seem capable of a whisper. However, he had enough strength in him—factitious no doubt—to very nearly make an end of us, as you shall hear directly.

"The manager appeared silently in the doorway; I stepped out at once and he drew the curtain after me. The Russian, eyed curiously by the pilgrims, was staring at the shore. I followed the direction of his glance.

"Dark human shapes could be made out in the distance, flitting indistinctly against the gloomy border of the forest, and near the river two bronze figures, leaning on tall spears, stood in the sunlight under fantastic head-dresses of spotted skins, warlike and still in statuesque repose. And from right to left along the lighted shore moved a wild and gorgeous apparition of a woman.

"She walked with measured steps, draped in striped and fringed cloths, treading the earth proudly, with a slight jingle and flash of barbarous ornaments. She carried her head high; her hair was done in the shape of a helmet; she had brass leggings to the knees, brass wire gauntlets to the elbow, a crimson spot on her tawny cheek,

† *Ms:* it open its

innumerable necklaces of glass beads on her neck; bizarre things, charms, gifts of witch-men, that hung about her, glittered and trembled at every step. She must have had the value of several elephant tusks upon her. She was savage and superb, wild-eyed and magnificent; there was something ominous and stately in her deliberate progress. And in the hush that had fallen suddenly upon the whole sorrowful land, the immense wilderness, the colossal body of the fecund and mysterious life seemed to look at her, pensive, as though it had been looking at the image of its own tenebrous and passionate soul.†

"She came abreast of the steamer, stood still, and faced us. Her long shadow fell to the water's edge. Her face had a tragic and fierce aspect of wild sorrow and of dumb pain mingled with the fear of some struggling, half-shaped resolve. She stood looking at us without a stir, and like the wilderness itself, with an air of brooding* over an inscrutable purpose. A whole minute passed, and then she made a step forward. There was a low jingle, a glint of yellow metal, a sway of fringed draperies, and she stopped‡ as if her heart had failed her. The young fellow by my side growled. The pilgrims murmured at my back. She looked at us all as if her life had depended upon the unswerving steadiness of her glance. Suddenly she opened her bared arms and threw them up rigid above her head, as though in an uncontrollable desire to touch the sky, and at the same time the swift shadows darted out on the earth, swept around on the river, gathering the steamer in a shadowy embrace.** A formidable silence hung over the scene.

"She turned away slowly, walked on, following the bank, and passed into the bushes to the left. Once only her eyes gleamed back at us in the dusk of the thickets before she disappeared.

" 'If she had offered to come aboard I really think I would have tried to shoot her,' said the man of patches nervously. 'I had been risking my life every day for the last fortnight to keep her out of the house. She got in one day and kicked up a row about those miserable rags I picked up in the storeroom to mend my clothes with. I wasn't decent. At least it must have been that, for she talked like a fury to Kurtz for an hour, pointing at me now and then. I don't understand the dialect of this tribe. Luckily for me,

† *Ms and Maga:* soul. And we men looked at her—at any rate I looked at her.
* *Ms:* implaccable brooding
‡ *Ms and Maga:* and she stopped. Had her heart failed her, or had her eyes veiled with that mournfulness that lies over all the wild things of the earth seen the hopelessness of longing that will find out sometimes even a savage soul in the loneliness [*Maga:* lonely darkness] of its being? Who can tell.

Perhaps she did not know herself. The young fellow, *etc.*
** *Ms:* embrace. Her sudden gesture was as startling as a cry but not a sound was heard. The formidable silence of the scene completed the memorable impression. *Maga:* embrace. Her sudden gesture seemed to demand a cry, but the unbroken silence that hung over the scene was more formidable than any sound could be. *1902:* embrace. A formidable silence hung over the scene.

I fancy Kurtz felt too ill that day to care, or there would have been mischief. I don't understand. . . . No—it's too much for me. Ah, well, it's all over now.'

"At this moment I heard Kurtz's deep voice behind the curtain: 'Save me!—save the ivory, you mean. Don't tell me. Save *me*! Why, I've had to save you. You are interrupting my plans now. Sick! Sick! Not so sick as you would like to believe. Never mind. I'll carry my ideas out yet—I will return. I'll show you what can be done. You with your little peddling notions—you are interfering with me. I will return. I . . .'

"The manager came out. He did me the honour to take me under the arm and lead me aside. 'He is very low, very low,' he said. He considered it necessary to sigh, but neglected to be consistently sorrowful. 'We have done all we could for him—haven't we? But there is no disguising the fact, Mr. Kurtz has done more harm than good to the Company. He did not see the time was not ripe for vigorous action. Cautiously, cautiously—that's my principle. We must be cautious yet. The district is closed to us for a time. Deplorable! Upon the whole, the trade will suffer. I don't deny there is a remarkable quantity of ivory—mostly fossil. We must save it, at all events—but look how precarious the position is—and why? Because the method is unsound.' 'Do you,' said I, looking at the shore, 'call it "unsound method"?' 'Without doubt,' he exclaimed hotly. 'Don't you?' . . . 'No method at all,' I murmured after a while. 'Exactly,' he exulted. 'I anticipated this. Shows a complete want of judgment. It is my duty to point it out in the proper quarter.' 'Oh,' said I, 'that fellow—what's his name?—the brickmaker, will make a readable report for you.' He appeared confounded for a moment. It seemed to me I had never breathed an atmosphere so vile, and I turned mentally to Kurtz for relief—positively for relief. 'Nevertheless, I think Mr. Kurtz is a remarkable man,' I said with emphasis. He started, dropped on me a cold heavy glance, said very quietly, 'He *was*,' and turned his back on me. My hour of favour was over; I found myself lumped along with Kurtz as a partisan of methods for which the time was not ripe: I was unsound! Ah! but it was something to have at least a choice of nightmares.

"I had turned to the wilderness really, not to Mr. Kurtz, who, I was ready to admit, was as good as buried. And for a moment it seemed to me as if I also were buried in a vast grave full of unspeakable secrets. I felt an intolerable weight oppressing my breast, the smell of the damp earth, the unseen presence of victorious corruption, the darkness of an impenetrable night. . . . The Russian tapped me on the shoulder. I heard him mumbling and stammering something about 'brother seaman—couldn't conceal—knowledge of matters that would affect Mr. Kurtz's reputation.' I waited. For him evidently Mr. Kurtz was not in his grave; I suspect that for him Mr. Kurtz was one of the immortals. 'Well!' said I at last, 'speak out. As it happens, I am Mr. Kurtz's friend—in a way.'

"He stated with a good deal of formality that had we not been 'of the same profession,' he would have kept the matter to himself without regard to consequences. He suspected 'there was an active ill-will towards him on the part of these white men that——' 'You are right,' I said, remembering a certain conversation I had overheard. 'The manager thinks you ought to be hanged.' He showed a concern at this intelligence which amused me at first. 'I had better get out of the way quietly,' he said earnestly. 'I can do no more for Kurtz now, and they would soon find some excuse. What's to stop them? There's a military post three hundred miles from here.' 'Well, upon my word,' said I, 'perhaps you had better go if you have any friends amongst the savages near by.' 'Plenty,' he said. 'They are simple people—and I want nothing, you know.' He stood biting his lip, then: 'I don't want any harm to happen to these whites here, but of course I was thinking of Mr. Kurtz's reputation—but you are a brother seaman and——' 'All right,' said I, after a time. 'Mr. Kurtz's reputation is safe with me.' I did not know how truly I spoke.

"He informed me, lowering his voice, that it was Kurtz who had ordered the attack to be made on the steamer. 'He hated sometimes the idea of being taken away—and then again . . . But I don't understand these matters. I am a simple man. He thought it would scare you away—that you would give it up, thinking him dead. I could not stop him. Oh, I had an awful time of it this last month.' 'Very well,' I said. 'He is all right now.' 'Ye-e-es,' he muttered, not very convinced apparently. 'Thanks,' said I; 'I shall keep my eyes open.' 'But quiet—eh?' he urged anxiously. 'It would be awful for his reputation if anybody here——' I promised a complete discretion with great gravity. 'I have a canoe and three black fellows waiting not very far. I am off. Could you give me a few Martini-Henry cartridges?' I could, and did, with proper secrecy. He helped himself, with a wink at me, to a handful of my tobacco. 'Between sailors—you know—good English tobacco.' At the door of the pilot-house he turned round—'I say, haven't you a pair of shoes you could spare?' He raised one leg. 'Look.' The soles were tied with knotted strings sandal-wise under his bare feet. I rooted out an old pair, at which he looked with admiration before tucking it under his left arm. One of his pockets (bright red) was bulging with cartridges, from the other (dark blue) peeped 'Towson's Inquiry,' etc. etc. He seemed to think himself excellently well equipped for a renewed encounter with the wilderness. 'Ah! I'll never, never meet such a man again. You ought to have heard him recite poetry—his own too it was, he told me. Poetry!' He rolled his eyes at the recollection of these delights. 'Oh, he enlarged my mind!' 'Good-bye,' said I. He shook hands and vanished in the night. Sometimes I ask myself whether I had ever really seen him—whether it was possible to meet such a phenomenon! . . .

"When I woke up shortly after midnight his warning came to my mind with its hint of danger that seemed, in the starred darkness, real enough to make me get up for the purpose of having a look round. On the hill a big fire burned, illuminating fitfully a crooked corner of the station-house. One of the agents with a picket of a few of our blacks, armed for the purpose, was keeping guard over the ivory; but deep within the forest, red gleams that wavered, that seemed to sink and rise from the ground amongst confused columnar shapes of intense blackness, showed the exact position of the camp where Mr. Kurtz's adorers were keeping their uneasy vigil. The monotonous beating of a big drum filled the air with muffled shocks and a lingering vibration. A steady droning sound of many men chanting each to himself some weird incantation came out from the black, flat wall of the woods as the humming of bees comes out of a hive, and had a strange narcotic effect upon my half-awake senses. I believe I dozed off leaning over the rail, till an abrupt burst of yells, an overwhelming outbreak of a pent-up and mysterious frenzy, woke me up in a bewildered wonder. It was cut short all at once, and the low droning went on with an effect of audible and soothing silence. I glanced casually into the little cabin. A light was burning within, but Mr. Kurtz was not there.

"I think I would have raised an outcry if I had believed my eyes. But I didn't believe them at first—the thing seemed so impossible. The fact is, I was completely unnerved by a sheer blank fright, pure abstract terror, unconnected with any distinct shape of physical danger. What made this emotion so overpowering was—how shall I define it?—the moral shock I received, as if something altogether monstrous, intolerable to thought and odious to the soul, had been thrust upon me unexpectedly. This lasted of course the merest fraction of a second, and then the usual sense of commonplace, deadly danger, the possibility of a sudden onslaught and massacre, or something of the kind, which I saw impending, was positively welcome and composing. It pacified me, in fact, so much, that I did not raise an alarm.

"There was an agent buttoned up inside an ulster and sleeping on a chair on deck within three feet of me. The yells had not awakened him; he snored very slightly; I left him to his slumbers and leaped ashore. I did not betray Mr. Kurtz—it was ordered I should never betray him—it was written I should be loyal to the nightmare of my choice. I was anxious to deal with this shadow by myself alone—and to this day I don't know why I was so jealous of sharing with any one the peculiar blackness† of that experience.

"As soon as I got on the bank I saw a trail—a broad trail through the grass. I remember the exultation with which I said to myself, 'He can't walk—he is crawling on all-fours—I've got him.' The grass was wet with dew. I strode rapidly with clenched fists. I fancy I had some vague notion of falling upon him and giving him a drubbing. I don't know. I had some imbecile thoughts. The knitting old woman with the cat obtruded herself upon my memory as a most improper person to be sitting at the other end of such an affair. I saw a row of pilgrims squirting lead in the air out of Winchesters held to the hip. I thought I would never get back to the steamer, and imagined myself living alone and unarmed in the woods to an advanced age. Such silly things—you know. And I remember I confounded the beat of the drum with the beating of my heart, and was pleased at its calm regularity.

"I kept to the track though—then stopped to listen. The night was very clear; a dark blue space, sparkling with dew and starlight, in which black things stood very still. I thought I could see a kind of motion ahead of me. I was strangely cocksure of everything that night. I actually left the track and ran in a wide semicircle (I verily believe chuckling to myself) so as to get in front of that stir, of that motion I had seen—if indeed I had seen anything. I was circumventing Kurtz as though it had been a boyish game.

"I came upon him, and, if he had not heard me coming, I would have fallen over him too, but he got up in time. He rose, unsteady, long, pale, indistinct, like a vapour exhaled by the earth, and swayed slightly, misty and silent before me; while at my back the fires loomed between the trees, and the murmur of many voices issued from the forest. I had cut him off cleverly; but when actually confronting him I seemed to come to my senses, I saw the danger in its right proportion. It was by no means over yet. Suppose he began to shout? Though he could hardly stand, there was still plenty of vigour in his voice. 'Go away—hide yourself,' he said, in that profound tone. It was very awful. I glanced back. We were within thirty yards from* the nearest fire. A black figure stood up, strode on long black legs, waving long black arms, across the glow. It had horns—antelope horns, I think—on its head. Some sorcerer, some witch-man, no doubt: it looked fiend-like enough. 'Do you know what you are doing?' I whispered. 'Perfectly,' he answered, raising his voice for that single word: it sounded to me far off and yet loud, like a hail through a speaking-trumpet. If he makes a row

† *Ms* and *Maga:* dismal blackness   * *Ms:* of; *Maga and 1902:* from

we are lost, I thought to myself. This clearly was not a case for fisticuffs, even apart from the very natural aversion I had to beat that Shadow—this wandering and tormented thing.† 'You will be lost,' I said—'utterly lost.' One gets sometimes such a flash of inspiration, you know. I did say the right thing, though indeed he could not have been more irretrievably lost than he was at this very moment, when the foundations of our intimacy were being laid—to endure—to endure—even to the end—even beyond.

"'I had immense plans,' he muttered irresolutely. 'Yes,' said I; 'but if you try to shout I'll smash your head with——' There was not a stick or a stone near. 'I will throttle you for good,' I corrected myself. 'I was on the threshold of great things,' he pleaded, in a voice of longing, with a wistfulness of tone that made my blood run cold. 'And now for this stupid scoundrel——' 'Your success in Europe is assured in any case,' I affirmed steadily. I did not want to have the throttling of him, you understand—and indeed it would have been very little use for any practical purpose. I tried to break the spell—the heavy, mute spell of the wilderness—that seemed to draw him to its pitiless breast by the awakening of forgotten and brutal instincts, by the memory of gratified and monstrous passions. This alone, I was convinced, had driven him out to the edge of the forest, to the bush, towards the gleam of fires, the throb of drums, the drone of weird incantations; this alone had beguiled his unlawful soul beyond the bounds of permitted aspirations. And, don't you see, the terror of the position was not in being knocked on the head—though I had a very lively sense of that danger too—but in this, that I had to deal with a being to whom I could not appeal in the name of anything high or low. I had, even like the niggers, to invoke him—himself—his own exalted and incredible degradation. There was nothing either above or below him, and I knew it. He had kicked himself loose of the earth.* Confound the man! he had kicked the very earth to pieces. He was alone, and I before him did not know whether I stood on the ground or floated in the air. I've been telling you what we said—repeating the phrases we pronounced—but what's the good? They were common everyday words—the familiar, vague sounds exchanged on every waking day of life. But what of that? They had behind them, to my mind, the terrific suggestiveness of words heard in dreams, of phrases spoken in nightmares. Soul! If anybody had ever struggled with a soul, I am the man. And I wasn't arguing with a lunatic‡ either. Believe me or not, his intelligence was perfectly clear—concentrated, it is true, upon himself with horrible intensity, yet clear; and therein was my only chance—barring, of course, the killing him there and then, which

† *Ms and Maga:* thing that seemed released from one grave only to sink forever into another. 'You will, *etc.*

* *Ms canceled:* of every restraint.

‡ *Ms and Maga:* mad man

wasn't so good, on account of unavoidable noise. But his soul was mad. Being alone in the wilderness, it had looked within itself, and, by Heavens! I tell you, it had gone mad. I had—for my sins, I suppose, to go through the ordeal of looking into it myself. No eloquence could have been so withering to one's belief in mankind† as his final burst of sincerity. He struggled with himself too. I saw it—I heard it. I saw the inconceivable mystery of a soul that knew no restraint, no faith, and no fear, yet struggling blindly with itself. I kept my head pretty well; but when I had him at last stretched on the couch, I wiped my forehead, while my legs shook under me as though I had carried half a ton on my back down that hill. And yet I had only supported him, his bony arm clasped round my neck —and he was not much heavier than a child.

"When next day we left at noon, the crowd, of whose presence behind the curtain of trees I had been acutely conscious all the time, flowed out of the woods again, filled the clearing, covered the slope with a mass of naked, breathing, quivering, bronze bodies. I steamed up a bit, then swung down-stream, and two thousand eyes followed the evolutions of the splashing, thumping, fierce river-demon beating the water with its terrible tail and breathing black smoke into the air. In front of the first rank, along the river, three men, plastered with bright red earth from head to foot, strutted to and fro restlessly. When we came abreast again, they faced the river, stamped their feet, nodded their horned heads, swayed their scarlet bodies; they shook towards the fierce river-demon a bunch of black feathers, a mangy skin with a pendent tail—something that looked like a dried gourd; they shouted periodically together strings of amazing words that resembled no sounds of human language; and the deep murmurs of the crowd, interrupted suddenly, were like the responses of some satanic litany.

"We had carried Kurtz into the pilot-house: there was more air there. Lying on the couch, he stared through the open shutter. There was an eddy in the mass of human bodies, and the woman with helmeted head and tawny cheeks rushed out to the very brink of the stream. She put out her hands, shouted something, and all that wild mob took up the shout in a roaring chorus of articulated, rapid, breathless utterance.

" 'Do you understand this?' I asked.

"He kept on looking out past me with fiery, longing eyes, with a mingled expression of wistfulness and hate. He made no answer, but I saw a smile, a smile of indefinable meaning, appear on his colourless lips that a moment after twitched convulsively. 'Do I not?'* he said slowly, gasping, as if the words had been torn out of

† to one's belief in mankind, *added*   * Ms and Maga: 'I will return.'
1902.

him by a supernatural power.

"I pulled the string of the whistle, and I did this because I saw the pilgrims on deck getting out their rifles with an air of anticipating a jolly lark. At the sudden screech there was a movement of abject terror through that wedged mass of bodies. 'Don't! don't you frighten them away,' cried some one on deck disconsolately. I pulled the string time after time. They broke and ran, they leaped, they crouched, they swerved, they dodged the flying terror of the sound. The three red chaps had fallen flat, face down on the shore, as though they had been shot dead. Only the barbarous and superb woman did not so much as flinch, and stretched tragically her bare arms after us over the sombre and glittering river.

"And then that imbecile crowd down on the deck started their little fun, and I could see nothing more for smoke.

"The brown current ran swiftly out of the heart of darkness, bearing us down towards the sea with twice the speed of our upward progress; and Kurtz's life was running swiftly too, ebbing, ebbing out of his heart into the sea of inexorable time. The manager was very placid, he had no vital anxieties now, he took us both in with a comprehensive and satisfied glance: the 'affair' had come off as well as could be wished. I saw the time approaching when I would be left alone of the party of 'unsound method.' The pilgrims looked upon me with disfavour. I was, so to speak, numbered with the dead. It is strange how I accepted this unforeseen partnership, this choice of nightmares forced upon me in the tenebrous land invaded by these mean and greedy phantoms.

"Kurtz discoursed. A voice! a voice! It rang deep to the very last. It survived his strength to hide in the magnificent folds of eloquence the barren darkness of his heart. Oh, he struggled! he struggled! The wastes of his weary brain were haunted by shadowy images now—images of wealth and fame revolving obsequiously round his unextinguishable gift of noble and lofty expression. My Intended,† my station, my career, my ideas—these were the subjects for the occasional utterances of elevated sentiments. The shade of the original Kurtz frequented the bedside of the hollow sham, whose fate it was to be buried presently in the mould of primeval earth. But both the diabolic love and the unearthly hate of the mysteries it had penetrated fought for the possession of that soul satiated with primitive emotions, avid of lying fame, of sham distinction, of all the appearances of success and power.

"Sometimes he was contemptibly childish. He desired to have kings meet him at railway stations on his return from some ghastly Nowhere, where he intended to accomplish great things. 'You show

† *Ms*: My Intended, my ivory, my station, my career, my ideas.

them you have in you something that is really profitable, and then there will be no limits to the recognition of your ability,' he would say. 'Of course you must take care of the motives—right motives—always.' The long reaches that were like one and the same reach, monotonous bends that were exactly alike, slipped past the steamer with their multitude of secular[9] trees looking patiently after this grimy fragment of another world, the forerunner of change, of conquest, of trade, of massacres, of blessings. I looked ahead—piloting. 'Close the shutter,' said Kurtz suddenly one day; 'I can't bear to look at this.' I did so. There was a silence. 'Oh, but I will wring your heart yet!'[†] he cried at the invisible wilderness.

"We broke down—as I had expected—and had to lie up for repairs at the head of an island. This delay was the first thing that shook Kurtz's confidence. One morning he gave me a packet of papers and a photograph—the lot tied together with a shoe-string. 'Keep this for me,' he said. 'This noxious fool' (meaning the manager) 'is capable of prying into my boxes when I am not looking.' In the afternoon I saw him. He was lying on his back with closed eyes, and I withdrew quietly, but I heard him mutter, 'Live rightly, die, die*[*] . . .' I listened. There was nothing more. Was he rehearsing some speech in his sleep, or was it a fragment of a phrase from some newspaper article? He had been writing for the papers and meant to do so again, 'for the furthering of my ideas. It's a duty.'

"His was an impenetrable darkness. I looked at him as you peer down at a man who is lying at the bottom of a precipice where the sun never shines. But I had not much time to give him, because I was helping the engine-driver to take to pieces the leaky cylinders, to straighten a bent connecting-rod, and in other such matters. I lived in an infernal mess of rust, filings, nuts, bolts, spanners, hammers, ratchet-drills—things I abominate, because I don't get on with them. I tended the little forge we fortunately had aboard; I toiled wearily in a wretched scrap-heap—unless I had the shakes too bad to stand.

"One evening coming in with a candle I was startled to hear him say a little tremulously,[‡] 'I am lying here in the dark waiting for death.' The light was within a foot of his eyes. I forced myself to murmur, 'Oh, nonsense!' and stood over him as if transfixed.

"Anything approaching the change that came over his features I have never seen before, and hope never to see again. Oh, I wasn't touched. I was fascinated. It was as though a veil had been rent.**[**]

---

9. A French form, like *serried* and *serviette* above, *secular* means simply "aged" or "ancient."
† *Ms:* 'Oh, but I will make you serve my ends.'
* *Ms:* die nobly

‡ *Ms and Maga:* querulously
** *Ms and Maga:* rent. I saw on that ivory visage the expression of strange pride, of mental power, of avarice, of blood-thirstiness, of cunning, of excessive terror, of intense and hopeless de-

I saw on that ivory face the expression of sombre pride, of ruthless power, of craven terror—of an intense and hopeless despair. Did he live his life again in every detail of desire, temptation, and surrender during that supreme moment of complete knowledge? He cried in a whisper at some image, at some vision—he cried out twice, a cry that was no more than a breath:

" 'The horror! The horror!'

"I blew the candle out and left the cabin. The pilgrims were dining in the mess-room, and I took my place opposite the manager, who lifted his eyes to give me a questioning glance, which I successfully ignored. He leaned back, serene, with that peculiar smile of his sealing the unexpressed depths of his meanness. A continuous shower of small flies streamed upon the lamp, upon the cloth, upon our hands and faces. Suddenly the manager's boy put his insolent black head in the doorway, and said in a tone of scathing contempt:

" 'Mistah Kurtz—he dead.'

"All the pilgrims rushed out to see. I remained, and went on with my dinner. I believe I was considered brutally callous. However, I did not eat much. There was a lamp in there—light, don't you know—and outside it was so beastly, beastly dark. I went no more near the remarkable man who had pronounced† a judgment upon the adventures of his soul on this earth. The voice was gone. What else had been there? But I am of course aware that next day the pilgrims buried something in a muddy hole.*

"And then they very nearly buried me.

"However, as you see, I did not go to join Kurtz there and then. I did not. I remained to dream the nightmare out to the end, and to show my loyalty to Kurtz once more. Destiny. My destiny! Droll thing life is—that mysterious arrangement of merciless logic for a futile purpose. The most you can hope from it is some knowledge of yourself—that comes too late—a crop of unextinguishable regrets. I have wrestled with death. It is the most unexciting contest you can imagine. It takes place in an impalpable greyness, with nothing underfoot, with nothing around, without spectators, without clamour, without glory, without the great desire of victory, without the great fear of defeat, in a sickly atmosphere of tepid scepticism, without much belief in your own right, and still less in that of your adversary. If such is the form of ultimate wisdom, then life

---

...spair. Did he live his life through in every detail of desire[,] temptation[,] and surrender during that short and supreme moment? [*Ms only continues:*] He cried at some image, at some vision, he cried with a cry that was no more than a breath—
  "Oh! the horror!"
  I blew the candle out and left the cabin. Never before in his life had he

been such a master of his magnificent gift as in his last on earth. [*Canceled:* The eloquence of it.]
  The pilgrims, *etc.*
† *Ms and Maga:* had so unhesitatingly pronounced.
* *Ms* p. 207 *ends here;* p. 75 (*sic*) *begins thirty-two words later,* the end, and to show my loyalty to Kurtz once more.

is a greater riddle than some of us think it to be. I was within a hair's-breadth of the last opportunity for pronouncement, and I found with humiliation that probably I would have nothing to say. This is the reason why I affirm that Kurtz was a remarkable man. He had something to say. He said it. Since I had peeped over the edge myself, I understand better the meaning of his stare, that could not see the flame of the candle, but was wide enough to embrace the whole universe, piercing enough to penetrate all the hearts that beat in the darkness. He had summed up—he had judged. 'The horror!' He was a remarkable man. After all, this was the expression of some sort of belief; it had candour, it had conviction, it had a vibrating note of revolt in its whisper, it had the appalling face of a glimpsed truth—the strange commingling of desire and hate. And it is not my own extremity I remember best— a vision of greyness without form filled with physical pain, and a careless contempt for the evanescence of all things—even of this pain itself. No! It is his extremity that I seem to have lived through. True, he had made that last stride, he had stepped over the edge, while I had been permitted to draw back my hesitating foot. And perhaps in this is the whole difference; perhaps all the wisdom, and all truth, and all sincerity, are just compressed into that inappreciable moment of time in which we step over the threshold of the invisible. Perhaps! I like to think my summing-up would not have been a word of careless contempt. Better his cry—much better. It was an affirmation, a moral victory paid for by innumerable defeats, by abominable terrors, by abominable satisfactions. But it was a victory! That is why I have remained loyal to Kurtz to the last, and even beyond, when a long time after I heard once more, not his own voice, but the echo of his magnificent eloquence thrown to me from a soul as translucently pure as a cliff of crystal.

"No, they did not bury me, though there is a period of time which I remember mistily, with a shuddering wonder, like a passage through some inconceivable world that had no hope in it and no desire. I found myself back in the sepulchral city resenting the sight of people hurrying through the streets to filch a little money from each other, to devour their infamous cookery, to gulp their unwholesome beer, to dream their insignificant and silly dreams. They trespassed upon my thoughts. They were intruders whose knowledge of life was to me an irritating pretence, because I felt so sure they could not possibly know the things I knew. Their bearing, which was simply the bearing of commonplace individuals going about their business in the assurance of perfect safety, was offensive to me like the outrageous flauntings of folly in the face of a danger it is unable to comprehend. I had no particular desire to enlighten them, but I had some difficulty in restraining myself from laughing in their faces, so full of stupid importance. I daresay I was not very well at that time. I tottered about the streets—there were various affairs to settle—grinning bitterly at perfectly respectable persons. I admit my behaviour was inexcusable, but then my temperature was seldom normal in these days. My dear aunt's endeavours to 'nurse up my strength' seemed altogether beside the mark. It was not my strength that wanted nursing, it was my imagination that wanted soothing. I kept the bundle of papers given me by Kurtz, not knowing exactly what to do with it. His mother had died lately, watched over, as I was told, by his Intended. A clean-shaved man, with an official manner and wearing gold-rimmed spectacles, called on me one day and made inquiries, at first circuitous, afterwards suavely pressing, about what he was pleased to denominate certain 'documents.' I was not surprised, because I had had two rows with the manager on the subject out there. I had refused to give up the smallest scrap out of that package, and I took the same attitude with the spectacled man. He became darkly menacing at last, and with much heat argued that the Company had the right to every bit of information about its 'territories.' And, said he, 'Mr. Kurtz's knowledge of unexplored regions must have been necessarily extensive and peculiar—owing to his great abilities and to the deplorable circumstances in which he had been placed: therefore——' I assured him Mr. Kurtz's knowledge, however extensive, did not bear upon the problems of commerce or administration. He invoked then the name of science. 'It would be an incalculable loss if,' etc. etc. I offered him the report on the 'Suppression of Savage Customs,' with the postscriptum torn off. He took it up eagerly, but ended by sniffing at it with an air of contempt. 'This is not what we had a right to expect,' he remarked. 'Expect nothing else,' I said. 'There are only private letters.' He withdrew upon some threat of legal proceedings, and I saw him no more; but another fellow, calling himself Kurtz's cousin, appeared two days later, and was anxious to hear all the details about his dear relative's last moments. Incidentally he gave me to understand that Kurtz had been essentially a great musician. 'There was the making of an immense success,' said the man, who was an organist, I believe, with lank grey hair flowing over a greasy coat-collar. I had no reason to doubt his statement; and to this day I am unable to say what was Kurtz's profession, whether he ever had any—which was the greatest of his talents. I had taken him for a painter who wrote for the papers, or else for a journalist who could paint—but even the cousin (who took snuff during the interview) could not tell me what he had been—exactly. He was a universal genius—on that point I agreed with the old chap, who thereupon blew his nose noisily into a large cotton handkerchief and withdrew in senile agitation, bearing off some family letters and memoranda without importance. Ultimately a journalist anxious to know something of the fate of his 'dear colleague' turned up. This visitor informed me Kurtz's proper sphere ought to have been politics 'on the popular side.' He had furry straight eyebrows, bristly hair cropped short, an eyeglass on a broad ribbon, and, becoming expansive, confessed his opinion that Kurtz really couldn't write a bit—'but Heavens! how that man could talk! He electrified large meetings. He had faith—don't you see?—he had the faith. He could get himself to believe anything—anything. He would have been a splendid leader of an extreme party.' 'What party?' I asked. 'Any party,' answered the other. 'He was an—an—extremist.' Did I not think so? I assented. Did I know, he asked, with a sudden flash of curiosity, 'what it was that had induced him to go out there?' 'Yes,' said I, and forthwith handed him the famous Report for publication, if he thought fit. He glanced through it hurriedly, mumbling all the time, judged 'it would do,' and took himself off with this plunder.

"Thus I was left at last with a slim packet of letters and the girl's portrait. She struck me as beautiful—I mean she had a beautiful expression. I know that the sunlight can be made to lie too, yet† one felt that no manipulation of light and pose could have conveyed the delicate shade of truthfulness upon those features.* She seemed ready to listen without mental reservation, without suspicion, without a thought for herself. I concluded I would go and give her back her portrait and those letters myself. Curiosity? Yes; and also some other feeling perhaps. All that had been Kurtz's had passed out of my hands: his soul, his body, his station, his plans, his ivory, his career. There remained only his memory and his Intended—and I wanted to give that up too to the past, in a way —to surrender personally all that remained of him with me to that oblivion which is the last word of our common fate. I don't defend myself. I had no clear perception of what it was I really wanted. Perhaps it was an impulse of unconscious loyalty, or the fulfilment of one of those ironic necessities that lurk in the facts of human existence. I don't know. I can't tell. But I went.

"I thought his memory was like the other memories of the dead that accumulate in every man's life—a vague impress on the brain of shadows that had fallen on it in their swift and final passage; but before the high and ponderous door, between the tall houses of a street as still and decorous as a well-kept alley in a cemetery,‡ I had a vision of him on the stretcher, opening his mouth voraciously, as if to devour all the earth with all its mankind. He lived then before me; he lived as much as he had ever lived—a shadow insatiable of

---

† *Ms and Maga:* yet that face on paper seemed to be a reflection of truth itself. One felt, *etc.*

* *Ms and Maga:* features. She looked out trustfully. She seemed ready, *etc.*

‡ *Ms and Maga:* well-kept sepulchre.

splendid appearances, of frightful realities; a shadow darker than the shadow of the night, and draped nobly in the folds of a gorgeous eloquence. The vision seemed to enter the house with me—the stretcher, the phantom-bearers, the wild crowd of obedient worshippers, the gloom of the forests, the glitter of the reach between the murky bends, the beat of the drum, regular and muffled like the beating of a heart—the heart of a conquering darkness. It was a moment of triumph for the wilderness, an invading and vengeful rush which, it seemed to me, I would have to keep back alone for the salvation of another soul. And the memory of what I had heard him say afar there, with the horned shapes stirring at my back, in the glow of fires, within the patient woods, those broken phrases came back to me, were heard again in their ominous and terrifying simplicity.† I remembered his abject pleading, his abject threats, the colossal scale of his vile desires, the meanness, the torment, the tempestuous anguish of his soul. And later on I seemed to see his collected languid manner, when he said one day, 'This lot of ivory now is really mine. The Company did not pay for it. I collected it myself at a very great* personal risk. I am afraid they will try to claim it as theirs though. H'm. It is a difficult case. What do you think I ought to do—resist? Eh? I want no more than justice.' . . . He wanted no more than justice—no more than justice. I rang the bell before a mahogany door on the first floor, and while I waited he seemed to stare at me out of the glassy panel—stare with that wide and immense stare embracing, condemning, loathing all the universe. I seemed to hear the whispered cry, 'The horror! The horror!'‡

"The dusk was falling. I had to wait in a lofty drawing-room with three long windows from floor to ceiling that were like three luminous and bedraped columns. The bent gilt legs and backs of the furniture shone in indistinct curves. The tall marble fireplace had a cold and monumental whiteness. A grand piano stood massively in a corner; with dark gleams on the flat surfaces like a sombre and polished sarcophagus. A high door opened—closed. I rose.

"She came forward, all in black, with a pale head, floating towards me in the dusk. She was in mourning. It was more than a year since his death, more than a year since the news came; she seemed as though she would remember and mourn for ever. She took both my hands in hers and murmured, 'I had heard you were coming.' I noticed she was not very young—I mean not girlish.

† *Ms and Maga:* simplicity: 'I have lived—supremely! [*Maga only:* What do you want here?] I have been dead—and damned.' 'Let me go—I want more of it.' More of what? More blood, more heads on stakes, more adoration, rapine, and murder. I remembered, *etc.*
* *Ms and Maga:* at my
‡ *Ms:* cry, 'Oh! the horror!'

She had a mature capacity for fidelity, for belief, for suffering. The room seemed to have grown darker, as if all the sad light of the cloudy evening had taken refuge on her forehead. This fair hair, this pale visage, this pure brow,† seemed surrounded by an ashy halo from which the dark eyes looked out at me. Their glance was guileless, profound, confident, and trustful. She carried her sorrowful head as though she were proud of that sorrow, as though she would say, I—I alone know how to mourn for him as he deserves. But while we were still shaking hands, such a look of awful desolation came upon her face that I perceived she was one of those creatures that are not the playthings of Time. For her he had died only yesterday. And, by Jove! the impression was so powerful that for me too he seemed to have died only yesterday—nay, this very minute. I saw her and him in the same instant of time—his death and her sorrow—I saw her sorrow in the very moment of his death.* Do you understand? I saw them together—I heard them together. She had said, with a deep catch of the breath, 'I have survived'; while my strained ears seemed to hear distinctly, mingled with her tone of despairing regret, the summing-up whisper of his eternal condemnation.‡ I asked myself what I was doing there, with a sensation of panic in my heart as though I had blundered into a place of cruel and absurd mysteries not fit for a human being to behold.** She motioned me to a chair. We sat down. I laid the packet gently on the little table, and she put her hand over it. . . . 'You knew him well,' she murmured, after a moment of mourning silence.

" 'Intimacy grows quickly out there,' I said. 'I knew him as well as it is possible for one man to know another.'

" 'And you admired him,' she said. 'It was impossible to know him and not to admire him. Was it?'

" 'He was a remarkable man,' I said unsteadily. Then before the appealing fixity of her gaze, that seemed to watch for more words on my lips, I went on, 'It was impossible not to——'

" 'Love him,' she finished eagerly, silencing me into an appalled dumbness. 'How true! how true! But when you think that no one knew him so well as I! I had all his noble confidence. I knew him best.'

" 'You knew him best,' I repeated. And perhaps she did. But with every word spoken the room was growing darker, and only her forehead, smooth and white, remained illumined by the unextinguishable light of belief and love.

" 'You were his friend,' she went on. 'His friend,' she repeated,

---

† *Ms:* pure brow, this candid brow, seemed, *etc.*
* *Ms:* death. It was too terrible.
‡ *Ms:* condemnation. I tell you it was

terrible. I asked, *etc.*
** *Ms and Maga:* behold. I wanted to get out. She motioned, *etc.*

a little louder. 'You must have been, if he had given you this, and sent you to me. I feel I can speak to you—and oh! I must speak. I want you—you who have heard his last words—to know I have been worthy of him. . . . It is not pride. . . . Yes! I am proud to know I understood him better than any one on earth—he told me so himself. And since his mother died I have had no one—no one—to—to——'

"I listened. The darkness deepened. I was not even sure whether he had given me the right bundle. I rather suspect he wanted me to take care of another batch of his papers which, after his death, I saw the manager examining under the lamp.† And the girl talked, easing her pain in the certitude of my sympathy; she talked as thirsty men drink. I had heard that her engagement with Kurtz had been disapproved by her people. He wasn't rich enough or something. And indeed I don't know whether he had not been a pauper all his life. He had given me some reason to infer that it was his impatience of comparative poverty that drove him out there.

" '. . . Who was not his friend who had heard him speak once?' she was saying. 'He drew men towards him by what was best in them.' She looked at me with intensity. 'It is the gift of the great,' she went on, and the sound of her low voice seemed to have the accompaniment of all the other sounds, full of mystery, desolation, and sorrow, I had ever heard—the ripple of the river, the soughing of the trees swayed by the wind, the murmurs of the crowds,* the faint ring of incomprehensible words cried from afar, the whisper of a voice speaking from beyond the threshold of an eternal darkness. 'But you have heard him! You know!' she cried.

" 'Yes, I know,' I said with something like despair in my heart, but bowing my head before the faith that was in her, before that great and saving illusion that shone with an unearthly glow in the darkness, in the triumphant darkness from which I could not have defended her—from which I could not even defend myself.

" 'What a loss to me—to us!'—she corrected herself with beautiful generosity; then added in a murmur, 'To the world.' By the last gleams of twilight I could see the glitter of her eyes, full of tears— of tears that would not fall.

" 'I have been very happy—very fortunate—very proud,' she went on. 'Too fortunate. Too happy for a little while. And now I am unhappy for—for life.'

"She stood up; her fair hair seemed to catch all the remaining light in a glimmer of gold. I rose too.

† *Ms and Maga:* lamp. But in the box I brought to his bedside there were several packages [*Maga only:* pretty well alike, all] tied with shoe-strings and probably he had made a mistake. And the girl, *etc.*
* *Ms, Maga,* and *1902:* the wild crowds; *1917:* the crowds

" 'And of all this,' she went on mournfully, 'of all his promise, and of all his greatness, of his generous mind, of his noble heart, nothing remains—nothing but a memory. You and I——'

" 'We shall† always remember him,' I said hastily.

" 'No!' she cried. 'It is impossible that all this should be lost—that such a life should be sacrificed to leave nothing—but sorrow. You know what vast plans he had. I knew of them too—I could not perhaps understand—but others knew of them. Something must remain. His words, at least, have not died.'

" 'His words will remain,' I said.

" 'And his example,' she whispered to herself. 'Men looked up to him—his goodness shone in every act. His example——'

" 'True,' I said; 'his example too. Yes, his example. I forgot that.'

" 'But I do not. I cannot—I cannot believe—not yet. I cannot believe that I shall never see him again, that nobody will see him again, never, never, never.'

"She put out her arms as if after a retreating figure, stretching them back and with clasped pale hands across the fading and narrow sheen of the window. Never see him! I saw him clearly enough then. I shall see this eloquent phantom as long as I live, and I shall see her too, a tragic and familiar Shade, resembling in this gesture another one, tragic also, and bedecked with powerless charms, stretching bare brown arms over the glitter of the infernal stream, the stream of darkness.* She said suddenly very low, 'He died as he lived.'

" 'His end,' said I, with dull anger stirring in me, 'was in every way worthy of his life.'

" 'And I was not with him,' she murmured. My anger subsided before a feeling of infinite pity.

" 'Everything that could be done——' I mumbled.

" 'Ah, but I believed in him more than any one on earth—more than his own mother, more than—himself. He needed me! Me! I would have treasured every sigh, every word, every sign, every glance.'

"I felt like a chill grip on my chest. 'Don't,' I said, in a muffled voice.

" 'Forgive me. I—I—have mourned so long in silence—in silence. . . . You were with him—to the last? I think of his loneliness. Nobody near to understand him as I would have understood. Perhaps no one to hear . . .'

" 'To the very end,' I said shakily. 'I heard his very last words. . . .' I stopped in a fright.

" 'Repeat them,' she murmured in a heart-broken tone. 'I want—

† *Ms:* I will
* *Ms:* the infernal stream that flows from the heart of darkness.

I want—something—something—to—to live with.'

"I was on the point of crying at her, 'Don't you hear them?' The dusk was repeating them in a persistent whisper all around us, in a whisper that seemed to swell menacingly like the first whisper of a rising wind. 'The horror! The horror!'†

" 'His last word—to live with,' she insisted. 'Don't you understand I loved him—I loved him—I loved him!'

"I pulled myself together and spoke slowly.

" 'The last word he pronounced was—your name.'

"I heard a light sigh and then my heart stood still, stopped dead short by an exulting and terrible cry, by the cry of inconceivable triumph and of unspeakable pain. 'I knew it—I was sure!'* . . . She knew. She was sure. I heard her weeping; she had hidden her face in her hands. It seemed to me that the house would collapse before I could escape, that the heavens would fall upon my head. But nothing happened. The heavens do not fall for such a trifle. Would they have fallen, I wonder, if I had rendered Kurtz that justice which was his due? Hadn't he said he wanted only justice? But I couldn't. I could not tell her. It would have been too dark— too dark altogether. . . ."

Marlow ceased, and sat apart, indistinct and silent, in the pose of a meditating Buddha. Nobody moved for a time. "We have lost the first of the ebb," said the Director suddenly. I raised my head. The offing was barred by a black bank of clouds, and the tranquil waterway leading to the uttermost ends of the earth flowed sombre under an overcast sky—seemed to lead into the heart of an immense darkness.

---

† *Ms:* wind. 'Oh! the horror!'
* *Ms:* I was sure!' She knew! She was sure! It seemed to me the house would collapse, the heavens would fall upon my head. But nothing happened. The heavens do not fall for such a trifle. Would they have fallen, I wonder, if I had rendered Kurtz justice. Hadn't he said he wanted only justice? But I couldn't. I could not tell her. It would have been too dark—too dark altogether."

Marlow ceased [*for canceled:* He was silent. *Then the following compounded predicate is added above the*

line] and sat in the pose of a meditating Vouddha. Nobody moved for a time. "We have lost the first of the ebb," said the Director suddenly. I looked around. The offing was barred by a black bank of clouds and the tranquil waterway that leads [*for canceled:* leading] to the uttermost ends of the earth flowing sombre under an overcast sky seemed to lead into the heart of an immense blackness.
Maga: like 1902 and Heinemann, except I looked around *for* I raised my head.

Note on the Text

Heart of Darkness first appeared in 1899 as "The Heart of Darkness" in *Blackwood's Magazine* in three parts (February, March, and April), after which it was revised for inclusion by Blackwood in a separate volume, *Youth: A Narrative, and Two Other Stories* (the third being *The End of the Tether*), published in 1902. All subsequent publication of *Heart of Darkness*, whether reprint or actual edition, stems from this version of the story, rather than from the one in *Blackwood's*. The next significant appearance was in 1917—the story had been reprinted in America in serial form and in three *Youth* volumes—when Conrad wrote an "Author's Note" for a reprint by Dent in London of the *Youth* volume of 1902. Then in 1920 Doubleday brought out the first collected works of Conrad in a limited, American edition, called the "Sun-Dial." At the same time William Heinemann in London was preparing a limited, English edition of the collected works, which appeared in 1921. The first general collected editions were brought out simultaneously in 1923 in New York and in London by Doubleday and by Dent. Because Conrad kept publishing, further collected editions were needed after his death in 1924, but an editor of *Heart of Darkness* cannot consider them authoritative, because the best copy-text by modern standards is the last edition which an author most likely had a chance to correct, revise, or merely approve in his lifetime.

We know from letters that Conrad took great interest in the 1923 Doubleday and Dent collected editions, and they have indeed served as the basis for all but one publication of *Heart of Darkness* since Conrad's death; however, Bruce Harkness, *Heart of Darkness and the Critics* (San Francisco, 1960) has shown (and the present editor has verified) that the *Youth* volumes in these two collections are printed from the same plates that were made in America for the 1920 "Sun-Dial" *Youth* volume, a work which is most unreliable both because there is no evidence that Conrad had a chance to oversee the publication and because it is filled with error. Hence, the 1921 Heinemann *Youth* volume would seem to afford the best copy-text for *Heart of Darkness* by default, but it does so not only by reason of date but also through merit.

The Heinemann *Collected Works* is not a reprint, but a separate edition, the type of which was distributed after 780 sets had been printed. Conrad kept abreast of the production, and worked closely with the editors on various of the volumes. The departures from the *Heart of Darkness* of 1902 are few, but do present a clarity of phrase and a consistency in matters such as tense, number, and punctuation found in no other state of the story. There is no direct proof that it was Conrad who made these final improvements, but his literary executor, Richard Curle, reported that although much of Conrad's work is "extant in at least six different states—the manuscript, the corrected typescript, the serial form, the American book form, the English book form, and the collected edition book form," it was "the last alone that Conrad considered his final text" (Richard Curle, *The Last Twelve Years of Joseph Conrad*, Garden City, N.Y., 1928).

Although the 1921 edition has been used, then, as the copy-text, the present edition contains four emendations, each of which appears before the bracket and after the page and line designation in the following list:

> 12. 9, observation . . .] observation. . .
> 19. 4, sent] set
> 38.18, 'Hurry up.'] Hurry up.
> 60. 6, forest] forests
> 60.37, Kurtz—Kurtz] Kurtz—Kirtz

In all other respects the present text follows that of 1921.

Backgrounds and Sources

Each of the following sections is interesting in its own right; however, each is intended primarily as a critical tool to be used in gaining a richer appreciation of *Heart of Darkness*. The first section sets the story within its historical context, but also provides the reader with the kind of information he needs to fully appreciate Conrad's irony. The second section offers all that Conrad ever biographically recorded concerning his Congo experience, the artistic projection of which is *Heart of Darkness*. The third reminds us that, autobiographical though it may be, the story was to Conrad a significant, but objective work of art; indeed, his concern for cash may come as a shock to the romantically inclined. And the fourth is not a medley of random Conradian opinions, but a carefully chosen group of statements which, because of their essay nature, give us insight into the themes and artistic methods of *Heart of Darkness*.

The titles and notes (except where labeled) are the editor's. The map of the Congo in 1890 (opposite) contains all the geographical references within the story proper and within the various essays and accounts which follow. Editorial omissions are indicated by three asterisks.

A Map of the
CONGO FREE STATE
1890

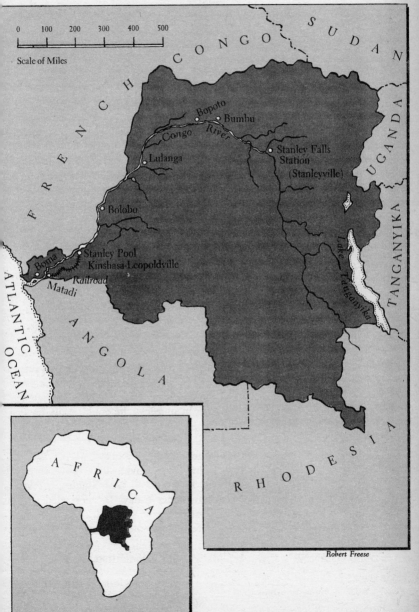

Scale of Miles

0 100 200 300 400 500

FRENCH CONGO

SUDAN

UGANDA

TANGANYIKA

Bopoto
Bumbu
Congo River

Lulanga

Stanley Falls
Station
(Stanleyville)

Bolobo

Lake Tanganyika

Stanley Pool
Kinshasa-Leopoldville

Boma
Railroad
Matadi

ATLANTIC
OCEAN

ANGOLA

RHODESIA

AFRICA

Robert Freese

THE CONGO

The mission which the agents of the State have to accomplish on the Congo is a noble one. They have to continue the development of civilisation in the centre of Equatorial Africa, receiving their inspiration directly from Berlin and Brussels. Placed face to face with primitive barbarism, grappling with sanguinary customs that date back thousands of years, they are obliged to reduce these gradually. They must accustom the population to general laws, of which the most needful and the most salutary is assuredly that of work.

—KING LEOPOLD II, OF BELGIUM, 1898.

Carlyle says that 'to subdue mutiny, discord, widespread despair by manfulness, justice, mercy, and wisdom, to let light on chaos, and make it instead a green flowery world, is beyond all other greatness, work for a God!' Who can doubt that God chose the King for His instrument to redeem this vast slave park. * * * King Leopold found the Congo * * * cursed by cannibalism, savagery, and despair; and he has been trying with a patience, which I can never sufficiently admire, to relieve it of its horrors, rescue it from its oppressors, and save it from perdition.

—H. M. STANLEY, 1898.

The kodak has been a sore calamity to us. The most powerful enemy that has confronted us, indeed. In the early years we had no trouble in getting the press to 'expose' the tales of the mutilations as slanders, lies, inventions of busy-body American missionaries and exasperated foreigners who had found the 'open door' of the Berlin-Congo charter closed against them when they innocently went out there to trade. * * * Yes, all things went harmoniously and pleasantly in those good days, and I was looked up to as the benefactor of a down-trodden and friendless people. Then all of a sudden came the crash!

—MARK TWAIN, "King Leopold's Soliloquy," 1905.

MAURICE N. HENNESSY: [The Congo: A Brief History, 1876–1908]†

Stanley was the most remarkable explorer of them all. A Welshman by birth, he was endowed with the fiery Celtic imagination of his ancestors. In his early years he went to America, became an American citizen and worked for the *New York Herald*. Although Stanley is best known for his African journeys, he could easily have claimed fame in another field for he was a great journalist. He had travelled most of the known world for his newspaper and proved himself to be one of the truly remarkable reporters of his time. When, between the years 1856 and 1871, Livingstone disappeared into the African bush, the *New York Herald* sent Stanley to the Congo to find him. After searching for 236 days he succeeded. He found something else also—an entirely new career and one which was to change not only his own life but the whole course of African history.

So clamorous was the exploration and colonisation vogue that it

† From *Congo*, by Maurice N. Hennessy (London: Pall Mall Press, 1961). Pp. 13–27. Reprinted by permission.

was quite evident that trouble was just around the corner. The Portuguese (the original pioneers), the British, the Dutch and the French were particular rivals, and to such an extent that there was serious danger of open war.

Sitting back in Europe watching the whole performance was a man who was monarch of a nation itself less than fifty years old. He was Leopold II of Belgium. He was a man of inordinate ambition, and centred his designs on Africa and particularly on the Congo. Possibly he saw that, due to its geographical position, its narrow approach to the sea, and the particular mystery of its interior, the Congo basin had escaped much of the depredation of the slave trade. Probably he also realised that he stood less likelihood of opposition if he set his heart on this particular area.

In 1876 Leopold called a conference in Brussels to examine the African situation and, as he expressed it, 'to open to civilisation the only part of our globe where Christianity has not penetrated and to pierce the darkness which envelops the entire population'. Here * * * we find the exalted language that was in reverse proportion to the nobility of the real intent. As a result of this conference, an International African Association was formed; very quickly it became, to all practical purposes, the personal organisation of Leopold. The success of this move encouraged the wily king to conceive another idea. He formed the International Association of the Congo.

* * *

While Leopold was looking to his own interests, the rivalry for Africa became more intense. The saner participants realised that the prize was too great to be lost by the risk of war, and consequently, in 1884, a conference was called in Berlin by Bismarck. Its purpose was to attempt to iron out the differences between the nations with territorial ambitions in Africa and at the same time to draw up a set of rules for would-be exploiters which would prevent open conflict. Up to this point the general pattern had been for each country's exploration parties to push inland from the coast until they met each other. They were then faced with the alternatives of making a gentleman's agreement or fighting it out there and then. The latter did not appeal very much in the bush, especially as all concerned were fully occupied fighting climatic conditions and the dread diseases of the tropics. On the other hand, many of the gentleman's agreements were of short duration and were by no means the kind of pacts that were likely to stand the test of time or form a firm basis for future peace. The conference at Berlin laid down certain rules, heard and decided on the claims of such nations as France and Portugal, and at the same time produced the most high-sounding resolutions, couched, according to pattern, in language as hypocritical as it was inapt. The main safeguard against an all-out clash was a unanimously approved resolution by the signatory nations that each nation should notify the others of its plans for colonisation, and at the same time outline the territories within which it proposed to operate.

* * *

The most surprising aspect of the Berlin Conference was that it agreed that the Congo should be the personal property of Leopold II. Less than three months later, on April 28th, 1885, the Belgian Parliament ratified this decision. The passing of the necessary legislation was unanimous, except for one dissentient. The text of the legislation was as follows: 'His Majesty, Leopold II, King of the Belgians, is authorised to be the chief of the state founded in Africa by the International Association of the Congo. The union between Belgium and the new State of the Congo shall be exclusively personal.'

Despite this amazing political decision, the Conference of Berlin tempered its magnanimity with certain regulations for the Congo basin. Their chief importance lies in the fact that they were, apparently, created to be disregarded; and when they were, they became the source of much dissension. The following constituted the main regulations:

1. The trade of all nations shall enjoy complete freedom.
2. All flags, without distinction of nationality, shall have free access.
3. All differential dues on vessels, as well as on merchandise, are forbidden.
4. No power which exercises or shall exercise sovereign rights in the above-mentioned regions shall be allowed to grant therein a monopoly of favour of any kind in the matters of trade.

It is really difficult to understand (unless, of course, Leopold had completely deceived most of Europe) how it could ever have been a serious consideration that he intended to abide by these decisions. A monarch demanding that nearly a million square miles of territory should be his own personal property could scarcely be described as a philanthropist. His personal life was quite appalling; even that most charitable of documents, the *Encyclopedia Britannica*, has an entry which reads: 'Leopold was a man of notoriously immoral life.'

It is even more difficult therefore to understand how he could ever be referred to by historians as an 'impractical kingly philanthropist'. At the actual conference, Prince Bismarck said of him: 'All of us here render justice to the lofty object of the work to which His Majesty The King of the Belgians has attached his name; we all know the efforts and the sacrifices by means of which he has brought it to the point where it is today; we all entertain the wish that the most complete success may crown an enterprise that must so usefully promote the views which have directed the Conference.'

* * *

Leopold retained control of the Congo Free State until [his death in] 1908. In a statement addressed to Monsieur Beernaert, Belgian Minister of Finance, on August 5th, 1889, he made known his intention of willing the state to the Belgians. He wrote: 'I have therefore made, as Sovereign of the Independent State of the Congo, the Will that I send you. I ask you to communicate it to the Legislative Chamber at the moment which shall appear to you the most opportune.' He used the words 'most opportune' with a reason; he was about to ask for a loan of one hundred and fifty million francs and was really offering the Congo as a *quid pro quo*. The money was granted—a fact which proved that whatever else may be said, the monarch had the confidence of the Belgian people in the early days of the state just as he had of his colleagues at Berlin.

* * *

Between 1885 and 1908, Leopold II was the supreme legislative and executive authority in the Congo Free State; his form of government was, of necessity, unique. He had never seen the Congo, nor was he ever in a position where he was likely to do so. In the early stages, he endeavoured to run the Congo state from Belgium through an Administrator General. This arrangement put him in a very fortunate position, for when trouble arose he was able to absolve himself from personal blame and attach it to his absent representatives.

Much power was vested in the Administrator General, but as there were no separate legal and executive bodies many quarrels, misunderstandings, and difficulties ensued. As was inevitable, numerous changes in personnel and tactics took place before the country was divided finally into fifteen districts, each of which had a Commissioner representing the Administrator General. While this arrangement limited the areas controlled by representatives, it still did not prevent almost unlimited power being placed in the hands of individuals—individuals who were, often, the least suitable to exercise such responsibility.

Adopting an entirely different approach from the British, who operated mainly through existing chiefs, through whom they strengthened local authority, the Congo administrators began to reduce steadily the power of their chiefs. They divided the chieftaincies into zones and later, these zones into sectors. * * * The mere reduction of a chief to the level of an ordinary individual, although a contributory factor, was not the real danger created by this system. It was the fact that the whole native tribe was frequently left at the mercy of a local officer or, in some cases, an African menial who was likely to carry out quite ruthlessly any orders passed on to him. All too frequently these officials used their position to pursue personal interests, avenge feuds, and, at times, even levy their own private taxes. In matters of routine administration this was not so serious, but when the economic drive to exploit the resources of the country was put into gear, then it became the source of serious trouble. In the first place, an African had no rights. The European residents had only a few limited ones, but they had on their side the basic principle that in any dispute between African and European, the latter's word (the accepted one) was law. This gave rise to every kind of abuse, and it was not unusual to find a local officer flogging mercilessly, without any legal right, any individual African who failed to comply with his wishes. As was to be expected, with development came an increase in outrageous abuses.

The granting of concessions to various companies was a natural sequel to the kind of rule Leopold established and to his lust for wealth. In all cases, he ensured that a large part of any profits went to himself, but in order to foster this end, an abundance of labour was a primary requirement. Consequently, quite early on a system of work as a tax medium was initiated. Each chief was authorised to collect taxes; he did so by demanding that individuals should work for a specific period of time for a minimum payment. This, of course, was another name for slavery. The so-called taxpayers were treated like prisoners; their work was carried out under the supervision of armed sentries, and, as can be easily imagined, the system lent itself to all kinds of tyranny, brutality and subsequent reprisals by the natives. In one concession alone one hundred and forty-two Africans were killed. The spirit of bitterness and hatred generated in the people was quite terrifying, but little could be done about it as there was not enough control in the area to prevent the various agents from misusing their power.

SIR HARRY JOHNSTON: [George Grenfell: A Missionary in the Congo]†

In December 1885, when the missionaries of all denominations had scarcely ceased acclaiming heartily the creation of the "Congo

† From *George Grenfell and the Congo* (2 vols.), I, 445–447. New York. Copyright 1910 by D. Appleton & Co. Reprinted by permission of the publisher.

Johnston (1858–1927) was a distinguished anthropologist and prolific writer on Africa.

Free State"[1] as an alternative to the extension of Portuguese influence (the Baptists being amongst the warmest friends of King Leopold's enterprise), Grenfell wrote a note at Stanley Pool complaining that the State was already beginning to infringe the provisions of the Act of Berlin by claiming all the land as State property and refusing sites to a missionary society as well as to the Dutch Trading House.

In 1890 he writes in his diary: "Bula Matadi has become disliked amongst the people of the Upper Congo, and is called Ipanga Ngunda, which means "Destroys the country." In May 1890 Grenfell first complains of the action of the Congo State officials in regard to ivory, which had been made a Government monopoly, in practice, if not in theory. The representative of the State at Bumba on the northern Congo was said to fire on all canoes carrying ivory westwards, whilst he also prevented canoes going eastwards from Bopoto to purchase ivory. "The State officers having a commission on the ivory they get, they are keen about securing all they can."

On June 17, 1890 Grenfell's diary records the first hint being given as to the possibility of *Concessionnaire* companies coming into existence on the Congo. He had received the information from an American, Colonel Williams, who went up the Congo as far as the Stanley Falls, and told Grenfell on his return that an American agent at Brussels (Mr. Sanford) had been discussing with the King in 1888 the idea of creating such companies to deal with the development of the State.

* * *

This method in the hands of a high-minded, conscientious potentate might at the start have been the best and simplest way of solving the land question of the Congo. King Leopold might then have proceeded to arrange in course of time a definite land settlement for the natives over whom he was the self-constituted suzerain or sovereign. By the issue of these decrees he was in a position to prevent any reckless or fraudulent buying up of native territories by uncontrolled adventurers.

* * * The fact is, not to waste too many words on this sad subject, the foundation of the Congo Free State has evinced a lack of statesmanship, and an incredible ignorance of African conditions on the part of theorists, amiable and unamiable, who have legislated for this million square miles of Central Africa from Brussels. Several of the Congo Secretaries of State or home administrators have never seen Africa, unless it has been in a winter visit to Algiers.

1. It is not clear how the official title of "L'Etat Indépendant du Congo" came to be rendered "Congo Free State," this translation not being strictly correct. Stanley—the wish being father to the thought—seems to have originated the common English name, "Congo Free State." The native name is "Bula Matadi," the nickname originally given to Stanley. [Johnston's note.]

JOHN DE COURCY MAC DONNELL: [The Visionary King]†

Nothing is more clear to the student of the history of Africa than the definite purpose which animated all King Leopold's legislation from the commencement of his rule over the Congo through all the changing years to the present moment. That purpose has ever been to secure the prosperity of the wide realm of the Congo and of its inhabitants. It is clearly shown and clearly observed in every decree the sovereign of the Congo has made. All that has been done in the Congo rests on the King's sole authority. In accepting the sovereignty of the Independent State King Leopold faced the greatest problem and undertook the weightiest responsibility of our age, but he faced it unfettered. The diplomatists who sat at the Congress of Berlin seem to have looked to no more than the interests of foreign traders and, in a somewhat vague way, the protection against slavery of the native races of Africa. It is well for mankind that the sovereign of the Congo looked farther, and that his views were wise.

King Leopold undertook to protect the native races from the raids of slave traders, and he undertook to free them from slavery; he undertook to open up Equatorial Africa to trade, and to establish a settled government in it; but these undertakings, great though they were, were but the least part of his task. Besides them, he had to regulate his government so that trade and industry would flourish profitably in the land in the future, and he had to educate and to civilise the negroes. Politicians and pamphleteers who deal only with the present moment are apt to overlook these, the main, points of King Leopold's great undertaking; but it is with regard to them, and not to any passing need, that King Leopold's rule in Africa and his legislation for the Congo must be judged.

RICHARD HARDING DAVIS: [His Brother's Keeper]‡

After one has talked with the men and women who have seen the atrocities, has seen in the official reports that those accused of the atrocities do not deny having committed them, but point out that they were merely obeying orders, and after one has seen that even at the capital of Boma all the conditions of slavery exist, one is assured that in the jungle, away from the sight of men, all things are possible. Merchants, missionaries, and officials even in Leopold's

---

† From *King Leopold II: His Rule in Belgium and the Congo* (London, 1905), pp. 162–63.

MacDonnell (1869–1915), an Irishman and Celtic scholar, was a Belgian civil servant.

‡ From *The Congo and the Coasts of Africa*, by Richard Harding Davis (New York: Charles Scribner's Sons, 1907), pp. 44–47. Davis (1864–1916) was a renowned, world-traveling journalist.

service told me that if one could spare a year and a half, or a year, to the work in the hinterland he would be an eye-witness of as cruel treatment of the natives as any that has gone before, and if I can trust myself to weigh testimony and can believe my eyes and ears I have reason to know that what they say is true. I am convinced that to-day a man, who feels that a year and a half is little enough to give to the aid of twenty millions of human beings, can accomplish in the Congo as great and good work as that of the Abolitionists.

Three years ago atrocities here were open and above-board. For instance. In the opinion of the State the soldiers, in killing game for food, wasted the State cartridges, and in consequence the soldiers, to show their officers that they did not expend the cartridges extravagantly on antelope and wild boar, for each empty cartridge brought in a human hand, the hand of a man, woman, or child. These hands, drying in the sun, could be seen at the posts along the river. They are no longer in evidence. Neither is the flowerbed of Lieutenant Dom, which was bordered with human skulls. A quaint conceit.

The man to blame for the atrocities, for each separate atrocity, is Leopold.

KING LEOPOLD II: [The Sacred Mission of Civilization]†

Our refined society attaches to human life (and with reason) a value unknown to barbarous communities. When our directing will is implanted among them its aim is to triumph over all obstacles, and results which could not be attained by lengthy speeches may follow philanthropic influence. But if, in view of this desirable spread of civilisation, we count upon the means of action which confer upon us dominion and the sanction of right, it is not less true that our ultimate end is a work of peace. Wars do not necessarily mean the ruin of the regions in which they rage; our agents do not ignore this fact, so from the day when their effective superiority is affirmed, they feel profoundly reluctant to use force. The wretched negroes, however, who are still under the sole sway of their traditions, have that horrible belief that victory is only decisive when the enemy, fallen beneath their blows, is annihilated. The soldiers of the State, who are recruited necessarily from among the natives, do not immediately forsake those sanguinary habits that have been transmitted from generation to generation. The example

† From Guy Burrows, *The Land of the Pigmies* (London, 1898), p. 286.
  The title for this selection is the title of a pamphlet prepared in 1953 by the Belgian government for presentation to the members of the U.N.

of the white officer and wholesome military discipline gradually inspire in them a horror of human trophies of which they previously had made their boast. It is in their leaders that they must see living evidence of these higher principles, taught that the exercise of authority is not at all to be confounded with cruelty, but is, indeed, destroyed by it. I am pleased to think that our agents, nearly all of whom are volunteers drawn from the ranks of the Belgian army, have always present in their minds a strong sense of the career of honour in which they are engaged, and are animated with a pure feeling of patriotism; not sparing their own blood, they will the more spare the blood of the natives, who will see in them the all-powerful protectors of their lives and their property, benevolent teachers of whom they have so great a need.

H. R. FOX-BOURNE: [New Forms of Slavery]†

In a report dated 16th July, 1891, by M. Van Eetvelde[1] credit was asked for the humane arrangements adopted in the interests of the inhabitants. "The Government," it was asserted, "has taken special precautions to prevent spoliation of the natives and infringement of their rights by fraud or violence. The lands occupied by blacks remain under local customs; the State leaves under this rule spaces extensive enough not only for maintenance but also, in view of increase of the population, for development of their institutions."[2] The worst interferences with native land rights have been subsequent to the date of this report, but even when it was written it was in flagrant contradiction not only of facts, but also of edicts signed by M. Van Eetvelde himself. As misleading was an earlier report, dated 24th October, 1889, in which he asked credit for the alleged and ostensible abolition of the status of slavery throughout the territories of the Congo State. "Slavery, even domestic," he said, "cannot be officially recognised. Indeed, it is not possible for a single man in the Congo to be subject to another, since every attempt on individual liberty is accounted an offence punishable by the articles of the Penal Code. Every one is punished who, by violence, tricks, or threats, removes or causes to be removed, arbitrarily arrests or causes to be arrested, detains or causes to be detained, any person whatever; or who disposes of any persons whatever by selling them as slaves. By these general arrangements the procuring, the transport, and the detention of individuals as slaves

† From *Civilisation in Congoland* (London, 1903), pp. 72–75. Fox-Bourne (1837–1909), historian, scholar, and man of letters, was active in the Aborigines Protection Society.

1. Administrator-General for foreign affairs: commerce, ports, and justice.
2. *Bulletin Officiel* [of the Free State], 1891, p. 180 [Fox-Bourne's note].

fall under the arm of the law."[3]

All this, it is true, was proposed in the Penal Code; just as much more was enjoined in the Ten Commandments and the Sermon on the Mount. But slavery was only abolished in name and forbidden as a matter of form. When the State officials were able and willing to enforce "these general arrangements," the bondsmen of black slave owners may have been taken from them, but only, or often, to fall into worse bondage under white masters; the cruellest and most plentiful employers of forced labour being generally the officials or the *protégés* of the State itself. On 8th November, 1888, a decree was issued according "special protection to the blacks." This "protection" took the form of allowing blacks, whether natives of the Congo or recruits from other parts, to be bound over for a term of seven years' service to any white masters or patrons (a term specially employed in the interests of missionaries and others) who satisfied the authorities that these blacks had voluntarily agreed to the conditions imposed upon them as regards wages and the like, and providing that the conditions should be set forth in writing. In case of ill-treatment or breach of contract the hireling was supposed to be able to obtain redress or to recover his liberty; and it was appointed that some supervision should be exercised by officers of the State over the relations between the hirelings and their masters, in the interests of the former.[4] It cannot be supposed, however, that, except in very rare cases, an effective check would thus be put upon any harsh treatment to which tyrannical employers might expose ignorant and unlettered natives in their service.

It was professedly in the interests of natives, as well as of traders, and "to repress abuses prejudicial to the regularity and security of transport between the Upper and Lower Congo," that another decree was issued on 12th March, 1889, applying especially to the Cataracts district, in which there was always the greatest demand for labourers and carriers until the railway was opened.[5] It was here provided that commercial societies and others wishing to recruit natives must first obtain a permit from the Governor-General, and must after that take out a licence for each native engaged, or, if the engagement was through a "capita" or head man, for each capita; the charges being 240 francs for an annual permit, 24 francs for not more than twenty-four recruits under one capita, and 3 francs for each labourer not engaged through a capita.[6] These licences and permits augmented the revenue; but it is not easy to see how they could benefit the natives, who, long after as well as before the

3. *Bulletin Officiel* [of the Free State], 1889, p. 199 [Fox-Bourne's note].
4. *Bulletin Officiel* [of the Free State], 1888, pp. 270–75 [Fox-Bourne's note].
5. From Matadi to Leopoldville (235 miles) the Congo River is not navigable. See *Heart of Darkness*, pp. 20–21 and Conrad's *Diary*, below, pp. 109–17.
6. *Bulletin Officiel* [of the Free State], 1889, pp. 66–69 [Fox-Bourne's note].

issuing of the decree, were at the mercy of the District Commissaries, and of the capitas who were practically slave-drivers at their beck and call. * * *

[The Testimony of the Kodak]†

March 10th, 1904.

DEAR MR. MOREL,[1]

In sending you the accompanying photographs of three mutilated natives who have come to my notice during my stay on the Congo, I wish to give you a few particulars of these cases.

Reading from left to right these victims are—

The youth standing up, with both hands gone—Mola Ekuliti. This boy was a native of Mokili, a town of the Lake Mantumba district.[2]

His town was attacked by the soldiers of the Government post of Bikoro, in 1898, under the command of an officer whom I knew and often met.

Several natives were killed, but Mola was tied up and taken away to the lake-side, where, owing to the tightness of the thongs round his wrists, the flesh had swollen. The officer directed the thongs to be beaten off, but his soldiers translated that into beating off the hands—which they did with the butt end of their rifles against a tree. The officer was standing by drinking palm wine. * * *

The woman sitting down was an old creature named Eyeka. I knew her well. She was the aunt of one of our best girls, who is now married to ———, and she often came here to visit her niece. She was the sister of ———'s mother—they came from the town of Mwebi, which is on the west shore of Lake Mantumba. Mwebi was attacked by the troops from Bikoro in pursuance of the customary punitive policy for not working rubber.

Eyeka more than once told us in the Mission how she lost her hand. When the soldiers came to Mwebi, she said, they heard a bugle blow, and she and her son and many people fled. While they ran shots were fired, and her son fell by her side. She fainted, and fell down too. Then she felt some one cutting at her wrist, and she was afraid to move, for she knew that if she moved her life would be taken.

When all was quiet she opened her eyes. Her son was lying dead

† From E. D. Morel, *King Leopold's Rule in Africa* (London, 1904), pp. 378–82.
1. Edmund Morel (1873–1924) was an outspoken critic of colonial abuse whether British, Belgian, or other. Nat-

urally he was much maligned as well as praised for his many writings and constant agitation against the authorities.
2. Between Bolobo and Lulanga off the left bank of the river.

beside her. His hand was gone, and hers was gone, and she was bleeding away.

This story of Eyeka's I have heard from many others. A small boy up in Banto had just the same experience when ——— led the soldiers from Wangata.

There are still many more poor beings around the Lake without hands, and I have heard these poor men tell the present Government officer at Bikoro, in my hearing, that their hands had been hacked off against the sides of canoes to which they were clinging, by the State soldiers. No one was ever punished for all these barbarities—that should be always remembered—and no attempt at providing for the mutilated victims of this rule of savagery, which, for nearly seven years, made Lake Mantumba a hell upon earth, has ever been attempted until the British Consul's visit last year.[3] * * * The third figure—the little boy on the right, whose right hand is gone—was a poor little fellow named Mwanza. * * *

When the British Consul was here in August last year, I know he was told by one of the State officers in the neighbourhood—I heard the officer tell him myself—that there were still a lot of mutilated people in the lake-side country, and that they often came in and told the officer how his predecessors had given orders for their mutilation.

The officer said that one of his predecessors, of whom he was speaking by name, had killed "thousands" of the people around the lake, and that the mutilation of those killed had gone on for a long time, until the scandal in the Belgian Parliament and the outcry in Europe stopped it.

Just after the Consul had gone away, three poor men—some of those this officer had referred to—came over the lake to try to see the Consul, and tell him. They hoped that he might be able to help them, *as the State officers had not done anything for them*. Mutilation of the dead is not now permitted *openly*, to the Government soldiers; but it must be remembered that the long spell of murder and massacre and pitiless destruction of life, which went on from 1893 to 1900, *has done its work*.

The people in the Lake *are entirely* broken, *and only a remnant of them remain*.

It was not a wise policy, apart from all other considerations, for

3. Roger Casement (1864–1916), whom Conrad met in the Congo in 1890, became the British consul at Boma in 1898. In 1903 he was asked by his government to make a report on conditions in the Congo as a result of the increasing number of complaints made by men such as H. R. Fox-Bourne and E. D. Morel. His report was long and detailed, and led to Casement's taking a personal interest in Congo reform. For his unsuccessful attempt to enlist Conrad's support, see *Life and Letters*, I, 325–26. Knighted in 1911 for his service to the crown, Casement served two more years before retiring to his native Ireland, where he became active in the nationalist movement. He was hanged for his attempt to get German support for the Easter uprising of 1916. See below, p. 110, and n. 2.

it has killed the goose that laid the golden egg, so far as this district is concerned, and it will take many years of peace and rest for the population to recover, while the native belief in the white man's truth, or justice, or decency, has gone for ever. They often say to me now, "Will he never go home to his own country? Has not the white man got enough rubber yet?" Poor people! a strange visitation —more dire than that which fell upon the Egyptians, for that was from above, with all its earthly plagues of loathsome nature; but who can say that what has come to the Congo people—whatever their faults may be—has been from above, or prompted by any love, but that of gain.

Believe me, dear Mr. Morel,
Yours faithfully,

CONRAD IN THE CONGO

On the 14th of August, 1879, I arrived before the mouth of this river to ascend it, with the novel mission of sowing along its banks civilised settlements, to peacefully conquer and subdue it, to remould it in harmony with modern ideas into National States, within whose limits the Europen merchant shall go hand in hand with the dark African trader, and justice and law and order shall prevail, and murder and lawlessness and cruel barter of slaves shall for ever cease.

—HENRY M. STANLEY, 1885.

"Night-time. We are slowly ascending the river. There are a few lights in the distance on the left bank; a bush fire on the horizon; at our feet the terrifying thickness of the waters."

—ANDRÉ GIDE, 1927.

MURIEL C. BRADBROOK: [Conrad: A Sketch]†

In the history of English literature there has never been anything like the history of Joseph Conrad; nor, so far as I am aware, has there been anything like him in any other European literature. He was a Pole of the landowning class, who became a Marseilles gun-runner at twenty, an English master mariner at twenty-nine, and one of the great English novelists at thirty-eight. Born in 1857, his childhood was darkened by the savage repressions which Tsarist Russia inflicted on the Poles after the abortive rebellion of 1863. His father, as a leader of the Polish people, was imprisoned and exiled; his mother, who elected to share the exile, was treated with ruthless barbarity and died in 1865. His father, a dying man, returned to Cracow in 1868 and died the next year. He had been a poet, a dramatist, and a translator of Hugo, de Vigny[1] and Shake-

† From *Joseph Conrad: Poland's English Genius*, by Muriel C. Bradbrook (New York: Cambridge University Press, 1941). Pp. 5–6. Reprinted by permission.

1. Victor Hugo (1802–85) and Alfred Victor de Vigny (1797–1863), French writers.

speare.

Konrad Korzeniowski was urged to seek his fortune abroad by his guardian and uncle, Tadeusz Bobrowski: but none of the family approved of his plan to be a sailor. However, in 1874, Joseph Conrad went to Marseilles, and here he became engaged in gun traffic for the Carlist party in Spain. Here also he met two people who were to count for more than anything as inspiration to his literature, whose portraits he drew again and again—a lovely Basque girl, whose name is unknown,[2] and Dominic Cervoni, the Corsican sailor.[3] Conrad sailed also to the West Indies and to Istanbul; and it was not until 1878 that he landed at Lowestoft, having joined an English vessel. Till 1894 he sailed in English ships with the one interlude of his Congo adventure in 1890; and though his original romantic impulse had sprung from a reading of Marryat,[4] his efficiency was recognised by the usual certificates from that very unromantic body, the Board of Trade, in 1880, 1883 and 1886, when he took his master's "ticket". The story of his seafaring life is told in his books. He sailed in Australian wool-clippers, traders in Malaya and the Gulf of Siam, and in Mediterranean and home waters. It was only in 1889 that Conrad began his first novel,[5] and not till five years later that he finally gave up the sea. He had a long struggle as an author, for though he was soon recognised by such people as Edward Garnett and Henry James, there was little money in his work, and for nearly twenty years he lived in poverty. Then came prosperity but also the Great War, agonising to Conrad: his son was in the British Army, his feelings triply engaged by his triple fidelity to England, France and Poland. Finally, after a few years of success and ease, he died suddenly in 1924, at the age of sixty-six.

JOSEPH CONRAD: Geography and Some Explorers†

The voyages of the early explorers were prompted by an acquisitive spirit, the idea of lucre in some form, the desire of trade or the desire of loot, disguised in more or less fine words. But Cook's three voyages are free from any taint of that sort.[1] His aims needed no disguise. They were scientific. His deeds speak for themselves with

2. Identified as Paula de Somogyi by Jerry Allen, *The Thunder and the Sunshine* (New York, 1958), but denied by Jocelyn Baines, *Joseph Conrad: A Critical Biography* (London, 1960).
3. The story is told most directly in *The Arrow of Gold* [Bradbrook's note].
4. Captain Frederick Marryat (1792–1848), British naval officer and novelist, who wrote *Mr. Midshipman Easy* and other stories of the sea.
5. *Almayer's Folly*.

† From *Last Essays*, ed. Richard Curle (London: J. M. Dent & Sons, Ltd., 1926). Pp. 10–17. Reprinted by permission.
1. Captain James Cook (1728–79), supported by the Admiralty and the Royal Society, made three trips around the world, 1768–71, 1772–75, and 1776–79, with the special purpose of exploring and charting the South Pacific. Cook was killed in the Hawaiian Islands, February 14, 1779.

the masterly simplicity of a hard-won success. In that respect he seems to belong to the single-minded explorers of the nineteenth century, the late fathers of militant geography whose only object was the search for truth. Geography is a science of facts, and they devoted themselves to the discovery of facts in the configuration and features of the main continents.

It was the century of landsmen investigators. In saying this I do not forget the polar explorers, whose aims were certainly as pure as the air of those high latitudes where not a few of them laid down their lives for the advancement of geography. Seamen, men of science, it is difficult to speak of them without admirative emotion. The dominating figure among the seamen explorers of the first half of the nineteenth century is that of another good man, Sir John Franklin,[2] whose fame rests not only on the extent of his discoveries, but on professional prestige and high personal character. This great navigator, who never returned home, served geography even in his death. The persistent efforts extending over ten years to ascertain his fate advanced greatly our knowledge of the polar regions.

As gradually revealed to the world this fate appeared the more tragic in this, that for the first two years the way of the *Erebus* and *Terror* expedition seemed to be the way to the desired and important success, while in truth it was all the time the way of death, the end of the darkest drama perhaps played behind the curtain of Arctic mystery.

The last words unveiling the mystery of the *Erebus* and *Terror* expedition were brought home and disclosed to the world by Sir Leopold McClintock, in his book, "The Voyage of the *Fox* in the Arctic Seas." It is a little book, but it records with manly simplicity the tragic ending of a great tale. It so happened that I was born in the year of its publication. Therefore, I may be excused for not getting hold of it till ten years afterwards. I can only account for it falling into my hands by the fact that the fate of Sir John Franklin was a matter of European interest, and that Sir Leopold McClintock's book was translated, I believe, into every language of the white races.

My copy was probably in French. But I have read the work many times since. I have now on my shelves a copy of a popular edition got up exactly as I remember my first one. It contains the touching facsimile of the printed form filled in with a summary record of the two ships' work, the name of "Sir John Franklin commanding the expedition" written in ink, and the pathetic underlined entry "All

2. Sir John Franklin (1786–1847) in 1845 led an exploring party in the *Erebus* and *Terror* in search of the Northwest passage. Franklin died while the ships were ice-bound from April 1846 to September 1848, at which point the crews tried their luck on foot. None survived. See *Heart of Darkness*, p. 4.

well." It was found by Sir Leopold McClintock under a cairn[3] and it is dated just a year before the two ships had to be abandoned in their deadly ice-trap, and their crews' long and desperate struggle for life began.

There could hardly have been imagined a better book for letting in the breath of the stern romance of polar exploration into the existence of a boy whose knowledge of the poles of the earth had been till then of an abstract formal kind as mere imaginary ends of the imaginary axis upon which the earth turns. The great spirit of the realities of the story sent me off on the romantic explorations of my inner self; to the discovery of the taste of poring over maps; and revealed to me the existence of a latent devotion to geography which interfered with my devotion (such as it was) to my other schoolwork.

Unfortunately, the marks awarded for that subject were almost as few as the hours apportioned to it in the school curriculum by persons of no romantic sense for the real, ignorant of the great possibilities of active life; with no desire for struggle, no notion of the wide spaces of the world—mere bored professors, in fact, who were not only middle-aged but looked to me as if they had never been young. And their geography was very much like themselves, a bloodless thing with a dry skin covering a repulsive armature of uninteresting bones.

* * *

Thus it happened that I got no marks at all for my first and only paper on Arctic geography, which I wrote at the age of thirteen. I still think that for my tender years it was an erudite performance. I certainly did know something of Arctic geography, but what I was after really, I suppose, was the history of Arctic exploration. My knowledge had considerable gaps, but I managed to compress my enthusiasm into just two pages, which in itself was a sort of merit. Yet I got no marks. For one thing it was not a set subject. I believe the only comment made about it to my private tutor was that I seemed to have been wasting my time in reading books of travel instead of attending to my studies. I tell you, those fellows were always trying to take my scalp. On another occasion I just saved it by proficiency in map-drawing. It must have been good, I suppose; but all I remember about it is that it was done in a loving spirit.

I have no doubt that star-gazing is a fine occupation, for it leads you within the borders of the unattainable. But map-gazing, to which I became addicted so early, brings the problems of the great spaces of the earth into stimulating and directing contact with sane

3. A marker formed by piling stones.

curiosity and gives an honest precision to one's imaginative faculty. And the honest maps of the nineteenth century nourished in me a passionate interest in the truth of geographical facts and a desire for precise knowledge which was extended later to other subjects.

For a change had come over the spirit of cartographers. From the middle of the eighteenth century on the business of map-making had been growing into an honest occupation, registering the hard-won knowledge, but also in a scientific spirit recording the geographical ignorance of its time. And it was Africa, the continent out of which the Romans used to say some new thing was always coming, that got cleared of the dull imaginary wonders of the dark ages, which were replaced by exciting spaces of white paper. Regions unknown! My imagination could depict to itself there worthy, adventurous and devoted men, nibbling at the edges, attacking from north and south and east and west, conquering a bit of truth here and a bit of truth there, and sometimes swallowed up by the mystery their hearts were so persistently set on unveiling.

Among them Mungo Park, of western Sudan, and Bruce, of Abyssinia,[4] were, I believe, the first friends I made when I began to take notice—I mean geographical notice—of the continents of the world into which I was born. The fame of these two had already been for a long time European, and their figures had become historical by then. But their story was a very novel thing to me, for the very latest geographical news that could have been whispered to me in my cradle was that of the expedition of Burton and Speke, the news of the existence of Tanganyika and of Victoria Nyanza.[5]

I stand here confessed as a contemporary of the Great Lakes. Yes, I could have heard of their discovery in my cradle, and it was only right that, grown to a boy's estate, I should have in the later sixties done my first bit of map-drawing and paid my first homage to the prestige of their first explorers. It consisted in entering laboriously in pencil the outline of Tanganyika on my beloved old atlas, which, having been published in 1852, knew nothing, of course, of the Great Lakes. The heart of its Africa was white and big.

* * *

4. Mungo Park (1771–1806), Scottish explorer of the Niger. Park's account of his first trip, *Travels in the Interior of Africa*, was published in 1799 and immediately proved popular. He drowned in the Niger while on a second exploration.

James Bruce (1730–94) was also a Scottish explorer in Africa who wrote in retirement *Travels to Discover the Source of the Nile in the Years 1768–73*, 5 volumes, 1790.

5. Sir Richard Francis Burton (1821–90), known for his translation of the "Arabian Nights" (*The Thousand Nights and a Night*, 16 volumes, 1885–86), was an adventurer who set the pattern for Stanley, Lawrence, and their kind. The Foreign Office and Royal Geographical Society commissioned Burton in 1856 to search for the sources of the Nile and to map what Burton called the "huge white blot" of Central Africa. In February he discovered Lake Tanganyika, and his assistant, Capt. J. H. Speke, discovered Victoria Nyanza. The discovery of these and the other Great Lakes drew David Livingstone into his own search for the sources of the Nile.

It must not be supposed that I gave up my interest in the polar regions. My heart and my warm participation swung from the frigid to the torrid zone, fascinated by the problems of each, no doubt, but more yet by the men who, like masters of a great art, worked each according to his temperament to complete the picture of the earth. Almost each day of my schoolboy life had its hour given up to their company. And to this day I think that it was a very good company.

Not the least interesting part in the study of geographical discovery lies in the insight it gives one into the characters of that special kind of men who devoted the best part of their lives to the exploration of land and sea. In the world of mentality and imagination which I was entering it was they and not the characters of famous fiction who were my first friends. Of some of them I had soon formed for myself an image indissolubly connected with certain parts of the world. For instance, western Sudan, of which I could draw the rivers and principal features from memory even now, means for me an episode in Mungo Park's life.

It means for me the vision of a young, emaciated, fair-haired man, clad simply in a tattered shirt and worn-out breeches, gasping painfully for breath and lying on the ground in the shade of an enormous African tree (species unknown), while from a neighbouring village of grass huts a charitable black-skinned woman is approaching him with a calabash[6] full of pure cold water, a simple draught which, according to himself, seems to have effected a miraculous cure. The central Sudan, on the other hand, is represented to me by a very different picture, that of a self-confident and keen-eyed person in a long cloak and wearing a turban on his head, riding slowly towards a gate in the mud walls of an African city, from which an excited population is streaming out to behold the wonder—Doctor Barth, the protégé of Lord Palmerston, and subsidized by the British Foreign Office, approaching Kano, which no European eye had seen till then, but where forty years later my friend Sir Hugh Clifford, the Governor of Nigeria, travelled in state in order to open a college.[7]

I must confess that I read that bit of news and inspected the many pictures in the illustrated papers without any particular elation. Education is a great thing, but Doctor Barth gets in the way.

6. A gourd.
7. Heinrich Barth (1821–65), German explorer, and author of *Travels and Discoveries in North and Central Africa*, 1857, visited Kano in Northern Nigeria in 1851 and 1854. The 3rd Viscount Palmerston (1784–1865), statesman and champion of Empire, was Prime Minister from 1855 until his death. Sir Hugh Clifford (1866–1941), a lifetime civil servant, was governor of Nigeria from 1919–25. He was author of several books, the first of which, *Studies in Brown Humanity* (about Malaya), was favorably reviewed by Conrad in the April 1898 *Academy*. The two then became and remained friends. See Clifford's review of the *Youth* volume (*The Spectator*, November 29, 1902).

Neither will the monuments left by all sorts of empire builders suppress for me the memory of David Livingstone. The words "Central Africa" bring before my eyes an old man with a rugged, kind face and a clipped, gray moustache, pacing wearily at the head of a few black followers along the reed-fringed lakes towards the dark native hut on the Congo headwaters in which he died, clinging in his very last hour to his heart's unappeased desire for the sources of the Nile.

That passion had changed him in his last days from a great explorer into a restless wanderer refusing to go home any more. From his exalted place among the blessed of militant geography and with his memory enshrined in Westminster Abbey, he can well afford to smile without bitterness at the fatal delusion of his exploring days, a notable European figure and the most venerated perhaps of all the objects of my early geographical enthusiasm.

Once only did that enthusiasm expose me to the derision of my schoolboy chums. One day, putting my finger on a spot in the very middle of the then white heart of Africa, I declared that some day I would go there. My chums' chaffing was perfectly justifiable. I myself was ashamed of having been betrayed into mere vapouring. Nothing was further from my wildest hopes. Yet it is a fact that, about eighteen years afterwards, a wretched little stern-wheel steamboat I commanded lay moored to the bank of an African river.

JOSEPH CONRAD: ["When I Grow Up I Shall Go There"]†

It was in 1868, when nine years old or thereabouts, that while looking at a map of Africa of the time and putting my finger on the blank space then representing the unsolved mystery of that continent, I said to myself with absolute assurance and an amazing audacity which are no longer in my character now:

"When I grow up I shall go *there*."

And of course I thought no more about it till after a quarter of a century or so an opportunity offered to go there—as if the sin of childish audacity was to be visited on my mature head. Yes. I did go there: *there* being the region of Stanley Falls which in '68 was the blankest of blank spaces on the earth's figured surface.

† From *A Personal Record* (London: J. M. Dent & Sons, Ltd., 1912). P. 13. Reprinted by permission.

JOSEPH CONRAD: Extracts from Correspondence, January 16–June 18, 1890†

London, 16 January 1890

Dear Uncle,[1]

I have just had a letter from Kazimierówka[2] in which, replying to a question of mine, Uncle Tadeusz tells me you are residing in Brussels and gives me your address. I deeply regret not having known of this sooner, for I was in Brussels last October. It may happen, however, that I shall have occasion to visit that city again. The purpose of this scribbling is to recall myself to a relative whose kindness—shown to me in Cracow[3]—I have by no means forgotten. I do not ask if you will allow me to visit you, for I permit myself not to doubt this, but I should like to know with certainty that you are in Brussels and that I can, in the course of the next month, find you there.

I returned to London six months ago after an absence of three years. Of these three years I spent one among the islands of the Malay Archipelago, after which, during the remaining two years, I commanded an Australian ship in the Pacific and Indian Oceans. Now I am, as it were, under agreement with the Société belge pour le commerce du Haut-Congo to command one of their river-steamers. I have not signed any contract, but M. A. Thys, the Company's manager, has promised me this position. Whether he will keep his promise and when he will send me to Africa I do not as yet know, but it will probably be in May.[4]

I intend to visit Uncle Tadeusz soon; that is, I wish to do so and he himself also wishes it, but it is difficult, he says, in winter. I expect a letter from him in a couple of days which will decide the

† From *Letters of Joseph Conrad to Marguerite Poradowska*, translated and edited by John A. Gee and Paul J. Sturm; copyright 1940 by Yale University Press; pp. 3, 7–14, 123–24. And from G. Jean-Aubry, *Joseph Conrad: Life and Letters* (London: William Heinemann Ltd., 1927), I, 124, 126–27. Selections reprinted by permission; *Life and Letters* by permission of J. M. Dent & Sons, Ltd. The present editor has regularized the style of the correspondence.

1. Alexandre Poradowski, first cousin of Conrad's maternal grandmother, was, like Conrad's father, an exile from Poland after the abortive revolution of 1863. He died February 7, 1890, but not before Conrad was able to see him again and meet his wife Marguerite, daughter of a distinguished scholar who was for a time the royal Belgian archivist. Mme. Poradowska, the "aunt"

of *Heart of Darkness*, because of her family's position had many friends within the royal government. Moreover, from the 1880's on she gained some minor fame as an author in her own right. In both respects, she was a beneficent spirit to Conrad at this stage in his careers as seaman and writer.
2. In the then, as now, Russian Ukraine, but formerly a part of Poland. The home of Conrad's uncle and guardian, Tadeusz Bobrowski.
3. Conrad's childhood home and the pre-revolutionary home of Poradowski.
4. The Trading Company of the Upper Congo was, under the terms of the Berlin agreement, an illegal *commissionaire* company founded in December 1888 by Albert Thys (1832–1913), who has been described as a long-time "henchman" of Leopold in Congo affairs. See above, pp. 90–91.

matter. If I do go home it will be via Hamburg, returning via Brussels. But should my visit be postponed, I shall at any rate go to Brussels in March in regard to the position in the Congo. So in any event I shall have the pleasure of seeing you, dear Uncle, and of making the acquaintance of Aunt Poradowska. * * *

London, 20 January 1890

Dear Uncle,

Most hearty thanks to you and my Aunt for the kindliness shown in your letter. * * * Along with your letter, I received this morning a letter from Uncle Tadeusz, who says "Come." * * *

London, 4 February 1890

My dear Aunt,

Ever so many thanks for your card. I am leaving London tomorrow, Friday, at nine in the morning and should arrive in Brussels at five-thirty in the afternoon. * * *

Kazimierówka, 10 March 1890

My dear Aunt,

* * * I beg your pardon for the shortness of this letter. The post leaves today and I have received a batch of mail requiring an answer. I believe that the recommendation in my behalf to the Company of the Congo was not strong enough[5] and that the affair will not go through. That vexes me somewhat. * * *

Kazimierówka, 14 April 1890

My dear Aunt,

I have received your charming, kind letter; and the proof of friendship you give me in concerning yourself with my African projects touches me more than I can say. Ever so many thanks for your kind pains; I impatiently await the moment when I shall be able to kiss your hands while thanking you in person.

I leave my uncle in four days; I have visits to make en route (among others one of forty-eight hours in Lublin) and so shall not be in Brussels before the 29th of this month. Then we shall discuss your idea of visiting Poland.[6] * * *

London, 2 May 1890

My dear Mariette,[7]

I have not been able to write sooner. I have been exceedingly busy and I still have much to do. I am sailing for the Congo in

5. Probably the letter from Conrad's previous employers which served as Conrad's letter of introduction to M. Thys in the fall of 1889.
6. Mme. Poradowska visited her late husband's (and Conrad's) relatives in Lublin, Poland during the summer of 1890.
7. One of the cousins whom Conrad had visited in Lublin.

three days, and have to prepare for a stay of three years in the middle of Africa, so you will easily understand that every moment is precious. * * *

Canary Islands, 15 May 1890

My dear little Aunt,

Suppose I tell you at the beginning that I have escaped the fever thus far! If I could only assure you that all my letters would start with this good news! Well, we shall see! Meanwhile I am comparatively happy, which is all one can hope for here on earth. We left Bordeaux on a rainy day. A dreary day, a not very merry sailing: haunting memories; vague regrets; still vaguer hopes. One is sceptical of the future. For indeed, I ask myself, why should anyone have faith in it? And so why be sad? A little illusion, many dreams, a rare flash of happiness; then disillusion, a little anger and much pain, and then the end—peace! That is the program, and we have to see this tragi-comedy through. We must resign ourselves to it.

The screw turns, taking me into the unknown. * * *

Freetown, Sierra Leone, 22nd May 1890

My Very Dear Charles,[8]

It is just a month to-day since you were scandalized by my hurried departure from Lublin. From the date and address of this letter you will see that I have had to be pretty quick, and I am only just beginning to breathe a little more calmly. If you only knew the devilish haste I had to make! From London to Brussels, and back again to London! And again to Brussels! If you had only seen all the tin boxes and revolvers, the high boots and the touching farewells; just another handshake and just another pair of trousers!—and if you knew all the bottles of medicine and all the affectionate wishes I took away with me, you would understand in what a typhoon, cyclone, hurricane, earthquake—no!—in what a universal cataclysm, in what a fantastic atmosphere of mixed shopping, business and affecting scenes, I passed two whole weeks. Two weeks spent at sea have allowed me to rest and I am impatiently waiting for the end of this trip. I shall reach Boma no doubt on the 7th of next month and then leave Boma with my caravan to go to Leopoldville. As far as I can make out from my "service letter" I am destined to the command of a steamboat, belonging to M. Delcommune's exploring party, which is being got ready;[9] but I know nothing for certain as everything is supposed to be kept secret. What makes me rather uneasy is the information that 60 per cent. of our Company's em-

---

8. Another cousin.
9. Alexandre Delcommune (1855–1922), who wrote a book on his twenty years in Africa. In 1890 he headed an expedition, the "Eldorado Exploring Expedition" of *Heart of Darkness*, up the Kassai River for the new Katanga Company.

ployees return to Europe before they have completed even six months' service. Fever and dysentery! There are others who are sent home in a hurry at the end of a year, so that they shouldn't die in the Congo. God forbid it! It would spoil the statistics which are excellent, you see! In a word, it seems there are only 7 per cent. who can do their three years' service. . . . Yes! But a Polish noble-man, cased in British tar! *Nous verrons!*[10] In any case I shall console myself by remembering—faithful to our national traditions—that it is of my own free will that I have thrust myself into this business.

When you see—with the help of a microscope, no doubt—the hieroglyphics of my handwriting, you will, I expect, wonder why I am writing to you. First, because it is a pleasure to talk to you; next, because, considering the distinguished personage who is penning this autograph, it ought to be a pleasure to you too. You can be-queath it to your children. Future generations will read it, I hope with admiration (and with profit). In the meantime, *trêve de bêtises!*[11]

* * *

Libreville, Gabon, 10 June 1890

Dear little Aunt,

As this is the last port of call before Boma, where my sea-voyage ends, I am beginning this letter here at the moment of departure, having in mind to continue it during the passage and end it the day of my arrival at Boma, where, naturally, I shall post it.

Nothing new as to events. As to feelings, nothing new either. And herein lies the trouble; for if one could get rid of his heart and memory (and also brain), and then get a whole new set of these things, life would become ideally amusing. * * *

While awaiting the inevitable fever, I am very well.—If my existence is to be at all bearable, I must have letters, many letters. From you, for one. Don't forget what I am telling you, my dear and good little Aunt.

After my departure from Boma there may be a long silence. I shall not be able to write until at Leopoldville. It takes twenty days to go there; afoot too! Horrors!

Probably you will write to my uncle; such was your intention, I believe. You will be very kind to tell him something of me. For example, that you saw me in Brussels, that I was well in body and mind. This will give him pleasure and make him easier on my account. He loves me dearly, and I grow as sentimental as an old fool when I think of him. Forgive this weakness.

When do you return to Brussels? What are your plans for the

10. "We shall see!" 11. "no more of this tomfoolery!"

future? Tell me of all this in your letters, but don't sit down at your writing-desk until you feel a hearty desire to chat with "the absent one." "The absent one" will be my official title in future. I shall be very happy to know that no one is bothering you, that you are working with a free mind. I await your new work with curiosity and impatience. You will send it to me, won't you?

I have discovered that my Company has an ocean-going vessel and will probably build others. If I could obtain the command of one, it would be much better than the river. Apart from the fact that it is more healthful, one always has the opportunity of returning at least every year to Europe. When you get back to Brussels I should like you to let me know whether any ships are being built, so that I can put in my request. You will be able to learn about this through M. Wauters,[12] while I in the depths of Africa won't have any news. I am sure you will do this for me. * * *

Matadi, 18 June 1890

Thank you! Thanks ever so much, dear Aunt, for your kind and charming letter, which came to meet me at Boma. * * * I leave tomorrow on foot. No donkey here except your very humble servant. A twenty-day caravan. Temperature very bearable here and health quite good. * * *

JOSEPH CONRAD: The Congo Diary†

The diary kept by Joseph Conrad in the Congo in 1890, or such of it as has survived (for there is no saying whether there was more or not), is contained in two small black penny notebooks, and is written in pencil. One carries his initials, J. C. K.—Joseph Conrad Korzeniowski. The first entry is dated June 13, 1890, but in the second notebook dates are practically discarded, and it is impossible to say when the last entry was made. And names of places, also, are practically discarded in the second notebook, while abounding in the first, so that, though we can see that the diary was begun at Matadi, we cannot discover where it was ended. The last place mentioned is Lulanga, far up the great sweep of the Congo River to the north of the Equator, but there remains some twenty-four pages of the diary beyond that entry in which no name whatsoever

12. A. J. Wauters was the general secretary for all the Belgian companies operating in the Congo, and was editor of two periodicals which furnish detailed information on all activities within the Free State, the *Mouvement Géographique* and the *Congo Illustré*.
† From *Last Essays*, ed. Richard Curle (London: J. M. Dent & Sons, Ltd., 1926). Pp. 155–71. Reprinted by permission.

The notes and introduction are by Curle (b. 1883) who became interested in Conrad in 1912 when he wrote his first of many critical appraisals of Conrad's work. The two met and became close friends. See Curle's *The Last Twelve Years of Joseph Conrad*, Garden City, N.Y., 1928.

appears. It must, indeed, have been continued into the very heart of that immense darkness where the crisis of his story, "Heart of Darkness," is unfolded. We know from "A Personal Record" that he reached ultimately somewhere to the neighbourhood of Stanley Falls; and Stanley Falls are farther from Lulanga than Lulanga is from Stanley Pool.

* * *

The following is a reproduction of the first notebook alone—not, however, of the list of names, persons, books, stores, and the calculations that fill the last pages—consisting of thirty-two manuscript pages, not all of which are full, and twelve of which are further curtailed by Conrad's sectional drawings of the day's march. The given spelling and abbreviations have been adhered to throughout—they help to heighten its true flavour—but the paragraphing and the punctuation have been freely altered.

* * *

As to the appended footnotes, their chief purpose has been to show how closely some of the earlier pages of "Heart of Darkness" are a recollection of Conrad's own Congo journey. * * * The pages which bear direct reference to the first volume of the diary, are only three * * * but in these few pages there are an astonishing number of touches strongly reminiscent of the diary. One would argue, indeed, that he must have consulted the diary when writing the story, but Mrs. Conrad assures me that it was not so. Twice had she saved it from the wastepaper basket, and probably by the time "Heart of Darkness" came to be written Conrad had forgotten all about it, or did not dream that it had survived. He never spoke to me of it, and I never heard of its existence until after his death. [*from Richard Curle's introduction*]

The Diary

Arrived at Matadi[1] on the 13th of June, 1890.

Mr. Gosse, chief of the station (O. K.) retaining us for some reason of his own.

Made the acquaintance of Mr. Roger Casement,[2] which I should consider as a great pleasure under any circumstances and now it becomes a positive piece of luck. Thinks, speaks well, most intelligent and very sympathetic.

1. On his voyage from Europe presumably. [All footnotes to the diary are Curle's.—*Editor*]
2. Afterwards the notorious Sir Roger Casement, who was hanged for treason on August 3, 1916—the very date on which Conrad died eight years later. At this period Casement was in the employ of a commercial firm in the Congo. In 1898 he became British Consul in the Congo Free State. [See above, p. 97, n. 3.—*Editor*]

Feel considerably in doubt about the future. Think just now that my life amongst the people (white) around here cannot be very comfortable. Intend avoid acquaintances as much as possible.

Through Mr. R. C. have made the acquain^{ce} of Mr. Underwood, the Manager of the English Factory (Hatton & Cookson) in Kalla Kalla. Av^{ge} com^{al}—hearty and kind. Lunched there on the 21st.

24th. Gosse and R. C. gone with a large lot of ivory down to Boma. On G.['s] return intend to start up the river. Have been myself busy packing ivory in casks. Idiotic employment. Health good up to now.

Wrote to Simpson, to Gov. B., to Purd.,[3] to Hope,[4] to Capt. Froud,[5] and to Mar. .[6] Prominent characteristic of the social life here; people speaking ill of each other.[7]

Saturday, 28th June. Left Matadi with Mr. Harou[8] and a caravan of 31 men.[9] Parted with Casement in a very friendly manner. Mr. Gosse saw us off as far as the State station.

First halt, M'poso. 2 Danes in Company.[10]

Sund[ay], 29th. Ascent of Pataballa sufficiently fatiguing. Camped at 11 A.M. at Nsoke river. Mosquitos [always spelt thus].

Monday, 30th. To Congo da Lemba after passing black rocks. Long ascent. Harou giving up.[11] Bother. Camp bad. Water far. Dirty. At night Harou better.

Tuesday, 1st July. Left early in a heavy mist, marching towards Lufu river. Part route through forest on the sharp slope of a high mountain. Very long descent. Then market place from where short walk to the bridge (good) and camp. V. G. Bath. Clear river. Feel well. Harou all right. 1st chicken, 2 P. [M.] No sunshine to-day.

Wednesday, 2nd July. Started at 5:30 after a sleepless night. Country more open. Gently undulating hills. Road good, in perfect

3. Probably Captain Purdy, an acquaintance of Conrad.

4. Conrad's old friend, now living in Essex, Mr. G. F. W. Hope. In 1900 Conrad dedicated "Lord Jim" to Mr. and Mrs. Hope, "with grateful affection after many years of friendship."

5. The then Secretary of the London Ship-Master's Society. See "A Personal Record" (Concord Edition), p. 7. "Dear Captain Froud—it is impossible not to pay him the tribute of affectionate familiarity at this distance of years—had very sound views as to the advancement of knowledge and status for the whole body of the officers of the mercantile marine."

6. Probably Marguerite Poradowska, his aunt.

7. This was also a failing of the white men at the "Central Station" in "Heart of Darkness."

8. Harou was an official of the Etat Indépendant du Congo Belge.

9. Compare "Heart of Darkness," p. 20: "Next day I left that station at last with a caravan of 60 men for a 200-mile tramp." On 13 out of the 19 travelling days taken by Conrad on this overland journey he kept a record of the distance covered, and it totals 197½ miles. [References to the story have been altered to designate pages of the present text.—*Editor*]

10. Curiously enough, the identity of these two Danes was discovered by Monsieur G. Jean-Aubry in Brussels early in 1925. Not knowing that they were mentioned in the diary, he omitted to take names or particulars.

11. He seems to have been constantly unwell and one may compare "Heart of Darkness," p. 20: "I had a white companion too, not a bad chap, but rather too fleshy, and with the exasperating habit of fainting on the hot hillsides, miles away from the least bit of shade or water."

order. (District of Lukungu.) Great market at 9:30. Bought eggs and chickens. Feel not well to-day. Heavy cold in the head. Arrived at 11 at Banza Manteka. Camped on the market place. Not well enough to call on the missionary. Water scarce and bad. Camp^g place dirty. 2 Danes still in Company.

Thursday, 3rd July. Left at 6 A. M. after a good night's rest. Crossed a low range of hills and entered a broad valley, or rather plain, with a break in the middle. Met an off^{er} of the State inspecting. A few minutes afterwards saw at a camp^g place the dead body of a Backongo. Shot?[12] Horrid smell.

Crossed a range of mountains, running N. W.—S. E. by a low pass. Another broad flat valley with a deep ravine through the centre. Clay and gravel. Another range parallel to the first mentioned, with a chain of low foothills running close to it. Between the two came to camp on the banks of the Luinzono river. Camp^g place clean. River clear. Gov^t Zanzibari[13] with register. Canoe. 2 Danes camp^g on the other bank. Health good.

General tone of landscape gray-yellowish (dry grass) with reddish patches (soil) and clumps of dark green vegetation scattered sparsely about. Mostly in steep gorges between the high mountains or in ravines cutting the plain.[14]

Noticed Palma Christi—Oil Palm. Very straight, tall and thick trees in some places. Name not known to me. Villages quite invisible. Infer their existence from calbashes [*sic*] suspended to palm trees for the "Malafu." Good many caravans and travellers. No women, unless on the market place.

Bird notes charming. One especially a flute-like note. Another, kind of "boom" ressembling [*sic*] the very distant baying of a hound. Saw only pigeons and a few green parroquets. Very small and not many. No birds of prey seen by me.[15]

Up to 9 A. M. sky clouded and calm. Afterwards gentle breeze from the Nth generally and sky clearing. Nights damp and cool. White mists on the hills up about half way. Water effects very beautiful this morning. Mists generally raising before sky clears.

Distance 15 miles. General direction N. N. E.—S. S. W.

Friday, 4th July. Left camp at 6 A. M. after a very unpleasant

12. Compare "Heart of Darkness," p. 20: "Once a white man in an unbuttoned uniform camping on the path . . . was looking after the upkeep of the road, he declared. Can't say I saw any road or any upkeep, unless the body of a middle-aged negro with a bullet-hole in the forehead, upon which I absolutely stumbled three miles further on, may be considered as a permanent improvement."

13. Compare "Heart of Darkness," p. 20, in which he mentioned his meeting with a white man, who was accompanied by "an armed escort of lank Zanzibaris."

14. In "Heart of Darkness," p. 20, the country of the march is described as "a stamped-in network of paths spreading over the empty land, through long grass, through burnt grass, through thickets, down and up hilly ravines, up and down stony hills ablaze with heat."

15. These natural history observations are curious, as Conrad practically never showed the slightest interest in such subjects.

night. Marching across a chain of hills and then in a maze of hills. At 8:15 opened out into an undulating plain. Took bearings of a break in the chain of mountains on the other side. Bearing N. N. E. Road passes through that. Sharp ascents up very steep hills not very high. The higher mountains recede sharply and show a low hilly country. At 9:30 market place. At 10 passed R. Lukanga and at 10:30 camped on the Mpwe R.

To-day's march. Direction N. N. E.½.—N. Dist^ce 13 miles.

Saw another dead body lying by the path in an attitude of meditative repose.[16]

In the evening three women, of whom one albino, passed our camp; horrid chalky white with pink blotches; red eyes; red hair; features very negroid and ugly. Mosquitos. At night when the moon rose heard shouts and drumming in distant villages.[17] Passed a bad night.

Saturday, 5th July. Left at 6:15. Morning cool, even cold, and very damp. Sky densely overcast. Gentle breeze from N. E. Road through a narrow plain up to R. Kwilu. Swift flowing and deep, 50 yds. wide. Passed in canoes. After^ds up and down very steep hills intersected by deep ravines. Main chain of heights running mostly N. W.—S. E. or W. and E. at times. Stopped at Manyamba. Camp^g place bad—in a hollow—water very indifferent. Tent set at 10:15. N. N. E. Dist^ce 12 m.

To-day fell into a muddy puddle—beastly! The fault of the man that carried me. After camp^g went to a small stream, bathed and washed clothes. Getting jolly well sick of this fun.

To-morrow expect a long march to get to Nsona, 2 days from Manyanga. No sunshine to-day.

Sunday, 6th July. Started at 5:40. The route at first hilly, then, after a sharp descent, traversing a broad plain. At the end of it a large market place. At 10 sun came out. After leaving the market passed another plain, then, walking on the crest of a chain of hills, passed 2 villages and at 11 arrived at Nsona. Village invisible.

Direction about N. N. E. Distance 18 miles.

In this camp (Nsona) there is a good camp^g place. Shady, water far and not very good. This night no mosquitos owing to large fires, lit all round our tent. Afternoon very close: night clear and starry.

Monday, 7th July. Left at 6, after a good night's rest, on the road to Inkandu, which is some distance past Lukunga Govt. station. Route very accidented.[18] Succession of round steep hills. At times

16. The most "Conradesque" phrase in the diary.
17. Compare "Heart of Darkness," p. 20: "Perhaps on some quiet night the tremor of far-off drums, sinking, swelling, a tremor vast, faint; a sound weird, appealing, suggestive, and wild—and perhaps with as profound a meaning as the sound of bells in a Christian country."
18. An odd Gallicism. Conrad knew French long before he knew English; moreover, he was naturally talking much French at this time.

walking along the crest of a chain of hills. Just before Lukunga our carriers took a wide sweep to the southward till the station bore N^th. Walking through long grass for 1½ hours. Crossed a broad river about 100 feet wide and 4 deep.

After another ½ hour's walk through manioc plantations in good order rejoined our route to the E^d of the Lukunga sta^on, walking along an undulating plain towards the Inkandu market on a hill. Hot, thirsty and tired. At 11 arrived on the m^ket place. About 200 people. Business brisk. No water; no camp^g place. After remaining for one hour left in search of a resting place. Row with carriers. No water. At last about 1½ P. M. camped on an exposed hill side near a muddy creek. No shade. Tent on a slope. Sun heavy. Wretched.

Direction N. E. by N.—Distance 22 miles.

Night miserably cold. No sleep. Mosquitos.

Tuesday, 8th July. Left at 6 A. M. About ten minutes from camp left main Gov^t path for the Manyanga track. Sky overcast. Rode up and down all the time, passing a couple of villages. The country presents a confused wilderness of hills, landslips on their sides showing red. Fine effect of red hill covered in places by dark green vegetation. ½ hour before beginning the descent got a glimpse of the Congo. Sky clouded.

To-day's march—3 h. General direction N. by E. Dist^ce 9½ miles.

Arrived at Manyanga at 9 A. M. Received most kindly by Messrs. Heyn and Jaeger. Most comfortable and pleasant halt.

Stayed here till the 25. Both have been sick. Most kindly care taken of us. Leave with sincere regrets.

Friday, the 25th July, 1890. Left Manyanga at 2½ P. M. with plenty of hammock carriers. H. lame and not in very good form. Myself ditto but not lame. Walked as far as Mafiela and camped—2 h.

Saturday, 26th. Left very early. Road ascending all the time. Passed villages. Country seems thickly inhabited. At 11 arrived at large market place. Left at noon and camped at 1 P. M.

General direction E ½ N-W ½ S. Sun visible at 8 A. M. Very hot. Distance 18 miles.

Sunday, 27th. Left at 8 A. M. Sent luggage carriers straight on to Luasi, and went ourselves round by the Mission of Sutili. Hospitable reception by Mrs. Comber. All the missio. absent. The looks of the whole establishment eminently civilized and very refreshing to see after the lots of tumbled down hovels in which the State & Company agents are content to live. Fine buildings. Position on a hill. Rather breezy.

Left at 3 P. M. At the first heavy ascent met Mr. Davis, Miss., returning from a preaching trip. Rev. Bentley away in the south with his wife. This being off the road, no section given.[19]

Distance traversed about 15 miles. Gen. direction E. N. E.

At Luasi we get on again on to the Gov[t] road.

Camped at 4½ P. M. with Mr. Heche in company. To-day no sunshine. Wind remarkably cold. Gloomy day.

Monday, 28th. Left camp at 6:30 after breakfasting with Heche. Road at first hilly. Then walking along the ridges of hill chains with valleys on both sides. The country more open and there is much more trees[20] growing in large clumps in the ravines.

Passed Nzungi and camped, 11, on the right bank of the Ngoma, a rapid little river with rocky bed. Village on a hill to the right.

General direction E. N. E.—Distance 14 miles.

No sunshine. Gloomy cold day. Squalls.

Tuesday, 29th. Left camp at 7, after a good night's rest. Continuous ascent; rather easy at first. Crossed wooded ravines and the river Lunzadi by a very decent bridge. At 9 met Mr. Louette escorting a sick agent of the comp[y] back to Matadi. Looking very well. Bad news from up the river. All the steamers disabled—one wrecked.[21] Country wooded. At 10:30 camped at Inkissi.

General direction E. N. E.—Dist[ce] 15 miles.

Sun visible at 6:30. Very warm day.

Inkissi River very rapid; is about 100 yards broad. Passage in canoes. Banks wooded very densely, and valley of the river rather deep, but very narrow.

To-day did not set the tent, but put up in Gov[t] shimbek. Zanzibari[22] in charge—very obliging. Met ripe pineapple for the first time. On the road to-day passed a skeleton tied up to a post. Also white man's grave—no name—heap of stones in the form of a cross. Health good now.

Wednesday, 30th. Left at 6 A. M. intending to camp at Kinfumu. Two hours sharp walk brought me to Nsona na Nsefe. Market. ½ hour after Harou arrived very ill with billious [sic] attack and fever. Laid him down in Gov[t] shimbek.

Dose of ipec[a]. Vomiting bile in enormous quantities. At 11 gave him 1 gramme of quinine and lots of hot tea. Hot fit ending in heavy perspiration. At 2 P. M. put him in hammock and started for Kinfumu. Row with carriers all the way.[23] Harou suffering much

19. Sections of the day's marches, with numerous names on them, were given under the following dates: July 3rd, 4th, 5th, 6th, 7th, 8th, 25th, 28th, 29th, 30th, 31st, August 1st.

20. One of the few un-English phrases in the diary. By 1890 Conrad had been a British subject for six years, but he never learnt the language until he was grown up.

21. Compare "Heart of Darkness," p. 21: "One of them [the white men at the Central Station] . . . informed me with great volubility and many digressions . . . that my steamer was at the bottom of the river."

22. See note 13.

23. Compare "Heart of Darkness," p. 21: "Then he [the white man with him] got fever, and had to be carried

through the jerks of the hammock. Camped at a small stream. At 4 Harou better; fever gone.

General direction N. E. by E. ½ E. Distance 13 miles.

Up till noon sky clouded and strong N. W. wind very chilling. From 1 P. M. to 4 P. M. sky clear and a very hot day. Expect lots of bother with carriers to-morrow. Had them all called and made a speech, which they did not understand.[24] They promise good behaviour.

Thursday, 31st. Left at 6. Sent Harou ahead, and followed in ½ an hour.[25]

Road presents several sharp ascents, and a few others easier but rather long. Notice in places sandy surface soil instead of hard clay as heretofore; think however that the layer of sand is not very thick and that the clay would be found under it. Great difficulty in carrying Harou. Too heavy—bother![26] Made two long halts to rest the carriers. Country wooded in valleys and on many of the ridges.

At 2:30 P. M. reached Luila at last, and camped on right bank. Breeze from S. W.

General direction of march about N. E. ½ E. Distance, est⁽ᵈ⁾ 16 miles.

Congo very narrow and rapid. Kinzilu rushing in. A short distance up from the mouth, fine waterfall. Sun rose red. From 9 A. M. infernally hot day. Harou very little better. Self rather seedy. Bathed. Luila about 60 feet wide. Shallow.

Friday, 1st of August, 1890. Left at 6:30 A. M. after a very indifferently passed night. Cold, heavy mists. Road in long ascents and sharp dips all the way to Mfumu Mbé. After leaving there, a long and painful climb up a very steep hill; then a long descent to Mfumu Kono, where a long halt was made. Left at 12:30 P. M. towards Nselemba. Many ascents. The aspect of the country entirely changed. Wooded hills with openings. Path almost all the afternoon thro' a forest of light trees with dense undergrowth.

After a halt on a wooded hillside, reached Nselemba at 4:10 P. M. Put up at Govᵗ shanty. Row between the carriers and a man, stating himself in Govᵗ employ, about a mat. Blows with sticks raining hard. Stopped it.

Chief came with a youth about 13 suffering from gun-shot wound in the head. Bullet entered about an inch above the right eyebrow, and came out a little inside the roots of the hair, fairly in the middle of the brow in a line with the bridge of the nose. Bone not damaged apparently. Gave him a little glycerine to put on the

in a hammock slung under a pole. As he weighed sixteen stone I had no end of rows with the carriers."
24. Compare "Heart of Darkness," p. 21: ". . . one evening, I made a speech in English with gestures, not one of which was lost to the sixty pairs of

eyes before me."
25. Compare "Heart of Darkness," p. 21: ". . . the next morning I started the hammock off in front all right."
26. Compare "Heart of Darkness," p. 21: ". . . he [the white man with him] weighed sixteen stone. . . ."

wound made by the bullet on coming out.

Harou not very well. Mosquitos—frogs—beastly! Glad to see the end of this stupid tramp. Feel rather seedy. Sun rose red. Very hot day. Wind S[th].

General direction of march N. E. by N. Distance about 17 miles.[27]

THE END

The second notebook, which is an entirely technical account of Congo navigation, written, no doubt, in relation to the then river charts, is not printed here, simply because it has no personal or literary interest. It is much longer than the first notebook, and is contained on seventy-nine pages, apart from several pages of rough outline maps. I reproduce a portion of one page, in order to show a sample:

> "11. N. (A) Long reach to a curved point. Great quantity of dangerous snags along the star[d] shore. Follow the slight bend of the shore with caution. The Middle of the Channel is a S—B— [sand bank] always covered. The more northerly of the two islands has its lower end bare of trees covered with grass and light green low bushes, then a low flat, and the upper end is timbered with light trees of a darker green tint."

It will be seen from this passage, which, though typical, is less technical than most, that the second notebook is not really, like the first, so much in the nature of a diary as of a specific aid to navigation. But those who recall the river journey in "Heart of Darkness," with its dangers and its difficulties, will perceive how this notebook, too, has played its special and impersonal part in the construction of that story.

The title-page of the first notebook is almost all torn out, but the title-page of the second reads, "Up-river Book, commenced 3 August 1890, S.S. *Roi des Belges*." [*from Richard Curle's introduction*]

* * *

JOSEPH CONRAD: [Stanley Falls, Early September 1890]†

Everything was dark under the stars. Every other white man on board was asleep. I was glad to be alone on deck, smoking the pipe of peace after an anxious day. The subdued thundering mutter of the Stanley Falls hung in the heavy night air of the last navigable

27. The journey from Matadi to this point by Stanley Pool took nineteen travelling days. Compare "Heart of Darkness," p. 21: "On the fifteenth day I came in sight of the big river [Congo]

again and hobbled into the Central Station."
† From "Geography and Some Explorers," *Last Essays*, ed. Richard Curle (London: J. M. Dent & Sons,

reach of the Upper Congo, while no more than ten miles away, in Reshid's camp just above the Falls, the yet unbroken power of the Congo Arabs slumbered uneasily. Their day was over.[1] Away in the middle of the stream, on a little island nestling all black in the foam of the broken water, a solitary little light glimmered feebly, and I said to myself with awe, "This is the very spot of my boyish boast."

A great melancholy descended on me. Yes, this was the very spot. But there was no shadowy friend to stand by my side in the night of the enormous wilderness, no great haunting memory, but only the unholy recollection of a prosaic newspaper "stunt"[2] and the distasteful knowledge of the vilest scramble for loot that ever disfigured the history of human conscience and geographical exploration. What an end to the idealized realities of a boy's daydreams! I wondered what I was doing there, for indeed it was only an unforeseen episode, hard to believe in now, in my seaman's life. Still, the fact remains that I have smoked a pipe of peace at midnight in the very heart of the African continent, and felt very lonely there.

JOSEPH CONRAD: Extracts from Correspondence, September 6–December 27, 1890†

Stanley Falls, 6 September 1890

M. Conrad Korzeniowski, Captain,

I beg herewith to ask you to take command of the S.S. *Roi des Belges* from this date until the recovery of Captain Koch.[1]

Believe me, etc.
Camille Delcommune

Ltd., 1926). P. 17. Reprinted by permission.

Conrad arrived in Kinshasa, the port for Leopoldville at Stanley Pool, on August 2 only to find that his ship was one of those which had been reported disabled on July 29 (see Diary). To learn the river while the ship was being repaired, Conrad was assigned on August 3 as second in command to Capt. Koch of the S.S. *Roi des Belges*, which left Kinshasa on August 4 for a relief trip up the river all the way to Stanley Falls, where it arrived September 1. On board with Conrad was Camille Delcommune (1859–92), the Acting Manager for the Trading Company of the Upper Congo and the brother of Alexandre, to whose Katanga exploring party Conrad had been assigned, in Brussels, as Captain.

1. Reshid was the nephew of the half-caste Arab Tipu-Tipu who ruled central Africa by force. Although Stanley had in the name of King Leopold made Tipu

Tipu the "governor" of the Stanley Falls area in 1887, by 1890 Tipu's incessant slaving and ivory raids had so incensed philanthropic and commercial interests alike that they for once joined power.

2. Stanley and Livingstone.

† From G. Jean-Aubry, *Joseph Conrad in the Congo* (London: William Heinemann, Ltd., 1926), pp. 67, 70–72. From *Life and Letters* (London: William Heinemann, Ltd.), 1927, I, 139. And from *Letters of Joseph Conrad to Marguerite Poradowska*, translated and edited by John A. Gee and Paul J. Sturm; copyright 1940 by Yale University Press; pp. 15–18. Selections reprinted by permission; *Life and Letters* by permission of J. M. Dent & Sons, Ltd. The style has been regularized by the present editor.

1. The manager was evidently anxious to return to Kinshasa because the agent at the Stanley Falls Station, Georges Antoine Klein, a Frenchman who had

Kinshasa, 24 September 1890

[My dear cousin Mariette,]

* * * I am very busy preparing for a new expedition on the Kassai River. I think that in a few days I shall once more leave Kinshasa for some months, perhaps more than ten months.[2] * * *

Kinshasa, 26 September 1890

Dearest and best of Aunts!

I received your three letters all at once on my return from Stanley Falls, where I went as supernumerary in the vessel *Roi des Belges* to learn the river. * * * My days here are dreary. Make no mistake about that! I am truly sorry to have come here. Indeed, I regret it bitterly. * * *

Everything is repellent to me here. Men and things, but especially men. And I am repellent to them, too. From the manager in Africa—who has taken the trouble of telling a good many people that I displease him intensely—down to the lowest mechanic, all have a gift for getting on my nerves; and consequently I am perhaps not as pleasant to them as I might be. The manager is a common ivory-dealer with sordid instincts who considers himself a merchant though he is only a kind of African shopkeeper. His name is Delcommune.[3] He hates the English, and I am of course regarded as an Englishman here. I can hope for neither promotion nor increase of salary while he remains here. Moreover, he has said that he is but little bound here by promises made in Europe, so long as they are not in the contract. Those made me by M. Wauters are not. Likewise I can look forward to nothing, as I have no vessel to command. The new boat will be finished in June of next year, perhaps. In the meanwhile my status here is vague, and I have been having troubles because of this. So there you are!

As a crowning joy, my health is far from good. *Keep the secret for me*, but the truth is that in going up the river I had the fever four times in two months, and then at the Falls (its native country) I had an attack of dysentery lasting five days. I feel rather weak physically and a little bit demoralized, and upon my word I think I am homesick for the sea and long to look again on the plains of that salt-water which has so often cradled me, which has so many times smiled at me under the glittering sunshine of a beautiful day, which many times too has flung the threat of death in my face with a whirl of white foam whipped by the wind under a dark December sky. I regret having to miss all that. But what I regret most of all

been in the Congo since early in 1889, was extremely weakened by dysentery; however, Klein died on board on September 21, and was buried at Bolobo. The *Roi des Belges*, pulling two barges probably full of ivory, made the return trip under Conrad's command.

2. With the Alexandre Delcommune Katanga expedition.

3. Camille Delcommune.

is having bound myself for three years. True, it is hardly likely I shall serve them out. Either those in authority will pick a German quarrel with me to ship me home (and on my soul I sometimes wish they would), or another attack of dysentery will send me back to Europe, if not into the other world, which last would be a final solution to all my troubles!

For four whole pages I have been talking about myself! I have said nothing of the delight with which I read your descriptions of men and things at home.[4] Truly, while reading your dear letters I forgot Africa, the Congo, the black savages and white slaves (of whom I am one) who inhabit it. I was happy for an hour. Know that it is not a small thing (or an easy thing) to make a human being happy for a *whole* hour. You may well be proud of having done it. And so my heart goes out to you in a burst of gratitude and sincerest, deepest affection. When shall we meet again? Alas, meeting leads to parting; and the more often one meets, the more painful become the separations. Fatality.

While seeking a practical remedy for the disagreeable situation into which I have got myself, I have thought of a little plan—still pretty much up in the air—with which you might perhaps help me. It seems that this Company or another affiliated with it is going to have some ocean-going vessels, and even has one already. Probably that big (or fat?) banker who rules the roost at home will have a sizeable interest in the other Company. If my name could be submitted for the command of one of their ships (whose home-port will be Antwerp), I might on each voyage run off to Brussels for a day or two when you are there. That would be ideal! If they decided to call me home to take a command, I should of course bear the expense of my return passage. This is perhaps not a very practical idea, but if you return to Brussels during the winter you might find out through M. Wauters what is going on, mightn't you, dear little aunt. * * *

I must close. I leave in an hour by canoe for Bamou, to select wood and have it cut to build the station here. I shall remain encamped in the forest two or three weeks, unless ill. I rather like that. Doubtless I can have a shot or two at buffalo or elephant. * * *

Lublin, Poland, 29 November 1890

[To Albert Thys, Director, Société du Haut Congo]

* * * I received a letter from Mr. Conrad Korzeniowski himself, who has just returned from Stanley Falls after two months' navigation on the up-river. * * * He tells me that his health is greatly affected, and he feels utterly demoralized. Further, the steamer of which he is to take command will not be ready before June, perhaps,

4. At Lublin in Poland.

and the Director, M. Delcommune, told him plainly that he was not to expect either promotion, or an increase in his salary, as long as he will be in the Congo. He also added that the promises made in Europe do not bind him in any way as long as they are not in the contract, and the promises which you were kind enough to make him are indeed not stated in the contract.

Mr. Korzeniowski's position, therefore, is as false as it can be, which is aggravated by these fevers and dysentery, which have greatly weakened him. Mr. Korzeniowski's family is naturally worried to hear this news; we all hoped that he would be able to stand the climate, but another voyage might destroy his health for always. You can understand that we are all very anxious, and that is why the family has asked me to write to you for advice so that we may know how to get this poor young man out of this dreadful position. * * *

It is sad to think that a capable man such as Mr. Conrad Korzeniowski, who has been used to commanding steamers for fifteen years, should be reduced to this subordinate position, and should be exposed to such fatal disease.

You seemed to have taken an interest in Mr. C. Korzeniowski, and during my stay in Brussels I was able to form an opinion of your kindness, and I hope that you will not withdraw your support, but that, on the contrary, you will advise him as to the steps he should take.

[Marguerite Poradowska]

Kazimierowka, 27 December 1890

My dear boy,

On the 24th I received your letter dated October 19th,[5] from Kinshasa, which informs me of the unfortunate end of your expedition to the Congo and your return to Europe. Mme. Marguerite (Poradowska) informed me also of it from Lublin, where she heard it through the Director of the Company, to whom she had written for news of you. * * *

[Tadeusz Bobrowski]

JOSEPH CONRAD: Two Final Notes†

I call to mind * * * a specially awkward turn of the Congo between Kinshasa and Leopoldville—more particularly when one had to take it at night in a big canoe with only half the proper

5. Early in October Alexandre Delcommune's Katanga party arrived in Kinshasa, and when it sailed on October 13 in the ship Conrad had been sent out to command, he was not aboard. Conrad sailed for Europe from Matadi on December 4, 1890.

† From *A Personal Record* (London: J. M. Dent & Sons, Ltd., 1912), p. 14. And from "Author's Note," *Tales of*

number of paddlers. I failed in being the second white man on record drowned at that interesting spot through the upsetting of a canoe. The first was a young Belgian officer, but the accident happened some months before my time, and he, too, I believe, was going home; not perhaps quite so ill as myself—but still he was going home. I got round the turn more or less alive, though I was too sick to care whether I did or not, and, always with "Almayer's Folly"[1] amongst my diminishing baggage, I arrived at that delectable capital Boma, where before the departure of the steamer which was to take me home I had the time to wish myself dead over and over again with perfect sincerity.

* * *

An Outpost of Progress is the lightest part of the loot I carried off from Central Africa, the main portion being of course the *Heart of Darkness*. Other men have found a lot of quite different things there and I have the comfortable conviction that what I took would not have been of much use to anybody else. And it must be said that it was but a very small amount of plunder. All of it could go into one's breast pocket when folded neatly. As for the story itself it is true enough in its essentials. The sustained invention of a really telling lie demands a talent which I do not possess.

ALBERT J. GUERARD: From Life to Art†

Heart of Darkness is the most famous of [Conrad's] personal short novels: a *Pilgrim's Progress* for our pessimistic and psychologizing age. "Before the Congo I was just a mere animal."[1] The living nightmare of 1890 seems to have affected Conrad quite as importantly as did Gide's Congo experience thirty-six years later.[2] The autobiographical basis of the narrative is well known, and its introspective bias obvious; this is Conrad's longest journey into self. But it is well to remember that "Heart of Darkness" is also other if more superficial things: a sensitive and vivid travelogue, and a comment on "the vilest scramble for loot that ever disfigured the history of human conscience and geographical exploration."[3] The Congo was much in the public mind in 1889, when Henry Stanley's

Unrest (London: J. M. Dent & Sons, Ltd., 1921), p. x. Selections reprinted by permission.
1. Conrad began his career as a writer quite unpremeditatedly one morning in London while looking for a ship in 1889. He continued to work on his manuscript during his visit to his Uncle Tadeusz early in 1890 and had seven chapters with him in the Congo.
† From *Conrad the Novelist*, pp. 33–38. Cambridge, Mass. Copyright 1958 by the Fellows of Harvard College. Reprinted by permission.
1. See below, p. 125.
2. See *Travels in the Congo*, Paris, 1927 and New York, 1929.
3. See above, p. 118.

relief expedition found Emin Pasha (who like Kurtz did not want to be rescued),[4] and it is interesting to note that Conrad was in Brussels during or immediately after Stanley's triumphant welcome there in April 1890. This was just before he set out on his own Congo journey. We do not know how much the Georges Antoine Klein who died on board the *Roi des Belges* resembled the fictional Kurtz, but Stanley himself provided no mean example of a man who could gloss over the extermination of savages with pious moralisms which were very possibly "sincere."

Heart of Darkness thus has its important public side, as an angry document on absurd and brutal exploitation. Marlow is treated to the spectacle of a French man-of-war shelling an unseen "enemy" village in the bush, and presently he will wander into the grove at the first company station where the starving and sick Negroes withdraw to die. It is one of the greatest of Conrad's many moments of compassionate rendering. The compassion extends even to the cannibal crew of the *Roi des Belges*. Deprived of the rotten hippo meat they had brought along for food, and paid three nine-inch pieces of brass wire a week, they appear to subsist on "lumps of some stuff like half-cooked dough, of a dirty lavender color" which they keep wrapped in leaves. Conrad here operates through ambiguous suggestion (are the lumps human flesh?) but elsewhere he wants, like Gide after him, to make his complacent European reader *see:* see, for instance, the drunken unkempt official met on the road and three miles farther on the body of the Negro with a bullet hole in his forehead.[5] *Heart of Darkness* is a record of things seen and done. But also Conrad was reacting to the humanitarian pretenses of some of the looters precisely as the novelist today reacts to the moralisms of cold-war propaganda. Then it was ivory that poured from the heart of darkness; now it is uranium. Conrad shrewdly recognized—an intuition amply developed in *Nostromo*—that deception is most sinister when it becomes self-deception, and the propagandist takes seriously his own fictions. Kurtz "could get himself to believe anything—anything." The benevolent rhetoric of his seventeen-page report for the International Society for the Suppression of Savage Customs was meant sincerely enough. But a deeper sincerity spoke through his scrawled postscript: "Exterminate all the brutes!" The conservative Conrad (who found Donkin[6] fit to be a labor leader) speaks through the journalist who says that

---

4. Emin Pasha, an agent of the Egyptian government, was perfectly content to sit in the center of Africa and amass large amounts of ivory. Naturally the commercial interests of Europe became "concerned" and started a private subscription to finance his relief—and the relief of his ivory.

5. Compare "The Congo Diary," above, p. 112. Conrad did not use the skeleton tied to a post that he saw on Tuesday, July 29. It might have seemed too blatant or too "literary" in a novel depending on mortuary imagery from beginning to end [from Guerard's note].
6. In *The Nigger of the "Narcissus."*

"Kurtz's proper sphere ought to have been politics 'on the popular side.' "

* * *

In any event, it is time to recognize that the story is not primarily about Kurtz or about the brutality of Belgian officials but about Marlow its narrator. To what extent it also expresses the Joseph Conrad a biographer might conceivably recover, who in 1898 still felt a debt must be paid for his Congo journey and who paid it by the writing of this story, is doubtless an insoluble question. I suspect two facts (of a possible several hundred) are important. First, that going to the Congo was the enactment of a childhood wish associated with the disapproved childhood ambition to go to sea, and that this belated enactment was itself profoundly disapproved, in 1890, by the uncle and guardian.[7] It was another gesture of a man bent on throwing his life away. But even more important may be the guilt of complicity, just such a guilt as many novelists of the Second World War have been obliged to work off. What Conrad thought of the expedition of the Katanga Company of 1890–1892 is accurately reflected in his remarks on the "Eldorado Exploring Expedition" of *Heart of Darkness:* "It was reckless without hardihood, greedy without audacity, and cruel without courage . . . with no more moral purpose at the back of it than there is in burglars breaking into a safe." Yet Conrad hoped to obtain command of the expedition's ship even after he had returned from the initiatory voyage dramatized in his novel. Thus the adventurous Conrad and Conrad the moralist may have experienced collision. But the collision, again as with so many novelists of the second war, could well have been deferred and retrospective, not felt intensely at the time.

WRITING THE STORY

But the Dwarf answered: 'No; something human is dearer to me than the wealth of all the world.'

—Epigraph to *Youth* (from Grimm's *Tales*).

The interview of the man and the girl locks in—as it were—the whole 30,000 words of narrative description into one suggestive view of a whole phase of life, and makes of that story something quite on another plane than an anecdote of a man who went mad in the Center of Africa.

—CONRAD, May 1902.

G. JEAN-AUBRY: [From Sailor to Novelist]†

Conrad's health was affected during all the rest of his life by this African expedition. He suffered from attacks of the gout which made

7. See *Life and Letters*, I, 137 [from Guerard's note].

† From *Life and Letters* (London: William Heinemann, Ltd., 1927), I, 141–42. Reprinted by permission of J. M. Dent & Sons, Ltd.

his life an intermittent martyrdom. But, on the other hand, it is a not unlikely supposition that this journey to the Congo and its unfortunate consequences gave us the great writer. * * * The illness which he brought back from the Congo, by limiting his physical activity and confining him to his room for several months, obliged him to withdraw into himself, to call up those memories with which his life, though he was only thirty-five, was already extraordinarily full, and to try to estimate their value both from the human and the literary point of view. * * * It may be said that Africa killed Conrad the sailor and strengthened Conrad the novelist.

EDWARD GARNETT: [Art Drawn from Memory]†

I agree with M. Jean-Aubry that Conrad's Congo experiences were the turning-point in his mental life and that its effects on him determined his transformation from a sailor to a writer. According to his emphatic declaration to me, in his early years at sea he had "not a thought in his head". "I was a perfect animal", he reiterated, meaning, of course, that he had reasoned and reflected hardly at all over all the varieties of life he had encountered. The sinister voice of the Congo with its murmuring undertone of human fatuity, baseness and greed had swept away the generous illusions of his youth, and had left him gazing into the heart of an immense darkness.

* * *

Great quickness of eye was one of Conrad's gifts. I remember while sitting one evening with him in the Café Royal I asked him, after a painted lady had brushed haughtily past our table, what he had specially noticed about her. "The dirt in her nostril", he replied instantly. On this acute sense rested his faculty of selecting the telling detail, an unconscious faculty, so he said. I remarked once of the first draft of *The Rescuer*, that as a seaman he must have noted professionally the details of the rainstorm at sea described in Chapter III. Conrad denied this, and asserted that all such pictures of nature had been stored up unconsciously in his memory, and that they only sprung into life when he took up the pen. That Conrad's memory had extraordinary wealth of observation to draw on I had an illuminating proof in *Heart of Darkness*. Some time be-

† From "Introduction," *Letters from Conrad 1895–1924* (London: The Nonesuch Press, 1928). Pp. xii, xviii–xix. Reprinted by permission.

Edward Garnett (1865–1937), essayist and dramatist, as a reader for the publishing house of Fisher Unwin "discovered" Conrad in 1894. After successfully arguing for the publication of Conrad's first work, *Almayer's Folly*, Garnett convinced Conrad that he should forsake the sea to become a writer. They remained lifelong friends. See Garnett's review of the *Youth* volume (*The Academy*, December 6, 1902) and Conrad's reaction (*Letters from Conrad*, pp. 187–88).

fore he wrote this story of his Congo experience he narrated it at length one morning while we were walking up and down under a row of Scotch firs that leads down to the Cearne.[1] I listened enthralled while he gave me in detail a very full synopsis of what he intended to write. To my surprise when I saw the printed version I found that about a third of the most striking incidents had been replaced by others of which he had said nothing at all. The effect of the written narrative was no less sombre than the spoken, and the end was more consummate; but I regretted the omission of various scenes, one of which described the hero lying sick to death in a native hut, tended by an old negress who brought him water from day to day, when he had been abandoned by all the Belgians. "She saved my life", Conrad said; "the white men never came near me." When on several occasions in those early years I praised his psychological insight he questioned seriously whether he possessed such a power and deplored the lack of opportunities for intimate observation that a sailor's life had offered him. On one occasion on describing to him a terrible family tragedy of which I had been an eye-witness, Conrad became visibly ill-humoured and at last cried out with exasperation: "Nothing of the kind has ever come my way! I have spent half my life knocking about in ships, only getting ashore between voyages. I know nothing, nothing! except from the outside. I have to guess at everything!" This was of course the artist's blind jealousy speaking, coveting the experiences he had not got, and certainly he could have woven a literary masterpiece out of the threads I held, had he known the actors.

RICHARD CURLE: [His Piercing Memory]†

He never kept any notes, and even his Congo diary, which gives so many hints for *Heart of Darkness*, survived only by chance and was, as I gather from Mrs. Conrad (who told me she had retrieved it from the waste-paper basket), never consulted by Conrad when writing that story.

* * *

This story was serialized in *Blackwood's Magazine* between February and April, 1899, and I remember Conrad telling me that its 40,000 words occupied only about a month in writing. When we consider the painful, slow labour with which he usually composed, we can perceive how intensely vivid his memories of this experience

1. The Cearne was Garnett's home in Surrey. This incident took place in early September, 1898.
† From *The Last Twelve Years of Joseph Conrad* by Richard Curle. Copyright © 1928 by Doubleday and Company Inc. P. 67. Reprinted by permission of the publisher. And from "The Congo Diary," *Last Essays*, ed. Richard Curle (London: J. M. Dent & Sons, Ltd., 1926). Pp. 158, 160. Reprinted by permission.

must have been, and * * * how intensely actual. But then the notebook only goes to prove the almost self-evident contention that much of Conrad's work is founded upon autobiographical remembrance. Conrad himself wrote of this story in his Author's Note [1917] to * * * the *Youth* volume in which it appeared: "*Heart of Darkness* is quite as authentic in fundamentals as *Youth* . . . it is experience pushed a little (and only a little) beyond the actual facts of the case."

* * *

No other diary of Conrad's is extant, and I am very sceptical as to whether he ever kept another. He was not at all that type of man, and his piercing memory for essentials was quite sufficient for him to recreate powerfully vanished scenes and figures for the purposes of his work.

FORD MADOX FORD: [The Setting]†

Heart of Darkness is a tale told *viva voce* by a ship's captain on the deck of a cruising yawl, to a Director of Companies, a Lawyer, and an Accountant, all of whom followed the sea to the extent of taking week-end cruises in the *Nellie*—the cruising yawl. They formed the society in which Conrad lived at Stamford-le-Hope[1] while, having left the sea but living near its verge, he was still quivering with his attempt, with the aid of the Director, the Lawyer, and the Accountant, to float a diamond mine in South Africa. For Conrad had his adventures of that sort, too—adventures ending naturally in frustration. And since, while waiting for that financial flotation to mature, he floated physically during week-ends in the company of those financiers on the bosom of that tranquil waterway, he really believed that all the bankers, lawyers, and accountants of the obscure square mile of city upstream were also seamen, or so near it as made no difference. He emerged, of course, from that conviction, but the tragedy was that, by the time he came to see life more collectively and less as a matter of Conway-trained[2] and steadfast individuals heroically fighting August northwesters, the unseeing and malignant destiny that waits on us writers set him in such circumstances as robbed him of the leisure in which *Youth* and *Heart of Darkness* could be written. For those two stories were written and

† From "Heart of Darkness," *Portraits from Life* by Ford Madox Ford. Copyright © 1936 and 1937 by Ford Madox Ford. Pp. 59–60. Reprinted by permission of Houghton Mifflin Company.

Ford Madox Ford (Hueffer) (1873–1939), English poet, novelist, and critic, knew Conrad intimately and collaborated with him on three books, the first of which was begun in the fall of 1898.
1. In Essex, from September 1896 to September 1898.
2. The *Conway* was an Admiralty training ship.

re-written and filed and thought over and re-thought over by a lei-
sured mind of a rare literary common sense.

* * *

While he was still under the spell of sea-following and the hypno-
tism of mariners, he did his best and, as it were, cleanest work. For
I think it is to *Youth, Heart of Darkness*, and the matchless *Nigger
of the "Narcissus"* that those epithets must be ascribed, leaving *Almayer* and *The Outpost of Progress* to be considered as his prentice
work.

JOSEPH CONRAD: Extracts from Correspondence, December 13, 1898–February 12, 1899†

13 December 1898

Dear Mr. Blackwood,[1]

I owe you a great many thanks for the *Maga*[2] which reaches me
with a most charming regularity. In truth it is the only monthly I
care to read, and each number is very welcome, though each is a
sharp jog to my conscience. And yet, God knows, it is wide-awake
enough and daily avenges the many wrongs my patient publishers
suffer at my hands.

And this is all I can say unless I were to unfold for the nth time
the miserable tale of my inefficiency. I trust however that in January I'll be able to send you about 30,000 words or perhaps a little
less, towards the Volume of short stories.[3] Apart from my interest
it is such a pleasure for me to appear in the *Maga* that you may well
believe it is not laziness that keeps me back. It is, alas, something—
I don't know what—not so easy to overcome. With immense effort
a thin trickle of MS is produced—and that, just now, must be kept
in one channel only lest no one gets anything and I am completely
undone.

18 December 1898

My dearest Garnett,

* * * Now I am at a short story for Blackwood which I must
get out for the sake of shekels.

† From G. Jean-Aubry, *Life and Letters* (London: William Heinemann,
Ltd., 1927), I, 265, 268. From *Joseph
Conrad: Letters to William Blackwood
and David S. Meldrum*, edited by William Blackburn; copyright 1958 by
Duke University Press; pp. 33–51.
From *Letters from Conrad 1895–1924*,
edited by Edward Garnett; copyright
1928 by the Nonesuch Press; pp. 142,
147. And from *Lettres Françaises*,
edited by G. Jean-Aubry; copyright
1929 by the Librairie Gallimard; p. 36.
Selections reprinted by permission; *Life*

and Letters by permission of J. M. Dent
& Sons, Ltd. The present editor has
regularized the style.
1. The fifth editor of the famed *Blackwood's Magazine*, established 1817 in
Edinburgh, as a monthly literary journal.
2. The nickname for *Blackwood's Magazine.*
3. Agreed to in May or June 1898 on
the strength of the just-completed
Youth and eighteen pages of "Jim:
A Sketch," which turned out to be *Lord
Jim*. See below, p. 134, n. 3.

21 December 1898

Dear Mr. Meldrum,[4]

* * * I am writing something for *Maga*, a tale (short) in the manner of *Youth*, to be ready in a few days.

30 December 1898

Dear Mr. Conrad,

* * * I am hoping to have the pleasure of seeing your hand in *Maga* again soon, and I should be specially pleased if you had anything on the stocks, or nearly ready, to send me for *Maga*'s Thousandth number, which you will have seen from the slip inserted in the January number takes place in February. It would give me pleasure to see something from your pen in that number, but I will require to know soon if you think of having something ready in time for it. Will you also let me know about what space you will require, so that I may arrange accordingly. * * *

Yours Very Sincerely,
William Blackwood

31 December 1898

Dear Mr. Blackwood,

Come this moment to hand is your good letter whose kind wishes, believe me, I reciprocate with all my heart.

Your proposal delights me. As it happens I am (and have been for the last 10 days) working for *Maga*. The thing is far advanced and would have been finished by this only our little boy fell ill, I was disturbed and upset and the work suffered. I expect to be ready in a very few days. It is a narrative after the manner of *Youth* told by the same man dealing with his experience on a river in Central Africa. The *idea* in it is not as obvious as in *Youth*—or at least not so obviously presented. I tell you all this, for tho' I have no doubts as to the *workmanship* I do not know whether the *subject* will commend itself to you for that particular number. Of course I should be very glad to appear in it and shall try to hurry up the copy for that express purpose, but I wish you to understand that I am prepared to leave the ultimate decision as to the date of appearance to your decision after perusal.

The title I am thinking of is *The Heart of Darkness* but the narrative is not gloomy. The criminality of inefficiency and pure selfishness when tackling the civilizing work in Africa is a justifiable idea. The subject is of our time distinctly—though not topically treated. It is a story as much as my *Outpost of Progress* was but, so to speak 'takes in' more—is a little wider—is less concentrated

4. Blackwood's literary advisor in London, whose office was on Paternoster Row.

upon individuals. I destine it for the volume which is to bear your imprint. Its length will be under 20,000 words as I see it now. If suitable and you wish to curtail it, a couple of paragraphs could be taken out—from the proof, perhaps. * * *

All I can do is to hurry up. Meantime many thanks for thinking of me.

2 January 1899

Dear Mr. Meldrum,

I enclose here a letter from Mr. Blackwood and a note (at the back of my reply).

This will make it clear to you how matters are. I am very pleased Mr. B'wood thought of me; but his letter coming just now makes it difficult for me to do what I intended doing—or at least I fancy so.

I began the story for *Maga* 10 days ago. It would have been finished yesterday had it not been our boy fell ill (he is better now) and thus knocked on the head my peace of mind and, say, inspiration. At any rate there is a delay. Now my intention was to ask Mr. Blackwood to let me have £40 before the 10th Jan. on the *general* account of my short stories (serial & book). The story would have covered the sum or more; but now the story is not quite ready and my necessity remains all the same. Still I would have asked for the cheque had it not been for this extremely pleasant letter. I don't want Mr. B'wood to think I am taking advantage of his ouverture. In this difficulty real or fancied may I ask you whether you could arrange the matter for me with Mr. B'wood. The story shall be in your hands shortly; it will be about 20,000 words (at the agreed rate for serial it would be about £50). My necessity is not a matter of life or death, but of the very greatest inconvenience of which I would fain be relieved by your good offices. If you think I could ask Mr. B'wood without gross indecency please mediate. I've just written to him and don't want to fire off another letter. And you can put a better look on the thing.

If you want to refer to the story its title so far is *The Heart of Darkness*.

A Central African narrative in the manner of *Youth*—told by the same man.

It would stand dividing into two instalments.

I would like you particularly to read the story and the type shall go to London. As I write this one in pencil my wife *must* type herself, or I would send you the MS of what is ready. A mere shadow of love interest just in the last pages—but I hope it will have the effect I intend. * * *

6 January 1899

Dear Mr. Blackwood,

Thanks very much for the cheque for £40 (on account of short stories) which I received to-day. * * *

I assure you I appreciate your prompt readiness. I am—alas! not so prompt. Still tomorrow I shall send off about 12,000 of H of D to Mr. Meldrum. * * *

Lots more of the story is written—not typed, and in a few days shall be dispatched. I am afraid it will be too long for one number. It has grown upon me a bit—and anyhow the value is in the detail.

6 January 1899

Dear Madam,[5]

* * * Only a word in great haste, for I am deeply entrenched in the midst of a piece which impatiently waits and waits for me ever since November when it should have been finished, and it is still there,—on my desk. * * *

9 January 1899

Dear Mr. Meldrum,

I send you pp. 1 to 35 typed of *The Heart of Darkness* and from 35 (typed) it goes on to p. 58 of Manuscript—pp. 58 to 90, which is all written up to yesterday. I am awfully sorry to send the pencil MS but my wife is not well enough to go on and I want you to have the first half of the story at once. May I ask you to have *the Whole* typed out on my account in at least 2 copies. One for Mr. McClure[6] and one for *Maga*. The type *from the MS* should be corrected by me before going to printers so you perhaps will let me have that portion for that purpose as soon as ready.

I had a friendly letter and cheque for £40 from Mr. Blackwood. I am in doubt as to the 1000th Number. There will be no time for U.S. Copyright. And I can't forego a penny. Are you angry with me for the bother I am giving? I am working under difficulties and that's the truth. * * *

12 January 1899

Dear Mrs. Bontine,[7]

* * * Pardon this hurried scrawl. I am finishing in a frightful hurry a story for *Blackwood* and it's an immense effort.

5. Baroness de Brunnow, a friend of Conrad's youth in Cracow, Poland.
6. Robert McClure, of S. S. McClure Co., Conrad's American publisher. Because McClure had failed to get an American copyright on *Youth* before it appeared in *Maga* the *Atlantic Monthly* was not able to carry out its plan to take it. Conrad was understandably upset that *Outlook* (New York) reprinted *Youth* in October and, in the absence of international copyright, he did not get a cent. However, McClure's secured the rights on "The Heart of Darkness" (the serial title) before the February number of *Maga* and published it in 1903 in the first American edition of the *Youth* volume.
7. Mother of Robert Bontine Cunninghame Graham (see note 12, below).

My dear Garnett,   13 January 1899

* * * Ah if I could only write! If I could write, write, write!
But I cannot. No 50 guineas[8] will help me to that. However I am
turning over some rotten stuff for Blackwood's 1000th Number.
Been asked to! * * *

William Blackwood and Sons   13 January 1899
Dear Sirs:

I have marked (on the last page, p. 65)[9] the place where the
first installment might end.

It would be about *half* of the whole story or perhaps a little more.
I shall hurry up the rest as fast as I can. * * *

My dear Mr. Meldrum,   13 January 1899

* * * I shall come up as soon as H of D is finished. I've sent
the balance of type to Edinburgh. * * *

Dear Mr. Meldrum,   16 January 1899

* * * As soon as I am done with the H of D I shall write you
and the day after call on you in Paternoster Row. It will be before
end of this month for certain.

The thing has grown on me. I don't think it will be bad. * * *

Dear Mr. Blackwood,   8 February 1899

Thanks very much for the wire. It put my mind at ease, for I
felt the balance of the story was a little too long for one installment.[10] * * *

I get letters from various people who seem to like the thing, so
far. * * *

Dear Mr. Meldrum,   8 February 1899

I had a wire from Mr. Blackwood advising me that the story is

8. The *Academy*, a literary review, had
awarded Conrad a prize for his five,
collected *Tales of Unrest* (1898).
9. This refers to the balance of the
manuscript (pages 58–90), which Mc-
Clure had had typed and sent back to
Conrad for correction. The thirty-five
pages which Mrs. Conrad had typed
McClure had already sent to Edinburgh.
William Blackburn, ed., *Joseph Conrad: Letters to William Blackwood and
David S. Meldrum* (Durham, N.C.,
1958), p. 45, mistakenly has dated this
letter February 7, 1899.

10. Some time toward the end of January Conrad sent through Meldrum to
Blackwood a part of the second (and
"final") installment of the story. At
that time the plan was still to run "The
Heart of Darkness" (the serial title) in
two parts, February and March, but
when Conrad finished the "balance of
the story" on 6 February he felt that
the whole would be too long for one
number and wired Meldrum asking that
the story be extended to the April number.

to go into three numbers.

I've sent the completed MS. to Edinburgh direct, by Tuesday's morning post.[11]

I think it will be 40,000 words. The first installment was about 14,000 (27 pages) and the two others should run to 12,000 each. I had £40 on account and (oppressed by my usual impecuniosity) would like to have the balance at once (£50–60). * * *

I like the story, tho' it is terribly bad in places and falls short of my intention as a whole. Still I am glad I wrote it. * * *

8 February 1899

Chérissime Ami,[12]

I am simply in the seventh heaven to find you like the "H. of D." so far. You bless me indeed. Mind you don't curse me by and by for the very same thing. There are two more installments in which the idea is so wrapped up in secondary notions that you,—even you!— may miss it. And also you must remember that I don't start with an abstract notion. I start with definite images and as their rendering is true some little effect is produced. So far the note struck chimes in with your convictions,—*mais après?* There is an *après*.[13] But I think that if you look a little into the episodes, you will find in them the right intention, though I fear nothing that is practically effective.

Somme toute, c'est une bête d'histoire qui aurait pu être quelque chose de très bien si j'avais su l'écrire.[14] * * *

11 February 1899

Dearest Jack,[15]

* * * The finishing of *H of D* took a lot out of me. I haven't been able to do much since.

12 February 1899

Dear Mr. Blackwood,

* * * Thanks very much for what you send and still more for what you say. The cheque for £60 now received and the previous one of £40 on account of the same tale (*H of D*) will probably overpay it as I do not think it will run to 40,000 words. I did write that number or even more but I've been revising and compressing

11. February 7, 1899.
12. R. B. Cunninghame Graham (1852–1936), Scottish writer, aristocrat, and socialist, who wrote Conrad an enthusiastic letter in the summer of 1897 when *An Outpost of Progress* first appeared. Although the two quickly became and remained close friends, the difference between them is signaled by the fact that when Conrad refused in 1903 to support Roger Casement's work in the Congo, he forwarded the appeal to Cunninghame Graham. See above, p. 97, n. 3, and *Life and Letters*, I, 324–26.
13. "—but later on? There is a sequel."
14. "In short, it is a silly story which might have been something quite fine if I had known how to write it."
15. John Galsworthy (1867–1933), British novelist and dramatist, who was at this time Conrad's neighbor. They remained lifelong friends.

the end not a little.[16] The proof of the second installment I kept only twelve hours—not knowing but it might have been wanted at once. I marked a place—on p. 24— where a break is, at least, practicable. If it does not commend itself to your judgment there may be a better place, somewhere within the last installment of typed MS, I've sent to Edinburgh on Tuesday last. My own MS copy is in such confusion and moreover so unlike the final 'type' that I could not venture on its authority to indicate any final sentence or paragraph for the ending of part 2[d].

I am delighted to hear you like the Story. * * *

I wonder what you will think of the end of the Story. I've been writing up to it and it loomed rather effective till I came to it actually. Still I am not altogether dissatisfied with the manner of it; but of course one cannot judge one's own *fresh* work—at any rate.

FORD MADOX FORD: [The Ending]†

I will add some further notations as to the passage I have quoted from *Heart of Darkness*.[1] It has always seemed to me—and still seems—one of the most perfect passages of prose in the language and it has for me a certain added significance from the fact that it must have been the first passage of Conrad's prose to which I ever paid minute and letter-by-letter consideration. He had come to stop with me at the Pent,[2] and had there received the proofs of the story in one or another of its stages.[3] And being worried over—and above all having the leisure to attend to—his closing passages, it was the last paragraph to which he first invited me to pay attention.

We must have argued over it for three whole days, going from time to time over the beginning and the body of the story, but always at the back of the mind considering that last paragraph and returning to it to suggest one or another minute change in wording or in punctuation.

If you will take the trouble to look back to the passage as I have quoted it, you will see that it begins, 'We have lost the first of the ebb.' Actually, in the copy from which I am quoting—Doubleday,

16. Conrad took advantage of the extension of the story into three parts by rewriting the ending. It is not possible to tell when he actually finished the manuscript.

† From "Heart of Darkness," *Portraits from Life* by Ford Madox Ford. Copyright © 1936 and 1937 by Ford Madox Ford. Pp. 61–63. Reprinted by permission of Houghton Mifflin Company.

1. The last three sentences of the story.
2. Ford's home in Kent, where Conrad moved at the end of September 1898 after having met Ford at the Garnetts the same month.
3. Probably the proofs for the projected Blackwood volume of three stories, only

two of which, *Youth* and *Heart of Darkness*, were completed. The third was to have been *Lord Jim*, but as the fall of 1899 and winter of 1900 passed *Jim* got to be so long that Blackwood decided that he would have to issue it separately as a novel after its serial appearance in *Maga*. Although Conrad returned proof on *Heart of Darkness* by the end of February 1900 and it was in plates by the middle of May, the *Youth* volume did not appear until late 1902, with *The End of the Tether* as the third story. No extant version of the story has a last paragraph such as Ford describes. See also Ford, *Joseph Conrad* (Boston, 1924), pp. 168–71.

Doran's Malay edition of 1928—the last paragraph begins, 'Marlow ceased and sat apart, indistinct and silent, in the pose of a meditating Buddha. Nobody moved for a time,' and then continues with the Director's speech.

In the original version, those last two sentences stood apart, the word 'time' ending the paragraph. And we tried every possible juxtaposition of those sentences, putting 'No one moved for a time' in front of Marlow's ceasing; running that sentence up to the end of the last paragraph of speech; cutting it out altogether—because the first principle of the technique of Conrad and myself at that time was that you should never state a negative. If nobody moves, you do not have to make the statement; just as, if somebody is silent, you just do not record any speech of his, and leave it at that.

However, that negative statement got itself left in at the end, I suppose as a matter of cadence, though I remember suggesting the excision of 'for a time'—a suggestion that Conrad turned down because that would have made the statement too abrupt and dramatic. The last paragraph of a story should have the effect of what musicians call a coda—a passage meditative in tone, suited for letting the reader or hearer gently down from the tense drama of the story, in which all his senses have been shut up, into the ordinary workaday world again.

In the interest of that tranquillity, either Conrad or I suggested the use of the adjectival-participle form in the last clause of the paragraph. I can't remember which of us it was, because we changed our position morning by morning, according as the one or the other of us had got up feeling the more French. We never read anything but French in those days, but sometimes Conrad, and less often I, would have a British reaction. . . . And to make that passage classic English prose, you would have to put it:

> . . . the tranquil waterway, leading to the uttermost ends of the earth, flowing sombre under an overcast sky, seemed to lead into the heart of an immense darkness.

Or, since Conrad—or, in the alternative, I—might object to the assonance of 'flowing' and 'leading':

> the tranquil waterway, leading to the uttermost ends of the earth, flowed sombre under an overcast sky, seemed to lead into the heart of an immense darkness.

Which last would be the version I should today adopt, as being, with its punctuation and all, the most tranquilly classic.

But I suppose that, in the end, we both of us got up one morning feeling unbridledly and unrepentantly Gallic—and so you have only one comma and a French dash for punctuation of the whole sentence and the relatively harsh 'seemed,' instead of the tender 'seeming.'

CONRAD'S MANUSCRIPT OF
HEART OF DARKNESS†

cried with a cry that was no more
than a breath —
— "Oh! The horror!"

I blew the candle out and left the
cabin. Never before in his life had
he been say ??? a master of
his magnificent ??? in this his last speech
on earth. The eloquence of ???

The pilgrims were dining in the mess
cabin and I went in and took my
place opposite the Manager who lifted his
eyes to give me a questioning glance
which I ignored. He leaned back serene
with that peculiar smile of his sealing
the unexpressed depths of his meanness.
A continuous shower of small flies streamed
upon the lamp, upon the cloth, upon
our hands and faces. Suddenly
the Manager's boy put his insolent
black face in the doorway and
said in a tone of scathing

"Oh! The horror!"

† Courtesy of Yale University Library

Contempt—

—"Mistah Kurtz—he dead."

All the pilgrims rushed out to see. I remained and went on with my dinner. I believe I was considered brutally callous. However I did not eat much. There was a lamp in there—light—don't you know—and outside it was so beastly, beastly dark. I went no more near the remarkable man who had so unhesitatingly pronounced a judgment upon the adventures of his soul on this earth. The voice was gone. What else had been there? The pilgrims buried something next day in a muddy hole.

"Mistah Kurtz—he dead."

whisper all around us in a whisper
that seemed to swell menacingly
like the first whisper of a rising
wind "Oh! the horror!"

—n this last word—to live with" she
murmured. "Don't you understand
I loved him — I loved him."

I pulled myself together and spoke slowly.

—"The last word he pronounced
was—your name".

I heard a light sigh and then
my heart stood still
a cry of inconceivable triumph
and of unspeakable pain.
"I knew it — I was sure!" She
knew. She was sure. It seemed to
me the house would collapse, the
heavens would fall upon my
head. But nothing happened. The
heavens do not fall for such a
trifle. Would they have fallen,
I wonder, if I had rendered Kurtz justice?

"The last word he pronounced was—your name."

He wanted only justice.

Hadn't he said, he wanted only justice? But I couldn't. I could not tell her. It would have been too dark too dark it would have been too dark — too dark altogether...

Marlow ceased and sat apart in the pose of a meditating Buddha. Nobody moved for a time. "We have lost the first of the ebb," said the Director suddenly. I looked around. The offing was barred by a black bank of clouds and the tranquil waterway leading to the uttermost ends of the earth flowing sombre under an overcast sky seemed to lead into the heart of an immense darkness.

The End

... into the heart of an immense darkness.

CONRAD ON LIFE AND ART

Most of the working truths on this earth are humble, not heroic; and there
have been times in the history of mankind when the accents of heroic truth have
moved it to nothing but derision.

—1912

My task which I am trying to achieve is, by the power of the written word,
to make you hear, to make you feel—it is above all, to make you *see*.

—1897

[Fidelity: Four Notes]†

Those who read me know my conviction that the world, the temporal world, rests on a few very simple ideas; so simple that they
must be as old as the hills. It rests notably, among others, on the idea
of Fidelity. At a time when nothing which is not revolutionary in
some way or other can expect to attract much attention I have not
been revolutionary in my writings. The revolutionary spirit is mighty
convenient in this, that it frees one from all scruples as regards ideas.
Its hard, absolute optimism is repulsive to my mind by the menace
of fanaticism and intolerance it contains. No doubt one should smile
at these things; but, imperfect Aesthete, I am no better Philosopher.
All claim to special righteousness awakens in me that scorn and
anger from which a philosophical mind should be free.

* * *

"Work is the law. Like iron that lying idle degenerates into a mass
of useless rust, like water that in an unruffled pool sickens into a
stagnant and corrupt state, so without action the spirit of men turns
to a dead thing, loses its force, ceases prompting us to leave some
trace of ourselves on this earth." The sense of the above lines does
not belong to me. It may be found in the note-books of one of the
greatest artists that ever lived, Leonardo da Vinci. It has a simplicity
and a truth which no amount of subtle comment can destroy.

---

† From "A Familiar Preface" (1912), *Conrad's Prefaces*, ed. Edward Garnett (London: J. M. Dent & Sons, Ltd., 1937), p. 208. From "Tradition" (1918) and "Well Done" (1918), *Notes on Life and Letters* (London: J. M. Dent & Sons, Ltd., 1921), pp. 194–95, pp. 189–91. Selections reprinted by permission of the publisher.

The Master who had meditated so deeply on the rebirth of arts and sciences, on the inward beauty of all things,—ships' lines, women's faces—and on the visible aspects of nature was profoundly right in his pronouncement on the work that is done on the earth. From the hard work of men are born the sympathetic consciousness of a common destiny, the fidelity to right practice which makes great craftsmen, the sense of right conduct which we may call honour, the devotion to our calling and the idealism which is not a misty, winged angel without eyes, but a divine figure of terrestrial aspect with a clear glance and with its feet resting firmly on the earth on which it was born.

And work will overcome all evil, except ignorance, which is the condition of humanity and, like the ambient air, fills the space between the various sorts and conditions of men, which breeds hatred, fear, and contempt between the masses of mankind and puts on men's lips, on their innocent lips, words that are thoughtless and vain.

* * *

It is my deep conviction, or, perhaps, I ought to say my deep feeling born from personal experience, that it is not the sea but the ships of the sea that guide and command that spirit of adventure which some say is the second nature of British men. I don't want to provoke a controversy (for intellectually I am rather a Quietist) but I venture to affirm that the main characteristic of the British men spread all over the world, is not the spirit of adventure so much as the spirit of service. I think that this could be demonstrated from the history of great voyages and the general activity of the race. That the British man has always liked his service to be adventurous rather than otherwise cannot be denied, for each British man began by being young in his time when all risk has a glamour. Afterwards, with the course of years, risk became a part of his daily work; he would have missed it from his side as one misses a loved companion.

The mere love of adventure is no saving grace. It is no grace at all. It lays a man under no obligation of faithfulness to an idea and even to his own self. Roughly speaking, an adventurer may be expected to have courage, or at any rate may be said to need it. But courage in itself is not an ideal. A successful highwayman showed courage of a sort, and pirate crews have been known to fight with courage or perhaps only with reckless desperation in the manner of cornered rats. There is nothing in the world to prevent a mere lover or pursuer of adventure from running at any moment. There is his own self, his mere taste for excitement, the prospect of some sort of gain, but there is no sort of loyalty to bind him in honour to consistent conduct. I have noticed that the majority of mere lovers of adventure are mightily careful of their skins; and the proof of it is that so many of them manage to keep it whole to an advanced age. You find them in mysterious nooks of islands and continents, mostly red-nosed and watery-eyed, and not even amusingly boastful. There is nothing more futile under the sun than a mere adventurer. He might have loved at one time—which would have been a saving grace. I mean loved adventure for itself. But if so, he was bound to lose this grace very soon. Adventure by itself is but a phantom, a dubious shape without a heart.

* * *

The successive generations that went out to sea from these Isles went out to toil desperately in adventurous conditions. A man is a worker. If he is not that he is nothing. Just nothing—like a mere adventurer. Those men understood the nature of their work, but more or less dimly, in various degrees of imperfection. The best and greatest of their leaders even had never seen it clearly, because of its magnitude and the remoteness of its end. This is the common fate of mankind, whose most positive achievements are born from dreams and visions followed loyally to an unknown destination. And it doesn't matter. For the great mass of mankind the only saving grace that is needed is steady fidelity to what is nearest to hand and heart in the short moment of each human effort. In other and in greater words, what is needed is a sense of immediate duty, and a feeling of impalpable constraint. Indeed, seamen and duty are all the time inseparable companions. It has been suggested to me that this sense of duty is not a patriotic sense or a religious sense, or even a social sense in a seaman. I don't know. It seems to me that a seaman's duty may be an unconscious compound of these three, something perhaps smaller than either, but something much more definite for the simple mind and more adapted to the humbleness of the seaman's task. It has been suggested also to me that this impalpable constraint is put upon the nature of a seaman by the Spirit of the Sea, which he serves with a dumb and dogged devotion.

Those are fine words conveying a fine idea. But this I do know, that it is very difficult to display a dogged devotion to a mere spirit, however great. In everyday life ordinary men require something much more material, effective, definite, and symbolic on which to concentrate their love and their devotion. And then, what is it, this Spirit of the Sea? It is too great and too elusive to be embraced and taken to a human breast. All that a guileless or guileful seaman knows of it is its hostility, its exaction of toil as endless as its ever-renewed horizons. No. What awakens the seaman's sense of duty, what lays that impalpable constraint upon the strength of his manliness, what commands his not always dumb if always dogged devotion, is not the spirit of the sea but something that in his eyes has a body, a character, a fascination, and almost a soul—it is his ship.

[The Cruel Sea]†

The love that is given to ships is profoundly different from the love men feel for every other work of their hands—the love they bear to their houses, for instance—because it is untainted by the pride of possession. The pride of skill, the pride of responsibility, the pride of endurance there may be, but otherwise it is a disinterested sentiment. No seaman ever cherished a ship, even if she belonged to him, merely because of the profit she put in his pocket. No one, I think, ever did; for a ship-owner, even of the best, has always been outside the pale of that sentiment embracing in a feeling of intimate, equal fellowship the ship and the man, backing each other against the implacable, if sometimes dissembled, hostility of their world of waters. The sea—this truth must be confessed—has no generosity. No display of manly qualities—courage, hardihood, endurance, faithfulness—has ever been known to touch its irresponsible consciousness of power. The ocean has the conscienceless temper of a savage autocrat spoiled by much adulation. * * *

[The Faithful River]†

The estuaries of rivers appeal strongly to an adventurous imagination. This appeal is not always a charm, for there are estuaries of a particularly dispiriting ugliness: lowlands, mudflats, or perhaps barren sandhills without beauty of form or amenity of aspect, covered with a shabby and scanty vegetation conveying the impression of poverty and uselessness. Sometimes such an ugliness is merely a repulsive mask. A river whose estuary resembles a breach in a sand rampart may flow through a most fertile country. But all the estuaries of great rivers have their fascination, the attractiveness of an open portal. Water is friendly to man. The ocean, a part of Nature farthest removed in the unchangeableness and majesty of its might from the spirit of mankind, has ever been a friend to the enterprising nations of the earth. And of all the elements this is the one to which men have always been prone to trust themselves, as if its immensity held a reward as vast as itself.

From the offing the open estuary promises every possible fruition to adventurous hopes. That road open to enterprise and courage invites the explorer of coasts to new efforts towards the fulfilment of great expectations. The commander of the first Roman galley must have looked with an intense absorption upon the estuary of the

† From *The Mirror of the Sea* (1905), pp. 136–37.   † From *The Mirror of the Sea* (1905), pp. 100–103.

Thames as he turned the beaked prow of his ship to the westward
under the brow of the North Foreland. The estuary of the Thames
is not beautiful; it has no noble features, no romantic grandeur of
aspect, no smiling geniality; but it is wide open, spacious, inviting,
hospitable at the first glance, with a strange air of mysteriousness
which lingers about it to this very day. The navigation of his craft
must have engrossed all the Roman's attention in the calm of a
summer's day (he would choose his weather), when the single row
of long sweeps (the galley would be a light one, not a trireme)
could fall in easy cadence upon a sheet of water like plate-glass, reflecting faithfully the classic form of his vessel and the contour of
the lonely shores close on his left hand. I assume he followed the
land and passed through what is at present known as Margate Roads,
groping his careful way along the hidden sandbanks, whose every
tail and spit has its beacon or buoy nowadays. He must have been
anxious, though no doubt he had collected beforehand on the shores
of the Gauls a store of information from the talk of traders, adventurers, fishermen, slave-dealers, pirates—all sorts of unofficial men
connected with the sea in a more or less reputable way. He would
have heard of channels and sandbanks, of natural features of the
land useful for sea-marks, of villages and tribes and modes of barter
and precautions to take: with the instructive tales about native
chiefs dyed more or less blue, whose character for greediness, ferocity,
or amiability must have been expounded to him with that capacity
for vivid language which seems joined naturally to the shadiness of
moral character and recklessness of disposition. With that sort of
spiced food provided for his anxious thought, watchful for strange
men, strange beasts, strange turns of the tide, he would make the
best of his way up, a military seaman with a short sword on thigh
and a bronze helmet on his head, the pioneer post-captain of an
imperial fleet. Was the tribe inhabiting the Isle of Thanet[1] of a
ferocious disposition, I wonder, and ready to fall, with stone-studded
clubs and wooden lances hardened in the fire, upon the backs of
unwary mariners?

Amongst the great commercial streams of these islands, the
Thames is the only one I think open to romantic feeling, from the
fact that the sight of human labour and the sounds of human industry do not come down its shores to the very sea, destroying the suggestion of mysterious vastness caused by the configuration of the
shore. The broad inlet of the shallow North Sea passes gradually into
the contracted shape of the river; but for a long time the feeling
of the open water remains with the ship steering to the westward
through one of the lighted and buoyed passage-ways of the Thames,
such as Queen's Channel, Prince's Channel, Four-Fathom Channel;

1. The Isle of Thanet lies off Kent in Southeast England.

or else coming down the Swin from the north. The rush of the yellow flood-tide hurries her up as if into the unknown between the two fading lines of the coast. There are no features to this land, no conspicuous, far-famed landmarks for the eye; there is nothing so far down to tell you of the greatest agglomeration of mankind on earth dwelling no more than five-and-twenty miles away, where the sun sets in a blaze of colour flaming on a gold background, and the dark, low shores trend towards each other.

[The World of the Living]†

This story, which I admit to be in its brevity a fairly complex piece of work, was not intended to touch on the supernatural.[1] Yet more than one critic has been inclined to take it in that way, seeing in it an attempt on my part to give the fullest scope to my imagination by taking it beyond the confines of the world of the living, suffering humanity. But as a matter of fact my imagination is not made of stuff so elastic as all that. I believe that if I attempted to put the strain of the supernatural on it it would fail deplorably and exhibit an unlovely gap. But I could never have attempted such a thing, because all my moral and intellectual being is penetrated by an invincible conviction that whatever falls under the dominion of our senses must be in nature and, however exceptional, cannot differ in its essence from all the other effects of the visible and tangible world of which we are a self-conscious part. The world of the living contains enough marvels and mysteries as it is; marvels and mysteries acting upon our emotions and intelligence in ways so inexplicable that it would almost justify the conception of life as an enchanted state. No, I am too firm in my consciousness of the marvellous to be ever fascinated by the mere supernatural, which (take it any way you like) is but a manufactured article, the fabrication of minds insensitive to the intimate delicacies of our relation to the dead and to the living, in their countless multitudes; a desecration of our tenderest memories; an outrage on our dignity.

[To Make You See]†

A work that aspires, however humbly, to the condition of art should carry its justification in every line. And art itself may be defined as a single-minded attempt to render the highest kind of justice to the visible universe, by bringing to light the truth, manifold and

† From "Author's Note," *The Shadow Line* (London: J. M. Dent & Sons, Ltd., 1920). Pp. ix–x. Reprinted by permission.

1. *The Shadow Line.*
† From the Preface (1897), *The Nigger of the "Narcissus,"* pp. vii–xiii.

one, underlying its every aspect. It is an attempt to find in its forms, in its colours, in its light, in its shadows, in the aspects of matter and in the facts of life, what of each is fundamental, what is enduring and essential—their one illuminating and convincing quality— the very truth of their existence. The artist, then, like the thinker or the scientist, seeks the truth and makes his appeal. Impressed by the aspect of the world the thinker plunges into ideas, the scientist into facts—whence, presently, emerging they make their appeal to those qualities of our being that fit us best for the hazardous enterprise of living. They speak authoritatively to our common-sense, to our intelligence, to our desire of peace or to our desire of unrest; not seldom to our prejudices, sometimes to our fears, often to our egoism —but always to our credulity. And their words are heard with reverence, for their concern is with weighty matters; with the cultivation of our minds and the proper care of our bodies: with the attainment of our ambitions: with the perfection of the means and the glorification of our precious aims.

It is otherwise with the artist.

Confronted by the same enigmatical spectacle the artist descends within himself, and in that lonely region of stress and strife, if he be deserving and fortunate, he finds the terms of his appeal. His appeal is made to our less obvious capacities: to that part of our nature which, because of the warlike conditions of existence, is necessarily kept out of sight within the more resisting and hard qualities—like the vulnerable body within a steel armour. His appeal is less loud, more profound, less distinct, more stirring—and sooner forgotten. Yet its effect endures forever. The changing wisdom of successive generations discards ideas, questions facts, demolishes theories. But the artist appeals to that part of our being which is not dependent on wisdom; to that in us which is a gift and not an acquisition—and, therefore, more permanently enduring. He speaks to our capacity for delight and wonder, to the sense of mystery surrounding our lives: to our sense of pity, and beauty, and pain: to the latent feeling of fellowship with all creation—and to the subtle but invincible, conviction of solidarity that knits together the loneliness of innumerable hearts to the solidarity in dreams, in joy, in sorrow, in aspirations, in illusions, in hope, in fear, which binds men to each other, which binds together all humanity—the dead to the living and the living to the unborn.

It is only some such train of thought, or rather of feeling, that can in a measure explain the aim of the attempt, made in the tale which follows,[1] to present an unrestful episode in the obscure lives of a few individuals out of all the disregarded multitude of the bewildered, the simple and the voiceless. For, if there is any part of truth in the

1. *The Nigger of the "Narcissus."*

belief confessed above, it becomes evident that there is not a place of splendour or a dark corner of the earth that does not deserve, if only a passing glance of wonder and pity. The motive, then, may be held to justify the matter of the work; but this preface, which is simply an avowal of endeavour, cannot end here—for the avowal is not yet complete.

Fiction—if it at all aspires to be art—appeals to temperament. And in truth it must be, like painting, like music, like all art, the appeal of one temperament to all the other innumerable temperaments whose subtle and resistless power endows passing events with their true meaning, and creates the moral, the emotional atmosphere of the place and time. Such an appeal to be effective must be an impression conveyed through the senses; and, in fact, it cannot be made in any other way, because temperament, whether individual or collective, is not amenable to persuasion. All art, therefore, appeals primarily to the senses, and the artistic aim when expressing itself in written words must also make its appeal through the senses, if its high desire is to reach the secret spring of responsive emotions. It must strenuously aspire to the plasticity of sculpture, to the colour of painting, and to the magic suggestiveness of music—which is the art of arts. And it is only through complete, unswerving devotion to the perfect blending of form and substance; it is only through an unremitting never-discouraged care for the shape and ring of sentences that an approach can be made to plasticity, to colour; and the light of magic suggestiveness may be brought to play for an evanescent instant over the commonplace surface of words: of the old, old words, worn thin, defaced by ages of careless usage.

The sincere endeavour to accomplish that creative task, to go as far on that road as his strength will carry him, to go undeterred by faltering, weariness or reproach, is the only valid justification for the worker in prose. And if his conscience is clear, his answer to those who, in the fulness of a wisdom which looks for immediate profit, demand specifically to be edified, consoled, amused; who demand to be promptly improved, or encouraged, or frightened, or shocked, or charmed, must run thus:—My task which I am trying to achieve is, by the power of the written word, to make you hear, to make you feel—it is, before all, to make you *see*. That—and no more, and it is everything. If I succeed, you shall find there according to your deserts: encouragement, consolation, fear, charm—all you demand and, perhaps, also that glimpse of truth for which you have forgotten to ask.

To snatch in a moment of courage, from the remorseless rush of time, a passing phase of life, is only the beginning of the task. The task approached in tenderness and faith is to hold up unquestioningly, without choice and without fear, the rescued fragment before all eyes and in the light of a sincere mood. It is to show its vibration, its colour, its form; and through its movement, its form, and its colour, reveal the substance of its truth—disclose its inspiring secret: the stress and passion within the core of each convincing moment. In a single-minded attempt of that kind, if one be deserving and fortunate, one may perchance attain to such clearness of sincerity that at last the presented vision of regret or pity, of terror or mirth, shall awaken in the hearts of the beholders that feeling of unavoidable solidarity; of the solidarity in mysterious origin, in toil, in joy, in hope, in uncertain fate, which binds men to each other and all mankind to the visible world.

It is evident that he who, rightly or wrongly, holds by the convictions expressed above cannot be faithful to any one of the temporary formulas of his craft. The enduring part of them—the truth which each only imperfectly veils—should abide with him as the most precious of his possessions, but they all: Realism, Romanticism, Naturalism, even the unofficial sentimentalism (which like the poor,[2] is exceedingly difficult to get rid of,) all these gods must, after a short period of fellowship, abandon him—even on the very threshold of the temple—to the stammerings of his conscience and to the outspoken consciousness of the difficulties of his work. In that uneasy solitude the supreme cry of Art for Art, itself, loses the exciting ring of its apparent immorality. It sounds far off. It has ceased to be a cry, and is heard only as a whisper, often incomprehensible, but at times and faintly encouraging.

Sometimes, stretched at ease in the shade of a roadside tree, we watch the motions of a labourer in a distant field, and after a time, begin to wonder languidly as to what the fellow may be at. We watch the movements of his body, the waving of his arms, we see him bend down, stand up, hesitate, begin again. It may add to the charm of an idle hour to be told the purpose of his exertions. If we know he is trying to lift a stone, to dig a ditch, to uproot a stump, we look with a more real interest at his efforts; we are disposed to condone the jar of his agitation upon the restfulness of the landscape; and even, if in a brotherly frame of mind, we may bring ourselves to forgive his failure. We understood his object, and, after all, the fellow has tried, and perhaps he had not the strength—and perhaps he had not the knowledge. We forgive, go on our way—and forget.

And so it is with the workman of art. Art is long and life is short,[3] and success is very far off. And thus, doubtful of strength to travel so far, we talk a little about the aim—the aim of art, which, like life itself, is inspiring, difficult—obscured by mists. It is not in the clear logic of a triumphant conclusion; it is not in the unveiling of one of

2. John xii:8.
3. Attributed to Hippocrates, fifth century B.C.

those heartless secrets which are called the Laws of Nature. It is not less great, but only more difficult.

To arrest, for the space of a breath, the hands busy about the work of the earth, and compel men entranced by the sight of distant goals to glance for a moment at the surrounding vision of form and colour, of sunshine and shadows; to make them pause for a look, for a sigh, for a smile—such is the aim, difficult and evanescent, and reserved only for a very few to achieve. But sometimes, by the deserving and the fortunate, even that task is accomplished. And when it is accomplished—behold!—all the truth of life is there: a moment of vision, a sigh, a smile—and the return to an eternal rest.

Books†

Of all books, novels, which the Muses should love, make a serious claim on our compassion. The art of the novelist is simple. At the same time it is the most elusive of all creative arts, the most liable to be obscured by the scruples of its servants and votaries, the one pre-eminently destined to bring trouble to the mind and the heart of the artist. After all, the creation of a world is not a small undertaking except perhaps to the divinely gifted. In truth every novelist must begin by creating for himself a world, great or little, in which he can honestly believe. This world cannot be made otherwise than in his own image: it is fated to remain individual and a little mysterious, and yet it must resemble something already familiar to the experience, the thoughts and the sensations of his readers. At the heart of fiction, even the least worthy of the name, some sort of truth can be found—if only the truth of a childish theatrical ardour in the game of life, as in the novels of Dumas the father. But the fair truth of human delicacy can be found in Mr. Henry James's novels; and the comical, appalling truth of human rapacity let loose amongst the spoils of existence lives in the monstrous world created by Balzac.[1] The pursuit of happiness by means lawful and unlawful, through resignation or revolt, by the clever manipulation of conventions or by solemn hanging on to the skirts of the latest scientific theory, is the only theme that can be legitimately developed by the novelist who is the chronicler of the adventures of mankind amongst the dangers of the kingdom of the earth. And the kingdom of this earth itself, the ground upon which his individualities stand, stumble, or die, must enter into his scheme of faithful record. To encompass

† From "Books" (1905), *Notes on Life and Letters*, pp. 6–10.

1. Alexandre Dumas (1802–70), French novelist, author of *The Three Musketeers* and *The Count of Monte-Cristo*.

Henry James (1843–1916), American novelist, friend and neighbor of Conrad when *Heart of Darkness* was written, became a British citizen at the outbreak of World War I.

Honoré de Balzac (1799–1850), French novelist, whose incomplete work of philosophical fiction, *The Human Comedy*, runs to forty volumes.

all this in one harmonious conception is a great feat; and even to attempt it deliberately with serious intention, not from the senseless prompting of an ignorant heart, is an honourable ambition. For it requires some courage to step in calmly where fools may be eager to rush. As a distinguished and successful French novelist once observed of fiction, "C'est un art *trop* difficile."[2]

It is natural that the novelist should doubt his ability to cope with his task. He imagines it more gigantic than it is. And yet literary creation being only one of the legitimate forms of human activity has no value but on the condition of not excluding the fullest recognition of all the more distinct forms of action. This condition is sometimes forgotten by the man of letters, who often, especially in his youth, is inclined to lay a claim of exclusive superiority for his own amongst all the other tasks of the human mind. The mass of verse and prose may glimmer here and there with the glow of a divine spark, but in the sum of human effort it has no special importance. There is no justificative formula for its existence any more than for any other artistic achievement. With the rest of them it is destined to be forgotten, without, perhaps, leaving the faintest trace. Where a novelist has an advantage over the workers in other fields of thought is in his privilege of freedom—the freedom of expression and the freedom of confessing his innermost beliefs—which should console him for the hard slavery of the pen.

* * *

Liberty of imagination should be the most precious possession of a novelist. To try voluntarily to discover the fettering dogmas of some romantic, realistic, or naturalistic creed in the free work of its own inspiration, is a trick worthy of human perverseness which, after inventing an absurdity, endeavours to find for it a pedigree of distinguished ancestors. It is a weakness of inferior minds when it is not the cunning device of those who, uncertain of their talent, would seek to add lustre to it by the authority of a school. Such, for instance, are the high priests who have proclaimed Stendhal for a prophet of Naturalism.[3] But Stendhal himself would have accepted no limitation of his freedom. Stendhal's mind was of the first order. His spirit above must be raging with a peculiarly Stendhalesque scorn and indignation. For the truth is that more than one kind of intellectual cowardice hides behind the literary formulas. And Stendhal was preeminently courageous. He wrote his two great novels, which so few people have read, in a spirit of fearless liberty.

It must not be supposed that I claim for the artist in fiction the freedom of moral Nihilism. I would require from him many acts of

2. "It is much too difficult an art."
3. Stendhal, pen name of Marie-Henri Beyle (1783–1842), French novelist and critic, author of *The Red and the Black* and *The Charterhouse of Parma*.

faith of which the first would be the cherishing of an undying hope; and hope, it will not be contested, implies all the piety of effort and renunciation. It is the God-sent form of trust in the magic force and inspiration belonging to the life of this earth. We are inclined to forget that the way of excellence is in the intellectual, as distinguished from emotional, humility. What one feels so hopelessly barren in declared pessimism is just its arrogance. It seems as if the discovery made by many men at various times that there is much evil in the world were a source of proud and unholy joy unto some of the modern writers. That frame of mind is not the proper one in which to approach seriously the art of fiction. It gives an author— goodness only knows why—an elated sense of his own superiority. And there is nothing more dangerous than such an elation to that absolute loyalty towards his feelings and sensations an author should keep hold of in his most exalted moments of creation.

To be hopeful in an artistic sense it is not necessary to think that the world is good. It is enough to believe that there is no impossibility of its being made so. If the flight of imaginative thought may be allowed to rise superior to many moralities current amongst mankind, a novelist who would think himself of a superior essence to other men would miss the first condition of his calling. To have the gift of words is no such great matter. A man furnished with a long-range weapon does not become a hunter or a warrior by the mere possession of a fire-arm; many other qualities of character and temperament are necessary to make him either one or the other. Of him from whose armoury of phrases one in a hundred thousand may perhaps hit the far-distant and elusive mark of art I would ask that in his dealings with mankind he should be capable of giving a tender recognition to their obscure virtues. I would not have him impatient with their small failings and scornful of their errors. I would not have him expect too much gratitude from that humanity whose fate, as illustrated in individuals, it is open to him to depict as ridiculous or terrible. I would wish him to look with a large forgiveness at men's ideas and prejudices, which are by no means the outcome of malevolence, but depend on their education, their social status, even their professions. The good artist should expect no recognition of his toil and no admiration of his genius, because his toil can with difficulty be appraised and his genius cannot possibly mean anything to the illiterate who, even from the dreadful wisdom of their evoked dead, have, so far, culled nothing but inanities and platitudes. I would wish him to enlarge his sympaties by patient and loving observation while he grows in mental power. It is in the impartial practice of life, if anywhere, that the promise of perfection for his art can be found, rather than in the absurd formulas trying to prescribe this or that particular method of technique or conception. Let him mature the strength of his imagination amongst the things of this earth, which it is his business to cherish and know, and refrain from calling down his inspiration ready-made from some heaven of perfections of which he knows nothing. And I would not grudge him the proud illusion that will come sometimes to a writer: the illusion that his achievement has almost equalled the greatness of his dream. * * *

[Fiction Is Human History]†

All creative art is magic, is evocation of the unseen in forms persuasive, enlightening, familiar and surprising, for the edification of mankind, pinned down by the conditions of its existence to the earnest consideration of the most insignificant tides of reality.

Action in its essence, the creative art of a writer of fiction may be compared to rescue work carried out in darkness against cross gusts of wind swaying the action of a great multitude. It is rescue work, this snatching of vanishing phases of turbulence, disguised in fair words, out of the native obscurity into a light where the struggling forms may be seen, seized upon, endowed with the only possible form of permanence in this world of relative values—the permanence of memory. And the multitude feels it obscurely too; since the demand of the individual to the artist is, in effect, the cry, "Take me out of myself!" meaning really, out of my perishable activity into the light of imperishable consciousness. But everything is relative, and the light of consciousness is only enduring, merely the most enduring of the things of this earth, imperishable only as against the short-lived work of our industrious hands.

When the last aqueduct shall have crumbled to pieces, the last airship fallen to the ground, the last blade of grass have died upon a dying earth, man, indomitable by his training in resistance to misery and pain, shall set this undiminished light of his eyes against the feeble glow of the sun. The artistic faculty, of which each of us has a minute grain, may find its voice in some individual of that last group, gifted with a power of expression and courageous enough to interpret the ultimate experience of mankind in terms of his temperament, in terms of art. I do not mean to say that he would attempt to beguile the last moments of humanity by an ingenious tale. It would be too much to expect—from humanity. I doubt the heroism of the hearers. As to the heroism of the artist, no doubt is necessary. There would be on his part no heroism. The artist in his calling of interpreter creates (the clearest form of demonstration) because he must. He is so much of a voice that, for him, silence is like death; and the

† From "Henry James: An Appreciation" (1905), *Notes on Life and Letters*, pp. 13–17.

postulate was, that there is a group alive, clustered on his threshold to watch the last flicker of light on a black sky, to hear the last word uttered in the stilled workshop of the earth. It is safe to affirm that, if anybody, it will be the imaginative man who would be moved to speak on the eve of that day without to-morrow—whether in austere exhortation or in a phrase of sardonic comment, who can guess?

For my own part, from a short and cursory acquaintance with my kind, I am inclined to think that the last utterance will formulate, strange as it may appear, some hope now to us utterly inconceivable. For mankind is delightful in its pride, its assurance, and its indomitable tenacity. It will sleep on the battlefield among its own dead, in the manner of an army having won a barren victory. It will not know when it is beaten. And perhaps it is right in that quality. The victories are not, perhaps, so barren as it may appear from a purely strategical, utilitarian point of view. * * * These warlike images come by themselves under the pen; since from the duality of man's nature and the competition of individuals, the life-history of the earth must in the last instance be a history of a really very relentless warfare. Neither his fellows, nor his gods, nor his passions will leave a man alone. In virtue of these allies and enemies, he holds his precarious dominion, he possesses his fleeting significance; and it is this relation in all its manifestations, great and little, superficial or profound, and this relation alone, that is commented upon, interpreted, demonstrated by the art of the novelist in the only possible way in which the task can be performed: by the independent creation of circumstance and character, achieved against all the difficulties of expression, in an imaginative effort finding its inspiration from the reality of forms and sensations. That a sacrifice must be made, that something has to be given up, is the truth engraved in the innermost recesses of the fair temple built for our edification by the masters of fiction. There is no other secret behind the curtain. All adventure, all love, every success is resumed in the supreme energy of an act of renunciation. It is the uttermost limit of our power; it is the most potent and effective force at our disposal on which rest the labours of a solitary man in his study, the rock on which have been built commonwealths whose might casts a dwarfing shadow upon two oceans. Like a natural force which is obscured as much as illuminated by the multiplicity of phenomena, the power of renunciation is obscured by the mass of weaknesses, vacillations, secondary motives and false steps and compromises which make up the sum of our activity. But no man or woman worthy of the name can pretend to anything more, to anything greater. * * * The earth itself has grown smaller in the course of ages. But in every sphere of human perplexities and emotions, there are more greatnesses than one— not counting here the greatness of the artist himself. Wherever he stands, at the beginning or the end of things, a man has to sacrifice his gods to his passions or his passions to his gods. That is the problem, great enough, in all truth, if approached in the spirit of sincerity and knowledge.

In one of his critical studies, published some fifteen years ago, Mr. Henry James claims for the novelist the standing of the historian as the only adequate one, as for himself and before his audience.[1] I think that the claim cannot be contested, and that the position is unassailable. Fiction is history, human history, or it is nothing. But it is also more than that; it stands on firmer ground, being based on the reality of forms and the observation of social phenomena, whereas history is based on documents, and the reading of print and handwriting—on second-hand impression. Thus fiction is nearer truth. But let that pass. A historian may be an artist too, and a novelist is a historian, the preserver, the keeper, the expounder, of human experience.

[The Symbolic Character of Fiction]†

Some critics have found fault with me for not being constantly myself. But they are wrong. I am always myself. I am a man of formed character. Certain conclusions remain immovably fixed in my mind, but I am no slave to prejudices and formulas, and I shall never be. My attitude to subjects and expressions, the angles of vision, my methods of composition will, within limits, be always changing—not because I am unstable or unprincipled but because I am free. Or perhaps it may be more exact to say, because I am always trying for freedom—within my limits.

Coming now to the subject of your inquiry, I wish at first to put before you a general proposition: that a work of art is very seldom limited to one exclusive meaning and not necessarily tending to a definite conclusion. And this for the reason that the nearer it approaches art, the more it acquires a symbolic character. This statement may surprise you, who may imagine that I am alluding to the Symbolist School of poets or prose writers. Theirs, however, is only a literary proceeding against which I have nothing to say. I am concerned here with something much larger. But no doubt you have meditated on this and kindred questions yourself.

So I will only call your attention to the fact that the symbolic conception of a work of art has this advantage, that it makes a triple appeal covering the whole field of life. All the great creations of liter-

1. "The Art of Fiction." James and Conrad admired each other's work greatly—and not only because they were good friends.
† From a letter to Barrett H. Clark, May 14, 1918, in G. Jean-Aubry, *Life*

and Letters (London: William Heinemann, Ltd., 1927), II, 204–5. Reprinted by permission of J. M. Dent & Sons, Ltd.
Clark (1890–1953), drama editor, translator, and critic.

ature have been symbolic, and in that way have gained in complexity, in power, in depth and in beauty.

I don't think you will quarrel with me on the ground of lack of precision; for as to precision of images and analysis my artistic conscience is at rest. I have given there all the truth that is in me; and all that the critics may say can make my honesty neither more nor less. But as to "final effect" my conscience has nothing to do with that. It is the critic's affair to bring to its contemplation his own honesty, his sensibility and intelligence. The matter for his conscience is just his judgment. If his conscience is busy with petty scruples and trammelled by superficial formulas then his judgment will be superficial and petty. But an artist has no right to quarrel with the inspirations, either lofty or base, of another soul.

[Explicitness Is Fatal to Art]†

I have this morning received the article for the *Blue Peter*.[1] I think I have given you already to understand the nature of my feelings. Indeed, I spoke to you very openly, expressing my fundamental objection to the character you wished to give to it. I do not for a moment expect that what I am going to say here will convince you or influence you in the least. And, indeed, I have neither the wish nor the right to assert my position. I will only point out to you that my feelings in that matter are at least as legitimate as your own. It is a strange fate that everything that I have, of set artistic purpose, laboured to leave indefinite, suggestive, in the penumbra of initial inspiration, should have that light turned on to it and its insignificance (as compared with, I might say without megalomania, the ampleness of my conceptions) exposed for any fool to comment upon or even for average minds to be disappointed with. Didn't it ever occur to you, my dear Curle, that I knew what I was doing in leaving the facts of my life and even of my tales in the background? Explicitness, my dear fellow, is fatal to the glamour of all artistic work, robbing it of all suggestiveness, destroying all illusion. You seem to believe in literalness and explicitness, in facts and also in expression. Yet nothing is more clear than the utter insignificance of explicit statement and also its power to call attention away from things that matter in the region of art.

There, however, I am afraid we will never agree. Your praise of my work, allied to your analysis of its origins (which really are not its origins at all, as you know perfectly well), sounds exaggerated

† From a letter to Richard Curle (April 24, 1922) in *Conrad to a Friend* by Richard Curle. Pp. 112–14. Copyright © 1928 by Doubleday & Company, Inc. Reprinted by permission of the publisher.
1. Richard Curle, "Joseph Conrad in the East." For a note on Curle, see above, p. 109.

by the mere force of contrast. I wouldn't talk like this if I did not attach a very great value to everything you write about me and did not believe in its wide influence. It isn't a matter of literary criticism at all if I venture to point out to you that the dogmatic, ex-cathedra tone that you have adopted in your article positively frightens me. * * * It is generally known that you are my intimate friend, that the text carries an air of authority and that a lot of dam-fools will ascribe to me the initiative and the sanction of all the views and facts expressed. And one really could not blame them if they thought and said that I must have wanted all those facts disclosed.

[My Manner of Telling]†

I am returning you the article[1] with two corrections as to matters of fact and one of style.

As it stands I can have nothing against it. As to my feelings that is a different matter; and I think that, looking at the intimate character of our friendship and trusting to the indulgence of your affection, I may disclose them to you without reserve.

My point of view is that this is an opportunity, if not unique then not likely to occur again in my lifetime. I was in hopes that on a general survey it could also be made an opportunity for me to get freed from that infernal tale of ships, and that obsession of my sea life which has about as much bearing on my literary existence, on my quality as a writer, as the enumeration of drawing-rooms which Thackeray frequented could have had on his gift as a great novelist. After all, I may have been a seaman, but I am a writer of prose. Indeed, the nature of my writing runs the risk of being obscured by the nature of my material. I admit it is natural; but only the appreciation of a special personal intelligence can counteract the superficial appreciation of the inferior intelligence of the mass of readers and critics. Even Doubleday was considerably disturbed by that characteristic as evidenced in press notices in America, where such headings as "Spinner of sea-yarns—master-mariner—seaman writer" and so forth predominated. I must admit that the letter-press had less emphasis than the headings; but that was simply because they didn't know the facts. That the connection of my ships with my writings stands, with my concurrence I admit, recorded in your book is, of course, a fact. But that was biographical matter, not literary. And where it stands it can do no harm. Undue prominence has been given to it since, and yet you know yourself very well that in the body of

† From a letter to Richard Curle (July 14, 1923) in *Conrad to a Friend* by Richard Curle. Copyright © 1928 by Doubleday & Company, Inc. Pp. 147–50. Reprinted by permission of the publisher.

1. A review article of the Dent Uniform Edition of Conrad's works for the London *Times Literary Supplement*. Doubleday had just published the Concord Edition in America.

my work barely one-tenth is what may be called sea stuff, and even of that, the bulk, that is *Nigger* and *Mirror*, has a very special purpose, which I emphasise myself in my Prefaces.

* * *

My manner of telling, perfectly devoid of familiarity as between author and reader, [is] aimed essentially at the intimacy of a personal communication, without any thought for other effects. As a matter of fact, the thought for effects is there all the same (often at the cost of mere directness of narrative) and can be detected in my unconventional grouping and perspective, which are purely temperamental and wherein almost all my "art" consists. That, I suspect, has been the difficulty the critics felt in classifying it as romantic or realistic. Whereas, as a matter of fact, it is fluid, depending on grouping (sequence) which shifts, and on the changing lights giving varied effects of perspective.

It is in those matters gradually, but never completely, mastered that the history of my books really consists. Of course the plastic matter of this grouping and of those lights has its importance, since without it the actuality of that grouping and that lighting could not be made evident any more than Marconi's electric waves could be made evident without the sending-out and receiving instruments. In other words, without mankind, my art, an infinitesimal thing, could not exist.

[Every Novel Contains Autobiography]†

This is one of his confessions. "May there not emerge at last the vision of a personality; the man behind the books so fundamentally dissimilar as for instance, *Almayer's Folly* and *The Secret Agent*—and yet a coherent justifiable personality both in its origin and in its actions?" In 1907 he wrote to me, thanking me for my "rejected address to the public on behalf of his art, and for the warm, living sincerity of my impression and of my analysis." He confesses that "fourteen years of honest work are not gone for nothing. A big slice of life that, which I may say is not altogether lost. There has been in all the time not ten minutes of amateurishness. That is the truth. For the rest I may say that there are certain passages in your article which have surprised me. I did not know that I had 'a heart of darkness' and 'an unlawful soul.' Mr. Kurtz had—and I have not treated him with easy nonchalance. Believe me, no man ever paid more for his lines than I have. But then I possess an inalienable right to the use of all my epithets. The fact is that I am really a much simpler

† From Arthur Symons, *Notes on Joseph Conrad: With Some Unpublished Letters.* Copyright 1925 by Arthur Symons and Myers & Co. Pp. 15–18. Reprinted by permission.

person. Death is a fact—and violent death is a fact too. In the simplicity of my heart I tried to realise these facts when they came in. Do you really think that Flaubert gloated over the death bed of Emma, or the death march of Mâtho, or the last moments of Félicité?[1] I've never looked into myself. There was no time in these years to turn my head away from the table. There are whole days when I did not know whether the sun shone or not. And, after all, the books are there! As for the writing of novels, delightful or not, I have always approached my task in the spirit of love for mankind. And I've rather taken it seriously. But I stand outside and feel grateful to you for the recognition of the work—not the man. Once the last page is written the man does not count. He is nowhere." * * *

"One thing that I am certain of, is that I have approached the object of my task, things human, in a spirit of piety. The earth is a temple where there is going on a mystery play childish and poignant, ridiculous and awful enough in all conscience. Once in I've tried to behave decently. I have not degraded the quasi religious sentiment by tears and groans: and if I have been amused and indifferent, I've neither grinned nor gnashed my teeth. In other words I've tried to write with dignity, not only out of regard of myself, but for the sake of the spectacle, the play with an obscure beginning and an unfathomable *dénouement*. I don't think this has been noticed. It is your penitent beating the floor with his forehead and the ecstatic worshippers at the rails that are obvious to the public eye. The man standing quietly in the shadow of the pillar if noticed at all runs the risk of being suspected of sinister designs. As I wrote to a friend I have been quarrying my English out of a black night, working like a coal miner in his pit. For fourteen years now I have been living as if in a cave without echoes. If you come shouting gloriously at the mouth of the same you can't really expect me to pretend I am not there."

Conrad wrote: "I know that a novelist lives in his work. He stands there, the only reality in an invented world, amongst imaginary things, happenings and people. Writing about them, he is only writing about himself. Every novel contains an element of autobiography—and this can hardly be denied, since the creator can only explain himself in his creations."

[On Marlow and *Heart of Darkness*]†

The three stories in this volume lay no claim to unity of artistic purpose. The only bond between them is that of the time in which

1. Gustave Flaubert (1821–80), French novelist, author of *Madame Bovary* (Emma), *Salammbô* (Mathô), and *Un Coeur Simple* (Félicité).

† From "Author's Note" (1917), *Youth* (London: J. M. Dent & Sons, Ltd., 1921). Pp. ix–xiii. Reprinted by permission.

they were written. They belong to the period immediately following the publication of *The Nigger of the "Narcissus,"* and preceding the first conception of *Nostromo,* two books which, it seems to me, stand apart and by themselves in the body of my work. It is also the period during which I contributed to *Maga;* a period dominated by *Lord Jim* and associated in my grateful memory with the late Mr. William Blackwood's encouraging and helpful kindness.

Youth was not my first contribution to *Maga.* It was the second. But that story marks the first appearance in the world of the man Marlow, with whom my relations have grown very intimate in the course of years. The origins of that gentleman (nobody as far as I know had ever hinted that he was anything but that)—his origins have been the subject of some literary speculation of, I am glad to say, a friendly nature.

One would think that I am the proper person to throw a light on the matter; but in truth I find that it isn't so easy. It is pleasant to remember that nobody had charged him with fraudulent purposes or looked down on him as a charlatan; but apart from that he was supposed to be all sorts of things: a clever screen, a mere device, a 'personator,' a familiar spirit, a whispering 'daemon.' I myself have been suspected of a meditated plan for his capture.

That is not so. I made no plans. The man Marlow and I came together in the casual manner of those health-resort acquaintances which sometimes ripen into friendships. This one has ripened. For all his assertiveness in matters of opinion he is not an intrusive person. He haunts my hours of solitude, when, in silence, we lay our heads together in great comfort and harmony; but as we part at the end of a tale I am never sure that it may not be for the last time. Yet I don't think that either of us would care much to survive the other. In his case, at any rate, his occupation would be gone and he would suffer from that extinction, because I suspect him of some vanity. I don't mean vanity in the Solomonian sense.[1] Of all my people he's the one that has never been a vexation to my spirit. A most discreet, understanding man. . . .

Even before appearing in book-form *Youth* was very well received. It lies on me to confess at last, and this is as good a place for it as another, that I have been all my life—all my two lives—the spoiled adopted child of Great Britain and even of the Empire; for it was Australia that gave me my first command. I break out into this declaration not because of a lurking tendency to megalomania, but, on the contrary, as a man who has no very notable illusions about himself. I follow the instincts of vain-glory and humility natural to all mankind. For it can hardly be denied that it is not their own deserts that men are most proud of, but rather of their prodigious

1. See Ecclesiastes i:14.

luck, of their marvellous fortune: of that in their lives for which thanks and sacrifices must be offered on the altars of the inscrutable gods.

Heart of Darkness also received a certain amount of notice from the first; and of its origins this much may be said: it is well known that curious men go prying into all sorts of places (where they have no business) and come out of them with all kinds of spoil. This story, and one other, not in this volume,[2] are all the spoil I brought out from the centre of Africa, where, really, I had no sort of business. More ambitious in its scope and longer in the telling, *Heart of Darkness* is quite as authentic in fundamentals as *Youth*. It is, obviously, written in another mood. I won't characterize the mood precisely, but anybody can see that it is anything but the mood of wistful regret, of reminiscent tenderness.

One more remark may be added. *Youth* is a feat of memory. It is a record of experience; but that experience, in its facts, in its inwardness and in its outward colouring, begins and ends in myself. *Heart of Darkness* is experience, too; but it is experience pushed a little (and only very little) beyond the actual facts of the case for the perfectly legitimate, I believe, purpose of bringing it home to the minds and bosoms of the readers. There it was no longer a matter of sincere colouring. It was like another art altogether. That sombre theme had to be given a sinister resonance, a tonality of its own, a continued vibration that, I hoped, would hang in the air and dwell on the ear after the last note had been struck.

After saying so much there remains the last tale of the book, still untouched. *The End of the Tether* is a story of sea-life in a rather special way; and the most intimate thing I can say of it is this: that having lived that life fully, amongst its men, its thoughts and sensations, I have found it possible, without the slightest misgiving, in all sincerity of heart and peace of conscience, to conceive the existence of Captain Whalley's personality and to relate the manner of his end. This statement acquires some force from the circumstance that the pages of that story—a fair half of the book—are also the product of experience. That experience belongs (like *Youth's*) to the time before I ever thought of putting pen to paper. As to its 'reality,' that is for the readers to determine. One had to pick up one's facts here and there. More skill would have made them more real and the whole composition more interesting. But here we are approaching the veiled region of artistic values which it would be improper and indeed dangerous for me to enter. I have looked over the proofs, have corrected a misprint or two, have changed a word or two—and that's all. It is not very likely that I shall ever read *The End of the Tether* again. No more need be said. It accords best with my feelings to part from Captain Whalley in affectionate silence.

2. *An Outpost of Progress.*

Criticism

The following collection of criticism ranges all the way from notes, through articles and essays, to selections from book-length studies of Conrad, and it varies in points of view taken, kinds of interest shown, and conclusions reached with regard to the art and theme of *Heart of Darkness*. But each of the pieces has in common a seriousness of critical intention. Proof of the high seriousness of the following writers is found in their lack of agreement about such matters as the tone of the story, the purpose of the frame, the significance of Kurtz, the role of Marlow, and whether the story is primarily literal, typal, or symbolic.

The selections have been gathered under two groupings: general essays and critical debates. Those in the first group have been arranged chronologically, with two exceptions. Because Robert Haugh reviews the main approaches taken to *Heart of Darkness* through 1954, I have placed his remarks before those essays which appeared in 1955 and after; although Albert Guerard's study appeared in 1958, his reading of the story was initially worked out in his introduction to the Signet edition of *Heart of Darkness* and *The Secret Sharer* (1950). Since particular aspects of the story have led to clear critical disagreement, the selections in the second part have been arranged by topic: "Structural Devices," "The Lie," and "The Russian."

Most of the items have been included in their entirety, those cuts which have been made being based mainly on two considerations. Because the story is bound with this collection of criticism, long quotations of Conrad's text have been eliminated where their absence does not weaken the presentation of a thesis; because the reader of this collection will be more interested in points of view and opinions, long demonstrations which take one through the story incident by incident have been shortened, but again only when the presentation of a thesis is not weakened. In no case should the editing be taken as a judgment on the quality of the omitted material. Finally, I have renumbered footnotes where necessary, eliminated page references to the text, omitted most notation of material included elsewhere in this collection of criticism, and added some cross-references to material outside the collection.

ROBERT F. HAUGH

[*Heart of Darkness*: Problem for Critics]†

Conrad's "Heart of Darkness" first appeared as a serial in *Blackwood's Magazine* for February, March, and April, 1899 [and] * * * received a mixed critical press. The story was taken by some as an attack upon Belgian colonial methods in the Congo; as a moral tract; and as a study in race relationships. *The Bookman* called it "a symbolic picture of the inborn antagonisms of two races, the white and the black." *The Spectator*, without indicating that it understood the story any better, praised the moral tone. Most of the other contemporary reviewers read it as a criticism of Belgian colonialism, an issue that remained alive until Conrad's death and got attention in his obituary notices.

Nearly three years after its initial magazine appearance, "Heart of Darkness" appeared in book form as one of the stories in the volume entitled *Youth*. Edward Garnett, Conrad's discoverer and friend in the publishing house of Fisher Unwin, came closer than anyone else up to that time. He wrote a review for *The Academy and Literature* for December 6, 1902, in which he said:

> A most amazing, consummate piece of artistic diablerie—an analysis of the white man's morale when let loose from European restraint, and planted down in the tropics as an "emissary of light" armed to the teeth to make trade profits out of subject races. The gulf between the white man's system and the black man's comprehension of its results—the unnerved, degenerating whites staring all day and every day at the heart of darkness which is alike meaningless and threatening to their own creed and conception of life—

Conrad was aware of certain obscurities in "Heart of Darkness," although he was quite willing to receive praise from those he puzzled. He wrote to Garnett: "My dearest fellow, you quite overcome me. And your brave attempt to grapple with the fogginess of H. of D., to explain what I myself tried to shape blindfold, as it were, has touched me profoundly." Conrad heard from his friend Cunninghame Graham, after the first installment had appeared, and warned him in reply:

> I am simply in the seventh heaven to find you like H. of D.

2. *The Advance of the English Novel.* New York, Dodd, Mead & Co., 1916, p. 215.
† From *Joseph Conrad: Discovery in*

Design by Robert F. Haugh. Copyright 1957 by University of Oklahoma Press. Pp. 35–40. Reprinted by permission.

so far. You bless me indeed. Mind you don't curse me bye and bye for the same thing. There are two more installments in which the idea is so wrapped up in secondary notions that you—even you—may miss it. And you must remember also that I don't start with an abstract notion. I start with definite images and as their rendering is true some little effect is produced.

No doubt many have missed the idea in "Heart of Darkness" and many have cursed Conrad for it. But as many have loved him for the wrong reasons. The fogginess in Conrad has been most memorably pointed out by E. M. Forster in *Abinger Harvest* [New York, 1936], reprinting his review of Conrad's *Notes on Life and Letters*. Forster meant his remarks to apply to Conrad generally:

> What is so elusive about him is that he is always promising to make some general philosophical statement about the universe, and then refraining in a gruff declaimer . . . there is a central obscurity, something noble, heroic, inspiring half-a-dozen great books, but obscure! Obscure! Misty in the middle as well as at the edges, the secret cask of his genius contains a vapour rather than a jewel; and that we needn't try to write him down philosophically, because there is, in this direction, nothing to write. No creed, in fact.

These impassioned mixed metaphors of Mr. Forster, which have been parroted many times, themselves veil the nature of the obscurity —which may be a fault in the viewer rather than in the object. Another who says, finally, that "Heart of Darkness" is one of Conrad's greatest, but who quotes the above sentiments from E. M. Forster, is F. R. Leavis. In *The Great Tradition* [London, 1948], Leavis recognizes that " 'Heart of Darkness' is, by common consent, one of Conrad's best things—an appropriate source for the epigraph of *The Hollow Men*: 'Mistah Kurtz, he dead.' " But the ultimate judgment of Mr. Leavis is drawn from Forster: the "disconcerting weakness or vice" by which the "Heart of Darkness" is marred. It remains to him a story obscure in its meanings, further damaged by an "adjectival and worse than supererogatory insistence upon 'unspeakable rites,' 'monstrous passions,' 'inconceivable mystery' and so on." My feeling about both Leavis and Forster is that they find a variety of metaphysical melodrama here; that they do not really understand the images and actions of the story. With a better understanding of what Conrad intends, objections to his language disappear.

Those who find in "Heart of Darkness" primarily a protest at colonial policies can read with ease and clarity, untroubled by ambiguities. Joseph Warren Beach says:

> Kurtz is a personal embodiment, a dramatization, of all that Conrad felt of futility, degradation, and horror in what the Europeans in the Congo called "progress," which meant the exploita-

tion of the natives by every variety of cruelty and treachery known to greedy man. Kurtz was to Marlow, penetrating this country, a name, constantly recurring in people's talk, for cleverness and enterprise. . . . The blackness and mystery of his character tone in with the savage mystery of the Congo, and they develop *pari passu* with the atmosphere of shadowy horror. This development is conducted cumulatively by insensitive degrees, by carefully correlated new items, new intimations; and all this process is controlled through the consciousness of Marlow. Thus we have a triumph of atmospheric effect produced with the technique of the limited point of view, a story in a class with "The Fall of the House of Usher" and "The Turn of the Screw." [*The Twentieth-Century Novel*, New York, 1932.]

We can agree with Mr. Beach if we concede that the Conrad who wrote "Heart of Darkness" is different, not only in conceptual interests, but in technical methods, from the Conrad who wrote *Lord Jim* and *The Nigger of the Narcissus*. But the assumption of centrality in the story of social and economic commentary, and the the assumption of a straightforward narrative pattern, are inadequate to extract the meaning from Conrad anywhere, and especially from "Heart of Darkness."

Finally, there is Paul Wiley, in his *Conrad's Measure of Man* [Madison, Wis., 1954], who finds the myth of the fall from innocence throughout Conrad, and who makes of Kurtz the man driven from the Garden of Eden. The awkwardness here is that a Christian myth leaves so much unexplained at important moments in the story, as it does elsewhere in Conrad. When Marlow went back to the ring of fire in the jungle to get Kurtz that night before they started back to civilization, he found that Kurtz had kicked himself loose from heaven and hell: "There was nothing above or below him." Only Kurtz himself, demonic being, can be invoked. This is not within the conceptual framework of Christianity. Kurtz has become pre-Christian, primal energy, demiurge. And he is capable of utterly destroying the ethical man, Marlow. Kurtz has no relationship with the Christian Satan. The Christian Satan has many ethical referents; he is a necessary and even cherished figure, often contemplated. Not so with Kurtz, whose "horror" is unthinkable. The Christian Satan is very much thinkable, a vital member of the moral household more real to many than Christ. He helps to define morality, and is brought forth upon every occasion to be examined for object lessons. Kurtz's horror is "too dark—too dark altogether" to be looked at. The enigma in "Heart of Darkness" is here; if we are to understand the story we must deal adequately with that "darkness" and its meaning. And what are these "surface truths" that Marlow finds saving, but which Kurtz can never find?

These enigmas cannot be resolved by a spot analysis of Kurtz at the very moment of his death. "Heart of Darkness" is an "epiphany" story, in the sense used by James Joyce, who introduced the term into literary criticism. "Epiphany" is a rather surprising word, the way Joyce uses it. The word comes from the language of salvation; it is the revelation of divinity, a "showing forth" of the Lord. The surprise in Joyce is that the structure is used again and again to reveal spiritual isolation. Its use is closer to Freud than to Christianity. That is, it describes the use of successive images in a non-causal, or a non-dramatic relationship; rather in a free associational appearance. Joyce sets up tangent structures—tangent, not parallel—curved shapes of idea or experience which touch and curve away. It is the calculus of art—the relationship of two curved shapes in motion. In *Dubliners*, Joyce uses the method again and again. For instance, in "Clay" he sets up small, unrelated (dramatically) relationships so ordered that as the warmth of the story increases, the terror grows that little Maria is to be cast out of human fellowship —even the tiny circle that she enjoys—and then she will die. Joyce did not invent the technique; he merely supplied the name by which it may be identified. Flaubert and Chekhov, both very dear to Conrad, were using this non-dramatic method long before Joyce.

The agent for the epiphanies in "Heart of Darkness" is Marlow, who is very much more than the "limited viewpoint" that J. W. Beach has him. He is a brother to Kurtz, identified with him in the climax of the story, impelled by the powerful attraction of the man —or demon—to something in himself, to search him out in the darkness. He must follow his demon to the nether regions, to the heart of darkness, take the talisman from his lips, and return to the city. Only the talisman turns out to be "The horror!" and it is too dark to contemplate. So Marlow takes back the word "love" to deliver, the truth being too dark for the Intended. It is not too dark for Marlow, though, nor for others with totems powerful enough to withstand its evil energies.

* * *

The true talisman was not carried back to the Intended. Her saving illusions could not have borne the demonic words; but then neither could many of those fidelities—surface truths—that we encountered on our way up the river. To Marlow [Kurtz] was a hero who had shown him the limits of the mortal spirit; and the situations penetrating into the human condition became more illuminating the closer we came to Kurtz's darkness. His remarkable energies, his stature, his amazing appeal to fellow humans in his moments of darkest savagery, the very magnificence of his plunge into the pit of the universe, all these showed Marlow a moral universe, dark though it was. Emerson's line: "Yawns the pit of the Dragon, Lit by rays from the Blest" indicates the nature of this final, blinding illumination: "that could not see the light of the candle, but was wide enough to penetrate all the hearts of the universe." This is why, to Marlow, Kurtz is a true hero; a vision downward, dark, may be as true as a vision upward into the light. * * * Conrad's hero may leap high into the rarefied air as does Jim, or plunge deep into the darkness of the pit as does Kurtz; in his remarkable actions he defines the mortal condition, and in his last moment of vision he sees all the scheme of the universe; and we share it in a moment of tragic exaltation. But for most of us fidelity to household gods is the clue to "how to be"; our leaky boilers hold us to surface truths, even as we learn the meaning of life from the moral adventurers who go to their deaths at the far rims of the universe.

ALBERT J. GUERARD

The Journey Within†

Conrad, * * * like many novelists today, was both drawn to idealism and repelled by its hypocritical abuse. "The conquest of the earth, which mostly means the taking it away from those who have a different complexion or slightly flatter noses than ourselves, is not a pretty thing when you look into it too much. What redeems it is the idea only. An idea at the back of it; not a sentimental pretence but an idea; and an unselfish belief in the idea . . ." Marlow commits himself to the yet unseen agent partly because Kurtz "had come out equipped with moral ideas of some sort." Anything would seem preferable to the demoralized greed and total cynicism of the others, "the flabby devil" of the Central Station. Later, when he discovers what has happened to Kurtz's moral ideas, he remains faithful to the "nightmare of my choice." In *Under Western Eyes* Sophia Antonovna makes a distinction between those who burn and those who rot, and remarks that it is sometimes preferable to burn. The Kurtz who had made himself literally one of the devils of the land, and who in solitude had kicked himself loose of the earth, burns while the others rot. Through violent not flabby evil he exists in the moral universe even before pronouncing judgment on himself with his dying breath. A little too much has been made, I think, of the redemptive value of those two words—"The horror!" But none of the company "pilgrims" could have uttered them.

The redemptive view is Catholic, of course, though no priest

† From *Conrad the Novelist* by Albert J. Guerard. Copyright 1958 by The President and Fellows of Harvard College. Pp. 35–48. Reprinted by permission of Harvard University Press.

was in attendance; Kurtz can repent as the gunman of [Graham Greene's] *The Power and the Glory* cannot. "Heart of Darkness" (still at this public and wholly conscious level) combines a Victorian ethic and late Victorian fear of the white man's deterioration with a distinctly Catholic psychology. We are protected from ourselves by society with its laws and its watchful neighbors, Marlow observes. And we are protected by work. "You wonder I didn't go ashore for a howl and a dance? Well, no—I didn't. Fine sentiments, you say? Fine sentiments, be hanged! I had no time. I had to mess about with white-lead and strips of woolen blanket helping to put bandages on those leaky steam-pipes." But when the external restraints of society and work are removed, we must meet the challenge and temptation of savage reversion with our "own inborn strength. [Principles?] Principles won't do." This inborn strength appears to include restraint—the restraint that Kurtz lacked and the cannibal crew of the *Roi des Belges* surprisingly possessed. The hollow man, whose evil is the evil of *vacancy*, succumbs. And in their different degrees the pilgrims and Kurtz share this hollowness. "Perhaps there was nothing within" the manager of the Central Station. "Such a suspicion made one pause—for out there there were no external checks." And there was nothing inside the brickmaker, that papier-maché Mephistopheles, "but a little loose dirt, maybe."

As for Kurtz, the wilderness "echoed loudly within him because he was hollow at the core." Perhaps the chief contradiction of "Heart of Darkness" is that it suggests and dramatizes evil as an active energy (Kurtz and his unspeakable lusts) but defines evil as vacancy. The primitive (and here the contradiction is only verbal) is compact of passion and apathy. "I was struck by the fire of his eyes and the composed languor of his expression . . . This shadow looked satiated and calm, as though for the moment it had had its fill of all the emotions." Of the two menaces—the unspeakable desires and the apathy—apathy surely seemed the greater to Conrad. Hence we cannot quite believe the response of Marlow's heart to the beating of the tom-toms. This is, I think, the story's minor but central flaw, and the source of an unfruitful ambiguity: that it slightly overdoes the kinship with the "passionate uproar," slightly undervalues the temptation of inertia.

* * *

Substantially and in its central emphasis "Heart of Darkness" concerns Marlow (projection to whatever great or small degree of a more irrecoverable Conrad) and his journey toward and through certain facets or potentialities of self. F. R. Leavis seems to regard him as a narrator only, providing a "specific and concretely realized point of view."[1] But Marlow reiterates often enough that he is re-

1. *The Great Tradition* (London, 1948), p. 183.

counting a spiritual voyage of self-discovery. He remarks casually but crucially that he did not know himself before setting out, and that he likes work for the chance it provides to "find yourself . . . what no other man can ever know." The Inner Station "was the farthest point of navigation and the culminating point of my experience." At a material and rather superficial level, the journey is through the temptation of atavism. It is a record of "remote kinship" with the "wild and passionate uproar," of a "trace of a response" to it, of a final rejection of the "fascination of the abomination." And why should there not be the trace of a response? "The mind of man is capable of anything—because everything is in it, all the past as well as all the future." Marlow's temptation is made concrete through his exposure to Kurtz, a white man and sometime idealist who had fully responded to the wilderness: a potential and fallen self. "I had turned to the wilderness really, not to Mr. Kurtz." At the climax Marlow follows Kurtz ashore, confounds the beat of the drum with the beating of his heart, goes through the ordeal of looking into Kurtz's "mad soul," and brings him back to the ship. He returns to Europe a changed and more knowing man. Ordinary people are now "intruders whose knowledge of life was to me an irritating pretence, because I felt so sure they could not possibly know the things I knew."

On this literal plane, and when the events are so abstracted from the dream-sensation conveying them, it is hard to take Marlow's plight very seriously. Will he, the busy captain and moralizing narrator, also revert to savagery, go ashore for a howl and a dance, indulge unspeakable lusts? The late Victorian reader (and possibly Conrad himself) could take this more seriously than we; could literally believe not merely in a Kurtz's deterioration through months of solitude but also in the sudden reversions to the "beast" of naturalistic fiction. Insofar as Conrad does want us to take it seriously and literally, we must admit the nominal triumph of a currently accepted but false psychology over his own truer intuitions. But the triumph is only nominal. For the personal narrative is unmistakably authentic, which means that it explores something truer, more fundamental, and distinctly less material: the night journey into the unconscious, and confrontation of an entity within the self. "I flung one shoe overboard, and became aware that that was exactly what I had been looking forward to—a talk with Kurtz." It little matters what, in terms of psychological symbolism, we call this double or say he represents: whether the Freudian id or the Jungian shadow or more vaguely the outlaw. And I am afraid it is impossible to say where Conrad's conscious understanding of his story began and ended. The important thing is that the introspective plunge and powerful dream seem true; and are therefore inevitably moving.

Certain circumstances of Marlow's voyage, looked at in these terms, take on a new importance. The true night journey can occur (except during analysis) only in sleep or in the waking dream of a profoundly intuitive mind. Marlow insists more than is necessary on the dreamlike quality of his narrative. "It seems to me I am trying to tell you a dream—making a vain attempt, because no relation of a dream can convey the dream-sensation, that commingling of absurdity, surprise, and bewilderment in a tremor of struggling revolt . . ." Even before leaving Brussels Marlow felt as though he "were about to set off for the center of the earth," not the center of a continent. The introspective voyager leaves his familiar rational world, is "cut off from the comprehension" of his surroundings; his steamer toils "along slowly on the edge of a black and incomprehensible frenzy." As the crisis approaches, the dreamer and his ship move through a silence that "seemed unnatural, like a state of trance"; then enter (a few miles below the Inner Station) a deep fog. "The approach to this Kurtz grubbing for ivory in the wretched bush was beset by as many dangers as though he had been an enchanted princess sleeping in a fabulous castle."[2] Later, Marlow's task is to try "to break the spell" of the wilderness that holds Kurtz entranced.

The approach to the unconscious and primitive may be aided by a savage or half-savage guide, and may require the token removal of civilized trappings or aids; both conceptions are beautifully dramatized in Faulkner's "The Bear." In "Heart of Darkness" the token "relinquishment" and the death of the half-savage guide are connected. The helmsman falling at Marlow's feet casts blood on his shoes, which he is "morbidly anxious" to change and in fact throws overboard.[3] * * * Here we have presumably entered an area of unconscious creation; the dream is true but the teller may have no idea why it is. So too, possibly, a psychic need as well as literary tact compelled Conrad to defer the meeting between Marlow and Kurtz for some three thousand words after announcing that it took place. We think we are about to meet Kurtz at last. But instead Marlow leaps ahead to his meeting with the "Intended"; comments on Kurtz's megalomania and assumption of his place among the devils of the land; reports on the seventeen-page pamphlet; relates his meeting and conversation with Kurtz's harlequin disciple—and only then tells of seeing through his binoculars the heads on the stakes surrounding Kurtz's house. This is the "evasive" Conrad in full

2. The analogy of unspeakable Kurtz and enchanted princess may well be an intended irony. But there may be some significance in the fact that this once, the double is imagined as an entranced feminine figure.

3. Like any obscure human act, this one invites several interpretations, beginning with the simple washing away of guilt. The fear of the blood may be, however, a fear of the primitive toward which Marlow is moving. To throw the shoes overboard would then mean a token rejection of the savage, not the civilized-rational. In any event, it seems plausible to have blood at this stage of a true initiation story.

play, deferring what we most want to know and see; perhaps compelled to defer climax in this way. The tactic is dramatically effective, though possibly carried to excess: we are told on the authority of completed knowledge certain things we would have found hard to believe had they been presented through a slow consecutive realistic discovery. But also it can be argued that it was psychologically impossible for Marlow to go at once to Kurtz's house with the others. The double must be brought on board the ship, and the first confrontation must occur there. * * * The incorporation and alliance between the two becomes material, and the identification of "selves."

Hence the shock Marlow experiences when he discovers that Kurtz's cabin is empty and his secret sharer gone; a part of himself has vanished. "What made this emotion so overpowering was—how shall I define it?—the moral shock I received, as if something altogether monstrous, intolerable to thought and odious to the soul, had been thrust upon me unexpectedly." And now he must risk the ultimate confrontation in a true solitude and must do so on shore. "I was anxious to deal with this shadow by myself alone—and to this day I don't know why I was so jealous of sharing with anyone the peculiar blackness of that experience." He follows the crawling Kurtz through the grass; comes upon him "long, pale, indistinct, like a vapor exhaled by the earth." ("I had cut him off cleverly . . .") We are told very little of what Kurtz said in the moments that follow; and little of his incoherent discourses after he is brought back to the ship. "His was an impenetrable darkness. I looked at him as you peer down at a man who is lying at the bottom of a precipice where the sun never shines"—a comment less vague and rhetorical, in terms of psychic geography, than it may seem at a first reading. And then Kurtz is dead, taken off the ship, his body buried in a "muddy hole." With the confrontation over, Marlow must still emerge from environing darkness, and does so through that other deep fog of sickness. The identification is not yet completely broken. "And it is not my own extremity I remember best—a vision of grayness without form filled with physical pain, and a careless contempt for the evanescence of all things—even of this pain itself. No! It is his extremity that I seem to have lived through." Only in the atonement of his lie to Kurtz's "Intended," back in the sepulchral city, does the experience come truly to an end. "I laid the ghost of his gifts at last with a lie . . ."

Such seems to be the content of the dream. If my summary has even a partial validity it should explain and to an extent justify some of the "adjectival and worse than supererogatory insistence" to which F. R. Leavis (who sees only the travelogue and the portrait of Kurtz) objects. I am willing to grant that the unspeakable rites and unspeakable secrets become wearisome, but the fact—at once literary and psychological—is that they must remain *unspoken*. A confrontation with such a double and facet of the unconscious cannot be reported through realistic dialogue. * * * When Marlow finds it hard to define the moral shock he received on seeing the empty cabin, or when he says he doesn't know why he was jealous of sharing his experience, I think we can take him literally . . . and in a sense even be thankful for his uncertainty. The greater tautness and economy of "The Secret Sharer" comes from its larger conscious awareness of the psychological process it describes; from its more deliberate use of the double as symbol. And of the two stories I happen to prefer it. But it may be the groping, fumbling "Heart of Darkness" takes us into a deeper region of the mind. If the story is not about this deeper region, and not about Marlow himself, its length is quite indefensible. But even if one were to allow that the final section is about Kurtz (which I think simply absurd), a vivid pictorial record of his unspeakable lusts and gratifications would surely have been ludicrous. I share Mr. Leavis' admiration for the heads on the stakes. But not even Kurtz could have supported many such particulars.

"I listened on the watch for the sentence, for the word, that would give me the clue to the faint uneasiness inspired by this narrative that seemed to shape itself without human lips in the heavy night air of the river." Thus one of Marlow's listeners, the original "I" who frames the story, comments on its initial effect. He has discovered how alert one must be to the ebb and flow of Marlow's narrative, and here warns the reader. But there is no single word; not even the word *trance* will do. For the shifting play of thought and feeling and image and event is very intricate. It is not vivid detail alone, the heads on stakes or the bloody shoes; nor only the dark mass of moralizing abstraction; nor the dramatized psychological intuitions apart from their context that give "Heart of Darkness" its brooding weight. The impressionist method—one cannot leave this story without subscribing to the obvious—finds here one of its great triumphs of tone. The random movement of the nightmare is also the controlled movement of a poem, in which a quality of feeling may be stated or suggested and only much later justified. But it is justified at last.

The method is in important ways different from that of *Lord Jim*, though the short novel was written during an interval in the long one, and though Marlow speaks to us in both. For we do not have here the radical obfuscations and sudden wrenchings and violent chronological ambiguities of *Lord Jim*. Nor are we, as in *Nostromo*, at the mercy of a wayward flashlight moving rapidly in a cluttered room. "Heart of Darkness" is no such true example of spatial form. Instead the narrative advances and withdraws as in a succession of long dark waves borne by an incoming tide. The waves encroach fairly evenly on the shore, and presently a few more feet of sand have been won. But an occasional wave thrusts up unexpectedly, much farther than the others: even as far, say, as Kurtz and his Inner Station. Or, to take the other figure: the flashlight is held firmly; there are no whimsical jerkings from side to side. But now and then it is raised higher, and for a brief moment in a sudden clear light we discern enigmatic matters to be explored much later. Thus the movement of the story is sinuously progressive, with much incremental repetition. The intent is not to subject the reader to multiple strains and ambiguities, but rather to throw over him a brooding gloom, such a warm pall as those two Fates in the home office might knit, back in the sepulchral city.

Yet no figure can convey "Heart of Darkness" in all its resonance and tenebrous atmosphere. The movement is not one of penetration and withdrawal only; it is also the tracing of a large grand circle of awareness. It begins with the friends on the yacht under the dark above Gravesend and at last returns to them, to the tranquil waterway that "leading to the uttermost ends of the earth flowed sombre under an overcast sky—seemed to lead into the heart of an immense darkness." For this also "has been one of the dark places of the earth," and Marlow employs from the first his methods of reflexive reference and casual foreshadowing. The Romans were men enough to face this darkness of the Thames running between savage shores. "Here and there a military camp lost in a wilderness, like a needle in a bundle of hay—cold, fog, tempests, disease, exile, and death—death skulking in the air, in the water, in the bush." But these Romans were "no colonists," no more than the pilgrims of the Congo nineteen hundred years later; "their administration was merely a squeeze." Thus early Marlow establishes certain political values. The French gunboat firing into a continent anticipates the blind firing of the pilgrims into the jungle when the ship has been attacked. And Marlow hears of Kurtz's first attempt to emerge from the wilderness long before he meets Kurtz in the flesh, and wrestles with his reluctance to leave. Marlow returns again and again, with increasing irony, to Kurtz's benevolent pamphlet.

The travelogue as travelogue is not to be ignored; and one of Roger Casement's consular successors in the Congo (to whom I introduced "Heart of Darkness" in 1957) remarked at once that Conrad certainly had a "feel for the country." The demoralization of the first company station is rendered by a boiler "wallowing in the grass," by a railway truck with its wheels in the air. Presently Marlow will discover a scar in the hillside into which drainage pipes for the settlement had been tumbled; then will walk into the grove where the Negroes are free to die in a "greenish gloom." The sharply visualized particulars suddenly intrude on the somber intellectual flow of Marlow's meditation: magnified, arresting. The boilermaker

who "had to crawl in the mud under the bottom of the steamboat
. . . would tie up that beard of his in a kind of white serviette he
brought for the purpose. It had loops to go over his ears." The
papier-maché Mephistopheles is as vivid, with his delicate hooked
nose and glittering mica eyes. So too is Kurtz's harlequin companion
and admirer, humbly dissociating himself from the master's lusts
and gratifications. "I! I! I am a simple man. I have no great
thoughts." And even Kurtz, shadow and symbol though he be,
the man of eloquence who in this story is almost voiceless, and
necessarily so—even Kurtz is sharply visualized, an "animated image
of death," a skull and body emerging as from a winding sheet, "the
cage of his ribs all astir, the bones of his arm waving."

This is Africa and its flabby inhabitants; Conrad did indeed have
a "feel for the country." Yet the dark tonalities and final brooding
impression derive as much from rhythm and rhetoric as from such
visual details: derive from the high aloof ironies and from a prose
that itself advances and recedes in waves. "This initiated wraith
from the back of Nowhere honored me with its amazing confidence
before it vanished altogether." Or, "It is strange how I accepted this
unforseen partnership, this choice of nightmares forced upon me
in the tenebrous land invaded by these mean and greedy phantoms."
These are true Conradian rhythms, but they are also rhythms of
thought. The immediate present can be rendered with great com-
pactness and drama: the ship staggering within ten feet of the bank
at the time of the attack, and Marlow's sudden glimpse of a face
amongst the leaves, then of the bush "swarming with human limbs."
But still more immediate and personal, it may be, are the meditative
passages evoking vast tracts of time, and the "first of men taking
possession of an accursed inheritance." The prose is varied, far more
so than is usual in the early work, both in rhythm and in the movements from the general to the particular and back. But the shaped
sentence collecting and fully expending its breath appears to be the
norm. Some of the best passages begin and end with them:

> Going up that river was like traveling back to the earliest begin-
> nings of the world, when vegetation rioted on the earth and the
> big trees were kings. An empty stream, a great silence, an im-
> penetrable forest. The air was warm, thick, heavy, sluggish.
> There was no joy in the brilliance of sunshine. The long stretches
> of the waterway ran on, deserted, into the gloom of over-
> shadowed distances. On silvery sandbanks hippos and alligators
> sunned themselves side by side.

The insistence on darkness, finally, and quite apart from ethical or
mythical overtone, seems a right one for this extremely personal
statement. There is a darkness of passivity, paralysis, immobilization;
it is from the state of entranced languor rather than from the

monstrous desires that the double Kurtz, this shadow, must be saved. In Freudian theory, we are told, such preoccupation may indicate fear of the feminine and passive. But may it not also be connected, through one of the spirit's multiple disguises, with a radical fear of death, that other darkness? "I had turned to the wilderness really, not to Mr. Kurtz, who, I was ready to admit, was as good as buried. And for a moment it seemed to me as if I also were buried in a vast grave full of unspeakable secrets. I felt an intolerable weight oppressing my breast, the smell of the damp earth, the unseen presence of victorious corruption, the darkness of an impenetrable night."

It would be folly to try to limit the menace of vegetation in the restless life of Conradian image and symbol. But the passage reminds us again of the story's reflexive references, and its images of deathly immobilization in grass. Most striking are the black shadows dying in the greenish gloom of the grove at the first station. But grass sprouts between the stones of the European city, a "whited sepulchre," and on the same page Marlow anticipates coming upon the remains of his predecessor: "the grass growing through his ribs was tall enough to hide his bones." The critical meeting with Kurtz occurs on a trail through the grass. Is there not perhaps an intense horror behind the casualness with which Marlow reports his discoveries, say of the Negro with the bullet in his forehead? Or: "Now and then a carrier dead in harness, at rest in the long grass near the path, with an empty water gourd and his long staff lying by his side."

All this, one must acknowledge, does not make up an ordinary light travelogue. There is no little irony in the letter of November 9, 1891, Conrad received from his guardian after returning from the Congo, and while physically disabled and seriously depressed: "I am sure that with your melancholy temperament you ought to avoid all meditations which lead to pessimistic conclusions. I advise you to lead a more active life than ever and to cultivate cheerful habits."[4] Uneven in language on certain pages, and lacking "The Secret Sharer" 's economy, "Heart of Darkness" nevertheless remains one of the great dark meditations in literature, and one of the purest expressions of a melancholy temperament.

4. *Life and Letters,* I, 148.

JEROME THALE

Marlow's Quest†

Conrad's "Heart of Darkness" has all the trappings of the conventional adventure tale—mystery, exotic setting, escape, suspense, unexpected attack. These, of course, are only the vehicle of something more fundamental, and one way of getting at what they symbolize is to see the story as a grail quest. Though Conrad is sparing in his explicit use of the metaphor ("a weary pilgrimage amongst hints for nightmares"), it is implicit in the structure of the action. As in the grail quest there is the search for some object, and those who find and can see the grail receive an illumination. Marlow, the central figure, is like a knight seeking the grail, and his journey even to the end follows the archetype. His grandiose references to the dark places of the earth, his talk of the secret of a continent, the farthest point of navigation, his sudden and unwonted sense that he is off not to the centre of a continent but to the centre of the earth —these, occurring before he starts his journey, give it the atmosphere of a quest.

And in the journey itself there are the usual tests and obstacles of a quest. After Marlow passes through the bizarre company head-quarters in Brussels and the inanity surrounding his voyage to the African coast, he makes a difficult and painful journey inland. At the central station he begins a seemingly routine task—going up the river to bring back a sick company agent—which will become his quest. Gradually he learns a little about Kurtz, at first a name; disgust with the manager and reports about the remarkable agent in the jungle make him increasingly eager to see the man. As Marlow's interest in Kurtz mounts, so do the trials and obstacles that are part of Marlow's test. The journey creeps on painfully in the patched ship. Near the end, just before the attack, Marlow realizes that Kurtz is the one thing he has been seeking, the "enchanted princess" in a "fabulous castle," whose approaches are fraught with danger.

The grail motif is of course connected with the profuse—and somewhat heavy-handed—light-darkness symbolism. The grail is an effulgence of light, and it gives an illumination to those who can see it. This is the light which Marlow seeks in the heart of darkness. The

† From *University of Toronto Quarterly*, XXIV (July, 1955), 351–58. Reprinted by permission of the editors and the author. See also Thale's companion study, "The Narrator as Hero," *Twentieth-Century Literature*, III (July, 1957), 69–73.

grail that he finds appears an abomination and the light even deeper darkness, yet paradoxically Marlow does have an illumination: "it threw a kind of light on everything about me." The manager and the others travelling with Marlow are constantly called pilgrims, "faithless pilgrims," and for the faithless there can be no illumination. At the end of his quest Marlow does not find what he had expected all alone, a good man in the midst of darkness and corruption. Instead he receives a terrible illumination. Such experiences are as ineffable as they are profound, and this is why the meaning of Marlow's tale must be expressed so obliquely, like the "glow that brings out the haze."

The nature of Marlow's illumination is determined by the remarkable man who is its occasion. And to comprehend Kurtz we must look into the reasons for Marlow's attitude towards him. Marlow is listening to the manager condemning Kurtz's methods as "unsound." "It seemed to me I had never breathed an atmosphere so vile, and I turned mentally to Kurtz for relief . . . it was something to have at least a choice of nightmares." Why must Marlow choose a nightmare at all? Because what he sees in one of the nightmares is so compelling that he cannot remain neutral before it.

Marlow's choice is made easier for the reader to accept by the fact that even before meeting Kurtz Marlow finds himself on Kurtz's side. Marlow has been disgusted by everything connected with the company; he learns that the manager schemes against Kurtz, because Kurtz, like Marlow, is one of the new gang, "the gang of virtue." The unseen apostle of light becomes the alternative to the cowardly plunderers. But Marlow is not trapped into an incredible allegiance; he knows what he is choosing when he later makes his real choice. Nor is it an unconsidered gesture of escape from the moral decay of the hollow men. His choice is a deliberate one.

Given Marlow's nature and his function in the story his choice must be based on something positive in Kurtz. There are strong hints in the story that Kurtz is a good man gone wrong in the jungle. But if he is merely a victim of unusual circumstances, a man to be pitied, then Marlow's choice is as sentimental as that of Kurtz's fiancée. The causes of Kurtz's tragedy are within—in his towering ambition, and his rootless idealism. Yet the jungle is important, for what happens to Kurtz can happen only under some such conditions. And what Marlow values in Kurtz is so paradoxical that it can be seen only against a dark and mysterious jungle and the corruption of colonial exploitation.

What is it in Kurtz that compels a choice and that produces such a profound change in the imperturbable Marlow? Simply that Kurtz has discovered himself, has become fully human; and Marlow's illumination, the light that is his grail, is a similar discovery about himself and all men.

* * *

And the discovery of the self is the discovery of one's freedom. Away from the grooves that society provides for keeping us safely in a state of subsisting, we can discover that we are free to be, to do anything, good or evil. For the mystic it means the freedom to love God. For Kurtz it means the freedom to become his own diabolical god. This radical freedom as it exists in Kurtz seems to Marlow both exalting and revolting. Exalting because it makes man human, revolting because in Kurtz it is so perverted and so absolute as to exceed all human limits and become inhuman. By distinguishing these two aspects of Marlow's response, we can make meaningful his commitment to Kurtz. To put it another way, we can sum up the two aspects of Kurtz's freedom in the phrase "I am." On the one hand, to say "I am," is to say that I exist, to say that I am free and have immense possibilities in my grasp. On the other, "I am" is the phrase which only God can utter, because only God exists simply and completely. For Kurtz to say "I am" is the ultimate and complete assertion of himself to the exclusion of all else, the assertion that he is a god.

Before Kurtz's discovery of his existence can become Marlow's illumination it has to be realized by both of them. The revelation proceeds through Kurtz to Marlow, and Marlow's full illumination, his full realization of what it means to be, must wait upon a realization in Kurtz that brings out and confirms what Marlow has already seen in him. A final awareness in Kurtz is needed to make meaningful and universalize Kurtz's experience. For Kurtz has accepted his freedom, has become human, but he has not evaluated what being human means. He must assent to the knowledge he has been trying to keep off. This realization, which must be distinguished from the agonizing discovery of his existence, can come only as its fruit. Authentic self-knowledge demands a real existent as its object. Having discovered that he can exist, Kurtz must now evaluate existence. "The horror! the horror" is this evaluation.

The most we can hope for in life, Marlow tells us, is "some knowledge of yourself—that comes too late." Marlow comes close to death and finds that he has nothing to say. Kurtz "had something to say. He said it. Since I had peeped over the edge myself, I understand better the meaning of his stare, that could not see the flame of the candle, but it was wide enough to embrace the whole universe, piercing enough to penetrate all the hearts that beat in the darkness."

Only after Marlow passes his final test, his brush with death, does the full significance of Kurtz come to him. Kurtz's last cry takes us to the meaning of the whole African venture for Marlow, the illumination he receives. For Marlow sees that Kurtz's cry is more than self-knowledge, more than an insight into the depths of his own evil. It is an insight into the potentialities in all men, it gives the perspective in which we must see Kurtz's discovery of himself. Kurtz's cry is no deathbed repentance which makes him a hero to whom Marlow can be loyal. It is for Marlow a terrible illumination, for in Kurtz Marlow discovers not simply one man become evil, but a universal possibility. Deprived of the insulation of society, the protecting surface, faced with the terrible challenge, we discover that we are free; the very fact is terrifying, for in that choice lies the unpredictable, even the Kurtzian.

Marlow's illumination comes only after Kurtz's last words and after Marlow's encounter with death; his choice of nightmares is not based on this evaluation. Marlow has chosen before Kurtz utters his cry, and the cry only enables Marlow to see more fully what he has already seen at the time of his choice. At the time he chooses Kurtz, Marlow declares that Kurtz is "remarkable," and to the end of the story he uses no stronger—indeed no other—epithet than this. Its occasional ironic uses only point up to its understatement. And "remarkable" is Marlow's comment on Kurtz's acceptance of his freedom.

And this is so remarkable that Marlow chooses it even in a man like Kurtz, a man who actualizes his existence only in the evil fulfilment of a monstrous megalomania. What Marlow values in Kurtz is both moral and non-moral. Moral because whether a man exists, has the capacity to act as a human being, is the most important moral fact about him. Non-moral because existence is prior to morality considered as a set of norms for acting and judging conduct. Kurtz's triumph is ontological. He existed as a human being capable of good and evil. His tragedy is moral, for he existed subject to no law or standard.

Marlow finds it hard to explain Kurtz and justify his own stand. He keeps telling his hearers, "You couldn't understand." His evaluation of Kurtz is presented through a series of contrasts and antitheses. The manager is a "flabby, pretending, weak-eyed devil," the brickmaker a "papier mâché Mephistopheles." Marlow prefers to these the devils of violence, greed, desire, for they are "strong, lusty, red-eyed devils, that sway and drive men," real devils that at least demand some commitment of the self. Kurtz is a genuine devil, a god in his Satanic rites. He can inspire horror and revulsion in Marlow, whereas the manager, neither feared nor loved, inspires only "uneasiness." Kurtz commits himself totally to evil, the manager keeps up appearances. Kurtz throws himself into action, though evil; the manager, ruled by caution, murmurs, and does evil by omission.

What is evil in the manager and his men is not their conniving, their opportunism, their neglect of Kurtz, but their moral impotence. In Kurtz evil is incarnate. In the company-men evil is a privation, not of goodness but of existence. Marlow condemns them on onto-logical as much as moral grounds. Too self-loving, too much the victims of their own life-killing prudence for a surrender even to evil, they are, like Leon Bloy's middle class, incapable of mortal sin. They are not evil, for they are not even alive, not capable of the humanity involved in making a choice for good or evil. Kurtz has made the journey to the depths of the self, he has responded to the fascinating and terrible appeal of existence. His choice is for evil, but it is a human choice—and it is to this humanity that Marlow turns with positive relief, even though it is a nightmare.

And it is a nightmare of enormous proportions. Kurtz fails so horribly because he has no "inborn strength," no capacity for faith-fulness, no code. Marlow's usual term for this is "restraint." The more one has realized himself, and become capable of all things, the more restraint is needed. And Marlow makes a great deal of restraint. He is amazed at the restraint in the cannibals that keeps them from eating the pilgrims. The manager's restraint, keeping up appearances, is but a parody that excites Marlow's scorn and makes the manager worse than Kurtz. The accountant immaculately dressed amidst moral and physical disintegration, keeping his books in apple pie order though a dying man lies on the floor, is admirable because he has some order, some code, some commitment outside the self. This is why the seamanship manual, with its "simple-hearted devotion to the right way of doing things," seems so precious to Marlow; it is a symbol of the restraint, the devotion, that both Kurtz and the man-ager lack.

Neither Kurtz with his abandon, nor the manager with his getting on in the world, has this restraint, this "devotion to the backbreak-ing business" rather than to the self. The self unharnessed must be used in terms of something outside itself. Better live by an absurd code, like the accountant, than by none at all. As Marlow says, "What redeems it is the idea only . . . an unselfish belief in the idea—something you can set up, and bow down before, and offer a sacrifice to." Marlow is ironic when he applies the phrase to the Romans, but the irony is lifted as the story progresses. And in Kurtz's final cry the "idea" becomes part of Marlow's illumination. Kurtz, living outside all norms, yet knows that they exist and condemn him. Implicit in his cry is an admission of what he has evaded, a realization of the insufficiency of his total commitment to himself and of the validity of the standards which condemn him. And through Kurtz, Marlow, the seaman who has always lived by a code, grasps its necessity and its validity.[1]

This is the last stage of Marlow's initiation, of his confrontation with what it means to be human. Kurtz is the grail at the end of Marlow's quest, and of all those who come into contact with Kurtz only Marlow—the faithful pilgrim—experiences an illumination. The manager reduces Kurtz to his own terms and cannot see him. The Russian sailor, who admires Kurtz, is too much a fool—perhaps a wise fool—to recognize the challenge that Kurtz has met. The two women each see and love Kurtz, but a false Kurtz, a lie, which Marlow must meet with another lie.

Most people are not capable of understanding Kurtz; the policeman and the two good addresses shelter them from the terror of being. But Marlow has had his illumination, and like Gulliver come back to England, he cannot stand the smug faces of the people walking down the streets, unaware of the challenge and the danger. Their knowledge of life seems "an irritating pretense." They do not know that they are and therefore they are not. Marlow scorns them because in the quest for Kurtz he has discovered the dreadful burden of human freedom. His full illumination, his grail, is not transcendent being but the heart of man. Yet it demands the same tests in the journey of purification and produces an illumination equally awful.

LILLIAN FEDER

Marlow's Descent Into Hell†

Marlow's journey in Conrad's "Heart of Darkness" is usually interpreted as a study of a descent into the unconscious self. Of course, the voyage into the heart of darkness is, on one level, a symbolic representation of an exploration of the hidden self and therefore of man's capacity for evil. However, Conrad is not merely narrating a

1. That it can be interpreted as a Freudian allegory testifies to the richness and validity of Conrad's story. Kurtz is like the id, the unharnessed primal forces. The manager represents a crushing amount of superego that destroys life by its timid and fearful unwillingness to release and use those forces. Marlow, at least at the end of the story, stands for ego, an awareness of the forces within him and a conscious use and control of them. His journey is a symbol of the process through which we discover the deepest recesses of the self and make use of its power. Whether the whole story could be adequately described in terms of some such allegory I do not know; certainly, much of the imagery of darkness and the jungle makes sense in those terms.

† From *Nineteenth-Century Fiction*, IX (March, 1955), 280–92. Copyright 1955 by the Regents of the University of California. Reprinted by permission of the editors and the author. The page references have been omitted by the present editor.

psychological experience; he is dealing with a significant moral conflict. If this were simply a story concerned with the two aspects of the mind of man, the conscious and the unconscious, what would be Conrad's point in treating so extensively the condition of the natives in the Congo? Moreover, without studying some of Conrad's most powerful and most consistent imagery, it is impossible to explain the role of Kurtz's "Intended," which is important in the development of the theme. In "Heart of Darkness," Conrad is depicting Marlow's discovery of evil and the responsibilities to himself and to others which this knowledge places upon him. In telling the story of Marlow's attainment of self-knowledge, Conrad does not use the language of psychology. Instead, he employs the imagery and symbolism of the traditional voyage into Hades.

By associating Marlow's journey with the descent into hell, Conrad concretizes the hidden world of the inner self. Through image and symbol, he evokes the well-known voyage of the hero who, in ancient epic, explores the lower world and, in so doing, probes the depths of his own and his nation's conscience. A study of "Heart of Darkness" from this point of view discloses some interesting parallels, but, more important, by setting Conrad's story in relief against a background rich in associations, it reveals the essential unity of his political and personal themes. Moreover, such a reading shows how Conrad, by combining the traditional imagery of the epic descent with realistic details from his own experience in the Congo, created an image of hell credible to modern man.

Though Marlow's journey recalls the epic descent in general, it is most specifically related to the visit to Hades in the sixth book of the *Aeneid*. In Vergil's poem, Aeneas' descent is part of his initiation for the role of leader of the Roman people. Vergil emphasizes the fact that truth is to be found in the heart of darkness; thus, the Sibyl who, in Vergil's words, "obscuris vera involvens" (hides truth in darkness), guides Aeneas. Moreover, just as Aeneas is about to enter Hades, Vergil interrupts his narrative to ask the very elements of hell, Chaos and Phlegethon, to allow him to reveal the secrets buried in the darkness and depths of the earth. Aeneas' voyage to Hades is one means by which he learns of the tragedy implicit in the affairs of men; this is the price he pays for fulfilling his duty as founder of Rome. In the lower world he looks both into past and the future and, having observed the penalties for personal crimes, he is told of the bloodshed and cruelty which are to weigh on the conscience of his nation—the cost of Rome's imperial power. Aeneas, the pious and worthy man, learns truth through a descent into darkness.

* * *

It is fairly obvious that "Heart of Darkness" has three levels of meaning: on one level it is the story of a man's adventures; on another, of his discovery of certain political and social injustices; and on a third, it is a study of his initiation into the mysteries of his own mind. The same three levels of meaning can be found in the sixth book of Vergil's *Aeneid*. Like Aeneas, Marlow comes to understand himself, his obligations, and the tragic limitations involved in any choice through this three-fold experience. Kurtz, like Aeneas, starts out as an "emissary of light," but, unlike Vergil's hero, he cannot conquer himself. Through Kurtz's experience, Marlow learns that a man is defined by his work: Kurtz's work has created a hell in the jungle, which destroys him. The symbol of the lower world suggests not only an imaginative union between the ancient world and the modern one, but a judgment on the morality of modern society.

From its beginning, Marlow's journey seems fated. He is destined by the needs of his own spirit, which Conrad concretizes in his response to the knitting "fates," to understand himself through a study of the world he lives in. By viewing that world indirectly, through an image, Marlow comes to closer grips with it than he has ever before been able to.

The epic descent is always a journey to find someone who knows the truth. Marlow realizes long before he has penetrated the Congo that the real purpose of his journey is to meet Kurtz and talk with him. When he discovers Kurtz, he finds, on one level, a man who has committed unspeakable crimes against his fellows. But on another and more important level, he finds a man who has allowed himself to sink to the lowest possible depths of evil, and, by observing Kurtz, Marlow realizes that in all men there is this possibility. In other words, he discovers the potential hell in the heart of every man.

In the Congo, there are no supernatural beings; all is credible on a purely realistic level. However, the imagery of hell, with its suggestion of the supernatural, implies the terror and violent suffering which Kurtz, the betrayer of light, must face. And, through the imagery of hell, Conrad makes Kurtz's struggle in the Congo symbolic of an inner defeat. Kurtz, on the one hand, has betrayed the natives and reduced them to poverty and subservience, but he has also betrayed the humanity in himself. He has reduced the natives to tormented shades, for he has robbed them of a living will and dignity and, in so doing, he has himself become a shade; his will is the victim and servant of his own hellish whims.

Marlow too has faced the terrors of hell, and, though he escapes, he learns wisdom at a price. He owes a debt to Kurtz, for Kurtz has been man enough to face the hell within him. Unlike the agents who turn away from the challenge of hell, Kurtz has gone all too far in his weird exploration. Through Kurtz's failure, Marlow learns about his own capacity for evil and his capacity to resist it. He realizes that without involvement, there is no restraint, and he makes his choice of "nightmares." He is even willing to experience a kind of spiritual death in the sacrifice of lying for Kurtz. Ironically, the reward of his victory over the elements of hell is his knowledge of human limitation; thus, while he repudiates Kurtz, he remains loyal to him. In this loyalty there is an acknowledgement of the eternal existence of the hell within, to be met and conquered again and again by every man; moreover, there is the tragic acceptance of the eternal possibility of defeat.

I have said that Kurtz's "Intended" is as much a shade as Kurtz is. Indeed, Conrad calls her by that name and identifies her, through his imagery, with the world of the dead. She, like the natives, has sacrificed all that is living in order to believe in Kurtz. Marlow refers to her at one point ironically as such a "thunderingly exalted creature as to be altogether deaf and blind to anything but heavenly sights and sounds." For such a person, the "earth . . . is only a standing place." By contrast, he says, for most people, the earth "is a place to *live* in, where we must put up with sights, with sounds, with smells, too, by Jove!—breathe dead hippo, so to speak, and not be contaminated." Kurtz's "Intended" sacrifices life to a dead ideal. She has not breathed "dead hippo"; she has not faced the darkness. Like Kurtz, she has chosen death. He has been conquered by his inhuman guilt; she by her inhuman innocence, by her unwillingness to pay the price of life, the acceptance of a knowledge of ugliness and evil. Marlow does not disillusion her, in part because of his loyalty to Kurtz, and in part because of the futility of telling the truth, brutal and ugly, like the "dead hippo" or the sights, sounds, and smells of the world, to a woman who, because of her unwillingness to face life, has become a shade. Thus, when she asks Marlow for Kurtz's last word, instead of repeating Kurtz's remark, "The horror," Marlow says that the last word he pronounced was her name. This is his final tribute to the world of the dead, his last "ceremony." For this reason the lie has a taint of mortality for him.

Speaking of the artist, Conrad says that "he must descend within himself, and in that lonely region of stress and strife, if he be deserving and fortunate, he finds the terms of his appeal." [1] And in *Victory*, he says, "It is not poets alone who dare descend into the abyss of infernal regions, or even who dream of such a descent." In "Heart of Darkness" Conrad used the imagery and symbolism of Hades to create that otherwise formless region into which not only the artist but every man must descend if he wishes to understand himself. Moreover, through the imagery of hell, with its timeless associations, the private struggle is united with man's public deeds, his responsibilities, and his history.

MARVIN MUDRICK

The Originality of Conrad†

Conrad offers himself from the first as a dogged innovator of fictional techniques, like his own Kurtz one of the first thorough explorers of a rather dark continent; and it is tempting to read him for the sophisticated pleasure one takes in recognizing novel and schematizable, if not necessarily expressive, method. A teacher once worked out for his students a chronological chart of the events in *Victory*. The chart proved, of course, Conrad's creative cleverness at mixing up the events and the teacher's critical astuteness at setting them right again. This is one pattern of Conrad criticism. That it is a seductive pattern appears from Henry James's professional admiration for the multiple viewpoints intruding, in *Chance*, between the reader and the events (James placed Conrad "absolutely alone as a votary of the way to do a thing that shall make it undergo most doing"): the only residual doubt being whether, at a fifth or even a second remove, the events of *Chance* have any interest in themselves; whether, for example, once we have pushed through layers of Marlow's gruff archness to arrive at Conrad's inevitable sweet silent slip of a girl and what Mr. Zabel notes as Captain Anthony's "touch of inscrutable sanctimony,"[1] our long attention seems worthwhile.

Length is usually, indeed, no advantage to Conrad. Albert Guérard has asserted that "Conrad's long stories and short novels are far more experimental and more 'modern' than his full-length novels"[2]; and, though it is an assertion that requires reservations, it points to the comparative economy and tact of Conrad's method in pieces like *Typhoon* and *The Nigger of the Narcissus*, to the unfailing grim power of Part I of *Under Western Eyes* (before the novel falls apart in a compulsion to extend itself beyond its normal novella length), as well as to the inert and wilful complications characteristic of such larger works as *Chance*, *Lord Jim*, *Victory*, *Nostromo*, and *The Secret Agent*. Everything Conrad wrote recalls everything else he wrote, in a pervasive melancholy of outlook, a persistency of theme ("the plight of the man on whom life closes down inexorably, divesting him of the supports and illusory protection of friendship, social privilege, or love"[3]), and a conscientious manipu-

† From *The Hudson Review*, XI (Winter, 1958–59), 545–53. Copyright 1959 by The Hudson Review, Inc. Reprinted by permission.

1. M. D. Zabel (ed.), *The Portable Conrad*, Viking, New York, 1952, pp. 40–41.
2. Conrad, *Heart of Darkness* and *The Secret Sharer*, introduction by Albert Guerard, Jr., Signet, New York, 1950, p. 8.
3. Zabel, *The Portable Conrad*, p. 26.

lation of innovational method; yet what marks Conrad as not a mere experimentalist or entertainer but a genuine innovator occurs only sporadically in his full-length novels, with discretion and sustained impulse only in several long stories or short novels: in *The Nigger of the Narcissus*, in *Typhoon*, in Part I of *Under Western Eyes*, and—with most impressive rich immediacy—in *Heart of Darkness*.

Conrad's innovation—or, in any case, the fictional technique that he exploited with unprecedented thoroughness—is the double-plot: neither allegory (where surface is something teasing, to be got through), nor catch-all symbolism (where every knowing particular signifies some universal or other), but a developing order of actions so lucidly symbolic of a developing state of spirit—from moment to moment, so morally identifiable—as to suggest the conditions of allegory without forfeiting or even subordinating the realistic "super-ficial" claim of the actions and their actors.

* * *

Conrad's symbolism, and his moral imagination, are, after all, as unallegorical as possible. When they function and have effect they are severely realistic: they nourish themselves on voices heard and solid objects seen and touched in the natural world, they contract into rhetoric as soon as the voices and objects begin to appear less than independently present; when Conrad is not describing, with direct sensuous impact, a developing sequence of distinct actions, he is liable to drift into the mooning or glooming that for some critics passes as Conrad's "philosophy" and for others as his style in its full tropical luxuriance.

Moreover, to assume, as Dr. Leavis seems to assume, that all symbolism works *only* as it is anchored to a record of immediate sensations, that it must totally coincide with "the concrete pre-sentment of incident, setting and image," is to transform Conrad's limitation (and gift) into a condition of fiction. To compare Conrad's symbolic method, his two-ply plot, with the methods of, say, Dostoievsky and Kafka is to become aware of radically different possibilities: on the one hand, Conrad's realistic mode; on the other, moral imaginations not necessarily anchored to objects and places, symbolic means capable of producing, for example, those vibrations of clairvoyant hallucination in Dostoievsky, and of mean-ingful enigma in Kafka, which move through and beyond immediate sensations into a world of moral meanings almost as independent as, and far more densely populated than, the other side of the mirror of traditional allegory. Of such effects, beyond the capacities of even the most evocative realism, Conrad is innocent; yet when, in *Heart of Darkness*, he approaches the center of a difficult moral situation (desperately more troublesome than the simple choices permitted the characters in *Typhoon*), when facts and details begin to appear inadequate as figurations of the moral problem, it is just such effects that he is at length driven to attempt.

The problem is, of course, Kurtz. It is when we are on the verge of meeting Kurtz that Marlow's "inconceivables" and "impenetrables" begin to multiply at an alarming rate; it is when we have already met him that we are urged to observe "smiles of indefinable meaning" and to hear about "unspeakable rites" and "gratified and monstrous passions" and "subtle horrors"—words to hound the reader into a sense of enigmatic awfulness that he would somehow be the better for not trying to find a way through:

> "Everything belonged to him—but that was a trifle. The thing was to know what he belonged to, how many powers of darkness claimed him for their own. That was the reflection that made you creepy all over. It was impossible—it was not good for one either—trying to imagine."

The problem, as Conrad sets it up, is to persuade the reader— by epithets, exclamations, ironies, by every technical obliquity— into an hallucinated awareness of the unplumbable depravity, the primal unanalyzable evil, implicit in Kurtz's reversion to the jungle from the high moral sentiments of his report:

> "The peroration was magnificent, though difficult to remember, you know. It gave me the notion of an exotic Immensity ruled by an august Benevolence."

Unhappily, though, the effect of even this minor irony is to bring to mind and penetrate Conrad's magazine-writer style as well as the hollowness of Kurtz's sentiments. Besides, Kurtz's sentiments must, to help justify the fuss Conrad makes about their author, radiate at least a rhetorical energy; yet all Conrad gives us of the report is a phrase or two of mealy-mouthed reformist exhortation that would not do credit to a Maugham missionary let alone the "extraordinary man" Kurtz is supposed by all accounts to be, so that the "irony" of the scrawled outcry at the end of the report— "Exterminate the brutes!" [*sic*]—is about as subtle and unexpected as the missionary's falling for the local call-girl.

In the effort to establish for Kurtz an opaque and terrifying magnitude, Conrad tends to rely more and more oppressively on these pat ironies. The very existence of the incredibly naïve young Russian is another such irony: the disciple who responds to Kurtz's abundant proofs of cruelty and mean obsession with the steadfast conviction—and no evidence for the reader—that Kurtz is a great man (" ' "he's enlarged my mind" ' "—another irony that cuts more ways than Conrad must have intended). And if the culminating irony of the narrative, Marlow's interview with Kurtz's Intended, is expertly anticipated long before, when Marlow remarks—

> "You know I hate, detest, and can't bear a lie, not because I am straighter than the rest of us, but simply because it appalls me. There is a taint of death, a flavor of mortality in lies—which is exactly what I hate and detest in the world—what I want to forget. It makes me miserable and sick, like biting something rotten would do."

—it is all the more disheartening, after such anticipation, to encounter in that interview sighs, heart stoppings, chill grips in the chest, exultations, the cheaply ironic double-talk (" 'She said suddenly very low, "He died as he lived." "His end," said I, with dull anger stirring in me, "was in every way worthy of his life." ' ") as well as the sentimental lie that provokes not only her " 'cry of inconceivable triumph and of unspeakable pain' " but the final cheap irony (" ' "I knew it—I was sure!" She knew. She was sure.' ")—a jumble of melodramatic tricks so unabashed and so strategic that in any less reputable writer they might well be critically regarded as earning for the work an instant oblivion.

Still, in *Heart of Darkness* at least, Conrad is neither cynical nor laxly sentimental in his failure of imagination and corresponding failure of technique. The theme itself is too much for him, too much for perhaps any but the very greatest dramatists and novelists. The sense of evil he must somehow project exceeds his capacity for imagining it; he strains into badness while reaching for verifications of a great and somber theme that is beyond his own very considerable powers. * * * [Nevertheless, *Heart of Darkness*] is one of the great originals of literature. After *Heart of Darkness* the craftsman in fiction could never again be unaware of the moral resources inherent in every recorded sensation, or insensitive to the need of making the most precise record possible of every sensation: what now appears an immemorial cliché of the craft of fiction has a date as recent as the turn of the century. If Conrad was never quite equal to his own originality, he was at least the first to designate it as a new province of possibilities for the novelist; and, in *Heart of Darkness*, the first to suggest, by large and compelling partial proof, the intensity of moral illumination that a devoted attention to its demands might generate. The suggestion was an historical event: for good and bad novelists alike, irreversible. After *Heart of Darkness*, the recorded moment—the word—was irrecoverably symbol.

STEWART C. WILCOX

Conrad's "Complicated Presentations" of Symbolic Imagery†

Conrad's exhaustive exploration of the imagery of *Heart of Darkness* accounts for its atmosphere, the "sinister resonances" of its symbols. The title of course sets the tone-color for the whole. Darkness is the unfathomable and the impenetrable; the savage, prehistoric past; the center of Africa, of the earth itself, even of man's consciousness, echoing from time to time passages from Dante's *Inferno* or Vergil's description of the underworld in the sixth book of the *Aeneid*.[1] In one of his letters Conrad remarks that to create a story "you must cultivate your poetic faculty . . . You must search the darkest corners of your heart . . . for the image."

As Marlow explores the spaces of the dark continent, he probes the depths of his unknown self to discover what is real. Leonard F. Dean observes: "Essentially the problem is the relation and disparity between appearance and reality, and hence the nature, the need, and the value of illusion."[2] Only through self-knowledge can man realize the "idea," the "illusion" which will save him from the dark powers he has faced within his being, and it is this need of ethical recognition that forces Marlow to search out his own hidden affinity with Kurtz, the *alter ego* who is his accusing conscience.

The setting of these adventurous and moral quests is the great jungle to which the story leads for its resolution. As a symbol the forest encloses all, for it is the heart of the African journey where Marlow enters the dark cavern of his own heart. Through the jungle, like a mighty pulse beating simultaneously with primitive and modern rhythms of savagery and commerce, the deadly Congo snakes to link itself with the sea and all other rivers of darkness and light, with the tributaries and source of man's being on earth. As will appear, it even becomes an image of a vast catacomb of evil, in which Kurtz dies but from which Marlow emerges spiritually reborn.

By such means does Conrad transform a tale that on one level of meaning is a travelogue telling of the economic exploitation of the Belgian Congo into a story with a profound theme—"the theme," says Albert Guerard, "of initiation and moral education, . . . of progress through temporary reversion and achieved self-knowledge,

† From *Philological Quarterly*, XXXIX (January 1960), 1–17. Copyright 1960 by the State University of Iowa. Reprinted by permission.
1. See Lillian Feder, "Marlow's Descent into Hell," * * * ; and Robert O. Evans, "Conrad's Underworld."
2. Dean, "Tragic Pattern in Conrad's 'The Heart of Darkness,'" *College English*, VI (1944), 100.

. . . of man's exploratory descent into the primitive sources of be-ing."[3] How aptly this comment sums up *Heart of Darkness* is fur-ther suggested by a remark of Conrad's own: "The artist descends within himself, and in that lonely region of stress and strife, if he be deserving and fortunate, he finds the terms of his appeal." As the teller of the story, Marlow thus becomes far more than a literary device to gain verisimilitude or shift points of narrative view. He is Conrad himself, for *Heart of Darkness* is based upon his experi-ences along the upper Congo in 1890, where, after trudging 250 miles of jungle, he became mate of a tiny sternwheeler and sailed to an Inner Station for ivory. Hence Marlow is both Conrad and all men who have taken the "night journey" into the primeval depths of their own and their racial consciousness. He has "voyaged alone among the temptations which entangle man in time,"[4] having to pay a price for his traffic with evil by telling two lies, one to the clerk of the company at the Central Station, the other to Kurtz's Intended. At the end, released from his fleshly ties, he "ceased his narration, sat apart, indistinct and silent, in the pose of the meditating Bud-dha." W. B. Stein writes: "A vision of spiritual reality is framed in the Buddha tableaux."[5]

* * *

Although [Stein's] observations upon the oriental ideal of selfless-ness signified in Marlow's posture during narration are fundamental in apprehending the spiritual outcome of *Heart of Darkness*, cer-tainly they do not include all its moral meanings. Perhaps just as fundamental to apprehension of them is Conrad's way of complicated presentation, a method that deepens the perspectives of his imagery as he foreshadows, suggests, works with an exhaustive steadiness to-ward the inner core of his own apprehension. "As a matter of fact," he wrote Richard Curle regarding his complicated presentations,

> the thought for effects is there . . . (often at the cost of mere directness of narrative), and can be detected in my unconven-tional grouping and perspective, which is purely temperamental and wherein almost all my 'art' consists. This, I suspect, has been the difficulty the critics felt in classifying it as romantic or real-istic. Whereas, as a matter of fact, it is fluid, depending on grouping (sequence) which shifts, and on the changing lights giving varied effects of perspective.
>
> It is in those matters gradually, but never completely, mastered that the history of my books really consists. Of course the plastic matter of this grouping and of those lights has its importance, since without it the actuality of that grouping and lighting could not be made evident. . . . (July 14, 1923)

3. Joseph Conrad, *Heart of Darkness and The Secret Sharer*, ed. Albert J. Guerard (New York, 1950), p. 14.

4. William Bysshe Stein, "The Lotus Posture and 'The Heart of Darkness.'"

5. See above, p. 199 [*Editor*].

It would follow from this statement that Conrad's technique of presentation is a basic principle in his meaning. "For him," says Robert Penn Warren, "the very act of composition was a way of knowing, a way of exploration."[6] To disclose the significance of this technique requires first the elucidation of a particular image, that of the "whited sepulchre" with its correlative image of the dead bones inside. * * * In conclusion will be offered comment upon its tragic outcome.

The metaphor of the whited sepulchre entombing dead men's bones interpenetrates both the narrative theme of economic exploitation and the archetypal theme of Marlow's exploration of himself. The significances of the figure also combine with the motif of moral purification in the Buddha posture so as ironically to blend Christian morality into its oriental religious implications. Indeed, the complexities of Conrad's presentation of the sepulchre image admirably illustrate what he means by the "plastic matter" of his fluid grouping, with the changing lights that give it perspective.

The source of this image is Christ's indictment of the Pharisees in Matthew, 23. 27-28: "Woe unto you, scribes and Pharisees, hypocrites! for ye are like unto whited sepulchres, which indeed appear beautiful outward, but are within full of dead men's bones, and of all uncleanness. Even so ye also outwardly appear righteous unto men, but within ye are full of hypocrisy and iniquity." The ancient Jews were accustomed to whitewash their tombs so that passersby would not accidentally be defiled by touching them. Hence the Pharisees were outwardly attractive but rotten within. In the strongest language he ever used, Christ reproved them for the false righteousness that covered their inward wickedness. In short, the warning here is against those evils which make modern Christians as contemptible as were the scribes and Pharisees themselves. Moreover, as the passage in Matthew emphasizes, the tombs contained dead men's bones, an image that Conrad turns to curiously effective use in *Heart of Darkness*. * * *

To Marlow "the meaning of an episode was not inside like a kernel but outside, enveloping the tale which brought it out only as a glow brings out a haze, in the likeness of one of these misty halos that sometimes are made visible by the spectral illumination of moonshine." Hence Conrad's "complicated presentations" have fundamental functions: the interplay of their imagery gives rise to the resonances of the recorded events—tomb, whiteness, blackness and darkness, bones, ivory, Time, nightmare, all contribute in their various meanings and overtones to a full understanding of Kurtz's tragedy and Marlow's journey in search of himself. They overlay

6. Joseph Conrad, *Nostromo*, "Introduction" by Robert Penn Warren (New York, 1951), p. xxxix.

and underlie the natural, just as the supernatural and the Hellish are above and below the snakelike river of Africa winding over the earth—flat on its map, penetrating a darkly passionate land. In short, they give *Heart of Darkness* dimension. Time and space, light and darkness, the dream and the night journey, bones and ivory (which is dental bone), the river, all are manipulated into symbolic relationships.

Kurtz figuratively becomes ivory, the image of his materialistic dedication and the symbol of his failure. The carved balls on the posts—the only image in the story Conrad specifically calls symbolic —signify one who looks like the heads of those he has murdered, bony death's heads entombed in the primeval darkness of the African catacomb, from whose labyrinth no moral thread leads to the light. Kurtz, whose journey ends in night, is in a sepulchre of his own making, for his earlier appearance of righteousness has disappeared along with his fleshly vestments. As a living skeleton he is the uncleanness within, a "disinterred body." The original image of the sepulchre Conrad has subtly worked forward so that what gave rise to perspectives upon Kurtz's spiritual death in the body of his life reveals him as the cenotaph of his better self. Conrad's method, then, rarely starts with the symbol. Rather it creates its atmosphere out of images in their implications. He works from a luminous periphery toward a central meaning, rather than from a center outward through static or conventionally arbitrary symbols.

* * *

The vision which emerges has its tragicalness, but it is not entirely pessimistic. Kurtz possessed potentialities for goodness, but lapsed into degradation. Furthermore, even though he is not the hero, he is psychologically linked to him in being Marlow's other self. Kurtz's momentary vision of his life is a moral victory, but what he sees is the horror of his total immorality. His tragedy is the irony of his insight. But Pharisees have no insight at all. Marlow on the other hand emerges, not unscathed, but tried to a temper of selflessness. Through his other self he sees evil laid bare. Had he not become a new man reborn from the old by the time he visited the Intended, had he not perceived that unlike Kurtz "she was one of those creatures that are not the playthings of Time," he would not have sacrificed his honesty to her illusion of love and faith. Marlow's quest for truth must therefore have an ironical culmination.

In facing reality Marlow seems to agree with Calderon that "life is a dream." Its illusions, however, are not negations; they are "a creation out of the images of the mind. In that sense the world *is* an illusion, though a vision perhaps, Conrad would say, of 'remote unattainable truth, seen dimly.' "[7] Kurtz, with his flaw of character,

---

7. Wilbur L. Cross, "Joseph Conrad" in *Four Contemporary Novelists* (New York, 1930), p. 46.

saw clearly beyond the false illusion of his life only at the end; his tragic judgment of himself was a victory, but short—like his name in German. Marlow faced a choice of illusions in addressing the Intended, but mustered the moral strength to resolve his dilemma by choosing charity at the expense of justice. Kurtz saw into his soul too late to save his life; Marlow saw his life soon enough to save his soul.

The tragic irony of *Heart of Darkness* is that a modern civilization of hypocrites professes to bring progress to remote regions in the name of the Christ who drove forth the Pharisees, saying, "Ye serpents, ye generation of vipers, how can ye escape the damnation of hell?" The tone of self-mockery of Marlow's narration is partly attributable to his retrospective awareness of his ignorance of and yielding to evil while he was the hero of his "epic" journey. Purchased by a lie, which was a merciful reversion to betrayal of his honesty, his attainment at last is Buddhistic purification. *Heart of Darkness* is an extended parable damning man's inhumanity to man, the highest hope of mankind lying in the sort of self-purification exemplified by Marlow. For "No eloquence could have been so withering to one's belief in mankind as . . . [Kurtz's] final burst of sincerity."

In his "Author's Note" to *Heart of Darkness* * * * Conrad says: "That sombre theme had to be given a sinister resonance, a tonality of its own, a continued vibration that, I hoped, would hang in the air and dwell on the ear after the last note had struck." This the tale has. Its symbolic conception gives it complexity, power, and depth and beauty, "a triple appeal covering the whole field of life": it may be read merely as a tale of adventure and exploration, or it may be interpreted as an indictment of capitalistic exploitation. As a moral discourse it damns Christian hypocrisy and materialism. Moreover, it combines the night journey of Dante and Vergil with the archetypal descent into the primeval and racial self, using the technique of the double for psychological confrontation and dramatic vividness. Finally, although Marlow remains among men, he is qualified to enter nirvana.

Conrad was a moralist who, like Hawthorne, saw the irony of technological change and progress without moral growth. His condemnation, as we have seen, savagely implies that without a "spark from the sacred fire" colonial capitalism is cruelly selfish. Yet he can see the "august light of abiding memories" of the Thames. Upon it the English, with their efficiency, set forth to conquer and colonize, redeemed in their snatching the earth "away from those who have a different complexion or slightly flatter noses" by an "unselfish belief" at the back of their "idea" of empire. For Conrad there were racial qualities in the British which in a showdown made them, for example, the finest seamen. Similarly he had at least superficial respect for the chief accountant; "in the great demoralization of the land he kept up his appearance." In an essay entitled "Well Done" Conrad said in addressing the Merchant Service in 1918: "For the great mass of mankind the only saving grace that is needed is steady fidelity to what is nearest to hand and heart in the short moment of each human effort." This steady application to duty and work in navigating the tin-pot steamer preserves Marlow's equilibrium: "There was surface truth enough in these things to save a wiser man," to save him from sinking back in Time into moral regression "for a howl and a dance." Thus navigation becomes a celebration of order, of sanity, and Towson's *An Inquiry into Some Points of Seamanship* is a book revealing "a singleness of intention, an honest concern for the right way of going to work. . . ." Its owner, a Russian in harlequin garb, is simple and innocent, unaware of moral issues in his involvement with Kurtz, an adventurer into space and time ignorant that he is engulfed in powers of darkness. The illumination can only come to one like Marlow, who sees the moral issue. Such lesser characters as the dandified accountant and the Russian with his volume on seamanship appropriately point up "surface truth" and the virtue of keeping up appearances in the midst of moral chaos. Yet, because it is merely an appearance, such a superficial quality is in Time. Wilfred Dowden says of the accountant:

> The thin mantle of civilization covering this man's inhumanity is symbolized by the white and brilliant perfection of his dress, which is juxtaposed to the devastation of the station and the misery of the black men who creep about in the gloom of the trees. It is also symbolized by the condition of his books, which were in "apple-pie order." The callousness which underlay this fantastic outward manifestation of his culture is emphasized by the irony of his greatest accomplishment; he had taught one of the native women, who "had a distaste for the work," to starch and iron his snowy white shirts. He was sensitive only to the amenities of the civilization of which he was a part and was conscious of the sufferings of the natives only when their noise disturbed his concentration on his books. Thus, he exhibited no sympathy for the dying man who was brought to the station and placed outside his window. In his strict adherence to the superficialities of his culture, he was isolated from the rest of mankind; his humanity had been forgotten in the process of keeping up appearances in the great demoralization of the land.[8]

The integrated functions of Conrad's minor characters reveal the care he took in weaving his complexities into a whole. Similarly, the firing of the gunboat into the coastal bush and the repetition of this

8. Dowden, "The Light and the Dark; Imagery and Thematic Development in Conrad's *Heart of Darkness*," in *The* *Rice Institute Pamphlet*, XLIV (1957), 41-42.

act by the Pilgrims shooting into the river forest are signs of futility. Exploiters so immersed in Time are aiming mere popguns into the heart of a vast, eternal darkness. No puny physical strength can breach Africa; even brute force, though it can subdue the blacks, is ultimately powerless. True strength can come only from a moral source above and out of the Time of which the jungle is the ancient embodiment.

As a foil to Kurtz's Intended, the native girl signifies his passionate involvement with Time and the flesh. Adorned with the ivory of his unholy quest, "She was savage and superb, wild-eyed and magnificent. . . . And in the hush that had fallen suddenly upon the whole sorrowful land, the immense wilderness, the colossal body of the fecund and mysterious life seemed to look at her, pensive, as though it had been looking at the image of its own tenebrous, passionate soul." F. R. Leavis's remark that Conrad was a "simple soul" in his attitude toward women is defensible, as the naive description of Rita in *The Arrow of Gold* discloses.[9] What is more to the present purpose, however, is the functions of the Intended and the native girl in *Heart of Darkness*. Marlow says of such women as the Intended: "We must help them to stay in that beautiful world of their own, lest our [world] get worse." The emphasis here is upon moral contrast, clearly imaged in the difference between the pale, pure forehead of the girl deserted by Kurtz and his own ivory-like "lofty frontal bone." The ivory-bedecked African girl is buried in primordial Time; the Intended, even though she lives in the atmosphere of the grave in a tomb-like, modern city, is, with her "mature capacity for fidelity, for belief, for suffering . . . , one of those creatures that are not the playthings of Time." The one is a partner in Kurtz's plunge into Satanic, unspeakable rites; the other an exemplar of the Fidelity to which man must cling for salvation. Because Kurtz could neither trust in nor be trusted by any other human being he is forever lost to both women, lost to both the flesh and the spirit.

The pattern of *Heart of Darkness* magnificently illustrates Conrad's view of man moving in space and in Time, over the earth. Mere adventurous movement, however, as the Russian's attitudes and life emphasize, ends in "the essential desolation of . . . futile wanderings." The movement must be a search for the illumination of values. The spatiality of the journey is linked through dream-consciousness with the temporal continuum.[1] The effect is a space-time dimension which encloses good and evil and gives unexpectedly profound perspective to the symbolic imagery. Complexity, power, depth and beauty lend a "sinister resonance" to Conrad's theme.

9. Leavis, *The Great Tradition* (London, 1948) p. 222.

1. Conrad once borrowed two volumes of Freud but returned them unread. Some of his symbolic imagery is anticipatory of Jung, just as his temporal ideas somewhat anticipate Bergson.

LEO GURKO

[Conrad's Ecological Art]†

Conrad not only perceives nature through his senses, but is aware of the profound parallelisms that link it with men. The ecological side of his art consists of demonstrating these parallelisms according to the demands of the particular scene. In his early period this demonstration reached its climax in the baffling and powerful story, "Heart of Darkness."[1] Marlow['s] * * * account of a journey up the Congo in fascinated search of a Belgian trader named Kurtz begins and ends on the Thames, with his four interlocutors sprawled on the deck of a yawl waiting in the gathering darkness for the tide to turn. The process of suturing nature with the mood of Marlow's African experience begins at once. "The sea-reach of the Thames stretched before us like the beginning of an interminable waterway," a waterway, we are informed a few paragraphs farther on, "leading to the uttermost ends of the earth." This continuum of nature, in which the rivers of the earth flow into one another indissolubly so that what happens on the Thames happens on the Congo also, is reinforced by the comment "the sea and the sky were welded together without a joint." The theme of all experience being one experience, transcending time and space, underlies the story, and appears in several variations. One variation on the theme is historical, one imperialist, one personal, and all rest on a vision of the earth as a single, interpenetrating whole. Conrad continuously evokes this idea by his fusions of landscape. Again the fusion is not manufactured to suit the purpose of his fiction, but a quality of nature organic to it which the author asks us to be aware of.

The historical note allies itself to the double movement of the tides. In Elizabethan times the Drakes and Franklins[2] sailed from

† From *Joseph Conrad: Giant in Exile*, pp. 148–53. Copyright 1962 by The Macmillan Co. Reprinted by permission.
1. Another of the Conrad tales which have supplied critics with a field day. They have found in Marlow's journey up the Congo a parallel to Aeneas's trip to Hades, a Freudian and/or Jungian passage into the subsconscious self, a disguised retelling of Passion Week, a return to the Garden of Eden, etc. Conrad invites all this sort of textual pearl-diving by his elaborate use of vaguely portentous and invitingly "significant" words like inscrutable, unspeakable, un-

earthly, incomprehensible, mysterious, impenetrable, inconceivable, intolerable, and incredible, for which the story has been criticized by F. R. Leavis. Other defects include a tendency to preachiness ("He must meet that truth with his own true stuff—with his own inborn strength") and an occasional disposition to the trite image ("a spark from the sacred fire"). These rhetorical and stylistic blemishes striate the text of the story without vitiating its impact.

2. For the corrective to this oft-repeated error, see above, p. 100 [*Editor*].

the light of England into the darkness of unknown seas, returning with the "round flanks" of their ships bulging with treasure. Nineteen centuries ago the incoming tide brought the Romans from the light of Rome into the darkness of England where decent young citizens in togas no doubt felt "the utter savagery" of the country closing round them. Modern imperialism is no different from ancient. "The conquest of the earth, which mostly means the taking it away from those who have a different complexion or slightly flatter noses than ourselves, is not a pretty thing when you look into it too much." Whereupon Marlow proceeds to look into it. He goes to Brussels, a city like "a whited sepulchre," headquarters of the Congo trade, to apply for a post as captain of a river steamer. He is hired at once to replace a man just killed in a skirmish with natives over two black hens. The natives flee their village in terror, and in time grass grows through the ribs of the dead man. The Brussels street where the company is located has grass sprouting between the stones, and in the anteroom of the office sit two women (the two black hens) knitting black wool. The repetition of sensory details and of symbolic analogues—in this instance the grass and the woman-hen concord—lends the story a central pulsation and reinforces the theme of indissolubility that lies at its heart.

The darkness of Africa has bleached Brussels into a sepulchral whiteness. Other death images of imperialism appear. On the trip down, Marlow's ship passes a French man-of-war firing into the empty bush. No sign of life is visible anywhere but "there she was, incomprehensible, firing into a continent. . . . There was a touch of insanity in the proceeding . . . not dissipated by somebody on board assuring me earnestly there was a camp of natives—he called them enemies!—hidden out of sight somewhere." After landing at the mouth of the Congo, Marlow runs into a grove filled with dying Negroes, too broken in health to work on their chain gangs any longer. Farther on, at the Central Station, he meets the manager and his henchmen, crassly devoted to extracting as much ivory as possible out of the country: "To tear treasure out of the bowels of the earth was their desire, with no more moral purpose at the back of it than there is in burglars breaking into a safe." Their naked rapacity fills Marlow with loathing, and this quickens his interest in Kurtz, who came to Africa with the "higher" aim of civilizing the natives and whom even his enemies acknowledge to be remarkable. He, too, is an imperialist trader (he sends out record-breaking quantities of ivory) but of a different sort, and Marlow is now confronted with "a choice of nightmares," between the systems of values represented by the manager and by Kurtz. The imperialist theme merges with the personal, and Marlow the observer-traveler now changes into Marlow the moral participant.

What redeems imperialism—it is again characteristic of Conrad that he should examine a generally repulsive process with an eye to salvage—is "an idea at the back of it; not a sentimental pretence but an idea; and an unselfish belief in the idea—something you can set up, and bow down before, and offer a sacrifice to. . . ." Kurtz has such an idea, of elevating the native, and the manager has not. Both are in the African darkness but on different levels of morality, and Marlow allies himself at once with Kurtz. If darkness it is to be, it had better be Kurtz's. His at least has intelligence, a noble purpose, and a touch of grandeur, while the manager's is rooted in a grubby, mean-spirited avarice. No matter that Kurtz has lost his footing and plunged into an abyss of degradation, that he has engaged in unspeakable rites, allowed the tribesmen to deify him, taken a savage mistress, slain Africans whose heads he awesomely impaled on posts outside his lodging, could exclaim "exterminate the brutes" after all his early intentions to civilize, and die with the cryptic words "the horror! the horror!" on his lips. If he has fallen, he has fallen from a considerable height, and Marlow finds in his fall a sign of his superiority. The manager, by contrast, is never ill, never varies his dead-level routine, never displays the slightest sign of humanness, has, in fact, nowhere to fall to. Marlow embraces the inescapable darkness of life, but it is a mark of his humanity that he maintains his powers of discrimination within it.

He discovers, also, that it is possible to function in darkness without falling satanically into its bottomless pit like Kurtz, or existing, like the manager, without the slightest awareness of light. He maintains himself by continually making moral judgments about the experience before him. The young Russian who is attached to Kurtz he recognizes as an admirable incarnation of youthful adventurousness, just as the manager's assistant, with his nose for influential connections back home, is a "papier-mâché Mephistopheles," a villain of the second grade ("it seemed to me . . . I could poke my forefinger through him, and would find inside nothing but a little loose dirt. . . .") The Company's chief accountant who, in the grueling heat of Africa, appears in starched collar, white cuffs, and snowy trousers, may look like a hairdresser's dummy, but he elicits Marlow's admiration: ". . . in the great demoralization of the land he kept up his appearance. That's backbone. His starched collars and got-up shirt-fronts were achievements of character." Marlow finds the physical act of refloating the sunken steamer a preservative in the jungle, as he does the unexpected discovery of a manual of seamanship in an abandoned hut up-river. The darkness of Africa embraces both demoralizing savagery and burgeoning life. Along the coast Marlow observes a boat being paddled by blacks: ". . . they had faces like grotesque masks—these chaps; but they had bone, muscle, a wild vitality, an intense energy of movement, that was as natural and true as the surf along their coast." In the end, Marlow returns to Europe and seals his commitment to Kurtz by lying to his fiancée. She wants to know what his last words were, and it seems to Marlow too dark altogether to tell her the truth. He tells her instead what she wants to hear, that the last word Kurtz uttered was her name. The lie, like the imperialism to which even Kurtz is allied, is an evil thing (lying makes Marlow "miserable and sick, like biting something rotten would do.") but is redeemed, as Kurtz's ivory activities were, by a benevolent and idealistic motivation. The truth would only have plunged her into needless disillusionment and pain. Marlow thus finally displays his heightened powers of discrimination, perhaps the ultimate benefit accruing from his trip to Africa.

If the historical theme expands into the imperialist, the imperialist into the personal, all of them are held aloft by the frame of external nature rooted at the bottom of the story. The Congo appears as "an immense snake uncoiled, with its head in the sea, its body at rest curving over a vast country, and its tail lost in the depth of the land." Its banks are lined with contorted mangroves; the water exudes the smell of primeval mud. And the wilderness in back waits in silence for the departure of rapacious men, a silence that "went home to one's very heart." For those outsiders who linger in it too long, or invade it too deeply, it is sure to wreak a terrible vengeance by exposing them, as it does Kurtz, to unbearable temptations. In the end it stamps the very flesh with its imprimatur, so that Kurtz's bald skull looked exactly like an ivory ball. The Thames, which seems at the start to be a waterway leading to the uttermost ends of the earth, merges into the Congo, which flows not so much in space as in time, "travelling back to the earliest beginnings of the world." The perils of such a journey are highlighted by the wreckage en route: an undersized railway truck lying on its back with its wheels in the air, looking "as dead as the carcass of some animal," the steamer Marlow drags up from the bottom, resembling "the carcass of some big river animal"; finally Kurtz himself, "lying at the bottom of a precipice where the sun never shines," a precipice into which Marlow himself nearly falls but is saved at the last moment.

All the while, Marlow tells this story, which he announces as "the farthest point of navigation and the culminating point of my experience," looking like a Buddha dressed in European clothes. The combination of east and west underlines the universality of his theme, linking the Thames and the Congo, Africa and Europe, the ancient Romans and latter-day British, streets in Brussels and mud paths in the heart of the wilderness. Kurtz as a pan-European figure, not simply a Belgian, is emphasized by the details of his parentage: "His mother was half-English, his father was half-French. All Europe contributed to the making of Kurtz." The spear, which to the astonishment of the natives "went quite easy between the shoulder-blades" of the white captain whom Marlow replaces, is the same spear which later passes through the body of the black helmsman, to the astonishment of Marlow himself. He compares the far-off drums of Africa to "the sound of bells in a Christian country." The disappearance of the Africans before the onslaught of the white men is described in terms of the emptying of farms in England "if a lot of mysterious niggers armed with all kinds of fearful weapons suddenly took to travelling on the road between Deal and Gravesend, catching the yokels right and left to carry heavy loads for them."

Throughout, Marlow pronounces the kinship between the howling, screaming Congolese and the rest of humanity, climaxed by the look given him by the dying Negro helmsman, a look creating a "subtle bond" between them: "And the intimate profoundity of the look he gave me when he received his hurt remains to this day in my memory—like a claim of distant kinship affirmed in a supreme moment." The match which the Buddha-like Marlow lights in the Thames night toward the end of his tale affirms not only the contrast between light and darkness but the flow between them, a flow establishing their subtle bond. The earth itself, with its rivers and continents, its jungles, seas, and peoples, covering its immense range in space and time, supplies "Heart of Darkness" with an ultimate source of reference. Behind the movement and symbolism of the story lies its ecology. Leaving the protective comforts of civilization for his plunge into barbaric darkness, Marlow learns to make his way about in it, to distinguish its noble and ignoble qualities, and by exposing himself to its pressures, he embraces the indivisibility of experience, reflected at every point by the indivisibility of the earth itself in all its manifestations. He and it are in the end "welded together without a joint."

PAUL L. WILEY

Conrad's Skein of Ironies†

The opening of *Heart of Darkness* sets the stage for an imposing theme. The yawl, upon which Marlow is about to preach to a small but select congregation of men of the world, rides in the perspectives of modern town and ageless sea, of history both near and far. Later the home office of the Congo trading company will seem to

† Published for the first time. By permission of the author.

have absorbed the sepulchral city wherein they gape. Yet as we move with Marlow from Europe to the wilderness, our crowding questions are likely to fix not only upon theme but also upon its treatment, upon literary classification of the story as a whole, since it represents a very modern blend of comic absurdity, tragedy, and satire almost Swiftian in manner. Binding all this is a controlling play of irony wholly fitted to the temper of Conrad's mind and imagination, an irony that grows in depth and complexity as the narrative proceeds and that never falters either in purpose or in relentless bite.

Granting, however, the ironic bent of Conrad's personal vision, the closing years of the Nineteenth Century, during which *Heart of Darkness* appeared, also nurtured an atmosphere conducive to skepticism. On the one hand, scientific and philosophical speculation had led to popular assumptions of an indifferent or malign nature. On the other, weakening religious faith had provoked doubt in traditional moral sanctions and had called forth in some quarters the demand for a new or different ethic, sometimes advocating the free expansion of purely human capacities. To these conflicts, often a spur to pessimism in the province of thought, the advance of Imperialism in world affairs added its practical complication; for seen at large, Imperialism raised and united the issues of European invasion of then often hostile parts of nature, especially in Africa, and of the moral justification for doing so—a shaky dualism for the reflective who discerned small morality under a chorus of *réclame* perhaps reflected in the babble of voices, the flow of journalistic eloquence, that echoes through *Heart of Darkness*. Of Conrad's thorough grasp of this dilemma in both its speculative and political aspects we need not doubt, since his story supplies the evidence. But active experience itself and the reserves of an aristocratic temperament gave him little patience with facile attempts at compromise between a wavering ethic and blind assaults on nature. On the untamed jungle, the rank wilderness of his early novels, he had looked with his own eyes; and he had observed its subjugation of the baffled or wretched specimens of civilization under its shadow. Whatever the inner equipment of men, whatever forms of action they take against it, primeval nature with its ancient darkness remains there permanent, seemingly destined to outlast most human illusions including, perhaps, the illusion of humanity's necessary survival.

For Conrad, then, the wilderness, as much as the sea, was a dominant image; and its recurrence in *Heart of Darkness* is less surprising than its subtler embodiment in the perfected artistry and the cunning skein of ironies in this late tale of the first and decisive phase of his literary career. Here again the wilderness of nature poses the question of man's methods of confronting it, but now

Conrad's purpose has in view a definite satirical objective—the complete rout of the fraudulent philanthropy of the trading company; and of main interest is his means of accomplishing this. Two considerations affect his procedure: the need to affirm his point dramatically in the action of the story and initial recognition of the fact that the morality of the company has no substance whatever. Hence the sequence of ironies originates in a bitter dilemma, or what Marlow will recognize eventually as "a choice of nightmares." In this situation ethics, what passes for restraint, is pure deceit whereas primitive nature, devoid of moral checks, is by contrast visibly true even in its frank destructiveness. Early in the tale Marlow's predecessor, Fresleven, dies in this predicament, since he must resort to beating natives to regain his self-respect after too long service in "the noble cause." Truth drives him at last to an ironical accord with nature as it is; and this step, finally, will justify Kurtz and explain his superiority to the feebler agents at the lower stations. Although for consolation we may wish this route to arrive at an implicit plea for an acceptable moral code, Conrad as artist refuses to weaken the force of his story by introducing irrelevancies; and, indeed, we may be left at the end disturbed by an intimation that the dilemma is not merely confined to the trading company but extends to the plight of modern man. In his posture on the yawl Marlow seems not only exhausted but also compelled to an almost frustrated renunciation of the world's evil; and in the closing melancholy cadences of the tale we are looking still into "the heart of an immense darkness."

As a kind of norm of integrity and as a guide line for the reader through a labyrinthine story, the Charlie Marlow of the central narrative detects at once the hypocrisy in his being called "a lower sort of apostle" in a profit-making concern; and under the increasing pressure of his wilderness education, his first uneasiness rises feverishly into that sense of unreality and hallucination which oppresses a man engaged in something secretly dishonest and which commonly results in breakdown and illness. Marlow has, of course, his seaman's standard of conduct—absolute fidelity to a physical task—to sustain him in his ordeal; but keeping the steamboat going is, in respect to the ultimate dilemma, only a means of clinging to what reality there is in the midst of nightmare, a stratagem like that adopted by many other men to busy themselves among incomprehensibles. It is, at best, a "surface truth" which will not prevent Marlow's collapse after the crisis of final disclosure.

With Marlow's arrival at the outer station at the mouth of the river we are well into the mainstream of Conrad's irony, which will deepen with the precisely marked advance from this to the two stations further on. At this stage Marlow's dismayed survey of his surroundings reveals waste and the pathos of the dying natives in the grove of death; but these details merely contribute to the main impression coming to focus in the Chief Accountant with his starched collars and umbrella. The salient point is the ironical fact that here the work advertised by the home company is being done and, in its purposeless fashion, done thoroughly. Blasting goes on, "criminal" workers are punished, and books are kept in apple-pie order. Routine masks the fundamental dilemma; and routine saves the timid Accountant who, as the stock time-server of old Europe, asks no questions and discreetly shuts his eyes to his company's output in death. A brilliantly sketched comic figure, he is, nevertheless, a commonplace good man; and we hear no more about him.

At the Central Station the terms of the looming dilemma become sharper as Marlow draws closer to the real inner darkness. Notable simply as comic creations of types of nullity are the manager, who manages only disorder, and his spy, the brickmaker without bricks. Yet despite his emptiness the manager is worth more consideration than the Chief Accountant because he is nearer the truth that nature offers no moral checks, and is taking some advantage of his opportunities. He wants the power that he attributes to Kurtz, and he is devising steps to get it; but as a passive intriguer, his tactic is to delay help reaching his rival until the latter perishes merely through solitude. Thus his weakness lies in his hesitance to bring himself into complete accord with nature and to exterminate Kurtz by outright violence, and we are amused to observe that his lukewarm measures succeed only after Kurtz has left nothing for the manager to control. Significantly, in contrast to the shock experienced by Marlow, the manager is virtually placid on encountering the awful transformation, the great unveiling of muffled truth, that the figure of Kurtz presents. Appropriately, therefore, the irresolutions of the manager urge Marlow towards his inevitable choice of nightmares.

On the river journey to the Inner Station the pettiness of the Central Station recedes, and the pilgrims become mainly nuisance as Marlow penetrates to the deeps of nature. Even hypocritical moral concerns have vanished, and Marlow struggles simply to meet the unpredictable as it comes, while the attacks on the steamer foreshadow the brute realities of Kurtz's compact with the wilderness. Now Marlow's reflections bear importantly on the mystery of human restraint in itself. What, for example, keeps his crew of hungry cannibals from making a meal of the outnumbered whites? Marlow cannot say. And, again, the question of motives applies to the wandering, and slightly sinister, Russian trader whose entry so finely heightens the tension before Kurtz manifests himself. What controls the Russian? Why is he alive at all? He likewise is an enigma at large in the wilderness, and Conrad lets him disappear still invested in uncertainties. Marlow's fog of confusion now only Kurtz can rend.

Kurtz and the crowning irony are wholly one. Never for an instant does Conrad bungle his long delayed climax nor commit the error of letting Kurtz melt into the waxwork bogy of the conventional horror yarn. For of the drama of moral ironies Kurtz is hero—or, if we like, anti-hero and certainly a main example of this modern type-figure. And he is tragic, with the shading of the term required by the complicated tone of the story, evoking from the barbaric woman of the forest her splendidly tragic gesture of farewell and from the sensitive Marlow feelings akin to the traditional emotions of pity and terror. Unlike the absurd characters at the lower stations Kurtz appallingly carries with him still the vestiges of a humanity whose illusions have not been mean. In fact, one of the many incidental artistries of *Heart of Darkness* is the skill holding us always in touch with the shade of the original Kurtz, loved by an innocent if ignorant girl and with all the human weakness of his excessive aspirations, this latter being epitomized, perhaps, in the curious painting left by him of the draped and blindfolded woman carrying a torch which might suggest the attempt to render a symbolic ideal warped in execution as if by an inkling of imminent fatality. To this aspect of Kurtz Marlow has reason to be loyal without a trace of sentimentalism. Neither does he admire Kurtz, nor does he invent a fictious grandeur to excuse an orgy of destruction. His tribute consists in seeing Kurtz strictly as he is, an act that, by provoking instinctive sympathy, enhances that tragic recognition which the reader must appreciate if Conrad is to bring off the denouement to his theme of moral frustration.

But to clinch the final irony Marlow's fidelity to Kurtz is a loyalty to the one possible choice between nightmares. The dilemma that has perplexed Marlow from the outset faces him terribly resolved in Kurtz, who had himself broken through to truth in his enlightened "Exterminate all the brutes!" annihilating in one stroke all the sham rhetoric of his report to the International Society for the Suppression of Savage Customs. In that phrase he had signified his determination to be at one with nature, to ravish and to master it; and he has been blessed by its every favor, including that of divesting himself entirely of human flesh except for the resonant voice for which the mute wilderness has no use. His brief career has been a triumph in the stripping away of all the rags of ethical self-deception with which men fatuously seek to confront the eternal powers of darkness; and, dying, he has won a further victory in his vision of "the horror." As Marlow rightly comprehends, this is a true expression of belief; and if it is immediately applicable to Kurtz and what his life has been, it is just conceivably true in itself. For what, indeed, have the sepulchral cities and all the trading companies of the world to cast in the scale against it? So "to the last, and even beyond" Marlow remains faithful to his choice of nightmares; and if, at the end, he does lie, it is in pity for a single glint of light among the shadows and in order that a statement of unbearable sincerity may not leave a house of sorrow "too dark—too dark altogether. . . ."

RALPH MAUD

The Plain Tale of *Heart of Darkness*†

Conrad wrote in May 1902 that "Heart of Darkness" is "something quite on another plane than an anecdote of a man who went mad in the Center of Africa." True enough: but at least we should get the anecdote straight, unravelling Marlow's garbled account of Kurtz. This essay has the limited aim of releasing Kurtz from the romantic double-talk with which Marlow shrouds his phantom. Marlow's problems—and whether or not *he* went mad in the Center of Africa—we leave to one side.

We have to make the effort to explain—as Marlow never does—certain crucial questions. For example, why does Kurtz turn back to his station after coming 300 miles down river? In what sense does Kurtz become a savage? What exactly makes him write "Exterminate all the brutes!" on his Report to the International Society for the Suppression of Savage Customs? And if his final cry of horror is a judgment on himself, what aspect of his behavior is he thinking of? Marlow tries to divine what was in Kurtz's soul, but we really want to know what was on Kurtz's mind.

* * *

We have to grant Kurtz's initial convictions about the civilizing function of Belgium in the Congo. The idea of performing miracles of benevolence at a sufficient distance from his present location is undoubtedly very compelling to him. * * *

Thus patriotic, Kurtz's ideals do not run counter to his personal ambition. At least, not in Brussels, where his ability to clothe the ideals with conviction, and with nothing more dangerously specific, so impresses the Authorities that he arrives in the Congo with special privileges and the expectation of early promotion.

Once in the Congo, of course, Kurtz's ideals would have been a liability had he allowed them to syphon his energies from the main job. Oil-painting at the Central Station, he alienates his fellows by preaching: "Each station should be like a beacon on the road towards better things"; but, safe to say, he has asked to be posted

† From *Humanities Association Bulletin*, XVII (Autumn, 1966), 13–17. Reprinted by permission of the editors and the author.

not to the station that affords the best opportunities for humanizing, improving, and instructing, but to the best station for trade, in the real ivory country. When Kurtz at the outpost immediately sends back his assistant with a curt reprimand, one knows it is not in any civilizing capacity that the poor fellow has failed. And when, after probably four or five months, Kurtz is returning with a fleet of canoes full of prime ivory, it is certainly not because he has finished civilizing the district, but because he is out of trinkets.

If all this is clear, then it should be equally clear why, after travelling with his ivory 300 miles of the way, he decides to turn back in a small canoe with but four paddlers against the current and leave the delivery of it (and the invoice for percentages) to an English half-caste clerk travelling with him. The Central Station is at a loss for an adequate motive: Kurtz is just about to return as any of them would, and then suddenly reverses himself. But surely this is the point: Kurtz, with the whole of Brussels expecting extraordinary things of him, cannot merely do the ordinary. The invoice is nowhere near big enough. Marlow, giving a flippant reason for lack of a better one, says: "Perhaps he was just simply a fine fellow who stuck to his work for its own sake." Near the mark, but it needs Kurtz's own later words: "You show them you have in you something that is really profitable, and then there will be no limits to the recognition of your ability." After 300 miles of indecision—he has run out of stores, too, so that real deprivation faces him—it becomes appallingly clear that no kings will meet him at railway stations for this bunch of tusks. And by this time he knows quite well how to get more, much more, no trinkets needed. He knows that his station is not desolate but filled with a serviceable tribe awaiting his return. By the end of a further seven or eight months not a tusk remains above or below ground in the whole district: it is all in Kurtz's mud hut.

We ask the question whether or not Kurtz was reduced to savagery during these months because this is the form in which the matter, following Marlow, is usually settled: "The wilderness had . . . sealed his soul to its own by the inconceivable ceremonies of some devilish initiation." Our only response to this interpretation must be that such devilish ceremonies *are* inconceivable. The story mentions no actual ceremonies beyond the obsequious protocol of lesser chiefs approaching the great chief. ("They would crawl" is the phrase used.) The French practice of using the guillotine for capital punishment would have required, in the case of the six heads before the hut, some rudimentary ceremony to publicize their crime as rebels. But in these matters Kurtz is acting as a statesman among savages rather than as a savage. The campfire vigil of the tribe, with its chanting, its drums, the abrupt yell to Kurtz on the steamboat, strikes one as no more savage than a football crowd rallying on behalf of a hurt player; and there is no reason to suppose (except for Marlow's amateur speculation) that Kurtz, in making for the firelight, intends to join the antelope-horned native on the native's own level.

What Kurtz really does in this productive period is to take over an area of the upper Congo in very much the same way as a Chicago gangster took over a segment of the city during Prohibition; he expands his empire by similar means, two shot-guns, a heavy rifle, and a light revolver-carbine, and for the same reason, profit. Again, Marlow misleads by suggesting there is "nothing exactly profitable" in the heads being there. To get ivory by raiding rather than trading, Kurtz had to impose martial law and dictatorial rule: this is motivated by the politics of the environment and not by its "darkness." There is nothing peculiarly African in the way Kurtz robs the Russian sailor, who describes the incident authentically, without recourse to "the victorious corruption, the darkness of an impenetrable night," etc., etc. Further, the Russian, who is the sole witness to Kurtz's empire-building, who is himself a gallant young person, does not consider Kurtz a savage; quite the opposite. Kurtz had broadened this young man's horizons; he had talked all night with him of noble things. Even after Kurtz's outburst of vile greed, the Russian does not flee, but waits for him to become friendly again; then actually nurses him through an illness. When Marlow deduces from his story that Kurtz must be mad, the Russian refutes him indignantly, saying that he had talked to Kurtz only two days before.

No one is likely nowadays to consider Kurtz mad for forgetting himself so far as to take a native girlfriend (who, by the way, seems a glorious creature in her public appearances but a shrew around the house). At most, one might say that Kurtz becomes mad in devoting himself to gang warfare. Certainly he had things out of proportion by the end of the affair—he even claims that the ivory is his own rather than the Company's. But one might equally say that he had things out of proportion before he ever left Brussels. He has the madness of an Eichmann devoting himself to the detailed execution of a "grand design"; but the madness, we must feel, is as much in the design as in the assiduousness of the individual. Kurtz's so-called unpermitted aspirations are hardly different from permitted ones; and his rule in the upper reaches is like nothing so much as King Leopold's claiming sovereignty of the Congo as a whole. Kurtz caught in the act is hardly as evil as the Manager, who seldom acts except to obstruct, and who is obviously incapable of being horrified. He speaks only of Kurtz's "unsound method" (largely because he misunderstands why the natives fire on the boat) and anticipates the petty triumph of reporting Kurtz to the proper authorities. Anyone who feels that Kurtz is at his worst in threatening the Russian might note that the Manager himself intends to get the young fellow hanged as unfair competition. Marlow is not wrong about the Manager when he turns "mentally to Kurtz for relief—positively for relief." Yes, Kurtz's career as a prima donna agent is much more easily stomached than the daily routine of the average station with its cruelties paraded as legal punishment or callously hidden in the shade of trees. So that one can imagine any one of the "pilgrims" writing "Exterminate all the brutes!"—but least of all Kurtz.

The seventeen closely written pages that Kurtz has time for in the early days, the Report undertaken for the International Society for the Suppression of Savage Customs, contains no details of how specifically to begin. What savage customs did the natives have before Kurtz set them marauding? In the story, at any rate, the yet unmolested villages seem quite pleasant—"a glimpse of rush walls, of peaked grass-roofs, a burst of yells, a whirl of black limbs, a mass of hands clapping, of feet stamping, of bodies swaying, of eyes rolling"—nothing in need of urgent suppression. Marlow feels a kinship with this passionate uproar; he thinks of his crew of cannibals as fine fellows; and would rather have seen any of the white men die in place of his helmsman. Given this kind of "savage," Kurtz might well have wondered what the International Society expected him to suppress. No doubt he does nothing, even in the early days. So his "Exterminate all the brutes!" cannot be the cry of a man exasperated to the uttermost in a vain effort to civilize recalcitrant savages. The exasperation must be from another source, perhaps sheer bad temper—even the accountant, well fortified with clean linen, responds to noise in the station yard with: "When one has got to make correct entries, one comes to hate those savages—hate them to the death." As a venting of bad blood the exclamation on the Report would indicate how far Kurtz had fallen from his ideal of himself; but surely the scrawl signifies more. It must be a moment of self-knowledge, a *recognition* of how far. * * * He had felt superior to the common bully and servant murderer; now he has finally recognized himself as part of the whole lethal system. Being in it—failing to be above it—he is not going to pretend that this exploitation amounts to much more than extermination. "Exterminate all the brutes!" becomes, then, not a disillusioned man's shocking prescription for future behavior, but a succinct rephrasing of what the International Society, if it were not blinded by hypocrisy, would see it is already proposing, in effect, to its best young men when it sends them out as agents of the Company. In intense mockery Kurtz is giving the benevolent Society its true slogan.

The mockery is not that of a prophet but of a victim, who, if he has failed to educate, will bitterly succeed in the more logical function. Perhaps he still feels that, when established as a super-agent, he can turn to amelioration—"right motives—always." But meanwhile the job in hand is ivory, whatever the cost in lives. Kurtz has travelled to an outpost of darkness where hypocrisy is easily detected. The Conradian test here is what you do when you are not only alone but also plagued by fever, covered with body sores, and your formal function as well as your personal ambition tells you to get more ivory. Hypocrisy ends there; unhypocritical cruelty begins. And the role of the wilderness, which Marlow leaves so mysterious, is simply to make Kurtz bald, to uncover him phys-ically, to make him ill and bad-tempered. His line of work does the rest. One might add that the wilderness has the venial fault of being too defenseless a victim, the cause of mortal sin in others. It makes a ravisher out of a missionary. But there's nothing really mysterious about that.

And one returns to the insistence that Kurtz's career in the Congo is not out of the ordinary. If Marlow had told the story without his editorial "incomprehensibles" it would have been too plain, too plain altogether. But Conrad means us to read the plain tale behind the other. Otherwise what is the point of "The horror! The horror!"? A man goes into the center of Africa and does extraordinarily horrible things, and then in a final moment admits they are horrible. That is no story of consequence. The point of Kurtz's likeness to Eichmann is that they both did horrible things which were considered common form by their peer group and supe-riors; the difference is that one never said "The horror! The horror!" and the other did, passing judgment on himself and all like him. If Kurtz's acts had been radically different from those of the other agents, his judgment would have been merely a condemnation of his peculiarities. This cannot be Conrad's intention. The horror is the whole dark system of imperialist exploitation masquerading as the spread of enlightenment.

What perversity, then, for Marlow on his return to Brussels—the real heart of darkness—to say to the Company official that "Mr. Kurtz's knowledge, however extensive, did not bear upon the prob-lems of commerce or administration." Is this guileless, or deliber-ately misleading? We wonder what Marlow has learned from "the journey of his soul" along one artery of darkness. He might at least have learned Kurtz's scorn of hypocrisy and rendered him justice on that score. But does he know what it would mean to render Kurtz justice? It would mean lancing the rotten system at its heart, burst-ing the sanctum, "the door of Darkness" guarded by the two fates knitting black wool, and transfixing "the pale plumpness in a frockcoat" with a tusk. Not that that would do much good; but Marlow doesn't even do the little bit of good that is very possible for him. If he had just told Kurtz's fiancee the truth in such a way that she had to believe him, she might, after some hysterics, have grown up into a healthy, useful woman, a member of the International Society for the Suppression of "Civilized" Customs. Instead, in a funk, in a feint of second-rate chivalry, he effectively seals her in darkness for ever.

DONALD R. BENSON

Heart of Darkness: The Grounds of Civilization in an Alien Universe†

The recent appearance of three casebooks on "Heart of Darkness"[1] is a remarkable testimony to the fascination of the story, as well as to the vogue of the casebook. The critical contents of the three books reveal a main reason for the story's fascination and for its aptness for casebook treatment: the critics are in solid agreement that the story is a profound account of "the journey within" and thus a rich source for essays in depth psychology.[2] "Marlow is questing for himself," says W. Y. Tindall. "That [he] saw his outer adventure as the archetypal embodiment of an inner adventure is clear" (Harkness, pp. 127–128). The result of Marlow's quest is a revelation of the darkness in the heart of every man—even an acceptance by Marlow himself of damnation. It is not my purpose to challenge this reading of "Heart of Darkness"; within limits, it seems to me valid and profitable. But it is not exhaustive, and it appears nearly to have obscured an equally important and perhaps more consciously intentional aspect of the story.

*   *   *

[To Guerard] "the story is not primarily about Kurtz or about the brutality of Belgian officials," and he proceeds to what he feels it really is about, Marlow's "inner journey." In fact, however, especially when it is viewed in light of the Victorian preoccupation with the issues raised by scientific and philosophical naturalism, by evolution theory—natural and cultural—and by colonial exploitation, "Heart of Darkness" is seen to be just as much about the nature, the possibilities, and the origins of civilization—that is, about what is distinctively and essentially human—in the alien uni-

† From *Texas Studies in Literature and Language*, VII (Winter, 1966), 339–47. Copyright 1966 by the University of Texas Press. Reprinted by permission of the editors.

1. Bruce Harkness, *Conrad's "Heart of Darkness" and the Critics* (San Francisco, 1960); Leonard F. Dean, *Joseph Conrad's "Heart of Darkness": Backgrounds and Criticisms* (Englewood Cliffs, New Jersey, 1960); Robert Kimbrough, *"Heart of Darkness": An Authoritative Text, Backgrounds and Sources, Essays in Criticism* (New York, 1963).

2. See above, Guerard [*Editor*].

verse of naturalism as it is about Marlow's inner journey. In the former aspect of the story, Marlow is more observer than protagonist.

The story's setting, the delineation of which is begun in the frame narrative and completed by Marlow, is the cosmos of naturalism: an indifferent infinitude of space and time, an elemental darkness momentarily relieved by a dying sun and the "running blaze" of lightning that is civilization. In the opening five paragraphs, by means of a few broad strokes reminiscent of impressionist painting, the setting is centered in cosmic space. * * * In the next eight paragraphs the setting is placed in cosmic time and the theme of civilization explicitly introduced. Beginning with the days when England had first served as warden of "the sacred fire" of civilization, when the Thames "had borne all the ships whose names are like jewels flashing in the night of time," from the *Golden Hind* forward, the narrative (here shifting from the unidentified frame-narrator to Marlow) moves backward to the time when England itself had been "one of the dark places on the earth . . . nineteen hundred years ago—the other day" and the Roman bearer of the sacred fire, moving up this same Thames, had felt "the utter savagery . . . closed round him,—all that mysterious life of the wilderness that stirs in the forest, in the jungles, in the hearts of wild men." The light of civilization itself, Marlow comments, "is like a running blaze on a plain, like a flash of lightning in the clouds. We live in the flicker—may it last as long as the old earth keeps rolling! But darkness was here yesterday." Thus the main thrust of the introduction—the thirteen paragraphs before Marlow actually launches into his tale—is cosmic rather than introspective; its burden is the tenuousness of civilization, of the distinctively human; the questions it calls to mind are about the nature, the possibilities, and the source of the civilized and human in such an alien universe. The remainder of the story, in one aspect at least, is a systematic testing of possible answers to these questions.

The first conclusion "Heart of Darkness" suggests about civilization is that taken abstractly, simply as a tradition to be passed from hand to hand, it is inadequate—highly liable to corruption by the forces of unrestraint. Marlow, speculating about the beginnings of British civilization, implies that corruption is inherent in the very act of imposing civilization on the darkness, and in the motivation necessary for such a formidable task. The Romans "grabbed what they could get for the sake of what was to be got. It was just robbery with violence, aggravated murder on a great scale, and men going at it blind—as is very proper for those who tackle a darkness. The conquest of the earth . . . is not a pretty thing when you look into it too much." There may be an ultimate justification for this conquest, but if so it involves continual *renewals* of the corrupted civilization by faithful individuals: "What redeems it [the conquest of the earth] is the idea only. An idea at the back of it; not a sentimental pretense but an idea; and an unselfish belief in the idea—something you can set up, and bow down before, and offer a sacrifice to." The inevitable tendency of expanding civilization itself, as the long and bitter exposition of the Belgian "civilization" of the Congo shows, is toward corruption. This is not simply a matter of brutal exploitation, though there is plenty of that, but of what Conrad elsewhere calls "the criminality of inefficiency and pure selfishness."[3] Marlow foresees that he will "become acquainted with a flabby, pretending, weak-eyed devil of a rapacious and pitiless folly"—a devil whose dominion extends from the "whited sepulcher" of Brussels to the dark heart of the Congo and whose disciples are met on every page of Part One, from the fatuous company doctor measuring the heads of prospective light-bringers, as his share in the Great Work, to the insane Eldorado Exploring Expedition setting forth from the Central Station "to tear treasure out of the bowels of the land," never to be heard from more.

Not that even at this level of conventional conduct and external restraint Conrad discounts civilization. On the contrary, even where they are merely external, the restraints of civilization are, for the mass of men, indispensable stays against chaos—against even the destructive *knowledge* of savagery, of unfettered impulse:

> You can't understand [says Marlow]. How could you? . . . stepping delicately between the butcher and the policeman . . . —how can you imagine what particular region of the first ages a man's untrammeled feet may take him into . . . without a policman . . . where no warning voice of a kind neighbor can be heard whispering of public opinion? These little things make all the great difference.

But these "external checks" are at best tenuously maintained, and how, in any case, do we account for their existence in the first place, in an alien universe whose very heart is darkness?

The idealisms so blandly professed by nineteenth-century colonials as the grounds of civilization—notably Progress and Religion—are mercilessly scrutinized in "Heart of Darkness" and rejected. It is by these sentimental pretenses that the exploiters of the Congo, the self-styled "emissaries of light," rationalize their rapacity. The first section of the story caustically documents the conclusion that sentimental pretenses won't do, but Marlow's assertion goes further: "*Principles* won't do. Acquisitions, clothes, pretty rags—rags that would fly off at the first good shake. No; you want a

3. In a letter to William Blackwood [see above, p. 129].

deliberate belief." Kurtz, it appears, is meant by Conrad for the real test of idealism. "He is a prodigy. He is an emissary of pity, and science, and progress," possessed of "higher intelligence, wide sympathies, a singleness of purpose," says the brickmaker ironically; but we are surely expected to admit some substance in the description, since Marlow does: "I was curious to see whether this man, who had come out equipped with moral ideas of some sort, would climb to the top after all and how he would set about his work when there." Kurtz's notorious failure as an idealist, an exemplar of principle, which is so concisely epitomized in his scribbled postscript "Exterminate all the brutes!" does not need to be elaborated here. Unfortunately a major flaw of "Heart of Darkness" is that Kurtz the idealist is as much a sentimental pretender as his flabby devils of Belgian colleagues. As Marvin Mudrick says, what we get of his report on the enlightenment of the heathen "is a phrase or two of mealy-mouthed reformist exhortation that would not do credit to a Maugham missionary," this despite Marlow's insistence on "the unbounded power of eloquence—of words—of burning noble words" in Kurtz, his essential gift. Marlow, we feel, would be a much better test case for the validity of principle as a defense against the darkness and a possible ground of civilization, and in fact except for the two white lies, both of them sacrificially altruistic, Marlow does stand firmly on principle. But Kurtz is Conrad's intended test-case; Marlow is not tested by solitude in the way Kurtz is, and, more important, he has the stay of work to maintain him.

Work, or craft as Conrad conceives it, is certainly one of civilization's disciplines—a product of civilization and a vital support of it. Both Marlow and, at a lower level, the starched-collar accountant are saved from dangerous introspections by their preoccupation with the details of their trades. And further, the demands of work honestly done constitute, for Conrad, a reality that sets it quite apart from pretenses and principles; it is, in fact, only to skilled and honest work and to elemental nature itself that he applies the word "reality" in "Heart of Darkness." Marlow finds in the *Inquiry into some Points of Seamanship* "a singleness of intention, an honest concern for the right way of going to work, which made these humble pages ... luminous with another than a professional light." The book makes him "forget the jungle and the pilgrims in a delicious sensation of having come upon something unmistakably real." Even in the drudgery of salvaging the sunken steamer Marlow sees "the chance to find yourself. Your own reality." Indeed, this notion of work and reality reflects the anti-idealism which we have already seen Conrad asserting directly in "Heart of Darkness": "You may," says Marlow, "be such a thunderingly exalted creature as to be altogether deaf and blind to anything but heavenly sights and sounds." But for most of us,

> the earth . . . is a place . . . where we must put up with sights, with sounds, with smells, too, by Jove!—breathe dead hippo, so to speak, and not be contaminated. And there, don't you see? your strength comes in, the faith in your ability for the digging of unostentatious holes to bury the stuff in—your power of devotion to an obscure, back-breaking business.

Thus work can be a means to salvation; but this does not really answer the question raised at the beginning of the story, for work is mainly a refinement of civilization's conventional restraints, and Conrad's ultimate intention is not only to see how civilization fares in confrontation with elemental nature but to get behind civilization itself, to reduce it to an essence as "real" as that of the confronting darkness.

Robert O. Evans aptly cites Graham Greene's assessment of Africa as a place where "you could measure what civilization was worth." The jungle—and the natural and primitive in general, both in man and his environment—is consistently presented as "real" in "Heart of Darkness," and it is thus the standard of measurement. On his trip down the coast, Marlow finds the sound of the surf "a positive pleasure, like the speech of a brother. It was something natural, that had its reason, that had a meaning." Later, at the Central Station, the silence of the brooding jungle goes home to his "very heart—its mystery, its greatness, the amazing reality of its concealed life." Here civilization seems unreality and illusion: one's past comes back to him "in the shape of an unrestful and noisy dream, remembered with wonder amongst the overwhelming realities of this strange world of plants, and water, and silence." And this reality is the reality of the naturalist's alien universe, for in this same passage Marlow specifies that the silence is not the silence of peace but of "an implacable force brooding over an inscrutable intention. It looked at you with a vengeful aspect." In this setting, certainly, such a phenomenon as civilization, as humanity itself, demands explanation. Some human reality must be discovered as "real" as the natural one.

Most readings of "Heart of Darkness" stress the identity of this jungle, and of darkness generally in the story, with the evil in the heart of man. But Conrad also insists, throughout Marlow's account of the trip up river, on its identity with the primeval in nature: "Going up that river was like traveling back to the earliest beginnings of the world," Marlow says. "We were wanderers on a prehistoric earth, on an earth that wore the aspect of an unknown planet. We could have fancied ourselves the first of men taking possession of an accursed inheritance." After describing savages sighted on the bank, he continues: "The prehistoric man was cursing us, praying to us, welcoming us—who could tell? We were cut off from the comprehension of our surroundings; we glided past like phantoms, wondering and secretly appalled. . . . We could not understand because we were too far and could not remember, because we were traveling in the night of first ages." But not too far to recognize an identity: "What thrilled you was just the thought of their humanity—like yours—the thought of your remote kinship with this wild and passionate uproar. . . . And why not [such recognition]? The mind of man is capable of anything—because everything is in it, all the past as well as all the future. What was there after all? Joy, fear, sorrow, devotion, valor, rage—who can tell?—but truth—truth stripped of its cloak of time."

Thus Marlow has reached the point in his journey backward where man faces the dark universe alone, bereft of the painfully wrought outer defenses of civilization. Kurtz, who has made the journey before him and submitted himself absolutely to the measurement of the jungle, must appear to him as the ultimate test case of civilization and humanity, and the desire to reach Kurtz becomes a passion. To have missed him would have been as if Marlow had "been robbed of a belief or had missed my destiny in life." Conrad has forewarned us in many ways (including Marlow's narrative anticipations of later events) that it cannot be by principle that Kurtz will triumph, if he does triumph, but by something more essential. The most essential human capacity given a name in "Heart of Darkness" is "restraint." In what is perhaps the most significant foreshadowing of Kurtz's confrontation with the darkness, the account of the near starvation of the steamer's cannibal crew, Marlow speculates at length on this capacity: "Restraint! What possible restraint? Was it superstition, disgust, patience, fear—or some kind of primitive honor?" But all these—and "principle" thrown in—are "chaff in a breeze" before the force of hunger. "It takes a man all his inborn strength to fight hunger properly. . . . Restraint! I would just as soon have expected restraint from a hyena prowling amongst the corpses of a battlefield. But there was the fact facing me—the fact dazzling . . . like a ripple on an unfathomable enigma, a mystery greater . . . than the curious, inexplicable note of desperate grief in this savage clamor that has swept by us on the river-bank." Here we are certainly close to solid ground, a mysterious human reality equal to the mysterious natural reality of the jungle. Though there is, to be sure, a primitivist tendency in Conrad's treatment of the jungle and its inhabitants, he is not driving here at a primitivist conclusion. These savages have no monopoly on restraint—though they may possess a purer strain of it; Marlow, certainly, has it. Further, it is Kurtz, the civilized man ("all Europe contributed to the making of Kurtz"), who is meant for the true test case, truer than the savages because civilization has equipped him, technologically and imaginatively, with a larger capacity for corruption. Marlow tells us that Kurtz "had no restraint"; yet he insists that Kurtz won a "victory," and we see that his whole attitude toward Kurtz, including his decision to tell the lie he so profoundly loathed and his compulsion later to tell Kurtz's story, are controlled by that victory. It is difficult, in light of this, to understand Evans' contention that Kurtz is, in any sense, "incidental" to "Heart of Darkness": whether we think of the story as a journey within or as a search for the essence of civilization and humanity, Kurtz's victory is its crux. From the latter point of view, his cry, "The horror! The horror!" reveals that Kurtz—though he lacked restraint, had "kicked himself loose of the earth"—by the strength of his essential humanity (which Marlow forbids us to call either "restraint" or its equivalent "inborn strength," though it must be related to both) managed in the final moment to regain a human vantage point from which to judge—and condemn—this unrestraint, this indulgence of worse than savage appetites. "It was an affirmation, a moral victory paid for by innumerable defeats, by abominable terrors, by abominable satisfactions. But it was a victory!"

Marlow's faithfulness to Kurtz, even to the point of the lie, can be mainly explained by his feeling that, in the very grasp of the dark forces of the universe—including those in his own heart—Kurtz, at the last, had not failed him, had vindicated his faith in an essential human quality. But his faithfulness must also be seen, so far as the lie is concerned, to be a consequence of his notion that women of the ideal type of Kurtz's intended are a luxury which civilization can afford to have and protect as a kind of ideal self-image—a notion which reflects something of the late nineteenth-century conception of woman, beauty, and the ideal. "It's queer how out of touch with truth women are," Marlow remarks early in the story. "They live in a world of their own, and there has never been anything like it, and never can be. It is too beautiful altogether, and if they were to set it up it would go to pieces before the first sunset." He first mentions the lie he had told the girl with the comment, "We must help them stay in that beautiful world of their own, lest ours gets worse." In the end, he bows "before the faith that was in her, before that great and saving illusion that shone with an unearthly glow in the darkness, in the triumphant darkness from which I could not have defended her," and tells his lie.

Three powerful currents of nineteenth-century life and thought converged upon the keepers of the humane tradition at the end of the century, and thus upon Conrad in his conception of "Heart of Darkness": scientific naturalism described a universe indifferent to man, an earth cooling under a darkening sun; evolution theory offered to account for man biologically and socially in terms of sub-human origins; and civilization, largely unaware of these profound challenges to itself, piously set forth on a final brutal assault on the unexploited corners of the earth. Conrad, caught in this convergence and keenly aware of its force, sought in "Heart of Darkness," as elsewhere, for some essential ground on which to base a belief in humanity. The alien universe he accepted and envisioned most powerfully as the setting for his story; it is indeed this convincing recognition and documentation of the forces ranged against the human that largely accounts for the story's authority. About civilization he remained ambivalent: though he mistrusted ideals, as an ideal he held civilization just short of sacred, and felt its ideal purity should find some sanctuary—even, if necessary, in illusion; in practice, he knew that, though it was tragically corruptible, civilization could provisionally save the great mass of mankind. But he refused to ascribe human origins (including the origins of civilization, a human product) to anything less than man. Kurtz's final residue of humanity is indeed small and his capacity for corruption vast, but this residue is irreducible, and in it Conrad finds the essence he has sought. This, of course, he does not and cannot explain; it is itself a final explanation, a point of faith. Except that Kurtz has been brought to his absolute confrontation by moving backward to the beginning of human time rather than forward to the end of it, he might be the man Conrad elsewhere envisions on the last day: "He is so much of a voice that, for him, silence is like death. . . . There is a group alive, clustered on his threshold to watch the last flicker of light on a black sky, to hear the last word uttered in the stilled workshop of the earth. It is safe to affirm that, if anybody, it will be the imaginative man who would be moved to speak on the eve of that day without to-morrow—whether in austere exhortation or in a phrase of sardonic comment, who can guess?"[4] Marlow has told us that Kurtz "had something to say," and that it was not "a word of careless contempt."

4. See above, pp. 152–53 [*Editor*].

CRITICAL DEBATE: STRUCTURAL DEVICES

ROBERT O. EVANS: Conrad's Underworld†

When T. S. Eliot prefaced "The Hollow Men" with the memorable, if brief, quotation from Conrad's "Heart of Darkness," "Mistah Kurtz—he dead," he was commenting, for his own reasons, on the finality of Kurtz's descent into the underworld, much as preachers have been known to indicate Hell as the reward for sinful life. But the poem does not really deal much with "lost, violent souls," but rather with the "stuffed men," a category to which Conrad's Marlow perhaps belonged before he made his journey up the great river in Hades. It is not entirely clear from the story whether Kurtz also began as one of the "hollow men" or not, but that point is not important, for Conrad's hero is Marlow, and the story deals with change in his character. Kurtz enters the picture, as it were, only incidentally at the end as an agent in Marlow's acquisition of knowledge. The "Heart of Darkness," like Eliot's poem, is written for the futile ones "gathered on this beach of the tumid river"; it is not much concerned with eternal damnation in the sense that the inhabitants of Dante's *Inferno* are dead and have gathered their deserts. The story is developed in terms of symbols, and it is, of course, not always possible to distinguish a clear separation between the symbolic and literal levels of meaning. For instance, Kurtz is plainly alive when Marlow begins his journey and still alive when Marlow reaches him, but symbolically there is no doubt that he is the arch-inhabitant of Hell or that Marlow, too, has been journeying through Hell, much as Dante did in the *Inferno*. Superficially there are differences; for example, Marlow travels alone while Dante had Virgil for his guide. But that Africa represents Hell and the great river, Acheron, Phlegethon, Styx, or all the rivers of Hell together is a traditional interpretation of the story.

Recently Miss Lillian Feder has pointed out a number of significant parallels with Virgil's descent in the sixth book of the *Aeneid*, but the "Heart of Darkness" is more than a reworking of an old theme in modern guise. There is no question that Conrad employed epic machinery borrowed from Virgil. Essentially the story is neither a recitation of Kurtz's awful degradation nor the simple history of Marlow's enlightenment. It is a journey through the underworld, for

† From *Modern Fiction Studies*, II (May, 1956), 56–62. Copyright by by permission of the editors and the author.

purposes of instruction as well as entertainment, calculated to bring into focus Conrad's moral vision, as it affects the mass of humanity struggling on the brink of the "tumid river." The story is really concerned with modern ethical and spiritual values and has far more significance for the reader than any transmutation of Virgil's descent could have. Clearly it was not possible for Conrad, writing in the twentieth century, to view the world with a disregard for Christian ethics, as Virgil had to do. Accordingly one would expect Conrad to have a deeper significance than Virgil. Moreover, as one of his main themes, the descent into Hell, was not Virgil's exclusive property, it would not seem likely that Conrad should owe Virgil more than Dante, or even Milton. I shall attempt to show that he did in fact make extensive use of the *Inferno* in the general structure of the story, and by his adoption of epic techniques and epic themes he accomplished something almost unique in the short story, or novelette. The "Heart of Darkness" is not the apex of a genre but rather a special use of form towards which Conrad had been painfully working in order to express his particular, ethical view of the universe.

* * *

It is not easy to determine exactly how closely Conrad relied on Dante. I do not mean to imply that he has slavishly enlisted under any master, but the structure of the "Heart of Darkness," at least from the moment of Marlow's arrival at the first station on the African coast, closely resembles a skeletalized version of the *Inferno*. And even prior to Marlow's landing the characters in the story would appear to fit nicely into Dante's threshold to Hell. Perhaps the knitters of black wool are slightly misplaced; Dante might have introduced them earlier. The directors themselves, though they do not realize it, belong in the Vestibule, as men whose lives have warranted neither great infamy nor great praise. Seamen who have abandoned the sea, they are now businessmen. * * * Actually Marlow has little space to devote to the directors; they serve as Marlow's audience, but they are not the audience the author is trying to convince. "Heart of Darkness" is not their story. They are really incapable of understanding it, as Conrad suggests when he puts in the narrator's mouth the insipid remark, "we knew we were fated . . . to hear about one of Marlow's *inconclusive* experiences" (italics mine). But at least they are capable of sensing something special about Marlow, for the same speaker relates that Marlow "had the pose of a Buddha preaching in European clothes and without a lotus flower." This is plain description of Marlow's mission.

The continentals, too, are "hollow men" living in or near the Vestibule, except perhaps for the guardians. Some, of course, are better than others. The doctor, like the narrator on the *Nellie*, has some realization of the importance of Marlow's journey, shown by his farewell, "Du calme, du calme. Adieu." The women in the story, beginning with Marlow's aunt, are not really damned but live in an unreal world of their own, incapable of understanding. Miss Feder has suggested that Kurtz's fiancée may occupy a special corner of Hades because she is related, through imagery, to Kurtz and, she says, has no separate existence apart from him. It is quite true that when the reader meets her she appears dressed in black, but I do not think the color alone enough to consign her to Hell. She is mourning for Kurtz in a mistaken, over-sentimental but not abnormal fashion. And her existence does not entirely depend on him. Conrad uses her primarily for an agent in Marlow's eventual discovery of the ethical nature of life. Structurally she is bound to Marlow. Symbolically Conrad simplified Marlow's problems until they are mostly bound in the experience of falsehood. The most distasteful action Marlow is capable of is a lie, but twice he is brought to tell one. On the first occasion he lies for practical reasons in order to obtain rivets to repair the steamer, symbolizing dishonesty in the course of the normal business of life. Of course, the lie is successful. But later, when he visits Kurtz's "Intended," Marlow tells another lie, this time with no ulterior motive, and this selfless though intrinsically sinful action, a sort of parable, completes his moral vision. Conrad needs the fiancée for Marlow far more than he does to explain Kurtz's presence in Africa. She, like Marlow's aunt, simply does not understand the real world. The women of this story live in a special, mythical realm of their own.

The close structural parallel between the "Heart of Darkness" and the *Inferno* is not explicit at the Vestibule stage. Moreover, Dante borrowed the Vestibule from Virgil, though Conrad's tenants resemble Dante's far more than the Latin poet's. But from the landing in Africa and Marlow's descent into Limbo the relationship becomes unmistakable. Immediately preceding the real descent, Conrad devotes several paragraphs to explanation, in symbolic terms, of his special Hades. He carefully separates Africa from modern civilization by describing machinery rusting uselessly on a hillside. * * *

Next Conrad turns to Marlow's meeting with the Chief Accountant, noteworthy for his gentle annoyance at having his work disturbed by a dying man on a litter placed in the office with him. The accountant is beyond the violence and the brutality. He keeps up appearances. He does not really suffer. Accordingly, he resembles Dante's tenants who have "sinned not; yet their merit lacked its chiefest // Fulfillment, lacking baptism, which is // The gateway to the faith which thou believest." The accountant belongs in Limbo.

From the coast up the river to the second station the characters in the story closely resemble the inhabitants of Upper Hell. Conrad does not follow Dante's eschatology strictly, but certainly the ivory traders belong with the lustful, gluttonous, wrathful. The second station is the abode of the fraudulent, through which blows, appropriately, "a taint of imbecile rapacity . . . like a whiff from some corpse." The idea is Dante's; the passage actually may have been drawn from a notation in the Congo Diary, "saw at a camp place the dead body of a Backongo. Shot? Horrid smell." He describes the station at length, its "air of plotting, [where the inhabitants] intrigued and slandered and hated each other," in terms that would be appropriate for Dante's City of Dis, that domain in the *Inferno* of those whose sins of violence and fraud involve exercise of the will.

From the second station on, up the river to Kurtz's outpost, Conrad carefully draws his characters as if they now inhabited Nether Hell. Nevertheless there is a fundamental difference between the "Heart of Darkness" and the *Inferno* at this stage. The inhabitants of Conrad's City of Dis actually travel further into the underworld; Dante's damned are fixed. I think this is an essential part of Conrad's solution to the problem of making Hell real though not actual. Moreover, the geography of Hell is, naturally, somewhat altered. As Marlow travels up the river on the steam launch, the natives are literally downtrodden blacks, but they resemble those who are violent against their neighbors. In fact, violence is one of their few distinguishing characteristics. The traders, now called Pilgrims primarily because they move about in Hell, take on the attributes of the circles they have entered. They too become violent, firing wickedly if ineffectually into the underbrush. The Russian trader that Marlow and his company encounter does seem slightly out of place in terms of Dante's scheme, for he appears to be a heretic. Conrad actually calls him a "harlequin," a verbal resemblance that is perhaps more than coincidental. He is not himself one of the violent; his real sin is accepting Kurtz as a false god. Their relationship is also in the foreground, though Conrad does not enlarge upon it. The trader merely remarks of Kurtz, "This man has enlarged my mind," suggesting intellectual sin, which heresy is. Conrad leaves little doubt about their relations in the readers' minds. The trader has not meditated about his connection with Kurtz; "it came to him, and he accepted it with a sort of eager fatalism." Marlow explains, "I must say that to me it appeared about the most dangerous thing in every way he had come upon so far." A writer could scarcely leave less to the imagination. Then, at the center of the underworld, Conrad presents Kurtz, perhaps something of a disappointment, because he does nothing but talk and die, to a reader schooled on the modern short story. But Kurtz fits Dante's scheme perfectly, as traitor to kindred, having put behind him all relations with Europe, to country, having abandoned even the platitudinous lip-service to the civilizing ideal upheld by the others, to guests, having turned upon the trader who nursed him, to God, having set himself up as a "graven image" in the center of Hades. In short Kurtz is the living Lucifer even without the unspeakable rites mentioned by Marlow.

His native queen, on the other hand, is an emendation to the complicated Dante-like system, though she completes Kurtz's degradation. In a sense she is not materially different from the aunt and the fiancée. In her ambitious dreams, which differ from theirs only because she is more primitive, she is out of touch with the real world. Another structural difference between the two works seems to lie in the fact that Conrad neglected the final circle of Dante's Hell, the frozen Lake of Cocytus. But Conrad's Hell is mythical. Literally Kurtz was alive when Marlow reached him. Death was still his immediate future, and perhaps he is not symbolically fixed in ice, like the Alberti brothers, because Conrad wished to suggest that evil as he was, a still worse fate awaited him. His final words, "the horror, the horror," may not only refer back to his Satanic service but may also look ahead to an everlasting horror.

I have devoted some time to showing that the structural basis of the "Heart of Darkness" resembles that of the *Inferno*. As Marlow descends deeper into Hades, he meets characters whose sins loosely correspond with those in the Italian epic. But Conrad by no means runs through the list of the seven deadly sins with their numerous subdivisions. In fact he does not conceive evil dialectically, but he roughly follows a tripartite division of sin of his own making, materially different from but not certainly related to the commonplace medieval conception. At the first station is the accountant, doomed but not suffering, in Limbo; at the next, the City of Dis, the ivory traders much as Dante would have treated them; finally, Kurtz, Lucifer himself, taking on the attributes of all the sins in which he has participated. Such a conception would be familiar to Dante, for superimposed on the complicated structure of his Hell is the threefold machinery of Vestibule, Upper Hell, Nether Hell. Conrad's structure is epic; he was not writing the usual sort of short story. As Miss Feder recognizes, he was heroically depicting "Marlow's discovery of evil and the responsibilities to himself and to others which this knowledge places upon him."

On the other hand, Miss Feder contends that Conrad employed the descent into Hell theme, at least to some extent, in order to "build up suspense, to tell the reader indirectly that this is no ordinary voyage." The voyage is certainly extraordinary, but, as I have pointed out, Conrad does not impart this information through implication. He states it so plainly and so often that the reader can scarcely mistake his meaning. Nor can I agree that the epic theme is employed to develop suspense. As I have shown, Conrad takes pains to adhere to epic structure, patterned after that of the *Inferno*. Suspense is a very slight element in both the classical epic and in Dante and of minor importance in the "Heart of Darkness." Conrad's goal, as Schiller said of Homer, is "already present in every point of his progress." From the first scene on the deck of the cruising yawl, *Nellie,* the reader is aware—even before the descent into Hell theme commences—that he is not listening to an ordinary sea-yarn. Marlow is no common sailor, any more than Christ's disciples were. He is described as sitting "cross-legged right aft . . . resembling an idol." The initial action is connected chronologically, through the epic list of ships, with heroic actions of the past. The Thames is geographically connected with all the other waters of the world and mythologically with the underworld. The preliminary scene, no mere enveloping action calculated to add verisimilitude, tends to do away with suspense.

In a geographical sense as well, the story progresses from incident through journey to further incident, avoiding climax by diversions of great intrinsic value, much as Dante progresses through the various circles of Hell. And because of this technique few experienced readers are likely to find themselves breathless as they journey with Conrad into the dark continent. The strength of the story lies not in the suspense it develops but in the power of its clear moral insight and in the readers' realization that they, too, could perhaps under trial follow in Marlow's footsteps.

* * *

For the development of Conrad's purpose, the promotion of ethical insight, the reader must be left emotionally free so that he can judge not only Kurtz's action but Marlow's as well, and draw the right conclusions from them. I contend that Conrad was fully aware of this problem and realized that a solution in modern prose form was extremely difficult. Throughout his career he struggled towards an answer. *The Shadow Line* and "The Secret Sharer" are attempts in the same direction, but it was only with the happy adoption of epic technique in "Heart of Darkness," based largely on the descent into Hell theme which Conrad borrowed from Dante and Virgil, that he achieved complete success.

WILLIAM BYSSHE STEIN: The Lotus Posture and
Heart of Darkness†

Although Robert O. Evans' "Conrad's Underground" offers some
interesting "epic" parallels to the "Heart of Darkness," it fails, I
think, to cope with the moral experience in terms of the structure of
the story. While I will not deny that there is a rough development of
the myth of the descent into the underworld, this pattern of action
cannot be viewed by itself and in itself. It must, rather, be seen in
the Jamesian frame Conrad provides. Mr. Evans, to be sure, takes
note of this important element of structure, but unfortunately he
does not consider it to have a function. I refer, of course, to the
Buddha tableaux, the positioning of which cannot be ignored, the
two at the beginning, the one near the middle, and the other in
the final paragraph of the work.

Mr. Evans even goes so far as to introduce his fragmentary cita-
tions from the tableaux into the context of Marlow's recital; actually
they belong to the perspective of the first person narrator who
acquaints us with the adventurer. Conrad deliberately restricts them
to the vision of the latter because, as Mr. Evans is aware, he is one
of the four auditors who cannot possibly understand the significance
of a subtle spiritual voyage. All four are blinded by their infatuation
with the material aspects of the world. Yet, as I shall show, the
tableaux of the lotus postures instruct the reader how to interpret
Marlow's descent into the underworld—his own, not Virgil's or
Dante's.

Most of us, I am sure, are familiar with the stylized postures and
gestures of Indian art, that is, with their appearance, not their
meaning. Conrad, if we can claim Marlow as his "altar" [sic] ego,
not only understood them; he believed in them. The first tableau,
for instance, catches the hero in the physical position prerequisite
to Yoga meditation, contemplation, and absorption. On the brink
of the spiritual fulfillment that comes with self-recollection (a mode
of personal salvation diametrically opposed to the Occidental belief
that perfection is acquired from without, for in the Indian view the
process is one of bringing into consciousness what lies in a dormant
and quiescent state, the timeless reality of one's being), Marlow's
lotus posture shows he is ready to engage in an exercise of intense
introspection; he is ready to contemplate the chaos out of which
order or cosmos comes: "Marlow sat *cross-legged* right aft. . . .
He had *sunken cheeks, a yellow complexion, a straight back*, an
ascetic aspect, and *with his arms dropped, the palms of hands out-*

† From *Modern Fiction Studies*, II
(Winter, 1956–57), 167–70. Copyright
by Purdue Research Foundation. Re-

ward, resembled an idol (italics are mine)." This description gives evidence of the self-mortification, the denial of the tyranny of physical matter, which precedes the introversion of consciousness. And surely the combination of gestures by the limbs is enough to command alert attention; or is Conrad, like Marlow, addressing himself to the inadvertent curiosity of a reader as dull as the observer? In effect, it seems to me that Conrad in setting up this tableau is ridiculing the moral complacency which, confronted by a form of religious discipline older by far than Christianity, is so incapable of expanding its understanding.

A similar irony asserts itself in the next tableau, for again Marlow's posture is the occasion for deprecation: "he had the pose of a Buddha preaching in European clothes and without a lotus-flower." But while we are engaged in a consideration of these blind impeachments, let us not forget that the springboard for Mr. Evans' treatment of the story as epic is this same narrative voice. It is he who invokes the romance of the sea: the *Golden Hind,* the *Erebus,* and the *Terror.* If he is also a representative of the class Conrad is mocking, then Mr. Evans is not justified in citing these images in proof of his thesis.

Indeed, the basic irony of the "Heart of Darkness" resides in the preoccupation of Marlow's auditors with the external aspects of the descent into the African underworld. Conrad's repetition of the word "meditation" is a rubric here. He wishes to stress that Marlow's journey is only important to the degree that he can vicariously relive Kurtz's lapse into primitive degradation. This emphasis is like-wise affirmed in Marlow's virtual obsession with Kurtz, the passionate interest in the man that grew as he proceeded towards the inner station. It is also manifest in Marlow's meticulous recreation of every facet of his trip, beginning with the interview on the continent. This recapitulation is necessary if he is to follow Kurtz's soul to the brink of utter damnation. After all, the latter's enlightenment consists of the sudden insight into his appalling inhumanity: " 'the horror' " and the "depths of his meanness." And Marlow leaves no doubt that he himself is party to the experience: "But his soul was mad. Being alone in the wilderness, it had looked within itself, and, by heavens! I tell you, it had gone mad. I had—for my sins, I suppose—*to go through the ordeal of looking into it myself* (italics mine)." But, of course, the nature of his enlightenment is different from Kurtz's, and at this point his lotus posture defines itself.

In an exercise of arduous spiritual discipline, symbolized in his physical bearing and studied introversion, "worn, hollow, with downward folds and drooped eyelids, with an aspect of concentrated attention," he lives through, to the very limit, a particular role in life. And in suffering its consequences, he fathoms and exhausts its contents. He descends into his own hell of fear, desire, and fleshly limitations, bearing all the suffering of his attachment to matter. At the last moment, he resists the attraction which Kurtz acknowledges. He breaks free from the forces of the flesh. With the story of his spiritual journey told, he sits in the inturned lotus posture, detached from the conditions, the victories, and the vicissitudes of time: "Marlow ceased, sat apart, indistinct and silent, in the pose of the meditating Buddha." And, as before, the narrator-observer is beguiled by outward appearance. Marlow has voyaged alone among the temptations which entangle man in time. He has not communicated with his auditors. He stands apart from them, the anonymous ascetic, cleansed and purged by his introspective ordeal.

This is all that Conrad tells the reader. The symbolic consecration to the ideal of Buddhahood constitutes the refinement of the experience in the heart of darkness. Whatever spiritual implications one finds in the story must be based on the tableaux. In effect, we have journeyed along "the way of the Bodhisattva." We have stood on the brink of time and eternity with Kurtz and Marlow, and we have seen the latter transcend this pair of opposites. We have also witnessed his triumph over inward suffering and toil. Although qualified to enter nirvana, like the true Bodhisattva, Marlow remains in the world to work for the salvation of all people. In his stage of enlightenment he teaches what his descent into the imperfections of the human soul has taught him—egoless compassion. Cancelling out all personal desire and fear, he has made available to humanity the gift of complete renunciation. To every suffering, striving creature, trapped in the karmic processes (enslavement to matter), he offers the inexhaustible wisdom of selflessness.

This interpretation, without the slightest exaggeration, emerges out of scrupulous focus on the structure of the story. A vision of spiritual reality is framed in the Buddha tableaux. Its meaning is not dependent upon any "epic" technique. If anything, consistent with Marlow's ironical attitude towards his audience, whatever parallels to the pagan and Christian underworlds that he broaches must be looked upon ironically. And here again I feel that Mr. Evans in his concern with a pattern of symbolism has slighted another of Conrad's conscious artistic practices. I refer in this instance to tone. Mr. Evans is quite aware of this device but never in the perspective of its effects upon thematic meaning. The self-mockery that pervades the Marlow recital, it seems to me, must operate to temper the ego climate of epic endeavor. Outward heroics are hardly a reflection of the compassionate Buddha.

SEYMOUR GROSS: [The Frame]†

Despite the frequency with which Conrad's "Heart of Darkness" has been discussed, the function of the frame in the novelette—the four men who sit on the deck of the *Nellie* and listen to Marlow's tale—has either been ignored or somewhat misconstrued. For example, Robert O. Evans in his "Conrad's Underworld" asserts that "actually Marlow [Conrad] has little space to devote to the directors. They serve as Marlow's audience, but they are not the audience the author is trying to convince. The 'Heart of Darkness' is not their story. They are really incapable of understanding it, as Conrad suggests when he puts in the narrator's mouth the insipid remark, 'We knew we were fated . . . to hear about one of Marlow's inconclusive experiences.'"

Similarly, William Bysshe Stein, in his "The Lotus Posture and 'The Heart of Darkness,'" recognizes the moral importance of the structure of the story and interestingly explicates the Buddha imagery in the frame, but nevertheless agrees with Mr. Evans that Marlow's story falls upon the spiritually deaf ears "of the four auditors who cannot possibly understand the significance of a subtle spiritual voyage."

I believe it is a mistake, however, to lump the four auditors together indiscriminately. As a matter of fact, Conrad subtly but emphatically differentiates one of the listeners—the first narrator—from the other three. What Evans and Stein say is true for the other three men, who, it turns out, are indeed incapable of comprehending the staggering implications of Marlow's tale. These three, in the frame, reflect all those in the actual experience—the corrupt pilgrims, the fantastic Russian, the company officials—who are unable to grasp the "hidden truth" of the moral abysm into which they have descended. For these three men, Marlow's tale (as Kurtz himself had been to the others in the story) is at worst ridiculous, at best an adventure story to listen to and forget. The only comment one of the three makes during the telling of Marlow's tale is "absurd," which understandably evokes from the experientially wiser Marlow the angry exclamation, "Absurd! . . . This is the worst of trying to tell. . . . Here you all are, each moored with two good addresses, like a hulk with two anchors, a butcher round one corner, a policeman round another, excellent appetites, and temperature normal—you hear—normal from year's end to year's end. And you say, Absurd! Absurd be—exploded! Absurd!" And

† From "A Further Note on the Function of the Frame in 'Heart of Darkness,'" *Modern Fiction Studies*, III (Summer, 1957), 167–70. Copyright by Purdue Research Foundation. Reprinted by permission of the editors and the author.

when the terrifying saga of human degradation and triumph is concluded, the only thing the Director can find to say is the practical but, in the context, morally obtuse comment, "We have lost the first of the ebb." This group in the frame reflects all those in the actual adventure, and by extension in life, who are "too much of a fool to go wrong—too dull even to know [they] are being assaulted by the powers of darkness."

The first narrator is something else again. He is hardly, as Mr. Stein asserts, "dull" and incorrigibly "beguiled by outward appearance," "a representative of the class Conrad is mocking." He, in the frame, stands in the same relationship to Marlow as Marlow stood to Kurtz in the actual experience. He is precisely "the audience the author is trying to convince," for he is a man, as becomes increasingly apparent, who is capable of "facing the darkness" and of accepting its black message. It is true, as Mr. Evans asserts, that his comment about Marlow's inconclusive tales is insipid; but it must be noted that this is the kind of superficiality he is capable of only *before* he has lived through Marlow's tale, just as Marlow considers his own judgment before he has lived through Kurtz as being that of "a silly little bird." Both Marlow and the first narrator, metaphorically speaking, start at the same place, take the same trip, and arrive at the same destination.

When we first meet the narrator, he is a potentially sensitive but essentially optimistic man—a man who sees and evaluates experience from a "*lightened*" (though hardly enlightened) point of view. Although we are told nothing directly about him, the manner in which Conrad has him describe things serves to reveal the delusion of his moral innocence, a delusion which Marlow's tale is to shatter in precisely the same way as the reality of Kurtz's degradation shattered Marlow's own "mournful and senseless delusion."

The imagery of light with which the first two pages of the story are studded serves both as an index to the narrator's innocence and as an ironic prologue to Marlow's opening comment—"And this also . . . has been one of the dark places on the earth." For the first narrator, the Thames is a "benign immensity of unstained light," enveloped in a mist of "gauzy and radiant fabric"; on her "luminous" waters the sails of the barges "seemed to stand still in red clusters of canvas sharply peaked, with gleams of varnished sprits." After the day ends "in a serenity of still and exquisite brilliance," "Lights of ships moved in the fairway—a great stir of lights going up and going down." Moreover, his conception of the history of the river—which Conrad ironically comments upon in Marlow's harrowing tale of the first Romans' struggle with "the fascination of the abomination"—is the epitome of bright, shadowless naiveté. For him, the history of the Thames is only "ships whose names are like jewels flashing in the night of time," carrying "bearers of a spark from the sacred fire" to glorious conquests. "What greatness had not floated on the ebb of that river. . . . The dreams of men, the seed of commonwealths, the germs of empires." Marlow is soon to give him another kind of vision of the men who go into the heart of darkness: "the growing regrets, the longing to escape, the powerless disgust, the surrender, the hate."

Although the narrator, with the others, at first merely sits back patiently to listen to Marlow's yarn, by the time Marlow has threaded his way through about a third of his experience, he suffers a severe shock to his moral equilibrium. In the symbolic darkness which has enveloped the group, Marlow becomes for the narrator "no more . . . than a voice," just as Kurtz, to Marlow, had also "presented himself as a voice." And it is a disturbing voice. "The others might have been asleep, but I was awake. I listened, I listened on the watch for the sentence, for the word, that would give me the clew to the faint uneasiness inspired by this narrative that seemed to shape itself without human lips in the heavy night air of the river." At this point, Marlow's tale seems to hold out for the narrator the promise of some moral revelation, which is exactly what Kurtz had come to represent for Marlow at an analogous point in his experience. (For example, when Marlow thinks that Kurtz is dead, he says, "I couldn't have felt more lonely desolation somehow, had I been robbed of a belief or had missed my destiny in life.")

The narrator's moral progress is completed in the final paragraph of the story. Marlow's tale of "diabolic love and unearthly hate" has literally bowed the narrator with the sheer immensity of its implications. Immediately after the Director's banal comment, he says, "I raised my head. The offing was barred by a black bank of clouds, and the tranquil waterway leading to the uttermost ends of the earth flowed somber under an overcast sky—seemed to lead into the heart of an immense darkness." The transformation has been complete: "the benign immensity of unstained light" has become "the heart of an immense darkness." Now he, like Marlow, will be set apart from all those who do not know the truth.

The recognition of the reflective function of the frame in "Heart of Darkness" not only serves to reinforce the thematic implications of the story in much the same way as, for example, Gloucester's tragedy reinforces Lear's, but adds a new aspect to the work as well. That the narrator is able to arrive at his moral insight through "literature," as Marlow had arrived at his through experience, demonstrates Conrad's faith in the moral efficacy of experience through literature. Louis Armstrong once remarked that there are people who if they don't know, you can't tell them. What Conrad seems to be saying is that these people can't be told either by life or literature. It seems to me, then, that the "Heart of Darkness" is not only an enduring comment on the nature of man, but a parable on the possibilities of moral knowledge as well.

ROBERT O. EVANS: [No Easy Clue]†

Two notes in MFS by Mr. Stein and Mr. Gross, both of which take issue with certain details in my article, "Conrad's Underworld," though not my thesis, deserve cautious amplification. No one would argue with Mr. Gross' conclusion that "the 'Heart of Darkness' is not only an enduring comment on the nature of man, but a parable on the possibilities of moral knowledge as well." I am not so sure this conclusion inevitably proceeds from the argument that the first narrator on the deck of the *Nellie* passes through a moral experience analogous to Marlow's own—with the same sort of beneficial results. If the speaker in the frame secures any moral knowledge whatsoever, it is purely vicarious and not the direct result of experience. I am willing to concede that Conrad's treatment of him is slightly different from that of the other directors; after all, he has a voice. But I do not think Mr. Stein misconstrues the story in lumping the directors together and considering the speaker, too, as "beguiled by outward appearance." Perhaps this narrator is sufficiently aware of the moral realm to recognize that they have "lost the first of the ebb," but he is not sufficiently aware to want to do anything about it or realize a prerogative has been presented to him. Conrad's vision is moral; thus I cannot believe, though he may wish to suggest parallels between the two narrators, that he intends for us to believe the speaker in the frame vicariously and almost idly profited from Marlow's yarn almost as much as Marlow himself. The tale, it still seems to me, is clearly directed at the reader, who may somehow apply the moral knowledge gleaned from it to his own experience.

There are other aspects in which the story in the frame parallels that in the center. Marlow's vision of the Roman commander ordered north from relative security to the Thames frontier, it seems to me, is a historical miniature of the main story, one in which, Conrad says, the Roman does his unpleasant duty because he was man "enough to face the darkness." Perhaps Mr. Stein, by concentrating on the "lotus posture" tableaux of Marlow as a cross-legged Buddha "preaching in western clothes," misplaces the emphasis Conrad desired when he concludes that "outward heroics are hardly a reflection of the compassionate Buddha." In the first place, there is really no doubt about the fact that Marlow was capable of outward heroics; the journey into darkness, itself, was one of the most heroic in literature. The moral courage required to

† From "A Further Comment on 'Heart of Darkness,'" *Modern Fiction Studies*, III (Winter, 1957–58), 358–60. Copyright by Purdue Research Foundation. Reprinted by permission of the editors and the author.

lie to Kurtz's Intended at the end of the story, despite the moral lessons Marlow has learned from Kurtz and despite his opinion of a lie as the epitome of evil, is not inconsiderable. Conrad seems to wish the reader to think of Marlow at the time he is telling the story as one making a recollection in tranquillity. Marlow has earned his godlike detachment by actively journeying up the Congo and into the depths of Hell; at the moment he is presented in "lotus posture" this aspect of his life is done, though Conrad deliberately suggests the role of prophet may not be an easy one.

There is a further difficulty in making Marlow a spokesman for Yoga. I find nothing in the description of Marlow's posture which makes it necessary to identify him with anything more than the commonplace image of Buddha. Such a statue carved in ivory and set on a black base can be purchased anywhere in the Orient for a few shillings. It seems unlikely that Conrad knew a great deal about eastern religion or that he intended to suggest that the end of life is contemplative self-abnegation, the anti-karmic way. But if he did intend to suggest anything beyond the fact of identification of Marlow with the god, there is no reason to believe that he meant for Marlow to advocate, as Mr. Stein implies, an end of life similar to that upheld by Krishna when he said: "The man who casts off all desires and walks without desire, with no thought of a *Mine* or an *I*, comes unto peace." So far as I can ascertain from the *Bhagavadgita*, Krishna was not obligated to alter his position to address the Arjuna, or fighting caste: "To a knight there is no thing more blessed than lawful strife" or "Make thyself ready for the fight; thus shalt thou get no sin." There are certainly no external reasons to assume that Conrad ever read deeply in the documents of eastern religion, but if he did he must certainly have known that there is more than one way to salvation. The one that best fits Marlow, not in "lotus posture" but throughout the action of the story, is the way of Karma, which leads to the end, as perhaps Marlow has been led, to contemplation—but contemplation of the ethical consequences of actions in terms of future existence. The way of the warrior, like the way of the Roman commander, resembles the way of the sailor who journeyed into Hell. Stated differently, it seems to me that Conrad would perforce subscribe to Milton's doctrine: "I cannot praise a fugitive and cloistered virtue."

Mr. Stein's suggestion that Marlow serves as Conrad's "altar" ego is also most interesting, aside from the play on words. It was once thought Conrad's Congo journey was the turning point of his career, after which he seriously took up writing, but it now seems that he took with him on that trip the MS of *Almayer's Folly*. Nevertheless, as M. Jean-Aubry, Conrad's biographer, points out, the journey may have shaken his confidence in the sea, as it robbed him of health. Marlow, however, has stuck with the sea, the real world of action; whereas the others on the deck of the *Nellie,* including Mr. Gross' candidate, have all deserted it. Thus while both explications are interesting and present valuable supplementary information about a story which now seems far more profound than readers have hitherto recognized, both, I think, deserve some qualification. Both depend too heavily on relatively minor matters of incident or image, at the expense of the primary image, the pervasive darkness. With Conrad there is no easy, Jamesian clue, as it were, to the pattern in the carpet.

R. KERF: Symbol Hunting in Conradian Land†

To look for symbols in Conrad's fiction has become quite a fashion in certain quarters. Since the revival of Conrad studies inaugurated shortly after World War II, an increasing number of articles dealing with Conrad's symbolic method have been published in various American magazines. Paul Wiley's *Conrad's Measure of Man,* published in 1954, was the first book-length study entirely devoted to an analysis of Conrad's use of imagery, symbol and myth. A second has just been published by another American critic, Ted E. Boyle, under the title *Symbol and Meaning in the Fiction of Joseph Conrad* [1965].

Symbolic interpretations of Conrad often make his symbolic method what it is not. Many critics tend to interpret all the details of a story in the light of the various symbolic or mythic referents they have discovered in the book. As a consequence they are apt not only to endow many details, or events with a symbolic significance for which the immediate context supplies very little evidence but also to distort the meaning of Conrad's works. In addition to this the hunt for symbols often makes these critics blind to the aesthetic value of the work under consideration: they seem to assume that provided symbols can be discovered, the work, or scene, or passage in which these appear gives evidence of consummate artistry. Two short extracts will show the kind of interpretations to which such "criticism" can lead.

In a note on "Buddhism and 'The Heart of Darkness' ", W. B. Stein considers that it is the comparisons of Marlow to a Buddha, and not the details Marlow gives about his journey through Africa, that bring us nearest to the meaning of the story. In a further note on "The Lotus Posture and 'The Heart of Darkness' "[1] he interprets Marlow's ordeal in the light of the Buddhist doctrine. * * * Not

† From *Revue des Langues Vivantes,* XXXII (1966), 266–77. Reprinted by permission of the editors.
1. *Modern Fiction Studies,* II (1956).

only does Stein's premise contradict Conrad's method, which aims at making the concrete details of the journey suggest the quality of Marlow's moral experience, but, by imposing the Buddhist doctrine on the meaning of the story, he would make Marlow the protagonist of a philosophy which contradicts the very idea he expresses several times in the course of the story—for example, after Conrad has compared him for the second time to a Buddha: —"What saves us is efficiency—the devotion to efficiency." The connotations of the Buddha metaphors must be taken into account to ascertain the exact shades of Marlow's "philosophy", but to stress them at the expense of other elements which are plainly stated is bound to distort the meaning of Marlow's experience.

In "Heart of Darkness" Conrad refers through his imagery to the old myth of the descent into the underworld and thereby deeply enriches the significance of the story. Yet not all details or events can be made to fit into the old mythical pattern. R. O. Evans, however, has argued from such metaphors as the comparison of the grove of death to "the gloomy circle of some Inferno" that Marlow's journey through the Congo "closely resembles a skeletalized version of The Inferno." The characters of the people Marlow meets at the various stages of his journey should indicate that Brussels is in The Vestibule, the First Station in Limbo and the Second Station in the Upper Hell. The critic is, however, prepared to admit that "the geography of Hell is, naturally, somewhat altered." Thus the Russian, whom he considers as a "heretic" (and as such belonging to the Sixth Circle of Dante's Hell) is found in the Seventh Circle, which is that of the "violent." Conrad is also shown to have neglected the final circle of Dante's Hell, the frozen lake of Cocytus. Apparently, the reader is not supposed to ask how such a lake could lie under the equator since the critic has warned him at the beginning that Marlow's Hell is a legendary rather than an actual place.

* * *

CRITICAL DEBATE: THE LIE

KENNETH A. BRUFFEE: The Lesser Nightmare†

Late in Conrad's story *Heart of Darkness*, Marlow expresses the belief that "some knowledge of yourself" is the only reward life offers. Thus the story implies that the self-knowledge Kurtz gains—his revelation of man's deficiency—is both a reward and a

† From *Modern Language Quarterly*, XXV (September, 1964), 322–29. Reprinted by permission of the editors and the author.

penalty, although obviously a vision of horror is no reward in the usual sense of the word. Furthermore, Marlow believes that this one reward which life offers is unique for each individual, that self-knowledge is a solitary knowledge which "no other man can ever know." Contrary to this belief, Marlow soon finds himself participating in Kurtz's self-revelation; and, sharing as he does in another man's experience, he is liable in some way to share the reward—and the penalty, the burden of the reward. His reward is to see and know, but not to die in terror; his penalty seems to come at the end of the story when, in telling Kurtz's Intended that the last word Kurtz spoke was her name, he sacrifices his integrity by lying.

Two paradoxes, then, seem fundamental to the story. First, a man participates in another man's self-revelation and both men profit by it. Second, the "profit" is an ironic one—that is, the original insight (Kurtz's) is both a reward of life and a terrible penalty for it, and the further insight (Marlow's), engendered by the first, is at the same time illuminating and apparently corrupting. These two paradoxes resolve themselves into one paradoxical action: a lie which establishes a condition of truth. This paradox, too, can be resolved in several ways.[1] The resolution I suggest here depends first of all on seeing the experience described in the story as a peculiarly twentieth-century kind of Faustian experience.

That Kurtz's experience is Faustian is quite clear. His "universal genius", his godlike power over the natives, his "forbidden knowledge" gained in the wilderness of the self—all suggest a parallel with Faust. More specifically, the wilderness of the jungle, Marlow says, had "sealed [Kurtz's] soul to its own by the inconceivable ceremonies of some devilish initiation." Once initiated, Kurtz takes to calling everything his own: "'My Intended, my ivory, my station, my river, my—' everything belong to him." And yet, Marlow says, "The thing was to know what he belonged to, how many powers of darkness claimed him for their own." After establishing that Kurtz is "no fool," Marlow implies just who it is Kurtz does belong to: "I take it, no fool ever made a bargain for his soul with the devil." Finally, after describing Kurtz's state of mind to be one of "exalted and incredible degradation," Marlow says, in language typical of descriptions of traditional Faustian characters, "the awakening of

1. A strong alternative interpretation of the story is Walter F. Wright's in *Romance and Tragedy in Joseph Conrad* (Lincoln, 1949). Wright says that since goodness and faith are as real as evil and despair, if Marlow had told the truth "he would have acknowledged . . . that goodness and faith were the unrealities," whereas Conrad wants us to believe "that not one, but both of these are reality" (p. 159). This remark appears to summarize neatly my contention in this paper, but it does so without showing the relevance of what Wright calls Conrad's "study of the nature of truth" in the final scene either to the rest of the story or to the peculiarly "modern" ethical nature of that truth.

forgotten and brutal instincts . . . had beguiled his unlawful soul beyond the bounds of permitted aspirations."

At the moment of self-revelation, however, Kurtz's Faustian experience initiates and begins to give way to an extension of that experience which is to be carried through and fulfilled by Marlow. It is to that extension that the story subordinates Kurtz's Faustian nature. Thus *Heart of Darkness* is not just a story in which a soul is sold and lost; the combined experience of Kurtz and Marlow represents a considerable departure from the "traditional" (that is, medieval and Renaissance) Faustian experience. But neither is this story one in which a soul is saved by outwitting the devil or by overcoming his evil with the powers of light. This characteristic of the romantic Faustus is, of course, also a considerable departure from the traditional Faustian experience. Goethe and Lessing made the inordinate pursuit of knowledge into the pursuit of wisdom, an ennobling human activity, the motive for the transformation being an identification with Faust, a desire to see Faust as Everyman, and the result being that Faust was not damned in the end, but saved.

Conrad's motive also seems to be redemption, even though he does follow the earlier tradition in that in his story the pursuit of forbidden knowledge remains an evil pursuit which does not ultimately ennoble man, but degrades him. Conrad departs from tradition in another way. Whereas Goethe and Lessing saved Faust by altering the story's assumptions, Conrad maintains the original assumptions (that there are such things in the world as forbidden knowledge and power), but alters the outcome of the experience by extending its effects. Once it is granted that the experience can be projected vicariously beyond the limits of one individual's soul to another's, it must be agreed that the benefits and penalties of the experience might project even further. Thus, through Marlow, the saving virtue brought to light by the experience he shares with Kurtz can be, and is, extended to their whole civilization—which includes, through Marlow's narration, his audience on the yawl and us, the readers. An important question arises, however, concerning the form of the extension: what, exactly, must the saving virtue be that results from their experience?

It is, of course, restraint, a virtue so simple and fundamental to humanity that the cannibal workmen on the riverboat under the pressure of extreme hunger incredibly and inexplicably exhibit it. It is exactly the virtue which Kurtz lacks, but which in Marlow is reinforced by vicarious revelation of "The Horror" until it becomes the most important, conscious, and compelling force in his character.

Restraint expresses itself, however, in a most peculiar way. Marlow confesses early in the story that "there is" for him "a taint of death, a flavour of mortality in lies" which makes him "miserable and sick, like biting something rotten would do." And yet in the end, Marlow lies. The fact of the lie, it would seem, is absolutely crucial to the meaning of the story. Conrad himself, in a letter to his publisher, William Blackwood, soon after the story was finished, described the last pages of *Heart of Darkness* as

> the interview of the man and the girl [which] locks in—as it were—the whole 30,000 words of narrative description into one suggestive view of a whole phase of life, and makes of that story something quite on another plane than an anecdote of a man who went mad in the Centre of Africa.[2]

It is this scene, however, which so often seems to miss being understood. In his book *Joseph Conrad: Achievement and Decline*, for example, Thomas Moser severely criticizes Marlow's apparent self-betrayal. He contends that "Marlow's lie certainly weakens the [final] scene; he has made truth seem too important throughout the novel to persuade the reader now to accept falsehood as salvation." One of the justifications Moser offers for the "weakness" is that "the scene can be read ... as an indictment of this woman, safe and ignorant in her complacent, Belgian bourgeois existence; she does not *deserve* to hear the truth." Furthermore, Moser insists that Marlow reaffirms his fellowship with Kurtz by lying and that thus he too accepts damnation.[3]

Marlow has certainly made a kind of truth seem extremely important throughout the story. Despite this, however, the lie weakens neither the final scene nor the story. It is not that the woman does not deserve to hear the truth, but rather that she does deserve not to hear the truth. In the course of the story, Marlow's lie is inevitable once his anger—frustrations and indignation caused by the girl's persistent illusions—"subsided before a feeling of infinite pity." This pity is Marlow's compassion for the fragility of the woman's illusions and the conventional "surface truth" upon which they are founded—for the fragility of the civilization, that is, however corrupt and hollow, the best of which the girl represents. Of course she is safe, complacent, and bourgeois. But she is also a "soul as translucently pure as a cliff of crystal," her "pure brow" is "illumined by the extinguishable light of belief and love," and the "halo" she seems surrounded with, however "ashy," is still a halo. To alleviate this woman's immediate grief is the first purpose of the lie. But more importantly, Marlow lies to relieve the suffering that she does not know she suffers. However hollow or dead the civilization she stands for may be, however ashy her halo, Marlow comes to believe in the last scene of the story that Kurtz's Intended is

2. See above [*Editor*].
3. Thomas Moser, *Joseph Conrad:*   *Achievement and Decline* (Cambridge, Mass., 1957), pp. 79–81.

nevertheless worthy, does nevertheless deserve not to have to face the truth about Kurtz.

This conviction shows how thoroughly Marlow, in spite of himself, has become identified with Kurtz. The girl represents all the best of Kurtz's ideals—all the best of what he had "intended" for the world as well as for himself. She is the medium through which the world has seen and will see what was best in him. Since by lying Marlow protects those intentions, he thereby reaffirms his fellowship with Kurtz. But he does not thereby accept damnation; on the contrary, he rejects it. Since Kurtz has taken a step that few are willing or able to take, offering himself up to be "rent"—"For nothing can be sole or whole / That has not been rent"—his final revelation of truth, which Marlow calls "an affirmation, a moral victory paid for by innumerable defeats," achieves for him at last a kind of wholeness—and after achieving this, he dies. Marlow achieves the same wholeness through self-revelation, but vicariously—and he does not die but, significantly, lives on to act upon what he has learned.

To make such an affirmation, Marlow has been thoroughly prepared. Earlier, he sided with Kurtz and was excluded from the society of pilgrims because of it. He found himself being "lumped along with Kurtz as a partisan of methods for which the time was not ripe: I was unsound! Ah! but it was something to have at least a choice of nightmares." In the corruption of the "pilgrims," who represent the worst of that safe, complacent, bourgeois civilization, Marlow has found something with a stronger "flavour of mortality," something more rotten to bite into than a lie. And after having himself experienced "all the wisdom, and all truth, and all sincerity" vicariously through Kurtz, when the choice comes again, he determines to choose the lesser nightmare.[4]

The choice comes again when he faces Kurtz's Intended. He chooses to lie (or rather finds himself compelled to lie) because at the last moment only by lying can he fulfill the "destiny in life" which he was earlier so afraid of missing. To fulfill his destiny he must act positively, because to act negatively would be to "accept damnation" passively. Marlow's positive act, then, is to place himself as an artificial barrier between the degraded and the exalted,

4. W. Y. Tindall notes that "forced to choose between 'nightmares,' that of the rapacious Belgians and that of Kurtz, Marlow chooses the latter," because Kurtz's last words seem to Marlow to be a "moral victory." Tindall does not, however, explain the choice, nor does he see its parallel in Marlow's final act. Marlow's lie is also far more positive an act than Tindall sees it to be when he says that Marlow tells "a white lie to keep the Intended in the dark by preserving her light." This interpretation gives both Marlow and Conrad less than they are due, since it depends on a defense of Kurtz by Marlow "out of loyalty to what is perhaps his own mistaken idea of light." Marlow's lie should not be seen to be the "defense of darkness" by a weakened man, but a defense of humanity by a newly strengthened one. See W. Y. Tindall, *From Jane Austen to Joseph Conrad* (Minneapolis, 1959), p. 279.

between the degraded and the ideal (or what passes for the ideal), that is, between Kurtz and his Intended. By the end of the story, Marlow alone bears that responsibility. All that falls between these contraries is Marlow and his lie. When the lily grows on the dunghill, only illusion, appearance, artifice, that is, only the lie, keeps us from seeing the dung. Marlow's destiny is to maintain that separation just because he has seen that, in reality, no separation exists.

It may still be difficult to see how we can be persuaded "to accept falsehood as salvation," because, as Moser says, there is an insistence on truth throughout this story. Marlow, however, makes a careful distinction between "surface truth" and "inner truth." As a result, it might be expected that the story's resolution would not be in terms of mere verbal truth. Furthermore, there are distinct signs of Marlow's disillusionment with words. Words first lead him to Kurtz: "I . . . became aware," he says, "that that was exactly what I had been looking forward to—a talk with Kurtz." But in the days after the rescue, he begins to hear "more than enough" of Kurtz's talk. He becomes less and less enamored of words as the verbose Kurtz talks, contradicts, effuses, and rambles, until "the memory of that time" lingers with him "like a dying vibration of one immense jabber, silly, atrocious, sordid, savage, or simply mean, without any kind of sense." After this, Marlow is only mildly astonished at the ease with which he can himself use words as the occasion demands. "It seemed to me," he says, after he lies to the girl, "that the house would collapse before I could escape, that the heavens would fall upon my head. But nothing happened." He discovers that "the heavens do not fall for such a trifle."

Marlow has discovered, then, a larger standard of truth, a standard according to which the lie, the ethically repulsive, dishonorable act, turns out to be a kind of honorable restraint. By lying, he affirms the artificiality of restraint at the same time as he affirms the necessity of restraint in maintaining the part of civilization worth saving. Unlike Kurtz, whose mission fails as his excessive aspiration fails, Marlow, by not denying that both the light and the dark exist, but by affirming that they must be carefully distinguished, represents his, the girl's, and all society's only salvation. The story's meaning, it finally appears, is a function not of the "surface truth" of a mere articulated falsehood, but of a man's seeing beyond a conventional "principle" to a necessity which demands of him a singularly unconventional act, an "unsound" act, the time for which, however, is all too ripe.

Thus, with the act which fulfills his own destiny, Marlow renders Kurtz "that justice which was his due." He would have accomplished neither had he not lied. Marlow has learned that when the heart speaks truest, it may speak not of light and harmony but of darkness and chaos. In his book on Thomas Mann, Erich Heller suggests something similar to this in a paraphrase of Adrian Leverkühn's conversation with the Devil in the novel *Doctor Faustus*:

> For four hundred years . . . all great music rested on the assumption that there could be harmony and peace between a universally established convention and the subjective concerns of the individual, that "soul" and "order" were profoundly at one, and that it was therefore possible for the human passions truly and freely to express themselves within prescribed formulae. But this "play" is over; the "law" no longer recognizes itself in the "mirror" of human inwardness, and the human heart refuses to be persuaded that there is a "universal order of things" with which it can live at peace; if it were to speak its true mind, its speech would not be of eternal harmonies but of chaos.[5]

Marlow is made aware of this chaos, the "inner truth" which the fragile beauty of Kurtz's Intended cannot be expected to bear, and he compulsively maintains the appearance of harmony.

Thus the paradox of the lie which establishes a condition of truth is resolved. By denying superficial "integrity," and by putting himself at the service of a passion to maintain, however tenuously, man's humanity, Marlow at last manifests the unexpectedly, wholly unideally devious forms that man's "innate strength" or "capacity for faithfulness" may take. Marlow's lie establishes a condition of truth, but of a special kind of truth, a special form of what Heller has called "a beautiful illusion": "The present state of our consciousness . . . as of our knowledge and sense of truth, ever more commandingly suggests . . . that art as 'a beautiful illusion' has simply become a 'fraud and a lie,' and the more a fraud and a lie the more beautiful it is" (p. 261).

Analogously, Conrad's hero, after his journey into the dark regions of the mind, after his insight, after participating vicariously in a kind of Faustian experience, chooses to mock truth. Preferring artifice to veracity, he establishes an ethic of his own according to which man, having been made aware of the truth, discovers also the necessity to cloak and conceal it for the sake of humanity. The traditional Faustian experience, which itself reaches "beyond the bounds of permitted aspirations," is thus pushed even further by an act which is godlike, by a creative act which ignores conventional principles and establishes its own. With one gesture, Marlow both proclaims his own values and acts according to them, just as in every creative act the artist, like the god, establishes a context of values for his work, a new "order" within which the work can be

5. Erich Heller, *Thomas Mann, The Ironic German* (Cleveland, 1961), p. 261.

said to be "true."[6]

Heart of Darkness concerns both the discovery and the act. The difficulty in reading the story arises because Conrad, to represent his theme honestly, had to make it an integral part of the work: he had to make the story itself in a sense "equal to, / Not true." That is why its resolution rests on artifice, why its culmination is a lie, and why contradiction and paradox seem to push their fingers into every corner of its frame. Kurtz's vision is horrifying, but at the same time it is "not extraordinary in any way," unheroic, and therefore hideously "disappointing"; Marlow finds life a "mysterious arrangement of merciless logic for a futile purpose," yet his word for it is "droll"; and even the story's narrator pretends to see Marlow's tale in its entirety to be a kind of fraud: he pretends to see it, that is, as just another one of somebody else's "inconclusive experiences."

TED E. BOYLE: Marlow's "Lie"†

In his letter of February 8, 1899, to Cunninghame Graham, Conrad implied that "Heart of Darkness" might well be too subtle for even the trained and perceptive critic. Conrad was correct. Only recently have criticisms of "Heart of Darkness" liberated themselves from the specious opinion that the story is Kurtz's. Again, only recently have critics recognized that in Conrad's complexly constructed tale Marlow makes an epic journey into the underworld symbolized by the Congo.

Most of us would now agree that Marlow is the central figure in "Heart of Darkness" and that critics have firmly established the importance of the epic machinery in the story. Yet the significance of Marlow's interview with Kurtz's Intended and the value of the "lie" which he tells her are still highly controversial.[1] There is an

---

6. Tindall points out that Marlow suggests the artist in still another way. Marlow, "more than an amateur philosopher," may be a kind of artist if as a teller of stories he represents "the artist at work" (pp. 284–85).

† From *Studies in Short Fiction*, I (Winter, 1964), 159–63. Reprinted by permission of the editors and the author.

1. Marvin Mudrick, in "The Originality of Conrad," *The Hudson Review*, XII (1958), p. 552, calls the lie "sentimental" and the final scene "cheaply ironic doubletalk." Thomas Moser, *Joseph Conrad, Achievement and Decline* (Cambridge, Mass., 1957), p. 79, writes: "Marlow has come there hoping to surrender to her the memory of

Kurtz. She instead maneuvers him into telling her a lie: that Kurtz's last words were, not 'The Horror,' but her name. . . . Marlow's lie certainly weakens the scene; he has made truth seem too important throughout the novel to persuade the reader now to accept falsehood as salvation." Lillian Feder, in "Marlow's Descent into Hell," *Nineteenth-Century Fiction*, says Marlow "experiences a kind of spiritual death in the sacrifice of lying for Kurtz." Robert Evans, "Conrad's Underworld," *Modern Fiction Studies*, says Marlow's action is "selfless though intrinsically sinful." Walter Wright, who almost alone among Conrad critics sees Marlow's "lie" as an act of truth, writes: "The scene in which Marlow conceals

apparent contradiction between what Marlow says about lying and what he actually does when placed in a situation in which a lie seems appropriate. When he completes the second leg of his journey into the Congo and observes the deceitful inhabitants of the Central Station, Marlow is quick to identify himself as a man of honor, a man so repulsed by lying that it makes him physically ill:

> "You know I hate, detest, and can't bear a lie, not because I am straighter than the rest of us, but simply because it appalls me. There is a taint of death, a flavour of mortality in lies—which is exactly what I hate and detest in the world—what I want to forget. It makes me miserable and sick, like biting something rotten would do."

But the man who hates, detests, and can't bear a lie tells Kurtz's fiancée a deliberate falsehood, a falsehood which, if we are to believe Conrad's severer critics, makes the ending of "Heart of Darkness" as aesthetically flawed as the ending of that other famous river adventure *Huckleberry Finn*.

It seems, however, that proper attention to one of the key symbols in the narrative and a full understanding of the way in which Marlow's interview with the Intended fits into the mythic framework of the tale would suggest that Marlow's "lie" does not contradict what he has said earlier about the nature of deceit. When he "lies" to Kurtz's fiancée, Marlow in fact accepts the trust of carrying the torch of a higher type of truth, a truth that neither Kurtz nor the uninitiated Marlow could understand.

We find a key to the more complicated type of truth which Marlow is able to comprehend after his Congo voyage in the associations called forth by Kurtz's painting of "justice." At the Central Station Marlow observes the picture which Kurtz had painted while waiting there for transportation to his post: "I noticed a small sketch in oils, on a panel, representing a woman, draped and blindfolded, carrying a lighted torch. The background was sombre—almost black. The movement of the woman was stately, and the effect of the torch-light on the face was sinister." Kurtz's

---

from the girl the nature of Kurtz's death is really a study of the nature of truth. If he had told the girl the simple facts, he would have acknowledged that the pilgrims in their cynicism had the truth, that goodness and faith were the unrealities. Marlow appreciates this temptation, and we are hardly to suppose that sentimental weakness made him resist it. He does not preach to us about the wisdom he has achieved; the fact is, he deprecates it, and now he says merely that to tell her would be 'too dark altogether.' He is still perplexed as to the ethics of his deception and wishes that fate had permitted him to remain a simple reporter of incidents instead of making him struggle in the realm of human values. Yet in leaving in juxtaposition the fiancée's ideal, a matter within her own heart, and the fact of Kurtz's death, Marlow succeeds in putting before us in his inconclusive way the two extremes that can exist within the human mind, and we realize that not one, but both of these are reality." Walter Wright, *Romance and Tragedy in Joseph Conrad* (Lincoln, Nebr., 1949), p. 149.

conception of justice is indeed sinister, a chiaroscuro representation, a black and white rendering untempered by mercy, a justice the light and truth of which only add to its threatening aspects. It is highly significant, then, that when Kurtz knows he is dying, he requests that Marlow render "justice" to his memory, and that when Marlow stands before the door of the Intended, he remembers Kurtz's plea: "I want no more than justice." In a mood both pensive and cynical, Marlow repeats: "He wanted no more than justice." It seems Marlow intends at this point to render Kurtz the jungle justice which is his due; but at the last moment, almost compulsively, the man who hates and detests a lie tells a lie. Marlow has not been false to himself but has completed the last stage of the journey which enlarges his sphere of moral consciousness. He at last perceives that Kurtz, in fact all mankind, wants not justice, but a complex kind of truth—a truth which is a mixture of illusion and love. Untempered justice, particularly the stark, sentimental type symbolized by Kurtz's painting, has a sinister countenance—destructive and "altogether too dark."

Further evidence that Marlow's falsehood represents not deceit but the highest type of truth is to be found within the mythic framework of the tale. In the mythic journey, the return from the underworld and the communication of the knowledge learned there are fully as important as the hero's descent and his adventures in the world of darkness. The hero, though he may imperfectly understand his motivation, descends to the nether world to gain knowledge which will redound to the good of his community or nation. If he does not communicate this knowledge after his return, his descent has been meaningless.[2]

The task of the returning hero is, moreover, not without its difficulties. He is constantly beset to keep his knowledge secret, to attempt no translation of his experience.[3] In his The Hero with a Thousand Faces, Joseph Campbell describes the problem of the returning hero:

> How teach again, however, what has been taught correctly and incorrectly learned a thousand thousand times, throughout the millenniums of mankind's prudent folly? That is the hero's ultimate difficult task. How render back into light-world language the speech-defying pronouncements of the dark? . . . The first prob-

2. See Joseph Campbell, *The Hero with a Thousand Faces*, Meridian Edition (New York, 1956), pp. 246–47, for a summary of the composite adventure of the mythological hero.

3. There are echoes of the refusal to render to the community what has been learned in the underworld in one of Kurtz's remarks to Marlow: "This lot of ivory now is really mine. The company did not pay for it. I collected it myself at a very great personal risk. I am afraid they will try to claim it as theirs though. H'm. It is a difficult case." Significantly enough, Marlow, the moment before he steps through the door of the house of Kurtz's fiancée, remembers these words of Kurtz.

lem of the returning hero is to accept as real, after an experience of the soul-satisfying vision of fulfillment, the passing joys and sorrows, banalities and noisy obscenities of life. Why re-enter such a world? Why attempt to make plausible, or even interesting, to men and women consumed with passion, the experience of transcendental bliss?[4]

Conrad's description of the psychological state of his returning hero closely enough resembles Campbell's summation of this segment of the archetypal pattern to deserve rather full quotation:

I found myself back in the sepulchral city resenting the sight of people hurrying through the streets to filch a little money from each other, to devour their infamous cookery, to gulp their unwholesome beer, to dream their insignificant and silly dreams. They trespassed upon my thoughts. They were intruders whose knowledge of life was to me an irritating pretence, because I felt so sure they could not possibly know the things I knew. Their bearing, which was simply the bearing of commonplace individuals going about their business in the assurance of perfect safety, was offensive to me like the outrageous flauntings of folly in the face of a danger it is unable to comprehend. I had no particular desire to enlighten them, but I had some difficulty in restraining myself from laughing in their faces, so full of stupid importance.

Marlow's experience with Kurtz is not precisely one of transcendental bliss; but Marlow, though he has learned about the darkness of the human heart, has also learned about the resiliency of the human spirit, for he speaks of Kurtz's dying exclamation as "an affirmation, a moral victory." Marlow has undergone a sort of imperfectly realized expansion of consciousness, and he senses that he must translate his own experience and that of Kurtz into some sort of meaningful pattern. The dark memories of Kurtz seem to enter the Intended's house with Marlow, but he realizes he must struggle with the powers of darkness: "It was a moment of triumph for the wilderness, an invading and vengeful rush which, it seemed to me I would have to keep back alone for the salvation of another soul." Marlow saves his own soul; he completes the salvation of Kurtz's soul, and saves the soul of Kurtz's fiancée; in fact, when Marlow "lies," he keeps back the darkness for an entire community of souls.

As Kurtz's savage consort symbolizes the soul of the jungle, Kurtz's fiancée, with her "great and saving illusion that shone with an unearthly glow in the darkness," symbolizes the soul of civilization. By lying to Kurtz's Intended, Marlow presents civilization with a slender ray of light with which to keep back the darkness.

4. Campbell, p. 218.

Kurtz's fiancée also stands as a symbol of the nobility which remained in Kurtz's soul when he died, the moral impulse which at the last allowed him to overwhelm his egoism and recognize "the horror" he had made of his life. When Marlow meets Kurtz's fiancée, he has a vision of her and Kurtz united in the same being; and when the woman says, "I have survived," though "the horror" still echoes in his ears, Marlow perceives that the noblest part of Kurtz, what he "Intended" when he undertook his missionary-like work in the Congo, has, in fact, survived the struggle with the powers of darkness. And Marlow becomes subconsciously aware that he must lie to preserve the small, frail truth inherent in Kurtz's dying exclamation.

"And this also has been one of the dark places of the earth," says Marlow before he begins the narrative of his Congo voyage. London, the city to which Marlow refers, is, however, no longer as devoid of light as the African jungle, for men like Marlow bring back light to it. A long and unbroken line of heroic adventurers has gazed into the pit and perceived light where there seemed to be none. The illumination these knights-errant have brought back with them is imperfect and fleeting, in fact may be enfolded in a lie: "Yes; but it is like a running glaze on a plain, like a flash of lightning in the clouds. We live in the flicker—may it last as long as the old earth keeps rolling!"

GERALD B. KAUVAR: Marlow As Liar†

The standard interpretation of the last scene in Conrad's *Heart of Darkness* is that Marlow pays for his knowledge of good and evil by lying, by, as he says, becoming mortal. Marlow understands that a lesser ethical value must yield to a greater, that the salvation of another soul is more important than rigid adherence to his personal code. Human compassion makes him deny himself. However, since we know that in Conrad's novels moral choices and judgments are not easy to make or comprehend, and that their contexts are murky and difficult to fathom, I suggest we need to consider the possibility that Marlow was not lying so patently as we often assume.[1]

The conflict as Marlow understands it prior to entering the mausoleum-like house is between Kurtz's request for justice and the

† From *Studies in Short Fiction*, V (Spring, 1968), 290–92. Reprinted by permission of the editors and the author.

1. Ted E. Boyle's article * * * is a persuasive reading of the work in terms of its ethical and symbolic structure. In a long note, Mr. Boyle recapitulates the positions various commentators have taken when considering Marlow's lie. The interpretation I offer differs from any I am aware of in emphasizing the psychological structure of the final scene. There are, as Conrad and his interpreters have taught us, many truths.

triumph of the wilderness that Marlow alone will have to keep back for the salvation of another soul. Marlow's initial description of the carriage of the Intended is important. "She carried her sorrowful head as though she were proud of that sorrow, as though she would say, I—I alone know how to mourn for him as he deserves." This description reveals Marlow's perception of how close the Intended feels to Kurtz and the depth of her love; but the description also contains Marlow's perception of the egotism of her love, the flaw in the cliff of crystal that is her soul. Her egotism exerts so powerful an effect on Marlow that he sees not her but it and feels as though he had "blundered into a place of cruel and absurd mysteries not fit for a human being to behold." To be sure the mysteries of such a love and such spiritual identity are so intense and private as to make a third party feel like a blunderer; its causes and effects seem unavailable to reason's inspecting eye. But these mysteries are not absurd in another sense: in much modern literature they are the one aspect of human existence that offers individuals a sense of identity, of place, of joy, in a world that is cruel and absurd. Such is not, however, the love of this woman for this man as perceived by Marlow.

The conversation between Marlow and the Intended begins in earnest, and it is obvious from the outset that Marlow is forcing himself. He has to repeat the sentence "He was a remarkable man" to her. But to Marlow and the reader the description is ironic: it has meant almost wholly different things to characters like the Russian and the papier-maché Mephistopheles, both of whom used it to describe Kurtz. Because of Marlow's consideration for the Intended, he is about to echo her statement that it was impossible not to admire Kurtz; but she interrupts and substitutes "love him." Then her love begins to gorge upon itself: "I had all his noble confidence. I knew him best." Marlow assents to this, too, and it may not be a lie; Marlow, though appalled by the words "love him" is not sure that he is lying by agreeing with her, for he says, "perhaps she did." The description that follows this equivocation is ominous: "But with every word spoken the room was growing darker, and only her forehead, smooth and white, remained illumined by the inextinguishable light of belief and love." The word *but* serves to remind us that the light of belief and love is not the same as the light of knowledge.

In her next speech the Intended admits her pride. She is proud to know that she understood Kurtz better than anyone on earth. Does Marlow agree? "I listened. The darkness deepened." The Intended is seeking corroboration, but Marlow has become so uncomfortable that he begins to think (wish?) that Kurtz had not wanted him to come here: "I rather suspect he wanted me to take care of another batch of his papers."

The Intended says that men were drawn to Kurtz by what was best in them; but because Marlow was not drawn by what was best but by the need to know what the worst was and what the best could be, he hears in her voice all the impenetrable "mystery, desolation, and sorrow" of existence. What is the nature of this sorrow? I suggest that it is man's limited ability "to know," to know himself, and his even more limited ability to communicate to another soul what one has discovered in the depths of one's own soul. This is, after all, one of Conrad's major themes and one of the constant refrains in the last scene of this novella.

Kurtz's Intended says that she and Marlow will remember his promise, his greatness, his generous mind, and his noble heart; but Marlow hastily says "We shall always remember him." She says that his words will live, but she does not know the "valuable postcriptum," "Exterminate all the brutes!" The Intended then says that Kurtz's example will remain, and Marlow's awkward response, "True . . . his example too. Yes, his example. I forgot that," shows that he who knew Kurtz as well as one man can know another is thinking of the totality of Kurtz's example. The half that the Intended does not know springs to Marlow's mind in a vision of the African woman.

When the Intended says, "He died as he lived," Marlow becomes dully angry and replies, more ambiguously and ironically than before, "His end . . . was in every way worthy of his life." Is Marlow lying? Not to himself, not to us, but to her. He speaks what he knows to be true, but he is also aware that his words will not indicate to her what he knows as truth; no matter how sourly he says what he does, she will take it as corroboration and Marlow knows it. His anger subsides, gives way to pity, when she invokes her illusion. But when she says that she should have been present at Kurtz's death, Marlow feels a chill grip on his chest and says, "don't." Marlow is being forced closer and closer to the point where it seems he will either have to tell a direct lie or else divest her of her illusions. We know that the Intended is not aware of Marlow's feelings because she asks forgiveness for spilling forth her feelings. But it is the nature of the feelings, not her spilling them, that Marlow resents.

Kurtz's Intended asks to hear his last words after she forces Marlow to admit he heard them. Marlow hears the words, "The horror! the horror!" echoing in the room as he heard them during his approach to the house. He hears them so vividly because the whole scene has been a horror to him, because he knows the woman's illusions are not in touch with reality, the understanding of which he so painfully earned.

But I think he also hears the words because this woman's misconception and distortion of the man Kurtz is so complete, so overwhelming, that by telling her Kurtz spoke her name, Marlow is not really lying. If Kurtz had heard this woman's judgment of him—since all he wanted was justice, which must be based on total understanding and knowledge—if Kurtz had seen this woman's illusion it would have been a horror to him. Her lack of ability to understand even had she been there to understand, her lack of insight, that this woman should carry the torch of her illusion as a proper memorial to him would have been a horror to Kurtz. Kurtz passed judgment not only on his activities in Africa, but also on his Intended, his station, his career, and his ideas, for these were all part of his life at a time when he lacked full knowledge of himself. Kurtz passes judgment, sums up, "the adventures of his soul on this earth." For these reasons, Marlow's telling the Intended that Kurtz's last word was her name is not a lie. Her name is a symbol for her lack of understanding that is similar to Kurtz's lack of self-understanding up to his last mortal moments; her name is a symbol for her illusions that were his illusions up to the time of his African adventures and his judgment. For those who quest for knowledge, this kind of illusion is no longer great and saving. Once again, Marlow speaks the truth, but he knows the woman cannot interpret his words the way he interprets them; he knows she will take them literally.

Marlow thought that the heavens were about to fall on him, but he knows now that "the heavens do not fall for such a trifle." We can take this to mean that the violation of Marlow's personal code is unimportant, but it can also mean that the lie itself was not so overwhelming. Marlow wonders whether the heavens would have fallen if he had done full justice to Kurtz. But in order for this to happen, the heavens would have to fall because he told the truth. Marlow did do justice to Kurtz, although in a peculiar way: he told the Intended a half-truth, as he had been doing throughout the scene. His words meant one thing to him—and to us—but another thing to her, and Marlow was aware that he was utilizing his ambiguity to defend himself and her from the darkness. They are defended by knowledge and illusion respectively, but the two are contained in each phrase he utters. Marlow knew the Intended could not know her name was symbolic of a kind of horror, but its symbolism remains for him and for us. He tells what we might call a half-truth; we might, that is, if we are audacious enough to try to categorize it in a moral system. If we consider the emotional needs of Marlow and the Intended, moral evaluations are intruders.

CRITICAL DEBATE: THE RUSSIAN

C. F. BURGESS: Conrad's Pesky Russian†

The presence of the Russian, that fantastic creature of clouts and patches, in Conrad's *Heart of Darkness* offers certain critical difficulties. With a nervous elusiveness that is characteristic of him, he manages to baffle efforts to find a place and a function for him in the story. Robert O. Evans, for example, who finds strong overtones of the *Inferno* motif in *Heart of Darkness*, confesses frankly that "The Russian trader that Marlow and his company encounter does seem slightly out òf place in terms of Dante's scheme, for he appears to be a heretic."

Marlow himself has some trouble coming to grips with the Russian, finding him at their first meeting, "altogether bewildering," "an insoluble problem." Ultimately, however, Marlow's bewilderment at this "phenomenon" which has burst upon him is intermixed with something akin to disgust, the disgust of the eminently practical man toward "the absolutely pure, uncalculating, unpractical spirit of adventure." This admixture of puzzled disdain reflects, it seems to me, the attitude of Polish patriot Teodor Korzenowski who spent his early years in unhappy proximity to Russians. In a letter to Constance Garnett, October 20, 1911, Conrad wrote: "But the fact is that I know extremely little of Russians. Practically nothing. In Poland we have nothing to do with them. One knows they are there. And that's disagreeable enough. In exile the contact is even slighter if possible if more unavoidable."[1]

Even so, enigmatic as he appears and artful dodger that he is, it is possible to account for the Russian in *Heart of Darkness* in two ways.

In the first place, on one level, the function of the Russian is a matter of technique. He is the friend of the author, much like Henry James's *ficelles*. He is there to bring the situation up to date for Marlow and the party on the steamboat: Kurtz, it must be remembered, has been out of contact with the trading company for some time now. Nothing definite as to his activities has filtered downstream—only the rumors concerning "unsound methods." Neither Marlow nor the manager have any idea what to expect

---

† From *Nineteenth-Century Fiction*, Vol. 18, No. 2, (September, 1963), 189–93. Copyright © 1963 by The Regents of the University of California. Reprinted by permission of The Regents.

1. Edward Garnett, *Letters from Joseph Conrad, 1895–1924* (Indianapolis, 1928), pp. 234–35.

here on the edge of the darkness. The Russian, then, is Conrad's device to fill in the time gap. It is through him that the relief party is made aware how badly the situation has deteriorated and in what peril they stand should Kurtz "not say the right thing." In effect, the Russian takes over Marlow's role as narrator, briefly, and plays a crucial part in preparing for the climactic meeting with Kurtz.

Yet it would be totally inadequate, artistically, to accept this as the sole reason for the Russian's being. Conrad is seldom obvious and in a work of enormous subtlety like *Heart of Darkness*, the presence of the Russian simply as a narrative expedient is scarcely to be subscribed to. There is another role the Russian plays which, while subservient to the main action, is a part of it. This function of the Russian, clearly suggested by the context, becomes apparent when the evidence is examined carefully.

Consider first the Russian's physical appearance. Conrad gives us several clues here. He is twice described as a "harlequin," a creature in motley, "who looked as though he had escaped from a troop of mimes." He reminds Marlow of "something funny I had seen somewhere." The over-all effect of his incredible accoutrement ("bright patches, blue, red, and yellow—patches on the back, patches on the front, patches on elbows, on knees; coloured binding round his jacket, scarlet edging on the bottom of his trousers") is somehow "extremely gay and wonderfully neat withall." In other words, all the Russian needs to make his costume complete for the role he plays is the cap and bells. With this single exception, he is perfectly drawn in the trappings of the Fool, the royal jester, the court buffoon.

He is, by his own admission, "a simple man. I have no great thoughts." He is completely adaptable, thoroughly malleable, and, as Marlow says, "uncalculating, unpractical, improbable, inexplicable." Like Marlow, he is one of those "curious men" who, Conrad tells us, "go prying into all sorts of places where they have no business."[2] There is, in fact, a direct analogy, intentional on Conrad's part I feel certain, between the Russian's and Marlow's reasons for being in the Congo. The Russian's badgering of old Van Shuyten until "he gave me some cheap things and a few guns, and told me he hoped he would never see my face again," is reminiscent of Charlie Marlow's harassment of his relatives on the Continent to procure for him the command of the steamboat. The difference, of course, is that Marlow has his "influential friend"—the steamboat—with him always whereas the Russian misplaces, or abandons, his hold on reality, "the simple old sailor, Towser or Towson."

2. See "Author's Note" to the *Youth* volume [above].

The Russian's moods range from frenetic exuberance to agitated uncertainty, his face, like the autumn sky, "overcast one moment and bright the next." Above all, he is completely selfless. The spirit of adventure, Marlow remarks, "seemed to have consumed all thought of self so completely, that, even while he was talking to you, you forgot that it was he—the man before your eyes—who had gone through these things." He is pathetically anxious to please, almost childlike in his desire to be understood and accepted. We see him first prancing about the river bank, shouting vaguely, "'Its all right. Its all right. I am glad.' . . . as cheerful as you please." In a moment, however, he is so overcome that he cannot claim kinship with Marlow as a fellow Englishman that, "The smiles vanished and he shook his head as if sorry for my disappointment."

The story he tells of his relationship with Kurtz, wavering (as he speaks) between enthusiasm and bewilderment, makes the wretchedness of his state all too clear to Marlow. But the Russian gives no evidence of a psychic scar; he has rolled with the punches magnificently. His only concern is for Kurtz's reputation, which he consigns to the hands of the unwilling Marlow. He goes off, rolling his eyes characteristically at the recollection of the "delights" he has encountered and innocently grateful for the enlargement of his mind. Marlow, groggy at the impact of his *jongleur* who has tumbled across the stage before him, can only shake his head in disbelief.

The Russian, thus, is ideally equipped in appearance and in temperament for his role as Fool. But when and where does he function in this capacity? During his meeting with Marlow, the Russian is much like the performer in the dressing room. He is still in the costume of the clown, his make-up intact, but the performance is over. He has already played his role as Fool.

It has been played, of course, in the court of Kurtz—king, god, journalist, ivory hunter, hollow man, what-have-you. Kurtz had an empire, a court, a consort, why not a Fool to complete the assemblage? The Russian played his role well—the fact that he had stayed alive is perhaps the best testimony to the quality of his performance. He was available at all times, in the best tradition of the jester, to amuse Kurtz when in an expansive mood, to nurse him when ill, and to stay out of his way when dangerous. The Russian reveals the whole sordid saga to Marlow while remaining himself completely unaware of its full implications. "Very often coming to this station, I had to wait days and days before he would turn up. Ah, it was worth waiting for!—sometimes." The tentative note struck by the word "sometimes" should not be overlooked. It suggests, of course, the measure of the Russian's dependence on the capricious temperament of Kurtz. The same note, again implying the necessity for the Russian to play fool to Kurtz's fancy, is heard again in the following passages. Note the force of "When I had a chance . . ." "I came up—took my chance."

> When he came down to the river, sometimes he would take to me, and sometimes it was better for me to be careful.

> When I had a chance I begged him to try and leave while there was time . . .

> I heard he was lying helpless, and so I came up—took my chance.

One is reminded of Lear's Fool who, despite his jauntiness, is still aware of the whip.

Marlow sums up the Russian as follows: "If it had come to crawling before Mr. Kurtz, he crawled as much as the veriest savage of them all." With a kind of fascinated revulsion, Marlow now sees that Kurtz's peculiar "gifts" are fatal alike to ignorant savage and educated white man. This commingling of disgust and awe on Marlow's part toward Kurtz's treatment of the Russian prefigures Marlow's final judgment of Kurtz. The Kurtz who was apparently gratified at the spectacle of the Russian playing Fool for him is indeed an "atrocious phantom." At the same time, the Kurtz who could secure the Fool's willing acquiescence is also something of a "remarkable man."

MARIO D'AVANZO:

Conrad's Motley as an Organizing Metaphor†

In identifying the role of the Russian as that of the fool who completes the "court" of King Kurtz, C. F. Burgess has settled an important problem of meaning in *Heart of Darkness*. However, the Russian motley signifies more than a traditional figure of drama cleverly employed by Conrad. In the context of the novel, motley radiates another and equally significant meaning, linking the incongruous and absurd presence of the fool to the equally checkered, disorganized, and contrarious presences of all the European countries in the geographical heart of darkness.

Marlow remarks, upon first seeing the startling figure of the bepatched Russian, "his aspect reminded me of something I had

† From *College Language Association Journal*, IX (March, 1966), 289–91. Reprinted by permission of the editor and author.

seen—something funny I had seen somewhere." One may presume, as Mr. Burgess has, that Marlow is referring only to an unrecorded experience in his past, at a time when he saw a harlequin. But Marlow has in fact seen Motley at an earlier occasion in the tale and is most likely trying to recall the context. I am referring to Marlow's taking rather extensive notice of a large map of Africa hanging in the company office in the sepulchral city:

> On one end a large shining map marked with all the colors of a rainbow. There was a vast amount of red—good to see at any time, because one knows that some real work is done there, a deuce of a lot of blue, a little green, smears of orange, and on the East Coast, a purple patch, to show where the jolly pioneers of progress drink the jolly beer. However, I wasn't going into any of these. I was going into the yellow. Dead in the center.

In tailoring the Russian in the motley colors of the map, Conrad, it would seem, creates the figure of the capitalistic everyman; he is a composite of fragmented, idiotic Europeans.[1] Motley is an appropriate symbol for the manifest disorder and lack of mortal congruence among the whites in the heart of darkness. Just as the fool appears, so he speaks—in fragments (and almost incoherent at that); so too do the heterogeneous colonists in the Congo show their confusion, inventing contradictory, deceptive arguments to explain why they are there. And Kurtz, we find, appears to be their spokesman. His gospel eloquently expresses in seventeen pages of "burning noble words" the ideals of the International Society for the Suppression of Savage Customs. But his deeds include, ironically, "unspeakable rites"—rites justified by a late entry or postscript to his gospel: "exterminate the brutes."

If "all Europe contributed to the making of Kurtz" (note particularly that Kurtz's father is half English and his mother is half French and that the map is predominantly in the colors of these two countries—red and blue), then there is something of his fragmented aims and checkered morality in the suicidal Swede, the sadistic Dane (Fresleven), the efficient and suspicious Dutchman (Van Shuyten), and even in Marlow, an Englishman working for the Belgian empire. Marlow avows that he too is not sinless, seeing

1. But why a Russian? This thorny question can be answered, it seems to me, in the light of Conrad's biography. Gerard Jean-Aubrey has recorded the effects on the young Conrad of Russia's total dominance of Poland. He knew terror, oppression, heartache, and exile, the results of his father's political dissent. Conrad knew the excesses of Pan-Slavism, an imperialistic movement attempting the Russification of Poland politically, religiously, and culturally.

The death of young Conrad's revolutionary father, whose epitaph read, "To Apollo Nalecz Korzeniowski/Victim of Muscovite Tyranny," may very well have left a lasting resentment in the mind of the boy—a resentment finding expression in the portrait of an imbecilic imperialist, the Russian fool of *Heart of Darkness*. See Gerard Jean-Aubrey, *The Sea Dreamer* (New York, 1957), pp. 22–27, 34, 45, 93.

in Kurtz something of himself.

In Kurtz and in the faceless "imbecilic" Pilgrims, all Europe professes to be "emissaries of light," but its light of progress, truth, and charity proves to be refracted symbolically into the contrarious colors adorning the fool's *holland* fabric (a whitish, *glazed* cotton material corresponding to the "*shining* map" of Africa hanging in Brussels), refracted and superimposed in a quilt of colors on the continent of Africa. Conrad suggests that this distortion of "light" proves worse for the souls of Europeans and the natives in the heart of darkness than the lack of it.

The perversion of Europe's aims is dramatized in Conrad's motley fool, who in being identified as the "son of an archpriest" fits in with all the other apostles and missionaries of capitalism. "His very existence was improbable, inexplicable, and altogether bewildering," just as the unholy presences of all colonial countries in Africa are indefensible and even absurd. And yet his "futile" presence, his unthinking and "unpractical spirit of adventure" will continue as will Europe's chaotic colonialism. In a final, parting criticism of all Europe, using his characteristic color symbolism, Conrad has the fool "vanish in the night":

> one of his pockets (bright red) was bulging with cartridges, from the other (dark blue) peeped 'Towson's Inquiry,' etc., etc. He seemed to think himself exceedingly well equipped for a renewed encounter with the wilderness.

Fortified with the materials of enlightened Europe—a wholly useless technical manual on seamanship, and equally worthless ammunition (he has no firearm)—the Russian fool represents a civilization whose means of enlightenment and whose ends are indeed motley, incongruous, and irreconcilable.

JOHN W. CANARIO: The Harlequin†

Next to Marlow and Kurtz, the most important character in Conrad's *Heart of Darkness* is the young Russian who meets the steamboat at Kurtz's station and soon thereafter is persuaded by Marlow to talk at some length about his life and his admiration for Kurtz. Marlow first describes this Russian as a harlequin, and he later reveals through frequent observation of harlequinesque qualities in the youth that this first impression was progressively strengthened during their conversation. Gauging the importance of

† From *Studies in Short Fiction*, IV (1967), 225–33. Reprinted by permission of the editors and the author.

the Russian's role in the novel by Marlow's description of his motley appearance, clownish mannerisms, and conspicuous gullibility, most interpreters have seen the Russian as one of several minor characters who serve chiefly to exemplify the extreme susceptibility of civilized Europeans to the corrupting influences of the Congo. However, there is considerable evidence in the story to show that this view misrepresents the Russian's thematic function. This view slights the fact that Marlow's insight into the youth's harlequinesque character moves from superficial matters to a discovery that has a crucial bearing on his initiation. The Russian, as Marlow comes to see, is not simply an irresponsible, light-headed buffoon, but rather, like the harlequin of the theatre, a modern representative of the European aborigine. When the harlequin is viewed in the light of this discovery, he assumes his true dimensions as one of the most important characters in the novel.

Although the Russian is twice mentioned by Marlow in the narrative of the journey up the river (once, vaguely, as another ivory trader " 'of whom the manager did not approve' " and again on the occasion of the pilgrims' discovery of the note on the woodpile), it is significant that Marlow does not meet the youth until he has traveled, figuratively speaking, back to the beginning of time. It is not until he is steering the steamboat into Kurtz's landing that Marlow sees on the river bank " 'a white man under a hat like a cart-wheel beckoning persistently with his whole arm'." At this point Marlow comments that the man struck him immediately as looking like a harlequin. As Marlow maneuvers the boat alongside the landing, he notices that the Russian's trousers and jacket, both made of a cheap brown material, are covered with blue, red, and yellow patches. He further observes that the Russian's face is beardless and fair with " 'no features to speak of, nose peeling, little blue eyes, smiles and frowns chasing each other over that open countenance like sunshine and shadow on a windswept plain.' " These observations of the Russian's physical appearance establish that Marlow first saw the man as simply a goodnatured but scatterbrained dunce.

That this condescending view of the Russian continues for a time to be uppermost in Marlow's mind is revealed by his comments on the childlike chatter, volatile temperament, and acrobatic agility displayed by the youth during his visit on the steamboat. Marlow notices that the Russian talks at a breathless rate, that he jumps abruptly from one subject to another, that his countenance changes mercurially " 'like the autumn sky, overcast one moment and bright the next' ", and that he gestures extravagantly, even leaping up at one point to grab both of his host's hands in his by way of showing gratitude for the offer of a pipeful of tobacco.

Reinforcing these suggestions that the Russian is a clownish simpleton, Marlow comments on the difficulty he has at the outset of the visit in getting the youth to discuss Kurtz. " ' "Don't you talk with Mr. Kurtz?" ' ", Marlow asks early in the conversation, but the question draws no information from his visitor beyond the fervid exclamation, " ' "You don't talk with that man—you listen to him" '." Then the Russian abruptly launches into the story of his life. When Marlow next finds an opportunity to ask a question about Kurtz, he receives another enthusiastic but uninformative reply, " ' "I tell you . . . this man has enlarged my mind" '." Thus, it is only slowly, by patient questioning and a tolerant acceptance of the Russian's many digressions, that Marlow eventually charms the youth out of his " 'mingled eagerness and reluctance to speak of Kurtz.' "

However, despite these evidences of amused condescension in Marlow's initial impressions of the Russian, it becomes clear as Marlow continues his relation of their conversation that his opinion of his visitor grew increasingly favorable as he learned more about him. One cause of his rise in Marlow's opinion is shown to be his appreciation of the Russian's loyalty to Kurtz and of his humane concern for the safety of both the white men and the natives. Marlow is favorably impressed, for example, by the Russian's urgent assurances that the natives are simple people who can be more effectively frightened away in case of trouble by a blowing of the boat's whistle than by firing rifles at them. A second cause is shown to be Marlow's respect for the Russian's devotion to doing a good job in his regular vocation as a sailor. When Marlow returns Towson's *An Inquiry into Some Points of Seamanship* to the Russian, he perceives that the man is ecstatically happy. But a third and clearly the dominant cause of Marlow's adoption of a more favorable view of his visitor is shown to be an awakening in him of an admiration for the Russian's reckless courage and adventurous spirit.

Marlow emphasizes the moment he first began to see the harlequin in a new light by interrupting his story to describe his fresh impressions. " 'I looked at him, lost in astonishment,' " Marlow exclaims. He then goes on to identify the Russian as an embodiment of the " 'glamour of the youth,' " a person " 'gallantly, thoughtlessly alive, to all appearances indestructible solely by virtue of his few years and his unreflecting audacity'." Summing up these impressions, Marlow continues, " 'If the absolutely pure, uncalculating, impractical spirit of adventure had ever ruled a human being, it ruled this be-patched youth. I almost envied him the possession of this modest and clear flame'." Finally, Marlow defines a limit to this newly discovered admiration by adding, " 'I did not envy him his devotion to Kurtz, though. He had not meditated over it. It came to him, and he accepted it with a sort of eager fatalism. I must say that to me it appeared about the most dangerous thing in every way he had come upon so far.' "

The intensity of feeling Marlow exhibits in this reassessment of the Russian reveals that his change of attitude towards the youth was not inspired merely by a desire to correct an unfair bias in his initial judgment of him. Instead, the degree of Marlow's astonishment, his admiration, and his envy establish that the traits of character he praises in the Russian were traits that he himself possessed and valued. Thus in essence Marlow's exclamations are an expression of his surprised recognition that he and the young vagabond were much alike.

The similarity between himself and the Russian that is obviously uppermost in Marlow's mind at this juncture is that they are both persons whose lives have been directed chiefly by a reckless hunger for adventure and by a rash self-confidence in the invulnerability of their youthful vitality. For Marlow's confession of envy is a reminder that his decision to command a steamboat on the Congo River was inspired by little more than boyish curiosity and a love of adventure. But Marlow's reporting of the conversation that led up to this recognition reveals that it was not the only similarity he had become aware of. A second point of resemblance between the two men is set forth in Marlow's earlier commentary on the Russian's joy at recovering Towson's book on seamanship. The reverence that the Russian exhibits toward this technical manual calls to mind Marlow's earlier remarks on his own single-minded devotion to the mechanical problems of getting his steamboat in operating condition and safely up the river. The point suggested by the parallel is Marlow's becoming aware that both his life and the Russian's were largely confined to surface reality, to the limited aspiration of skillfully and conscientiously performing the mechanical duties of their occupation. Still a third point or resemblance that Marlow is shown to have become aware of is that both men shared a tendency to regard intellectuals with awe. Marlow conveys his recognition of this likeness between himself and the Russian in the similarity that he reveals between the youth's adulation of Kurtz and his own early development of an intense curiosity about the man.

However, at the same time that Marlow reveals that he sees something of himself in the harlequin's enthusiastic and unsophisticated outlook, he also makes it a point to introduce the reservation that he does not envy the Russian his naïve devotion to Kurtz. This reservation serves two important purposes. First, it makes absolutely clear that Marlow's attitude towards Kurtz, which was strongly inclined toward approbation when he first heard of the man, had become seriously qualified by the time he met Kurtz's disciple. Secondly, it establishes that the likenesses Marlow observes between himself and the Russian no longer existed by the time of his encounter with the youth because of the maturing effect on Marlow of his experiences in the Congo. Consequently, what Marlow is conveying in his praise of the Russian is more, finally, than the discovery that the harlequin had a youthful glamour that he admired; he is simultaneously expressing a regretful realization that his own adventures in the Congo had taught him, beyond any possibility of a return to a light-hearted view of life, a dark truth about man's potentialities for evil.

The truth that had robbed Marlow of his own harlequinesque innocence only shortly before he met the Russian is shown in his earlier descriptions of the white colonials in Africa; it is his discovery that Europeans who lack self-discipline and a strong commitment to unselfish life goals quickly degenerate to a level of brutality below that of an aborigine when their fortunes place them in an environment where there are no external checks on their behavior. Marlow's encounters with a French man-of-war firing six-inch shells at an invisible native village, with black railroad workers dying of disease and starvation, with the station manager who was determined to destroy any rival for his position, with the manager's scheming assistant, and with the unlimited greed of the Eldorado Exploring Expedition are shown to have taught him this truth by negative example. On the other hand, his encounters with the company accountant who kept his books and his dress in apple-pie order and with the black crewmen who did their work loyally and efficiently out of a primitive sense of honor even when starving are shown to impress upon him the same truth in positive terms. Marlow's reservation about the Russian's devotion to Kurtz implies that it is because Marlow had only recently learned this lesson himself that he could be both envious of the youth's innocence and apprehensive about his adulation of Kurtz.

But the growth of Marlow's insight into the harlequinesque character of the Russian does not end with his discovery that the youth personified his own lost innocence and boyish love of adventure. In his account of the remainder of his conversation with the Russian, Marlow reveals that he continued to gain new insight into the youth's character until he arrived finally at the essence of his clown-like nature. Marlow makes clear that this ultimate revelation came to him only after he at last succeeded in getting the Russian to tell him something of his life with Kurtz. In the middle of his retelling of the youth's story, Marlow digresses to comment, " ' . . .

never, never before, did this land, this river, this jungle, the very arch of this blazing sky, appear to me so hopeless and so dark, so impenetrable to human thought, so pitiless to human weakness'." And at the end of the story, when the youth tries to impress Marlow with a description of how the natives had to crawl when they approached Kurtz, Marlow reflects, " 'I suppose that it did not occur to him that Kurtz was no idol of mine. He forgot I hadn't heard any of these splendid monologues on, what was it? on love, justice, conduct of life—or what not. If it had come to crawling before Mr. Kurtz, he crawled as much as the veriest savage of them all.' "

In this equation of the Russian with the black followers of Kurtz, Marlow is pointing back to his own earlier reported impressions of the interior of the Congo and revealing in the light of these his discovery at the end of the youth's story of a fundamental harmony between the harlequin's character and his environment. Lying behind Marlow's statement is the opening sentence of his description of the steamboat expedition, " 'Going up that river was like travelling back to the earliest beginnings of the world . . .'," and his comment on the general feeling of isolation he experienced as the boat progressed through the jungle, " 'We were wanderers on a prehistoric earth, on an earth that wore the aspect of an unknown planet'." Against the background of this perspective on the Congo, Marlow's statement equating the Russian with the savages becomes recognizable as a revelation that his curiosity about the youth led him ultimately to see that he was confronted with a white aborigine, a living example of the atavistic European from which the harlequin of the theatre evolved.

Although Marlow says nothing anywhere in his narrative about the history of the harlequin as a type, his repeated references to the prehistoric environment of the Congo and his characterization of the Russian as essentially aboriginal suggest that he was familiar at least with the general theory that the races of Europe evolved through migrations of nomadic tribes from the interior of Asia and possibly Africa. And there is even evidence to suggest that Marlow's knowledge of the type encompassed more than the broadest generalities, for the history of the harlequin in the theatre supports the assumption implicit in Marlow's characterization of the Russian that the type is a representation of aboriginal man. Some historians believe that the harlequin originated in the depictions by strolling players of the Middle Ages of the demon or earth spirit of German folk legend. However, a larger number believe that he evolved through the *commedia dell' arte* from the aboriginal satyrs of Greek Old Comedy. Thelma Niklaus, in her detailed study of the harlequin's beginnings in primitive Greek comedy, asserts that the satyr types in this drama always represented slaves and that the Young Satyr, the satyr type from which she believes the modern harlequin evolved, was invariably dressed in an animal skin, a brown mask suggesting an African slave, and a Greek peasant hat.[1]

But it is not necessary to establish the limits of Marlow's historical knowledge to show that he was profoundly influenced by his discovery of the aboriginal nature of the harlequinesque Russian. For Marlow provides several prominent guideposts to the meaning of this discovery in the philosophical observations he makes during his voyage up the river. One of these observations is a reflection on the meaning of the howling of savages in the jungle:

> The mind of man is capable of anything—because everything is in it, all the past as well as all the future. What was there after all? Joy, fear, sorrow, devotion, valour, rage—who can tell?—but truth—truth stripped of its cloak of time. Let the fool gape and shudder—the man knows, and can look on without a wink. But he must at least be as much of a man as these on the shore. He must meet that truth with his own true stuff—with his own inborn strength. Principles? Principles won't do. Acquisitions, clothes, pretty rags—rags that would fly off at the first good shake. No; you want a deliberate belief.

A second is a reflection on the inner strength that restrained the starving cannibal crew of the steamboat from overpowering their white overseers:

> Yes; I looked at them as you would on any human being, with a curiosity of their impulses, motives, capacities, weaknesses, when brought to the test of an inexorable necessity. Restraint! What possible restraint? Was it superstition, disgust, patience, fear—or some kind of primitive honor? No fear can stand up to hunger, no patience can wear it out, disgust simply does not exist where hunger is; and as to superstition, beliefs, and what you may call principles, they are less than chaff in a breeze.

A third is a comment on how civilized man little understands the extent to which his moral stability is dependent on his existence in a society of civilized institutions:

> These little things make all the difference. When they are gone you must fall back upon your own innate strength, upon your own capacity for faithfulness. Of course you may be too much of a fool to go wrong—too dull even to know that you are being assaulted by the powers of darkness. I take it, no fool ever made a bargain for his soul with the devil; the fool is too much of a fool, or the devil too much of a devil—I don't know which. Or

1. Thelma Niklaus, *Harlequin, or the Rise and Fall of a Bergamask Rogue* (New York, 1956), p. 18.

you may be such a thunderingly exalted creature as to be altogether deaf and blind to anything but heavenly sights and sounds. Then the earth for you is only a standing place—and whether to be like this is your loss or your gain I won't pretend to say. But most of us are neither one nor the other.

In light of these observations, it becomes evident that Marlow's recognition that the Russian was a white aborigine brought with it a profound realization that aboriginal man possesses a capacity for humane behavior and a primitive sense of honor that makes him impervious to the greed that corrupts civilized Europeans. From the moment of this discovery onward, Marlow emphasizes by mentioning several acts of friendly assistance to the harlequin that he thereafter allied himself with the aboriginal humanity of the youth against the greed and cruelty of the company manager and the pilgrims of the Eldorado Exploring Expedition.

However, it is not the contrast between the harlequin and the pilgrims, but a contrast between the harlequin as aborigine and Kurtz as a representative of man in his most civilized state that leads Marlow to his fullest understanding of the human potential for good and evil. Marlow first suggests the importance of this contrast when he is on the threshold of describing his experiences at Kurtz's station. It is then that he makes his statement that fools and saints are impervious to the powers of darkness, but that most men do not fall into these extreme categories. Marlow's subsequent portrayal of the Russian and Kurtz in close conjunction with one another confirms the suggestion implicit in this statement that he is about to describe two very different men who exemplify contrasting stages of human development almost beyond the limits of vulnerability to the forces of evil.

The harlequin is portrayed as a youth so slightly exposed to the influences of civilization that he approaches in his naïveté and childlike exuberance the behavior of a fool. On the other hand, he is shown to possess the inner strength of a man uncorrupted by greed and vanity to act humanely and responsibly even when he is not externally compelled to do so. In contrast, Kurtz, who is shown to possess a superior intelligence and to have enjoyed all of the humanizing benefits of a university education, is finally exhibited as an idealist who, in spite of an original motivation to devote his life to the advancement of civilization, has become the victim of an insatiable hunger for power out of a vanity freed from any external restraints upon it. Through this portrayal of two men representing opposite ends of the scale of human development, Marlow makes clear that the capstone of his initiation is the realization that there are two kinds of darkness in the world: the darkness of ignorance

represented by the primeval environment and aboriginal inhabitants of the Congo and a greater darkness of undisciplined greed
and vanity represented by the city of the whited sepulcher in
Europe.

The last section of the story reveals Marlow's belief that against
these two kinds of darkness man has ultimately only the defense of
a steadfast faith in the essential goodness of human nature and in
the ultimate potential of civilization to make this goodness prevail.
It is a recovery of this faith, objectified in the flame of a single
candle produced by Marlow in an otherwise pitch-black cabin, that
motivates the dying Kurtz, looking back on his corrupted life, to
whisper, "The horror! The horror!" It is also Marlow's understanding that these words express Kurtz's final victory over the loss of
faith that had undermined his youthful idealism that explains Marlow's lie to Kurtz's betrothed. For it is in women—in the aunt who
obtained Marlow his job, in Kurtz's black mistress, and in Kurtz's
betrothed—that Marlow shows the most enduring faith in man's
goodness to reside. In telling the young woman that Kurtz died
pronouncing her name, Marlow merely chose to adhere to vital
truth rather than to literal accuracy.

Bibliography

I. BIBLIOGRAPHICAL AIDS

The most complete bibliographies on Conrad are Kenneth A. Lohf and Eugene P. Sheehy, *Joseph Conrad at Mid-Century: Editions and Studies, 1895–1955* (1957) and Theodore G. Ehrsam, *A Bibliography of Joseph Conrad* (1969). More helpful to the student, however, is Maurice Beebe, "Criticism of Joseph Conrad: A Selected Checklist," *Modern Fiction Studies*, I (February, 1955), 30–45, revised and updated, X (Spring, 1964), 81–106. George T. Keating, *A Conrad Memorial Library* (1929) describes the largest single collection of Conrad manuscripts, editions, and studies, now at Yale. Thomas Wise, *A Bibliography of the Writings of Conrad 1895–1921* (1921, 2nd ed. 1964) describes both the first English and the first American editions of Conrad's works. The bibliography of Ludwik Krzyzanowski in *Joseph Conrad: Centennial Essays* (1960) corrects and adds to the Polish items in Lohf and Sheehy; the annual bibliography in PMLA may be used to bring all of the above up to date. Useful for bibliographical as well as critical purposes is the new periodical *Conradiana*, published by the Department of English, University of Maryland.

II. BIOGRAPHY

Much primary material on Conrad's life is readily available. Of autobiographical value are *The Mirror of the Sea* (1906), *A Personal Record* (1912), *Notes on Life and Letters* (1921), *Last Essays* (1926), and *Conrad's Prefaces*, ed. Edward Garnett (1937). The greatest body of letters by Conrad is in G. Jean-Aubrey, *Joseph Conrad: Life and Letters*, 2 vols. (1927), but other important edited collections are Richard Curle, *Conrad to a Friend* (1928), Edward Garnett, *Letters From Conrad, 1895–1924* (1928), G. Jean-Aubrey, *Lettres Françaises* (1929), John A. Gee and Paul J. Sturm, *Letters of Joseph Conrad to Marguerite Poradowska, 1890–1920* (1940), and William Blackburn, *Joseph Conrad: Letters to William Blackwood and David S. Meldrum* (1958). Of testimonial value are two books by Conrad's wife Jessie, *Joseph Conrad as I Knew Him* (1926) and *Joseph Conrad and His Circle* (1935, 2nd ed. 1964), various studies by Richard Curle, the most important of which is *The Last Twelve Years of Joseph Conrad* (1928), and the many reminiscences by literary friends, the fullest of which are by Ford Madox Ford, *Joseph Conrad: A Personal Remembrance* (1924) and *Portraits from Life* (1937). Two studies which concentrate on a particular period of Conrad's life are Jerry Allen, *The Sea Years of Joseph Conrad* (1965), and Norman Sherry, *Conrad's Eastern World* (1966). Engaging full biographies are G. Jean-Aubrey's 1947 recasting of the biographical part of his pioneer *Life and Letters*, which was translated by Helen Seeba as *The Sea Dreamer. A Definitive Biography of Joseph Conrad* (1957), and Jerry Allen, *The Thunder and the Sunshine: A Biography of Joseph Conrad* (1958). Bernard C. Meyer in *Joseph Conrad: A Psychoanalytic Biography* (1967) presents a psychoanalytic approach. To date, however, the excellent work of Jocelyn Baines, *Joseph Conrad: A Critical Biography* (1960), still remains the fullest and most accurate account of Conrad's life.

III. IMPORTANT GENERAL STUDIES

The first detailed, scholarly study of Conrad's work was John Dozier Gordan, *Joseph Conrad: The Making of a Novelist* (1940) which provides a careful survey of the milieu, chronological progression, and artistic development of Conrad's early work, with special emphasis on *Almayer's Folly, The Nigger of the "Narcissus,"* and *Lord Jim*. Although Morton D. Zabel has written extensively on Conrad, probably his most useful and important work is *The Portable Conrad* (1947), useful for its introduction and generous sampling of Conrad, important for its role in the post-World-War-II renaissance of interest in Conrad. Like Zabel's work, much of F. R. Leavis' first appeared in periodicals before it was synthesized within *The Great Tradition: A Study of the English Novel* (1948), a work which places Conrad along with Jane Austen, George Eliot, and Henry James as the major defining forces in the evolution of the English novel. The moral bias of *Scrutiny* and Leavis is picked up in Douglas Hewitt, *Conrad: A Reassessment* (1952), the two main theses of which are that Conrad's greatness lies in a technique of presentation which forces the reader to see "that the plight of his [Conrad's] central characters is but one manifestation of the working of universal spiritual and moral laws," and that Conrad's work suffered a serious decline with *Chance* (1914) and after. Two other writers followed these ideas independent of each other and of Hewitt: Paul Wiley, *Conrad's Measure of Man* (1954) explores the archetypal, emblematic aspects of Conrad's art, while Thomas Moser, *Joseph Conrad: Achievement and Decline* (1957) searches psychoanalytically for the reasons for Conrad's falling off. More recently Ted Eugene Boyle, *Symbol and Meaning in the Fiction of Joseph Conrad* (1965) concentrates on detailed symbolic analysis of individual works, and J. I. M. Stewart, *Joseph Conrad* (1968) suggests in his epilogue that the inferiority of the later novels may be due to the influence on them of the Polish romantic literature of Conrad's boyhood. Leo Gurko, *Joseph Conrad: Giant in Exile* (1962) feels that the tensions in Conrad's personal life which led eventually to exhaustion and decline of artistic quality also contributed to his twentieth-century view of the bleakness of the universe. Robert H. Haugh, *Joseph Conrad: Discovery in Design* (1957) passes by the question of artistic change to focus on the twelve major works of 1897–1917 in a "new critical" analysis of Conrad's style and structure. Three writers have examined Conrad's political novels. Eloise Hay, *The Political Novels of Joseph Conrad: A Critical Study* (1963) investigates the transformation of political vision into artistic vision, and Claire Rosenfield, *Paradise of Snakes: An Archetypal Analysis of Conrad's Political Novels* (1967) discusses the function which myth and archetype perform in such a process. Avrom Fleishman, *Conrad's Politics: Community and Anarchy in the Fiction of Joseph Conrad* (1967) stresses the complexity of Conrad's political imagination as seen both in Conrad as man and as artist. Concern with Conrad's shorter works is seen in Edward Said, *Joseph Conrad and the Fiction of Autobiography* (1966) and Lawrence Graver, *Conrad's Short Fiction* (1968). Said approaches the works through an examination of Conrad's letters, and Graver notes the role of financial need in Conrad's composition of his stories and novelettes. To date, Albert J. Guerard's *Conrad the Novelist* (1958) remains the most influential and significant single study on Conrad, for the numerous approaches he takes within his work enable him to discover in a comprehensive and thorough manner the complexities of Conrad's art. Of more recent studies, only that of J. I. M. Stewart mentioned above can compare. Finally, three centennial symposia may be mentioned: Oliver Warner, John Wain, W. W. Robson, Richard Freislich, Tom Hopkinson, Jocelyn Baines, and Richard Curle, "Joseph Conrad: A Critical Symposium," *London Magazine*, IV (November, 1957), 21–49; Ludwik Krzyzanowski, ed., *Joseph Conrad: Centennial Essays* (1960); and Robert Stallman, ed., *The Art of Joseph Conrad: A Critical Symposium* (1960), which is the fullest and mose useful.

IV. STUDIES OF *HEART OF DARKNESS*

Neither the articles included in nor the articles cited in the footnotes of the present work have been included.

Andreas, Osborn. *Joseph Conrad: A Study in Non-conformity*. New York, 1959. Pp. 46–54, 193–94. In *Heart of Darkness* "Conrad's art takes a great leap upward to a higher level of performance and meaning." Through Kurtz and Marlow, Conrad makes "his personal declaration of independence from that centripetal force in society which tends to make conformists of us all." Although Kurtz is great because he has the courage to condemn and reject his "natal group," Marlow (as does Conrad) works out a modus vivendi.

Bernard, Kenneth. "The Significance of the Roman Parallel in Joseph Conrad's *Heart of Darkness*." *Ball State Teacher's College Forum*, V (Spring, 1964), 29–31. In the opening frame of *Heart of Darkness*, Marlow, in comparing modern to Roman colonization, says that only efficiency and "the idea" redeem us. The story may be seen as Conrad's revelation of the falsity of this theory, stating that evil is permanent in the nature of man and the only difference between Romans and moderns is the greater hypocrisy of the latter.

Bowen, Robert. "Loyalty and Tradition in Conrad." *Renascence*, XII (1960), 125–131. Though Conrad is committed to tradition and loyalty as qualities which will lead to proper action, he is not authoritarian. There are various systems of tradition, and the man who has the ability is free to make his choice and accept his responsibility.

Brady, Marion B. "Conrad's Whited Sepulcher." *College English*, XXIV (October, 1962), 24–29. Demonstrates the unity of the story and the double theme of public and private guilt by tracing the imagery of whiteness and death, but does not seem to be aware of the earlier and more impressive articles by Wilford S. Dowden and Stewart C. Wilcox. (See also a rebuttal by Thomas C. Kishler and answer by Brady, *College English*, XXIV (April, 1963), 561–63.)

Brown, Douglas. "From *Heart of Darkness* to *Nostromo*: An Approach to Conrad." *The Modern Age* (The Pelican Guide to English Literature, Volume 7). London and Baltimore, 1961. Pp. 119–137. Conrad must be read with full attention paid to the texture of the prose and "the shifting viewpoints." For example, Kurtz is a hero only to Marlow, a romantic adventurer who has just recovered from a "nervous breakdown," not to the narrator; hence, the final scene in the sepulchral city should strike the reader as "absurd" and "grotesque."

Collins, Harold R. "Kurtz, the Cannibals, and the Second-Rate Helmsman." *The Western Humanities Review*, VIII (Autumn, 1954), 299–310. In anthropological terms, the cannibal-crewmen have "dignity and self-assurance" because they "still have the comfortable feeling of being valued members of some native social order"; however, both Kurtz and the native helmsman run amuck because they are "detribalized."

Crews, Frederick. "The Power Of Darkness." *Partisan Review*, XXXIV (Fall, 1967), 507–25. In this Freudian approach to *Heart of Darkness*, Marlow's journey into Africa, a continent symbolic of "the maternal body," is analyzed as "voyeuristic and incestuous." Kurtz is a "vindictive reconstruction of Conrad's father." What Marlow discovers in the very heart of darkness is the father performing an unspeakable sexual rite on the mother. He lies at the end to "suppress the father's misdeeds and re-establish the pure mother-son dyad." (See McCall, below.)

Dahl, James C. "Kurtz, Marlow, Conrad and the Human-Heart of Darkness." *Studies in the Literary Imagination*, I (1968), 33–40. Kurtz disintegrates because he does not recognize the potential savagery in himself, and the only thing which prevents Marlow's own disintegration is work. Marlow emerges disillusioned with "idealism," believing life absurd.

Dean, Leonard F. "Tragic Pattern in Conrad's *The Heart of Darkness*." *College English*, VI (November, 1944), 100–104. The potential tragic impact of Kurtz's realization that demonic powers lie in the heart of life is muted because Marlow never changes, but clings to a world of illusion on the surface of life.

Dudley E. J. "Three Patterns of Imagery in Conrad's *Heart of Darkness*." *Revue des Langues Vivantes*, XXXI (1965), 568–578. The image patterns of darkness, wilderness, and death, increasingly symbolic in the course of the story, culminate in Kurtz, whom Marlow has come to see as a representation of certain elements within himself.

Farmer, Norman. "Conrad's *Heart of Darkness*." *The Explicator*, XXII (March, 1964). The symbolism of the "serpent-river is fundamental to Conrad's depiction of the workings of evil in man." Marlow is charmed by this symbol and is driven to envelop himself in evil in order to analyze it and define it for himself.

Gillon, Adam. *The Eternal Solitary: A Study of Joseph Conrad.* New York, 1960. Pp. 103–08. In this existential approach to Conrad, Marlow is seen as an "isolato" who by the end of the story "has come to believe that 'we live as we dream—alone.'"

Gross, Harvey. "Aschenbach and Kurtz: The Cost of Civilization." *Centennial Review*, VI (Spring, 1962), 131–4. *Heart of Darkness* and Thomas Mann's *Death in Venice* show, following Freud, that "man cannot live at peace in his culture; he dies without it." Even though these "allegories of culture" depict a disintegrating civilization, their authors are examples of hope for humanity because, through their art, they are able to control "the disordered materials which provide their subject."

Guetti, James. "*Heart of Darkness* and The Failure of the Imagination." *Sewanee Review*, LXXIII (Summer, 1965), 488–504. In *Heart of Darkness* there are two realities, one which concerns surface, practical features of existence, and another which concerns the inner truths of the heart. Because the imagination cannot fully comprehend the latter, it is ultimately inexpressible.

Hoffman, Stanton De Voren. "The Hole in the Bottom of the Pail: Comedy and Theme in *Heart of Darkness*." *Studies in Short Fiction*, II (1965), 113–123. Marlow's use of comic images reveals a paradox in his role of narrator and protagonist; as detached narrator he attempts to render confusion and darkness as ordered and intelligible, but as protagonist he is drawn by an "unconscious pull" toward Kurtz's "confusion."

Hollingsworth, Alan M. "Freud, Conrad, and the Future of an Illusion." *Literature and Psychology*, V (1955), 78–82. Maintains that *Heart of Darkness* exposes the "white façade and inner dark corruption * * * of Christian imperialism" embodied in Kurtz who, "representing the genius of Europe," manages to pervert naive cannibals. Back in civilization Marlow attempts to maintain the Christian illusion by lying to Kurtz's intended.

Karl, Frederick. "Introduction to the Danse Macabre: Conrad's *Heart of Darkness*." *Modern Fiction Studies*, XIV (Summer, 1968), 143–156. The story focuses "on the Kurtz-Marlow polarity as a definition of our times." Conrad shows that "the most dutiful of men, Marlow, can be led to the brink of savagery * * * the most idealistic of men, Kurtz, can become a sadistic murderer." Marlow, a man of "moral courage and order," loses his innocence when he discovers that elsewhere "men do not share his belief in an orderly society," practice no moral restraints, and thrive on naked power, as does Kurtz. Still, while Marlow abhors those qualities in Kurtz, he is simultaneously fascinated by them and lies about Kurtz in the end to protect both him and his own illusions.

Kreiger, Murray. "Joseph Conrad: Action, Inaction, and Extremity: *Heart of Darkness.*" *The Tragic Vision,* New York, 1960, Pp. 154–65. "Thanks to Mr. Kurtz, Conrad's magnificently proportioned Marlow never need pay the full price himself for so costly a victory and a vision. * * * For, having lived through Kurtz's extremity, Marlow can retain" his own sense of workaday reality without ever mistaking it for ultimate reality and without being tempted to follow the way of Kurtz.

Levine, Paul. "Joseph Conrad's Blackness." *South Atlantic Quarterly,* LXIII (1964), 198–206. With reference to some of Conrad's other works and to those of other authors, especially Melville, Levine discusses *Heart of Darkness,* defining "blackness" as that state in which man succumbs to the realm of the id, ignoring the superego.

McCall, Dan. "The Meaning in Darkness: A Response To a Psychoanalytical Study of Conrad." *College English,* XXIX (May, 1968), 620–627. In a thorough and carefully reasoned criticism of Frederick Crews' "The Power Of Darkness," McCall criticizes Crews for "creating false dichotomies" and misusing biographical evidence in his Freudian analysis of *Heart Of Darkness.* Furthermore, Crews uses psychological analysis exactly as Freud warned that it not be used, to elucidate "the nature of the artistic gift," to "explain the means by which the artist works—artistic technique." (See Crews, above.)

McConnell, Daniel J. " 'The Heart of Darkness' in T. E. Eliot's *The Hollow Men.*" *Texas Studies in Literature and Language,* IV (Summer, 1962), 141–53. Mainly on Eliot, but sees Kurtz as a hero within a dying Western civilization.

Mellard, James. "Myth and Archetype in *Heart of Darkness.*" *Tennessee Studies in Literature,* XIII (1948), ed. Richard B. Davis and Kenneth L. Knickerbocker. In view of the several mythical interpretations of *Heart of Darkness,* Mellard attempts to reduce the story to its lowest common denominators by application of the principles of Joseph Campbell stated in *The Hero With a Thousand Faces.*

Ober, Warren. "*Heart of Darkness*: 'The Ancient Mariner' a Hundred Years Later." *Dalhousie Review,* XLV (Autumn, 1965), 333–337. A comparison of "Rime of the Ancient Mariner" and *Heart of Darkness* reveals that Conrad's view toward man and man's place in nature is a reversal or a parody of Coleridge's. The vision is not that of man seeking universal love but of man seeking power in a world of horror.

Perry, John. "Action, Vision, or Voice: The Moral Dilemmas in Conrad's Tale-Telling." *Modern Fiction Studies,* IX (Spring, 1964), 3–14. Perry discusses Conrad's inability to make a moral judgment concerning his characters because of his realization of the "complexities of understanding, interpreting, and communicating the direct and single experience of meaning that the situation has for the person most involved."

Raskin, Jonah. "Heart of Darkness: The Manuscript Revisions." *Review of English Studies,* XVIII (1967), 30–39. Concerns revisions of the manuscript connected with theme and technique.

Reid, Stephen. "The 'Unspeakable Rites' in *Heart of Darkness.*" *Modern Fiction Studies,* IX (Winter, 1963), 347–356. Kurtz participates in cannibalism to maintain his position as god-man among the natives.

Ridley, Florence. "The Ultimate Meaning of *Heart of Darkness.*" *Nineteenth-Century Fiction,* XVIII (June, 1963), 43–53. "The story is built upon the balance of opposites, a core of faith vs. hollowness, restraint vs. its lack, civilization vs. savagery, light vs. darkness." Marlow's "lie" to Kurtz's Intended ironically implies that it is necessary "to protect the saving illusion" lest man become "de-civilized and in the process less human."

Sanders, Charles. "Conrad' *Heart of Darkness.*" *The Explicator,* XXIV (September, 1965). "Conrad's development of the 'knitter's episode' . . . can be shown to be a *specific* variation on the legend of Clotho, Lachesis, and Atropos." Only two fates are present because the third, Atropos, who cuts the thread, would suggest Marlow's death, which would result from complete submission to the evil in the "heart of darkness."

Spinner, Kaspar. "Embracing the Universe: Some Annotations to Joseph Conrad's 'Heart of Darkness.' " *English Studies,* XLIII (October, 1962), 420–23. As its title implies, this note is a series of suggestions, most of which have been made before, but of particular interest is the comparison of Kurtz to Orpheus.

Stallman, Robert W. "Conrad and *The Great Gatsby.*" *Twentieth Century Literature,* I (April, 1955), 5–12. Shows the influence of Conrad on Fitzgerald by, in part, paralleling the structure of *Heart of Darkness* with *Gatsby,* the role of Marlow with Nick, and Kurtz with Gatsby. Concludes, however, that Marlow more fully understands Kurtz than Nick, Gatsby.

Stein, William. "Conrad's East: Time, History, Action, and 'Maya'." *Texas Studies in Literature and Language*, VII (Autumn, 1965), 265–283. Conrad records the "pathos of the struggle to exist in time without any organizing principles to cope with the disillusionments of experience." The article focuses on those works with an Eastern setting, but generalizations are applicable to *Heart of Darkness* and to Conrad's art as a whole.

Tick, Stanley. "Conrad's *Heart of Darkness*." *The Explicator*, XXI (April, 1963). The several references to the Congo River as a serpent establish the Biblical pattern of man's temptation to evil and forbidden knowledge. Marlow, unlike Kurtz and the pilgrims, placates the "devil-god" of the river by the symbolic sacrifice of his blood-stained shoes and in the process of his experiences learns of "good and evil."

Tindall, William York. "Apology for Marlow." *From Jane Austen to Joseph Conrad*, ed. Robert C. Rathburn and Martin Steinmann, Jr. Minneapolis, 1958. Pp. 274–85. A discussion of the growth and development of Marlow both as personality and as author's mask. In *Heart of Darkness* "Marlow is questing for himself"; but because he does not gain complete knowledge both his story and Conrad's story emerge ambiguous and ironic: "darkness in white fog seems a fitting symbol."

Williams, George. "The Turn Of The Tide in *Heart Of Darkness*." *Modern Fiction Studies*, IX (Summer, 1963), 171–72. The moral transformation of the narrator between the beginning and end of the story is mirrored structurally "by a natural, nautical event—the turn of the tide," and "the 180° swing of the Nellie." All of these changes transfer the reader from the "particular to the universal."

NORTON CRITICAL EDITIONS